THE GUINNESS BOOK OF

CAR

FACTS & FEATS

FOURTH EDITION

THE GUINNESS BOOK OF

CAR

FACTS & FEATS

FOURTH EDITION

David Hodges ■ David Burgess-Wise
John Davenport ■ Anthony Harding

GUINNESS PUBLISHING

Acknowledgements

The majority of the illustrations were supplied by David Hodges
and David Burgess-Wise and the publishers are also grateful to *Autocar* Archives
and Maurice Rowe, manufacturers and sponsors.

Editor: Beatrice Frei
Design and Layout: Stonecastle Graphics Ltd

First published in 1971 by Guinness Superlatives Ltd
Second Edition revised, 1976
Second Impression, 1977
Third Edition revised, 1980
Second Impression, 1983
Third Impression, 1985
Fourth Edition, 1994 by Guinness Publishing Ltd

Published in Great Britain by Guinness Publishing
Ltd, 33 London Road, Enfield, Middlesex

Typeset in Great Britain by
Ace Filmsetting Ltd, Frome, Somerset
Printed and bound in Great Britain by
The Bath Press, Bath

A catalogue record for this book is available from the
British Library

ISBN 0–85112–768–1

CONTENTS

IN THE BEGINNING   7
David Burgess-Wise

ORIGINS   29
David Hodges

MILESTONES   42
Marques; Bodywork and Accessories; Brakes;
Chassis, Tyres and Wheels; Under the Bonnet;
Transmissions; Lighting; In-Car Entertainment

David Burgess-Wise

MEN OF MOTORING   98
David Burgess-Wise and David Hodges

RACING AND RECORDS   114
David Hodges

RALLIES   182
John Davenport

THE DRIVERS   204
David Hodges and John Davenport

MOTORING MISCELLANY   218
David Burgess-Wise

INDEX   244

IN THE BEGINNING

Few of man's inventions have so changed society as the motor car. Once regarded as a rich man's eccentricity, it has now become an essential part of everyday life throughout the world. The freedom of movement bestowed by the motor car has created the modern town, with its sprawling suburbs and its shopping precincts, and created a restless desire to travel where once people were content to remain in the community into which they were born.

The motor car industry has become a prime indicator of national wealth and a major employer. Enthusiasm for motoring in all its aspects has engendered a whole 'support industry' of books, magazines, models, items of clothing, and artefacts of all kinds right down to novelty soaps and chocolates.

Cars have always had their detractors, usually the more earnest sort of political activist who either denounces the motor car as a symbol of wealth and privilege or as a source of brain-numbing pollution. They have also provided a seemingly inexhaustible milch cow for governments, which disproportionately tax their use. But many of the problems blamed on the car are really due to the population explosion and to government inability to tailor public transport to public needs, so that people whose mode of life does not call for a motor car as a necessity, buy one anyway to enable them to go about their business with the expectancy of reaching their destinations on time.

But to regard the motor car as an alternative to public transport demeans both the vehicle and its inventors, whose motives were many and varied, ranging from a humanitarian wish to end the cruel overworking of horses to the desire to produce a universal power source. What the car has given man, should he choose to exercise it, is freedom. Freedom from timetables and set routes, freedom to stop (subject, these days, to parking restrictions) where and when he wants.

The car has also been an instrument of democratisation, for while there have always been the exclusive super cars for the super rich, very early in the history of motoring there were also cars within reach of anyone who could afford to keep a pony and trap.

These days, hedged around as we are with restrictions and regulations, it is difficult to realise the vision opened by the first generation of motor cars – or the amazing speed with which those motor cars developed. Today's cars are much like their predecessors of a decade ago, and some models can be in production for twenty or thirty years and still remain acceptable to the car buying public. In the early days, however, the change in motor car design was as fast as the development of computers nowadays. In 1894 no car could move significantly faster than a horse: ten years later the fastest car on earth was capable of over 100 mph and even production models (at a considerable price) could reach 80 mph.

Fortunately, we can still see that amazing pageant of change in action in the annual London–Brighton Run for Veteran Cars, when over 400 cars – all built before 1905 – make a pilgrimage to the sea to commemorate the emancipation of British motorists from a foolish law that compelled them to be preceded by a man on foot. With a rich diversity of power plants – petrol, steam or electricity – and a wonderful variety in shapes, styles and colours, those pioneer cars are a tribute to the engineers and craftsmen who designed and made them. They may look quaint alongside today's aerodynamic saloons, but the one could not have happened without the other.

This first chapter tells how and when those first steps were made.

The first full-scale vehicles moved by 'artificial' power were:

FRANCE

■ In 1769 the Minister of War authorised the Commandant of Artillery to make a steam truck (or *fardier*) for carrying cannon, to the designs of Nicolas-Joseph Cugnot. A reduced-scale prototype tested early in 1770 could carry four people at 2½ mph, but had to stop every 15 minutes for the boiler to be refilled. The full-sized truck, designed to carry a 4 to 5-ton payload, was finished by May 1771, by which time the government had lost interest. Nevertheless, the *fardier* survived the French Revolution and is now a prized exhibit in the Conservatoire National des Arts et Métiers in Paris. Sadly, since the days of Napoleon, no one has ever tried to make it run (even on high-pressure air) to see just how well it worked.

ENGLAND

■ Richard Trevithick, the Cornish engineer and inventor of the steam railway engine, made a primitive steam 'Travelling Engine' which climbed part way up Beacon Hill, Camborne, with several men aboard on Christmas Eve 1801 (but terminally caught fire while the party was celebrating in a nearby hotel 'with a roast goose and proper drinks'!). In 1803, partnered by his cousin Andrew Vivian, 'Captain Dick' patented a greatly improved steam carriage. Its engine and boiler were made in Cornwall and shipped to London to be fitted with a stagecoach-like body. Trevithick's 'London Carriage' could reach 5–6 mph and went (on occasion) 'capitally well' but when funds ran out in 1804 it was dismantled and its boiler and engine were used to drive a rolling-mill. The first purpose-built 'private car' (as opposed to massive steam carriages or rolling test beds) was the 'steam gig' built by Walter Hancock of London and demonstrated by him in Hyde Park in July 1838.

AMERICA

■ Oliver Evans, 'America's James Watt' – who coincidentally developed a high-pressure steam engine at the same time as Trevithick – was granted a steam wagon patent by the State of Maryland on 21 May 1787, but it was not until 1805 that he actually made a self-moving steam conveyance, and even then it was marginal. Commissioned by the Philadelphia Board of Health to build a steam dredger for the city docks, Evans had to move it about 1½ miles from his workshop to the River Schuykill. So he fitted a stout wheeled undercarriage beneath the stern-wheeler's hull and powered one wheel by a make-shift belt and pulley drive from its 5 hp engine. Eventually the grandiosely named 'Orukter Amphibolos' ('Belching Amphibian') was persuaded to trundle down into the water and floated off its undercarriage. America's oldest surviving steam carriages are an improbable device built around 1867

by Richard Dudgeon of New York and currently on display in the Smithsonian Institution, Washington – it looks like the offspring of a night of passion between a traction engine and a couple of park benches – and the altogether more practical Roper steam carriage, built around 1865 and preserved by the Henry Ford Museum in Dearborn, Michigan. Stephen Roper became the first fatal casualty of an automobile accident in America when he crashed a two-wheeled steamer at the Charles River cycle track in Massachusetts on 1 June 1896.

CANADA

■ In 1867 watchmaker Henry Seth Taylor of Stanstead, Quebec, built a steam buggy which ran as fast as a trotting horse. Unfortunately, he omitted to equip it with brakes and it inevitably ran away down a hill and crashed. The wreck gathered dust in a barn until 1960, when the property changed hands and the steamer was acquired for restoration by the president of Anaconda American Brass Company. In 1869 another watchmaker, Myer Moss, of Truro, Nova Scotia, built a steam wagon, which ran often enough to become notorious for frightening horses (but had an emergency pedal drive in case it broke down . . .). A third pioneer, John B. Kelly of Blyth, Ontario, built a chain-driven oil-fired steam buggy in the early 1880s: this one was noted for frightening cows, chickens, horses – 'and especially women'!

The horseless carriage having been invented, it took no time at all for accidents to happen . . .

■ The first recorded accident was in 1771 when Cugnot's steam truck hit a low wall in the grounds of the Paris Arsenal. Excessive speed was hardly a factor, but examination of the *fardier*'s rudimentary steering linkage shows that it must have taken a very long time for even the most furious turning of the steering handles to be translated into action at the single front wheel.

■ The first fatal accident occurred on 20 December 1832 when Richard Outridge, an engineer employed by the steam coach builder Walter Hancock, was killed by a boiler explosion while conducting final tests on a newly-built steam omnibus, the 'Enterprise'. As Outridge had wired the safety-valve shut in order to build up the pressure in the boiler, the Coroner brought in a verdict of 'Accidental death occasioned by the deceased's own negligence'.

Hancock's next steam omnibus, built for the London & Brighton Steam Carriage Company, was unfortunately named 'Autopsy'. The word is merely Greek for 'see for yourself', but the choice seems a trifle insensitive.

■ America's first recorded road accident took place in 1864 when the Cleveland-built Grant steam carriage ran into a woman and child.

■ The first fatal road accident occurred on 29 July 1834 when the wheel of a coach operated by the Steam Carriage Company of Scotland on the Glasgow to Paisley service broke as a result of sabotage by the Turnpike Trustees, who tried to stop the service by heaping loose stones across the road. The boiler hit the road and exploded, flinging the passengers from the vehicle and causing the death of four of them.

■ The first fine for a traffic accident involving a self-propelled vehicle was a penalty of £5 inflicted upon John Hall, driver of the Paddington horse omnibus, on 3 May 1833 for 'driving against and wantonly damaging the steam omnibus recently started upon the Paddington Road'. Because of Hall's previous good character, his sentence was cut to £2 and costs. Half the fine was given 'for the use of the poor'.

■ Parliament first concerned itself with 'coaches and other vehicles propelled by steam or gas' in the autumn of 1831 when a Select Committee of the House of Commons examined a number of steam carriage pioneers.

■ The first 'motoring magazine' was *The Journal of Elemental Locomotion (and of Advantages resulting from the application of Steam and other Power as connected with Arts, Sciences, Manufactures, Commerce & Agriculture, Reporter of all Projects of Inventions,*

The Dudgeon of around 1867; it is difficult to work out which of the passengers is actually in charge!

Discoveries, Patents, & c., & c., of National Utility), first published in October 1832. It was edited by Alexander Gordon, a civil engineer whose father David had patented both a carriage driven by a small steam railway engine running inside a 9 ft diameter wheel like a squirrel in a cage and a steam carriage equipped with six jointed iron legs. *The Journal of Elemental Locomotion* only ran to six issues.

■ The first 'motor club' was the Institution of Locomotion, formed on 23 April 1833 by Alexander Gordon. It was intended 'to ameliorate the Distress of the Country by means of Steam Transport and Agriculture' but failed to achieve its lofty intentions.

■ The first vehicle to cover over 100 miles in a day without mechanical trouble was Francis Hill's 'common road steam carriage' which he drove in 1840 from London to Hastings and back – a distance of 128 miles/206 km – without breakdown. Capable of 16 mph/26 kph on the level, this was the first successful road vehicle fitted with a differential gear.

■ The first British motoring legislation to be enacted was the Locomotives on Highways Act of 1865 – the so-called 'Red Flag Act' – which was intended to regulate the use of heavy steam-driven traction engines pulling loads. The Act required three persons in attendance: one to steer, one to stoke and one to walk 60 yards ahead with a red flag to warn oncoming traffic and help control restive horses. Maximum speeds allowed were 4 mph in open country and 2 mph in towns. A new Act in 1878 slightly modified the earlier legislation, but still failed to recognise that what made sense for a 15-ton traction engine, drawing a 30-ton load, made no sense for the light 'horseless carriages' which inventors would otherwise have been encouraged to develop.

■ In 1878 the Locomotives on Highways Amendment Act ordered that self-propelled vehicles should be preceded by 'some person at least 20 yards ahead who shall, in case of need, assist horses in passing the same'. While the red flag requirement was relaxed, flags were still regularly carried as a sort of 'badge of office' by the compulsory pedestrian. It was under this act that the first motor cars were to venture forth upon the roads of Britain.

After the first uncertain attempts, the steam carriage became a moderately viable means of transport. In the early 19th century attempts were even made to run regular steam carriage services in England and France, though they eventually petered out in the

face of the more reliable (and profitable) railway engine. Astoundingly, one such steam carriage survives in perfect condition in the Biscaretti Museum in Turin. Built in the local arsenal in 1852 by one Virginio Bordino, it is based on the stagecoach-like machines he saw running in London as a student engineer in the 1830s. But such machines were too big and clumsy for everyday use. A new power source was required – the internal combustion engine:

Ancestral people-mover: Amédée Bollée's l'Obéissante of 1872–3 had forward control (and independent front suspension).

ENGLAND

■ In 1824 Samuel Brown of Brompton made an ingenious road vehicle driven by his patent 'gas-vacuum engine' which burnt coal gas. His carriage engine was a true internal-combustion machine in which the combustion space was combined with the cylinder. Brown's carriage climbed Shooter's Hill, Blackheath, London, but as its 89-litre twin-cylinder engine (12-in bore by 24-in stroke) only developed 4 hp, the gas-vacuum engine proved so much more expensive to run than a comparable steam engine that nothing came of it. In 1884 Edward Butler of Erith, Kent, patented a three-wheeled 'Petrolcycle' which was actually built around 1887–8 and ran

'fairly satisfactorily' though lack of development funds caused the project's abandonment. In 1889 Butler also made the first float-feed carburetter. The oldest surviving British cars are the toy-like Bremer, built in Walthamstow, London, in 1894, and the Knight motor carriage, which first ran in July 1895. The first British-built prototype to lead (eventually) to production was the 1895–6 Lanchester.

FRANCE

■ The first commercially practicable gas engine was patented by J.-J. Etienne Lenoir in 1860. Though more efficient types became available, the Lenoir gas engine was still being made in the 1890s as it was

simple and reliable. Lenoir's engine could run on 'liquid petroleum spirit'; in 1862–3 he made a primitive 'motor car' powered by a 1.5-hp gas engine and drove it several times between his works and his home. The car was heavy and underpowered – it took about 90 minutes to make the 6-mile/9½-km journey. Subsequently, it was claimed, it was bought by the Czar of Russia and exported to St Petersburg (though a search made in 1905 failed to find it). In 1984 France fêted the centenary of Edouard Delamarre-Deboutteville's 'invention of the motor-car' in 1884, but this dilettante inventor's most successful motor vehicle – a gas-powered tricycle – actually ran (and exploded!) in 1883. A replica of the vehicle described in his 1884 patent for a motorised brake was built in 1984 and ran after a fashion, but whether such a vehicle had previously existed is, as the French say, *très discutable*.

AUSTRIA

■ Siegfried Markus was formerly described as the 'inventor of the motor car' from claims that, following experiments with an atmospheric gas engine fitted in a handcart in 1863–5, he had built a motor car in 1875. But his crude vehicle (which still exists) was actually constructed in 1888–9: the '1875' date displayed on it at the 1900 Paris Exposition was a falsehood.

GERMANY

■ Carl Benz was the first man to sell horseless carriages made to a set pattern – not one-off experi-

The first petrol car to be offered for sale to the public was the 1887–8 Benz three-wheeler.

ments – to the public. Benz made stationary gas engines in Mannheim and in 1885 built a two-seater tricycle powered by a four-stroke gas engine with electric ignition and surface carburetter, which he patented on 29 January 1886. Gottlieb Daimler had already patented his 'high-speed' petrol engine, but though Daimler built a motor cycle test bed in 1885 and fitted an engine in a carriage in 1886, there was no regular production of Daimler cars until 1892. On the other hand, Benz developed his original design through 1886–7 and offered an improved and more powerful version of his 'Patent Motor Wagon' for sale, though customers were noticeably lacking in his native Germany. He made his first sale at the beginning of 1888, to Emile Roger of Paris, granted Roger sole French agency rights – and the modern motor industry was under way. An 1888-type Roger-Benz car is preserved in running order in the Science Museum, London (nobody knows how or when it came to England).

DENMARK

■ In 1887 Albert Hammel, who had been making gas engines since 1882, had a 'carriage which can move without horses' built by his foreman Urban Johansen 'to drive Mr Hammel all the way to Skokshoved where he lives, if they can get that far'. Since its 2.7-litre two-cylinder four-stroke engine developed just 3.5 hp and had only one forward speed, hill-climbing ability was almost nil . . . and turning the steering wheel to the left turned the car right, and vice versa! Nevertheless, in 1954 the Hammel successfully completed the London–Brighton Veteran Car Run at a heady 6 mph.

AMERICA

■ Forget the bogus claims of George Baldwin Selden to have invented the motor car in 1877; this was an exploitation of the US patent laws to attempt to create a monopoly over the infant American automobile industry. The so-called '1877 Selden' was not built until 1904 as part of a legal case against Henry Ford, who refused to pay the Selden patent royalties and the longest run it made under its own power was 3520 ft/1073 m, with two stops en route. In riposte, Ford built a 3.3-litre Lenoir-engined car and drove it round New York at speeds of up to 10 mph. The Selden patent was ruled invalid in 1911. In 1904 Reuben Plass of Brooklyn claimed to have built a car in the 1860s with cylinders 'cast like Civil War cannon' but it seems to have been a flight of fancy.

Anyway, in 1891 John William Lambert, of Ohio City, had built a three-wheeled 'gas-buggy' which ran successfully, though attempts to market the machine at $550 failed. The first American petrol car leading to actual production was built by the brothers Frank and Charles Duryea in 1893; the Duryea Motor Wagon Co. was formed in Springfield, Massachusetts, in September 1895 and 13 cars were built in 1896, the first series-production vehicles in America. A Duryea was featured in the parade at Barnum & Bailey's Circus on 2 April and two of them came to England and took part in the November 1896 London–Brighton Emancipation Day Run (one finished first and was awarded a gold medal 'for punctual arrival at Brighton', despite having knocked down a little girl named Dyer at Crawley en route). During 1896 Detroit's first cars made their appearance: on 6 March a car built by Charles Brady King ran though the streets, followed on a bicycle by 33-year-old Henry Ford, whose Quadricycle made its maiden run that June. Incidentally, Ford found that his little car was too wide to get through the doorway of the shed in which he had built it, so he took an axe and widened the opening, creating America's first garage door.

JAPAN

■ Despite the country's domination of the world motor industry in recent years, the first all-Japanese car did not appear until 1904 and was an inchoate ten-seat steam car built to transport the many offspring of one Torao Yamaba. The Takuri, first of many millions of Japanese petrol cars, did not appear until 1907. It seems to have been a close copy of the contemporary Darracq.

AUSTRALIA

■ Australia's first cars – the Shearer built between 1885 and 1895 and the 1896–7 Thomson – were steamers and the country's first petrol car was the 1897 Pioneer which, despite worldwide publicity and talk of 'sufficient orders for six months', was the first and last product of the Australian Horseless Carriage Syndicate and possibly the only car ever designed by a practising dentist (Henry Austin of Fitzroy, Victoria).

CANADA

■ Canada's first successful 'gas buggy' was built during the winter of 1896–7 by George Foote Foss,

who owned a machine shop in Sherbrooke, Quebec and made its first run the following spring. Its top speed of 12 mph/19 kph so incensed the local inland revenue collector that he threatened to have Foss put in jail. Foss eventually became a car dealer and sold his buggy for $75 to a man wanting cheap transport (who drove off owing $5 on the deal and was never seen again). Around the same time as Foss, an inventor named Tom Doherty, of Sarnia, Ontario, began experimenting with a gasoline vehicle, and by 1901 it had been developed to the point where it ran reliably. Alas, it also frightened the horses and the

Though the date on the side says '1877', Selden's car was actually built in the early 1900s to uphold his 'master patent'.

local judge declared Doherty's car 'a dangerous nuisance'. This had not been Doherty's first horseless carriage: in 1895 he had built a three-wheeled vehicle driven by clockwork, but its limited range, low speed (it was far quicker to walk) and the effort needed to rewind the massive spring doomed the project to an early demise.

The horseless carriage having arrived, the legislators inevitably decided to limit its use as best they could, and so the first motoring laws began to pass through Parliament. . . .

■ The 1896 Locomotives on Highways Act – the so-called 'Emancipation Act' – at last recognised a new class of vehicle, the 'light locomotive' with an unladen weight of less than 3 tons, and did away with the need for three persons in attendance. The maximum speed limit was raised to 14 mph/22.5 kph (though the Local Government Board promptly had it cut to 12 mph/19 kph). A 'bell or instrument capable of giving audible and sufficient warning of the approach or position of the carriage' had to be carried and lights were required at night.

■ Until the 1896 Act, motor cars had been taxed as carriages: from 1 January 1897 the first specific motor car licence duties were introduced, cars weighing between 1 and 2 tons paying 2 guineas and cars of 2–3 tons paying 3 guineas in addition to the 2-guinea annual carriage tax.

■ Construction & Use Regulations for cars began with the 1896 Act and have been developed ever since. Where it is now illegal to drive with tyres with a tread pattern less than 1.6 mm deep, the 1896 Act specified that tyres should have smooth treads (though 'projections or bosses' were permitted on pneumatic or 'soft and elastic' tyres). Two independent braking systems were also mandatory.

■ Exhaust emission regulations now involve complex analysis of exhaust gases, but they were once very simple. The 1896 Act said merely that 'light locomotives' must be so constructed 'that no smoke or visible vapour is emitted except from some temporary or accidental cause'.

■ Road tax is far older than the motor car. The earliest vehicle tax was imposed on private carriages and hackney cabs by Charles I in 1637; it was levied on coachbuilders. Toll roads were instituted in 1706, when duties began to be collected on turnpikes. The last Turnpike Act expired in 1896 but politicians seem incapable of learning from history: in the 1993 Autumn Budget it was announced that tolls would be introduced on motorways – paid for many times over by the so-called road tax – in the near term.

Despite many problems and hindrances, the pioneers succeeded, and the horseless carriage movement gathered pace. . . .

■ The world's first long-distance journey by a petrol car (and the first solo trip by a lady driver) was made in August 1888 when Frau Berta Benz borrowed the 1886 Benz tricar without asking her husband's permission. She took her two young sons to visit relatives in Pforzheim, 75 miles (120 km) from the Benz home in Mannheim. They arrived safely, though en route the resourceful Frau Benz had bought dry-cleaning fluid from a chemist's shop when the car ran out of fuel, repaired a shorting ignition wire with elastic from her garters, unblocked a fuel line with her hatpin and had the brake relined with leather by a cobbler. Five days later, she drove home again.

■ America's (and probably the world's) first press launch took place on 13 May 1897 when journalists were invited to an 'open house' at the Pope Manufacturing Company's HQ at Hartford, Connecticut at which they could test-drive the firm's products.

■ The first long-distance journey by a petrol car in Great Britain was made by the Hon. Evelyn Ellis – a pioneer motorist and Member of Parliament who backed the 1896 'Emancipation Act' – who had owned a 5-hp Panhard & Levassor in France in 1894 and brought it into Britain in 1895 to promote the cause of 'mechanical transit'. In August 1895 he drove from Micheldever to his home near Datchet, a distance of 56 miles/90 km, and subsequently travelled to Malvern, Worcestershire.

■ At the beginning of November 1896 Charles MacRobie Turrell was the first person to drive a motor car – a 'magnificently built and equipped' imported Daimler – in the Lord Mayor of London's procession. He was accompanied by Harry J. Lawson. The police unsuccessfully tried to issue a summons for a breach of the Locomotives on Highways Act (though a week later they were successful in prosecuting a driver who went out at 10.00 p.m. on the eve of the Emancipation Act's coming into force).

■ The first London to Brighton motor run was organised on 14 November 1896 by H. J. Lawson and his Motor Car Club to celebrate the emancipation of the horseless carriage. Of the 54 vehicles entered, 32 are believed to have started from the Metropole Hotel in Northumberland Avenue after Lord Winchelsea had symbolically torn up a red flag, and 20 (or 22, depending on whom you believe) reached Brighton in time for a dinner that evening at the seaside Metropole Hotel. However, it was rumoured that some of them had actually made the journey by train.

■ Pioneer motorists often met blank incomprehension from a public unused to motor vehicles. After W. G. Windham had been taught to ride a De Dion-Bouton tricycle in Battersea Park, London, by a youthful 'motor expert' named Percival Perry (later chairman of Ford Britain) in 1896, he set off to ride to Scotland after unofficially taking part in the Emancipation Run. Inevitably, he broke down, and decided to send the tricycle by train from Berwick-upon-Tweed, Northumberland. The booking clerk, who had never seen a motor vehicle, booked the De Dion as a child's perambulator.

■ The first hotel to cater especially for motorists was the 'Villa des Cyclistes' at Poissy (Seine-et-Oise), which in 1897 was advertised as a 'Rendez-Vous des Cyclistes et Automobilistes' and kept a stock of motor oil and fuel on the premises.

■ The enforcement of the speed limit has always been a bone of contention between police and motorists and in the days when limits were checked with stopwatches there were justified complaints of police persecution of alleged speeders. The first road patrols were instituted to warn drivers of police

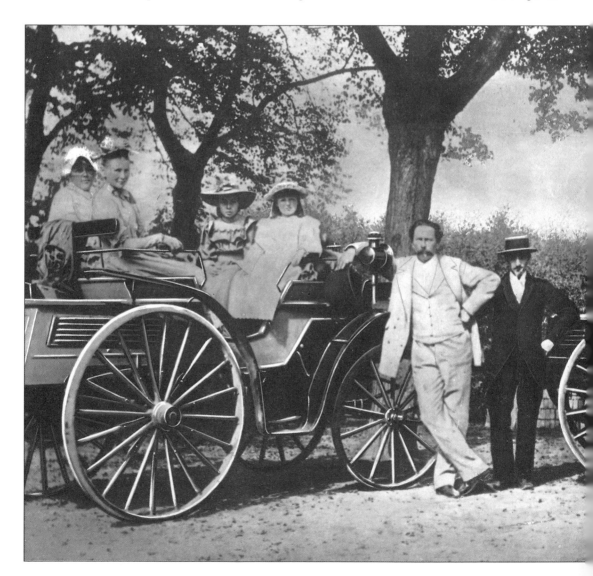

traps. The earliest were a free patrol service operated by the importers of Panhard & Levassor cars during 1901 and a paid service operated by the Brighton Road Motor Patrol from the weekend of 2–3 November 1901. The 'BRMP' had a fleet of motor cars and cyclists with red flags patrolling the Brighton Road to warn of police traps. It is not known how long these services lasted, but the Panhard patrol – organised by P & L importer Charles Jarrott – was indirectly the ancestor of today's Automobile Association. When the AA was instituted in 1905 it grew out of a later cycle patrol operated by Jarrott &

Letts Limited and Charles Jarrott was the leading figure on the AA's original committee.

■ Despite protests from many motorists, who objected to being 'numbered like convicts and labelled like hackney carriages', the Motor Car Act passed by the British Parliament in August 1903 required all cars to be registered and carry a number plate. Moreover, every motorist had to have a driving licence. The Act, which came into force on 1 January 1904, also made dangerous driving an indictable offence. Registration cost £1 and the driving licence 5s, but there was no driving test to pass and the licence was obtained by filling up a form and paying the fee at a Post Office. Earl Russell queued all night to obtain A1, the first London number, for his Napier and Lord Justice Advocate Kingsburgh was given S1, the first number in Scotland. The original intention of the 1903 Act was to abolish the open road speed limit but the House of Commons insisted on a general speed limit of 20 mph/32 kph, which remained in force until 1930.

■ Until the 1903 Act laid down a minimum age of 17 for driving a car (14 for a motorbike), anyone could drive a powered vehicle in Britain and in 1903 Peugeot boasted of a nine-year-old who drove a Baby Peugeot voiturette.

■ The world's first car number plates were issued by the Paris police from 14 August 1893. Each car had to have a licence describing its mechanical layout and carry a metal plaque bearing its 'distinctive number' (and the owner's name and address) on its left-hand side. However, numbering did not become universal in France until 17 December 1901 and even then was only compulsory on cars capable of exceeding 30 kph. The letters in the registration indicated whether the car had been registered in Paris, Lyon, Arras or Bordeaux. Numbering had been compulsory for pedal cycles since 1899.

■ The examination of motor vehicles and drivers in France was carried out by the Ministry of Mines for the simple reason that the first steam engines in general use in France had been used in mines. Thus mining engineers had special expertise in this field in the pre-automobile era.

Carl Benz (white suit, centre), his wife Berta (second from left) and members of their family gather for an outdoor motoring party near Gernsheim, Germany in August 1894.

■ The first driving licence issued in France was held jointly by Léon Serpollet and his assistant Averard. Issued on 7 April 1891, it permitted them to drive Serpollet's steam tricar, tested by the Service des Mines on 15 August 1889 and 8 January 1891.

■ The first lady motorist to pass her driving test was the Duchess d'Uzès, who was issued with her licence in Paris on 21 May 1898, several days after demonstrating her skill at the tiller of her Delahaye 'automobile break' (now in the Compiègne Museum) accompanied by an official examiner. In 1932, the Duchess – then aged 85 – remained an active motorist who competed in rallies and was president of the French Ladies' Automobile Club.

■ America's first recorded woman motorist was Mrs John Howell Phillips of Chicago, who was issued with her driving licence (Illinois No. 24) in 1899.

■ The first police pursuit of a criminal by motor car seems to have taken place at Moor Edge, Newcastle-upon-Tyne on 15 August 1900 when F. R. Goodwin's Gladiator voiturette was commandeered by a police constable. The policeman ordered the driver to chase a drunken horse-rider, who was caught and arrested after a mile.

■ The first recorded fine imposed on a drunken driver of a private car was the £1 mulcted from a 'gentleman named Kelly' at the Dublin Police Court in April 1900 for 'being intoxicated while in charge of a motor car in Dame Street and driving the car recklessly and furiously'. An electric cab driver named George Smith had been fined £1 for being drunk in charge on 10 September 1898.

■ The first American to receive a traffic ticket was Elwood Haynes of Kokomo, Indiana. In 1895 he was driving a motor car which he had built in conjunction with the Apperson brothers when he was ordered off the street by a bicycle-riding policeman in Chicago.

■ The first person to appear in court on a motoring charge was almost certainly John Henry Knight of Farnham, Surrey, who was convicted of using his

Originally built as a three-wheeler, Knight's 1895 carriage was later converted to a four wheeler (with independent front suspension).

three-wheeled motor carriage on the public highway in 1895. On 22 December that year Birmingham perambulator manufacturer Leon l'Hollier, who also claimed to be a car maker (though he actually imported Benz cars from Germany) was summoned for driving a 'locomotive' on the road without being preceded by a man on foot. He was fined 1s plus costs.

■ America's first recorded speeding fine was $10, imposed on L. T. Shevlin of Minneapolis in 1902 for exceeding 10 mph in his automobile.

■ Under a law passed in Chicago in 1902, drivers were permitted to wear spectacles (but *pince-nez* glasses were forbidden).

■ American cars were first registered on a state-wide basis in New York and California in 1901. The first American number plates were issued in New York and carried the owner's initials; nearly $1000 was collected in the first year. 'Personalised' number plates can still be purchased in American states.

■ The first photographic speed trap was invented in 1900 when a camera which took a sequence of photographs 'to prove the pace of autocars' was submitted to the Parisian Prefect of Police for trials.

■ Britain's first motor insurance policy was issued in November 1896 by the General Accident Fire & Life Assurance Company at the instigation of a young executive named Francis Norie-Miller (who subsequently became the company's chief executive).

■ The first American to take out motor insurance was Gilbert A. Loomis of Westfield, Massachusetts, who in 1897 paid $7.50 for $1000-worth of liability insurance on his own-make single-cylinder automobile.

■ America's first independent car dealer was William E. Metzger of Detroit, who opened for business in 1898.

■ The first motor car accident in Britain resulting in the death of the driver occurred on 25 February 1899 when the rear wheels of a Daimler car under test by the Army & Navy Stores collapsed under heavy braking while descending Grove Hill, Harrow-on-the-Hill, London. The driver, a Daimler employee named E. R. Sewell, was killed instantly; one of the five passengers, Major Richer, died later.

■ There was irrational dislike of the first horseless carriages. When the Hon. Evelyn Ellis visited his father (Lord Howard de Walden) in his 1895 Panhard & Levassor, Papa was furious and complained: 'If you must bring that infernal thing here, kindly bring a little pan to put under it to catch the filthy oil it drips.' 'Certainly, Father,' replied Ellis, 'if you'll bring a big pan for your carriage horses when you visit me.'

■ One of the big problems faced by pioneers was what to call their vehicles. Among the terms proposed were horseless carriage, autobain, automobile carriage, automatic carriage, self-propelled carriage, motocycle and autocar, but Britons finally chose 'motor car' as the most appropriate name for the new invention. The name had been coined by consulting engineer Frederick R. Simms in a letter he wrote to his partner as early as 8 February 1891. France and America chose a name of more classical derivation: 'automobile'. The Scots-born pioneer car maker Alexander Winton is said to have introduced the term 'automobile' into the American vocabulary. Frederick Simms also gave the English language the word 'petrol', which he coined in 1890 when people were beginning to worry about storing inflammable motor spirit. Simms's logic was that since 'petrol' was a meaningless word, it would allay these fears. It was registered as a trade name to describe motor spirit marketed by Carless, Capel & Leonard of London, but eventually came to describe motor fuel in general in Britain. In America the universal term has always been 'gasoline'.

■ Pioneer British motorists also objected to the use of French motoring terms. They particularly disliked 'garage' but the suggested alternatives were universally ugly. 'Carhome', 'carrepose', 'carrest', 'cardomain', 'cardom', 'dock', 'motor mews', 'motories' and 'motostore' were some of the better efforts, while the Greek word 'muron' – a perfume store – was a definite non-starter. No wonder we still use 'garage' . . .

■ The oldest surviving car companies in the world are: Mercedes-Benz (Germany 1886), Peugeot (France 1889), Daimler (England 1896), Oldsmobile (USA 1896), Fiat (Italy 1899), Renault (France 1899) and Tatra (Czech Republic 1899).

■ The first company to sell private cars, made to a set pattern, to the public was De Dion, Bouton & Trépardoux of Paris, who issued a catalogue in 1886 and actually sold light steam tricars and other steam-powered vehicles as a result. They began selling petrol tricycles in 1895 and light cars two years later.

■ The first American company to offer automobiles made to a set pattern to the public was the Moto-Cycle Manufacturing Company of 1529 Arch Street, Philadelphia, which issued a catalogue in the spring of 1886. The firm was set up to make and sell steam tricycles and other vehicles to the designs of Lucius D. Copeland, who had fitted a 'Star' high-wheeler bicycle with a tiny steam engine in 1884 and later built a delicate three-wheeled 'Phaeton Moto-Cycle': but there were no takers. The only known relics of Copeland's machines are the engine and boiler of the 1884 bicycle, which survive in a museum in Arizona.

■ The world's biggest manufacturer of motor vehicles in the late 1890s and early in the 20th century was De Dion-Bouton of Paris, a partnership between aristocrat, politician and noted duellist Comte Albert de Dion and diminutive mechanic Georges Bouton. Their company's growth was astounding: at the end of 1898 it had 250 employees and a year later there were 600, turning out 200 petrol tricycles and 300 engines a month, as well as quadricycles, voiturettes and steam omnibuses. By the turn of the century it had built some 22 000 engines, many of which were supplied to other manufacturers, such as Renault and Delage. In May 1901 its staff had grown to 2000, and 200 voiturettes a month were built, while in 1903 its Puteaux factory turned out 30 000 engines.

■ De Dion-Bouton was probably the first factory to employ female labour; early in 1901 women were assembling batteries in its Puteaux works.

■ France was the world's most prolific producer of motor vehicles until 1904 when its output – 16 900 automobiles – was overtaken by America (22 130); nevertheless, France remained the world's biggest exporter of motor vehicles for another decade.

■ The first self-propelled vehicle to be shown at a public exhibition was the light steam tricycle built by A. H. Bateman & Co. of Greenwich for Sir Thomas Parkyn, displayed at the 1881 Stanley Bicycle Show and still in running order 20 years later.

■ The first indoor British exhibition featuring a display of motor vehicles was the Stanley Cycle Show in the Agricultural Hall, London, on 22–30 November 1895. The five cars displayed included a l'Hollier-Benz, Gladiator 'mineral naphtha' tricycle, a Facile

Production of Cannstatt Daimlers in 1900: shortly after, the company produced the first Mercedes and a new marque was born.

'heavy oil' carriage and the Hon. Evelyn Ellis's Panhard & Levassor.

■ The first public exhibition of motor vehicles in Britain was organised by Sir David Salomons on the showground of the Tunbridge Wells Agricultural Society on 15 October 1895. Peugeot, Panhard & Levassor and De Dion-Bouton vehicles were demonstrated.

■ America's first National Automobile Show was held between 3 and 10 November 1900 in Madison Square Garden, New York, by the Automobile Club of America. Some 300 vehicles were on display, at prices ranging from $280–4000.

■ Britain's first motoring organisation was The Motor Car Club (MCC), founded in 1896 by the entrepreneur Harry J. Lawson. The MCC promoted London's first exhibition dedicated entirely to motor vehicles, held at the Imperial Institute in South Kensington from 9 May to 8 August. Four motor cars were demonstrated in action – petrol-driven Daimler, Acme and Kane-Pennington machines and an electric carriage.

■ The world's oldest motoring organisation is the Automobile Club de France, founded at a meeting in the Paris town house of the Comte de Dion on the Quai d'Orsay on 12 November 1895. A house rented as club premises in the Bois de Boulogne in 1896 soon proved inadequate and the Club bought the former Hôtel de Plessis-Bellière in the Place de la Concorde for 1.5 million francs in 1899: the ACF is still based in this former palace, the most sumptuous clubhouse imaginable.

■ The first motor club in the USA was the American Motor League of Chicago, which held its first meeting in November 1895. Membership cost $2. The Automobile Club of America was organised in 1899.

The main aisle of the 1899 Automobile Club de France Paris Show, held in a marquee in the Tuileries Gardens.

The first Easter tour of the ACGBI (predecessor of the RAC) paused in Farnham, Surrey, on Good Friday, 1898: the three nearest cars are Benz dog carts.

■ On 27 January 1897 the Automobile Club of Great Britain & Ireland was founded by Frederick R. Simms. It had 163 members. In 1907, under the patronage of King Edward VII, it became the Royal Automobile Club. The RAC is now Britain's oldest motoring organisation and has a membership of 5.6 million.

■ The first motor journey from Land's End to John O'Groats was made by Henry Sturmey, Editor of *The Autocar*, between 9 and 18 October 1897, in a 4½-hp Coventry Daimler. His actual running time over the 929 miles/1495 km was 93 hours, an average speed of nearly 10 mph. While Sturmey described his trip as 'trouble free', he took no account of routine chores such as putting in new inlet valves, wiring on loose solid tyres and taking links out of worn driving chains.

■ In April 1900 the 1000 Miles' Trial, organised by Claude Johnson in his capacity as secretary of the Automobile Club of Great Britain & Ireland, put motoring on the map and gave many people their first sight of a motor car. The route started in London and then headed west to Bristol before turning up the west coast to Edinburgh. The return route was via the east coast and the Midlands, and there were static displays, hill-climbing trials and a speed contest in Welbeck Park en route.

■ The first car to enter the precincts of the House of Commons was a 12-hp four-cylinder Daimler owned by the Hon. John Scott Montagu MP (father of the present Lord Montagu), who drove it into Old Palace Yard on 3 July 1899 after successfully appealing to the Speaker against a ban on 'spirit-powered vehicles' imposed by the Office of Works. This was also the first car to be fitted with a mascot, a small bronze St Christopher sculpted by Charles Sykes. In 1910 Rolls-Royce commissioned Sykes to create the 'Spirit of Ecstasy' mascot first seen in March 1911 (and apparently modelled on Eleanor Thornton, Montagu's secretary and secret lover).

■ The first British Prime Minister to own a motor car was the Conservative A. J. Balfour (1902–5) who rode a motor tricycle before buying a 3½-hp De Dion-Bouton voiturette at the end of 1900. In April 1901 he ordered a 7-hp Panhard & Levassor which was delivered the following August, and shortly after he succeeded Lord Salisbury as PM in July 1902, he took delivery of a new 9-hp Napier. While the elderly Salisbury had ridden on his son's Locomobile steamer when he was still PM, he preferred his Humber pedal tricycle.

■ The first US President to travel in a motor car was William McKinley, who rode in a steamer driven by its maker, Freelan O. Stanley, in November 1899. He first rode on the public road in July 1901 aboard a Winton driven by Zib Davis. After he was fatally wounded by an assassin in September 1901, McKinley was taken to hospital in Buffalo by 'automobile ambulance'. It was not until the presidency of William Howard Taft that the White House switched from horse carriages to motor cars and a fleet of four automobiles was purchased for $12 000, arriving in Washington the day before Taft's inauguration in 1909. One of the cars was a White Steamer, and White celebrated the honour by bringing out a 40-hp 'Presidential Model' in 1911.

■ The first French prime minister recorded as owning a motor car was René Waldeck-Rousseau in 1901. He was driving through Le Havre when 'a ruffian' threw a rotten orange at his car and hit the Premier's wife in the face. Waldeck-Rousseau was so angry that he turned the car round, chased and caught the man and handed him over to the police.

■ The first motor car to be used in warfare was a 1901 Locomobile steam car belonging to Captain R. S. Walker of the Royal Engineers. The car was used during the Boer War as a searchlight tender and for mine disposal work in the Transvaal. It was also the first car to be fitted with a telephone (but this only had a range of a mile, which was the length of the wire connecting the car to its base station . . .).

■ The first car to climb the 17-mile/27-km road to the 14 147-ft/4312-m summit of Pike's Peak, Colorado, was a Locomobile steamer driven by W. B. Felker and C. A. Yont in August 1901.

■ The first magazine totally devoted to motor cars was the monthly *La Locomotion Automobile*, launched by Raoul Vuillemat on 1 December 1894. The magazine was subsequently published twice monthly and then weekly. Exactly two months later, on 1 February 1895, Paul Meyan brought out the weekly *La France Automobile*. A less successful venture of 1895 was *L'Automobile Journal*, published in Lyon by a M Vitou; only a few issues appeared.

■ The first British magazine entirely devoted to motor cars, *The Autocar*, appeared on 2 November 1895. It was published by Iliffe, Sons & Sturmey and edited by J. J. Henry Sturmey. On 15 October 1896, *The Automotor and Horseless Vehicle Journal* made its bow. It was edited by Stanley Spooner, who ran *Automotor Journal* for well over 20 years before he learned to drive! In October 1898 Charles Cordingley, who ran the annual laundry exhibition in the Agricultural Hall, Islington, launched *Motor Car Journal*, with a cover price of only one penny against the three pence charged by its two rivals. *Autocar* (now amalgamated with its long-term rival *Motor*, founded 1903) is still published weekly and is thus the longest-running title in motoring history.

■ The first crossing of the United States by car was achieved in 1903 when a Winton car, driven by Dr H. Nelson Jackson and Sewell K. Crocker, started from San Francisco on 23 May and arrived in New York on 26 July. More than 20 days out of the 65-day total were spent making repairs, mostly due to the rough going, though the longest delay was caused by a broken connecting-rod, which burst through the crankcase. They were followed on 20 June by Tom Fetch, who drove his Packard 'Old Pacific' from San Francisco to New York in 53 days.

■ America's first automobile parts and supply company was founded by Andrew Lee Dyke, the 'Automobile Doctor' of St Louis, Missouri, in 1899.

■ America's first car rental business was the Back Bay Cycle & Motor Company of Boston, Massachusetts, who began renting motor vehicles in 1899.

■ The first Royal motorist was the Prince of Wales – later King Edward VII – who rode in a Serpollet steam car belonging to Gaston Menier, the chocolate manufacturer, at Bad Homburg, Germany, in the summer of 1893. The Prince first took the wheel of a motor car – an English-built Daimler – in the grounds of Buckingham Palace on 27 November 1897. His first long car journey came on 25 June 1898 when J.S. Critchley of the Daimler Motor Company drove him from Warwick Castle to Compton Verney, about 10 miles away. He ordered his first motor car – another Daimler – in 1899 and it was delivered on 28 March 1900. Since then the British Royal Family has bought more than 100 Daimlers.

■ The first reigning monarch to drive a motor car on the public highway was King Leopold II of the Belgians (the monarch who purchased the Belgian Congo out of his own pocket), who was stopped for

speeding in the Bois de Boulogne in Paris in October 1900. 'Name? Address?. . . Sorry to have troubled you, Your Majesty. . .' The once-fashionable curvaceous 'Roi des Belges', or 'tulip phaeton' body-style was named after King Leopold, though the credit for it should really go to Cléo de Merode, the King's *amie intime*. She was present when the King was discussing (in her apartment) with the representative of Rothschild & Cie, the famous Parisian coachbuilders, what kind of body to have on his new 1902 Panhard & Levassor. Mlle de Merode placed two prettily curved small easy chairs side by side and suggested that the seating of the new car should be shaped to correspond. The design was executed by Ferdinand Charles of Rothschild, who deserves credit as the first car stylist. Charles later achieved fame as a mezzotint artist.

■ America's biggest producer at the beginning of the century was Ransom Eli Olds who made 425 'Merry' Oldsmobiles in 1901, 2500 in 1902, 3000 in 1903 and 5508 in 1904.

■ Dr Thomas Roberts became the first doctor in Britain to own a car when he imported a two-year-

This Winton was the first car driven across the United States, in 1902.

old 3½-hp Benz in 1896. In November he made his own unofficial 9-hour drive from London to Brighton, preceded by a boy with a red flag on a bicycle.

■ Early manufacturers insisted on payment in full on delivery of a car, but hire purchase schemes were operated from 1900 by companies like the SS Motor Company of London, which offered a 12-month hire purchase scheme, and United Motor Industries. Instalment plans for car purchase only seem to have started in America in 1905.

■ Engine and chassis design have changed out of all recognition over the past 100 years and modern tyres are very different from the short-lived rubberware of pioneer days, but the most constant component of the motor car is the spark plug – its basic design and 18-mm thread were standardised by De Dion-Bouton in the 1890s. Today, well over 90 years later, 18-mm spark plugs are still in production, though the majority of modern car engines use plugs with a thread of 14 mm or less.

■ Petrol distribution was somewhat haphazard in the early days, so the opposed-piston engine introduced by Gobron-Brillié in 1898 offered pioneer motorists the distinct advantage of being able to operate on fuels such as pure alcohol, benzene 'or any good spirit such as gin, brandy or whisky' as well as petrol. Operating on a mixture of methylated spirit and benzol, the exhaust had a novel odour, according to *The Autocar*: 'The olfactory excitation is exasperatingly akin to the fragrant vapours of hot punch.'

■ The most improbable method of propelling a car to reach the road was liquid air, proposed by a Boston, Massachusetts, company in 1900. Wild claims were made and a British depot established near Victoria Station in London, but the 'Liquid Air' car was no more than a mildly adapted steam car and the purpose of the exercise was to separate gullible investors from $1.5 million by the sale of shares.

■ The now familiar design of petrol can was introduced by Pratt & Company around 1900; prior to

Ransom Eli Olds – at the tiller of his 'Merry Oldsmobile' – was America's biggest producer of automobiles in the early 1900s.

that, petrol was distributed in 40-gallon barrels or 10-gallon drums. These cans were of 2-gallon capacity and were the principal means of selling petrol until petrol pumps became common in the 1920s.

■ The first motor cab fleet in the world was operated by the London Electrical Cab Company, founded in November 1896 (though it did not put its first 12 cabs into service until 19 August 1897). The cabs proved expensive and unreliable to run – the weight of the cab and its batteries was too much for any available solid rubber tyres to bear – and the company was wound up at the end of May 1900. At its peak their fleet numbered 77 battery-electric cabs, designed by Walter C. Bersey.

■ The first recorded purpose-built private garage was the 'motor house' attached to the residence of Dr

W. W. Barrett of Park Crescent, Hesketh Park, Southport, Lancashire and in use to house the doctor's two Daimler cars in 1898. The garage had hot-water heating and an inspection pit. The doctor – an inveterate inventor – devised the quick-lift jack, still in use by racing car mechanics for rapid tyre changes today. One of his Daimlers was probably the first fully-enclosed saloon car.

Hubert W. Egerton reaches Land's End on 22 December 1900, after driving from John o'Groats to Land's End in 12 days on his Locomobile steam car.

■ The first 'motor wedding' with cars used to transport the bride and groom took place in August 1897, using Benz automobiles. The guests were conveyed in a farm wagon hauled by a traction engine. However, since the groom's car bore an advertising placard, one is forced to the sad conclusion that it was all a publicity stunt.

■ The first 'motor funeral' took place in Coventry in August 1901 when the coffin of an elderly Daimler employee named William Drakeford was carried to the cemetery on a hearse based on an obsolete Daimler fitted with a flatbed body and painted black.

■ The first motor car to cover a distance of 1000 miles/1609 km without stopping was a 5-hp Decauville which completed the distance in 48 h 24 min 4 s – an average speed of 20.66 mph/33.25 kph – on the banked Crystal Palace cycle track on 21–22 November 1900. Its drivers, Théry and Gabriel, subsequently achieved fame as racing drivers.

■ The first road surveyor to use a car for his work was Percy J. Sheldon, county surveyor of Essex County Council, who provided a 4½-hp De Dion-Bouton for his use in 1901.

■ In 1904 there were 28 842 vehicles registered in Britain. A year later the figure had risen to 66 703. Figures for cars licensed and in use were respectively 8465 and 16 895.

■ Dust sucked up from the unsurfaced roads was a major problem for early motorists (it still is in places like the Australian outback). Various road dressings were tried in the early days – in 1903 the 'Westrumite' company's product was used to lay the dust on the Gordon Bennett race circuit in Ireland – but tar was first applied to a Macadam surface in 1902 in Monte Carlo. It was the idea of Dr Guglielminetti, a Swiss, who became known as 'Dr Goudron' ('Dr Tar'). At first the tar was brushed on cold; soon it was being applied hot. In the United States Amzi Lorenzo Barber's Trinidad Asphalt Company had a virtual monopoly in the use of this material between 1888 and 1908 and had laid asphalt roads in Washington as early as 1878. However, as late as 1904, some 93 per cent of America's 2.2 million miles of rural roads were still unsurfaced.

■ The strangest layout of any early car was that of the 1901 Sunbeam Mabley, designed by architect Mabberley Smith. The wheels were arranged diamond fashion to 'overcome sideslip'; the offset front and rear wheels steered, the centre pair of wheels drove, and the seats were arranged in an 'S' shape like a Victorian sociable settee, with their occupants sitting sideways to the line of travel. The driver sat at the rear, steering the machine by a short tiller. Though the engine was at the front, the starting handle was under the driving seat.

■ The most horrendously bad design of the early days of motoring was unquestionably the Pennington 'Raft' of 1899. It flew in the face of reason with a degree of foolhardiness that deserved a medal. Where every other car on the road steered with the front wheels, the Raft steered with the back. Needless to say, it drove with the front – by a twisted rope belt. Its engine had no form of cooling, was mounted in the centre of the chassis well away from any current of air, and its crankshaft was vertical, so that the primary drive chain was perpetually tempted by gravity to fall off the sprockets – which it frequently did. Tightening the chain (of course) loosened the belt, and vice versa. It had neither steering wheel nor tiller, just a vertical lever like a hand-brake moving fore-and-aft, a totally unnatural motion for steering. Nor was there a carburetter, just a simple drip valve which let neat petrol trickle into the immensely long cylinder. And if that wasn't enough sheer enjoyment for the most dedicated of sado-masochists, it got through spark plugs at a rate that beggars belief. In 1899 a brave soul named Hubert Egerton – first man to ride from Land's End to John O'Groats on a motor cycle – set out to drive a Pennington Raft from Manchester to London. He gave up after having covered 16 miles in 9 hours; he had used up all the spares on board and burnt out no fewer than 48 spark plugs.

ORIGINS

Alfa Romeo (I) Founded by Ugo Stella as Anonima Lombardo Fabbrica Automobili in 1909, produced its first ALFA cars in 1910. Taken over by Nicola Romeo in 1915, and the name Alfa Romeo adopted after World War I. Gained splendid racing record. Became part of the Fiat empire in 1986.

American Motors (AMC) (USA). Formed by the merger of the ailing Nash and Hudson companies in 1954, and from 1958 a Nash marque name, Rambler, was used for the range. AMC badging came from 1968, and was even used on imported Renaults. Acquired by Chrysler in 1987, effectively becoming the Jeep-Eagle Division.

Aston Martin (GB) The first car built by Bamford & Martin appeared in 1914 and the Aston Martin name was adopted in 1915 (the Aston prefix derives from Aston Hill, where Martin achieved hill climb success). Specialised in sports and high-performance cars. The company survived several crises and changes of ownership, but since 1987 has been revitalised as a Ford subsidiary.

Audi (D) The first Audi company was set up by August Horch in 1910, and lasted until 1928 when Rasmussen took over. In the 1930s it was part of the Auto Union combine, and the name was not revived after World War II until 1965. Under VW control it became a consistently successful marque.

Austin (GB) The first car completed by Herbert Austin's company appeared in 1906. Austin survived receivership after World War I, and from 1922 small cars under-pinned its prosperity. Merged with Morris in 1952, forming BMC and it was then absorbed into BLMC. The last Austin introduced as such was the Montego of 1984, but in 1988 this was badged as a Rover, when the Austin-Rover Group gave way to Rover.

Austro-Daimler (A) The Austrian branch of the Daimler company became independent in 1906 and built some outstanding cars, designed by Paul Daim-

ler and Ferdinand Porsche. Amalgamated with Puch from 1928, and Steyr from 1930, Austro-Daimler lasted only until 1934.

Bentley (GB) W. O. Bentley announced his first model in 1919, and production cars appeared in 1922. Through the 1920s Bentley built high-performance cars, but the company was hardly sound in business terms. Rolls-Royce acquired it from the receiver in 1931, and the marque identity was allowed to fade. However, in the late 1980s distinctive Bentleys started to appear.

Benz (D) Karl Benz' pioneering company dated from 1885, but by the end of the century his conservatism meant it was stagnating. After he left, it built some outstanding cars. Benz was merged with Mercedes in 1926.

BMW (D) The established aero engine and motorcycle manufacturer produced its first cars in 1928 (Austin Sevens built under licence). Increasingly refined models in the 1930s pointed toward BMW's future, but in the immediate post-World War II period old designs were built in East Germany. BMWs were built at Munich from 1951, and from the late 1960s the company became a substantial force, acquiring Rover in 1994.

Bollée (F) Amédée Bollée *père* built self-propelled vehicles at Le Mans from 1873. Amédée Bollée *fils* produced small numbers of cars 1896–1914 (a few were assembled later). Léon Bollée built notable light cars 1895–1901, then larger, staid, cars until Morris took over 1924–31; an attempt to revive the marque 1931–3 failed.

Bugatti (F) Ettore Bugatti's company was German when it was established at Molsheim in 1909, became French when Alsace was returned to France after World War I. It produced a few notable models between the wars, but is often overrated. A few cars were built after World War II. In the late 1980s Romano Artioli chose to revive the Bugatti name for an Italian-based supercar venture, with a first launch in 1991.

Buick (USA) David Buick formed his company in 1903 but William Durant took control late in 1904. Four years later he set up General Motors, with Buick as a 'founder company'. Buick continues as an important GM marque.

Cadillac (USA) Founded by Henry M. Leland in 1902, Cadillac became part of GM in 1909 and tended to produce its 'quality cars', with V8s standardised from 1914, V12s and V16s coming for the 1930s. Post-World War II models have been V8s, some technically advanced and all aimed at the luxury end of the market.

Chevrolet (USA) When he lost control of GM in 1910, William Durant set up a new manufacturer with racing driver Louis Chevrolet in 1911. Their first car came in 1912, the one millionth in 1923. Success meant that Durant regained control of GM (only to lose out again), and Chevrolet challenged Ford as market leader. In the 75th year of production it was America's best-selling marque, and had built more than 110 million vehicles.

Chrysler (USA) Formed by Walter Chrysler on the basis of the Maxwell company, the first Chryslers were sold in 1924. The name was to be used for prestige models, with the related Plymouth and Dodge names used for 'popular' types. Chrysler survived a slump in the 1960s, withdrew from Europe in the late 1970s, returning in the 1990s.

Citroën (F) One-time Mors chief engineer André Citroën produced his first car in 1919, then introduced American-style mass production methods to Europe. Less successful in business terms was the revolutionary Traction Avant in 1934 – it bankrupted the company, which was taken over by Michelin. It continued to produce individualistic cars, since 1974 with considerable interchange with Peugeot, which then controlled the company.

Daimler (GB) The British Daimler company was founded in 1896, and was to become known for its majestic cars. Merged with BSA in 1910, taken over by Jaguar in 1960.

De Dion-Bouton (F) One of the earliest companies in the industry, dating from 1883 as the Comte Albert de Dion backed mechanics Bouton and Trépardoux in a steam carriage business. Petrol engines came in the mid-1890s, and the company built the first worthwhile production V8 in 1910. The company struggled to survive in the 1920s, completing its last car in 1932.

Delage (F) One of the great marques of France in the 1920s and 1930s, although Louis Delâge's company produced few cars of note during its early years, from 1905. Delâge was forced to sell out to Delahaye

The first Chevrolet leaving the company's Detroit plant in 1912.

in 1935, and nominal production continued until Hotchkiss acquired the remnants in 1954.

Delahaye (F) Emile Delahaye built his first car in 1894, left his company in 1901. After World War I Delahaye concentrated on commercial vehicles, until the mid-1930s when it entered the *grand' routier* market. That theme was half-heartedly picked up after World War II, but when the end came in 1954 Delahaye was building lorries again.

Dodge (USA) Dodge Brothers' first cars were built in 1914, the company was bought by Chrysler in 1928 and for years Dodge cars were closely related to

Plymouth models. In the 1970s the name was used for cars with Mitsubishi origins, and in the 1980s for sporty cars.

Ferrari (I) The first cars bearing Enzo Ferrari's name appeared in 1946, and the marque has always been known for its high-performance road cars and its racing cars. These have often been seen as representing Italian auto engineering, hence Fiat sometimes helped Ferrari, took a 50 per cent holding in 1969 to ensure the marque's survival. Since Ferrari's death, his company has become a high-profile member of the group.

Fiat (I) Giovanni Agnelli founded Fabbrica Italiana Automobili Torino (FIAT) in 1899, and it became Fiat in 1906, growing into an industrial giant with car manufacture just one of its activities. Its first popular model did not come until 1912, but it has since been successful with mass-produced types, leaving the tiny prestige sectors to companies it took under its wing, nowadays notably Alfa Romeo, Ferrari and Lancia.

Ford (USA) Henry Ford's early companies and cars were at best modestly successful, but the Ford Motor Co. founded in 1903 grew into a multi-national giant. The Model A was cheap and simple, but among early Fords the best known was the simple and slightly eccentric Model T, which sold some 16½ million. A British Ford company came in 1909, started manufacture in 1911 and by the mid-1920s there were Ford factories all around the world. The empire became large enough to shrug off some real lemons, and particularly in Europe, underwent rationalisation.

General Motors In production terms, the world's largest producer, dating from 1908 and comprising marques such as Buick, Cadillac, Chevrolet, Oldsmobile and Pontiac, Vauxhall and Opel in Europe, and Holden in Australia.

Hispano-Suiza (E) Set up in Spain in 1904, with a title recognising the important contribution of its Swiss designer, Marc Birkigt, the company opened a French plant in 1911. In the 1920s and 1930s this was to produce some notable cars. The Barcelona factory built a few cars until 1944, the French operation lasted until 1938.

Holden (AUS) An Australian body-building company was absorbed by GM in 1931 to become General Motors-Holden, which launched its first car

Fiat turned to small cars with the 500 'Topolino', and has generally been most successful when it has followed this theme.

in 1948. It was developed into a major producer and exporter, but also a serious loss maker in the 1980s. Part of the solution was found in marketing Nissans and Suzukis to run under local names alongside GM-H products.

Honda (J) The first Honda cars in 1962 reflected the company's motor-cycle background, then through the 1970s and 1980s it developed a range of sophisticated models. Established a close collaboration with Rover – at least until the BMW take over of that company – and set up a Honda operation in Britain in the 1990s.

Humber (GB) Thomas Humber's motor tricycles gave way to a light car in 1903, and the solid middle-class cars for which the company is recalled came in the 1920s. Rootes took over in 1930, and after a period of 'badge engineering' under Chrysler ownership the last Humber was delivered in 1976.

Jaguar (GB) Following Swallow Sidecars (SS) bodies for various small cars in the late 1920s, the first SS car, using Standard components, came in 1931. 'Jaguar' was added to SS in 1935, and the company became Jaguar Cars in 1945. Acquired Daimler/Lanchester in 1960, was in turn merged with BMC in 1966, when Sir William Lyons largely retained control. Survived difficult periods, regained independence in 1984, was taken on by Ford at the end of the decade.

Lamborghini (I) Tractor manufacturer Ferruccio Lamborghini reputedly intended to 'out-Ferrari' Ferrari when he launched his first car in 1966. A string of high-performance models followed, some successful, some flashy and short-lived, none the basis for a good business. Lamborghini sold out in 1972; 15 years later Chrysler took it on, despaired and sold the faltering enterprise to the Indonesia-based MegaTech in 1994.

Lanchester (GB) The Lanchester brothers were pioneer automotive engineers, built their first car in 1895, with distinctive production cars following from 1900. More conventional prestige models came in the 1920s, before Daimler took over in 1931. The name survived until 1956.

Lancia (I) Vincenzo Lancia left Fiat in 1906 and the first production model bearing his name came in 1907 (Alpha, introducing the practice of using letters of the Greek alphabet as designations). Lancias were advanced, particularly the Lambda of the 1920s, and fine engineering was a hallmark after World War II. The business results were not so good; eventually

Fiat took on the debts, and while the badge survived the take over eventually spelled the end for the 'pure' Lancia line.

Lincoln (USA) Henry Leland formed Lincoln in 1920, and sold the bankrupt company to Henry Ford two years later. Ford maintained the 'quality' image; after World War II some Lincolns were handsome prestige cars, others were just very large, then downsizing came in the 1980s.

Lotus (GB) Colin Chapman's cars were never built in remarkable quantities, but some had outstanding qualities, were highly original and efficient. In the 1970s he moved the range up-market, not altogether successfully. GM gained control in 1986, Romano Artioli's Bugatti company took over in 1993.

Maserati (I) From the late 1950s, this company was far removed from the motoring boutique the Maserati brothers set up in 1912, built tiny numbers of cars from 1926, and sold to Omer Orsi in 1937. It nearly went down some twenty years later, then had affiliations with Citroën, de Tomaso, the Italian government and Chrysler, generally building 'supercars' until the 1980s when lack of success led to a realignment.

Mazda (J) Toyo Kogyo (founded in 1920) built three-wheel trucks from 1931 and its first production Mazda car in 1960. From 1967 through to the 1990s it was the only car manufacturer to persevere with the Wankel-type rotary engine, although its expanding range of increasingly sophisticated small and medium cars with conventional power units was more important. The company is quarter-owned by Ford.

Mercedes-Benz (D) The Mercedes name as such was used 1901–26 – earlier there were Daimlers, and after that there was Mercedes-Benz. Through a century the companies enjoyed reputations for sound, but usually conventional, high-quality engineering, and enlivened by bursts of sporting success.

Mercury (USA) Created as Ford-Mercury by Henry Ford in 1938, to fill a market gap between Ford and Lincoln. Continued in that vein, but gradually moved closer to Lincoln (in the Lincoln-Mercury Division). Later used as a badge for some imported European Fords, as well as clean-lined compacts.

MG (GB) Specials built by Cecil Kimber of Morris Garages led to the first MG (the 14/28) late in 1924. The famous Abingdon factory was opened in 1929, and lasted until 1980. Morris took over in 1935, after

Three early Lamborghini models – the Espada, the exemplary Miura and the Jarama.

World War II MG therefore passed through the BMC and BL phases until, seemingly, the last 'traditional' sports car was completed in 1980, and the badge was used on saloons. Then Rover tentatively returned to tradition with the MG RV8.

Mitsubishi (J) Apart from a handful of Model As in 1917, Mitsubishi did not enter the car market until 1959, and from 1969 was part-owned by Chrysler – hence collaborative programmes in the USA and Australia, and sometimes confusing model names (complicated as for some time Colt was used as a make name in Europe).

Morgan (GB) H. F. S. Morgan built his first three-wheeler in 1908–9, but the first four-wheeled production car with the famous independent front suspension did not come until 1936. Essentially, all subsequent Morgans have followed similar lines, albeit with much more powerful engines, and the company has carefully kept production within known demands, thus avoiding motor industry expansion pitfalls.

Morris (GB) The first Morris Oxford was sold in 1913, and the model name was used for many years, on best-selling cars in the 1920s. Absorbed companies such as Wolseley and MG, was merged with traditional rival Austin to form BMC in 1952, and that in turn became part of British Leyland. The name was allowed to lapse in 1983.

Nash (USA) Charles W. Nash built his first car under his own name in 1917. His company survived the recession and setbacks, built some quite advanced models, set up an association with Healey in the early 1950s, became one arm of AMC. Then the name faded away, and was dropped altogether in 1957.

Nissan (J) The origins of the Japanese company were in a prototype built by Kwaishinsha in 1912, and in the production DAT from 1915. The name was changed to Datsun in 1932; the first car to carry it was based on the Austin Seven, and came in 1933. The company name became Nissan in 1937, but until the start of the 1980s cars were still marketed as Datsuns. Nissan was the first Japanese manufacturer to set up in Europe, opening its UK plant in 1986.

Oldsmobile (USA) Ransom Eli Olds built a car in 1895, a company was established, and made its name

An early Morgan 4/4, priced at 185 guineas (£194.25) in 1937.

The '£100 Morris', the simplest two-seater version of the 1930 Minor.

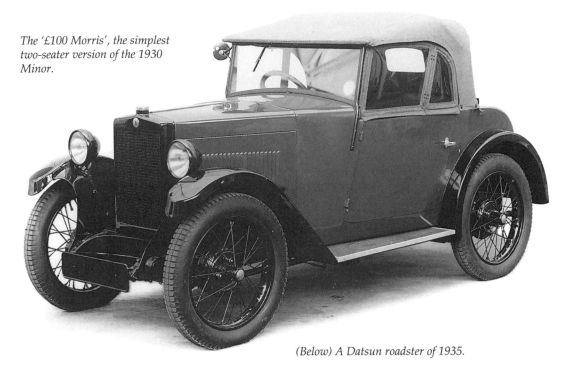

(Below) A Datsun roadster of 1935.

with the Curved Dash that appeared in 1901. Oldsmobile was acquired by General Motors in 1909 (the millionth GM car was an Olds, in 1916, and so was the 100 millionth, in 1966). After World War II it built some notable performance cars – the 1966 Toronado was the most powerful front-wheel drive car – and the 1990s range was wide.

Opel (D) The first Opels were on Lutzmann lines, from 1898, and the first true Opels came in 1902. The company embraced mass-production in 1924, but with a car that was too similar to the Citroën 5CV and had to be modified. GM took control in 1929, and production reached a million by 1940. Three decades on Opel was GM's European flagship company.

Packard (USA) Formed in 1899, taken over in 1901, Packard became established as a leading manufacturer of luxury cars during the Edwardian period. That position was held through to World War II, but never regained after it. Studebaker was acquired in 1951, then the ailing group was taken over, and the last Packards were sold in 1958.

Panhard (F) Pioneer French manufacturer, prominent in early racing. It concentrated on sleeve-valve engines from 1912 and into the 1930s, and after World War II turned to distinctive small cars. Citroën took over, for Panhard's factory premises rather than its car designs, and the last Panhard car was built in 1967.

Peugeot (F) Another French company with roots in the horseless carriage era – Armand Peugeot built his first steam car in 1889. Petrol-engined cars followed from 1891 and a range developed. Robert Peugeot broke away and set up Lion-Peugeot in 1906, but this became part of the main company in 1910. Peugeot set high-performance standards with its 1912 GP car (after 1914 it stayed away from racing's top category until 1994). After World War I its products were generally staid, after World War II tough and reliable rather than exciting, until the 1980s. Peugeot took control of Citroën in 1974 and Chrysler's European companies in 1979 (briefly reviving the Talbot name for them).

Pierce-Arrow (USA) One of America's great marques, Pierce-Arrow introduced a light car in 1901, and the first of its large cars three years later. That set the standard for the next 30 years, but a five-year merger with Studebaker undermined the product; lost ground could not be recovered in a final independent period and production ended in 1938.

Plymouth (USA) Introduced as Chrysler's popular marque in 1928, a position maintained through to the 1960s, when the departure was the introduction of 'performance' models. More recently Plymouth's few large models have shadowed equivalent Dodges, or been rebadged Mitsubishis.

Pontiac (USA) The only marque formed by General Motors to have stamina, Pontiac came in 1926 to cater for the cheap end of the market. That did not apply so strongly after World War II, and from the 1960s it was responsible for semi-sporting and high-performance cars.

Porsche (D) Almost from the start, in 1948, Porsche cars had a strong image despite the early close relationship with the humble VW Beetle (itself a product of Ferdinand Porsche's pre-World War II design bureau). Its air-cooled, rear-engined cars came in many forms, and in some respects outlived their day, through a refusal to recognise changing times or worthwhile developments outside Porsche. Successful in most branches of motor sport, except the two highest single-seater racing categories where its cars made little impact. Porsche eventually adopted front-engined layouts, and water cooling. It was hurt by sales downturns from the late 1980s.

Renault (F) Louis Renault built the first car of the marque in 1898, and demand for replicas led to his brothers backing a production company. Prominent in early racing, but more importantly in building popular cars (and also some very grand ones). At the end of World War II Renault was nationalised. Between the wars it had produced many dull cars; its little rear-engine 4CV (1946–61) was the first Renault to sell a million and the Dauphine that followed sold two million, despite shortcomings and its dismal failure in America (where Renault was rebuffed more than once). Eventually, Renault turned to front-wheel drive cars. The R5 was a best seller from 1972, and was timely as others in the range were not selling well. There were sporting enterprises, in rallies, with Alpine sports cars and turbocharged GP cars, and the association supplying Formula 1 engines to Williams that at last brought championships, in the

The first Porsche, a 356 roadster, with its creator Ferry Porsche (left) and his father Ferdinand, whose Volkswagen was the basis of this Porsche.

early 1990s. Meanwhile, there was a collaborative PRV (Peugeot-Renault-Volvo) arrangement, and the setback of an unconsummated merger with Volvo.

Riley (GB) Notable for its high-quality medium-size cars in the 1920s and 1930s. Riley's first car had been built in 1898, and after a take over by Morris in 1938 the long-term destiny of the diamond badge was to fade away on variants of BMC models in 1969.

Rolls-Royce (GB) Henry Royce, engineer, improved on the Decauville he owned, in 1903–4. The Royce car impressed the Hon. C. S. Rolls, and Rolls-Royce came into being. It produced some sound cars, then the 40/50 that came to be known as the Silver Ghost, which with modest upratings was continued until 1925. The company weathered the recession, although its American offshoot did not, and nor did Bentley

which Rolls-Royce acquired in 1931. After World War II car production was moved from Derby to Crewe, where the first complete R-R cars (Silver Dawns) were built in 1949 – previously only chassis had been built. Production reached 100 000 in 1985, when the company had been part of the Vickers group for five years.

Rover (GB) Like many car companies, Rover had its origins in bicycle manufacture. Its first car was produced in 1904, and in the 1930s its reputation came safely to rest on middle-class models. After World War II the inspired Land Rover became its leading production model; in developed forms it was continued into the 1990s, with the more refined Range Rover alongside it from 1970. In 1986 the Rover Group took on the mantle of British Leyland, and a fruitful collaboration with Honda was developed, at least until Rover's owners, British Aerospace, sold the company to BMW in 1994.

Saab (S) This Swedish aircraft manufacturer showed its first car in 1947, and production of this distinctive

(Above) One of the three Royce cars built in 1904
before Rolls joined Royce.

(Below) Four decades of gradual development separate
the Land Rover of 1948 and the 1988 Land Rover
County Station Wagon.

92 started in 1949. It had an unusual aerodynamic body and two-stroke engine. Saab's first four-stroke engines were offered in 1967. During the 1960s the Saab team built up a great rally record. The company merged with Scania-Vabis in 1969, survives in the 1990s despite its theoretically uneconomic production levels with GM involvement.

SEAT (E) The Sociedad Española de Automóbiles de Turismo had its origins in Fiat's Spanish subsidiary, as early as 1922, but was formally established in 1950 as a joint venture between Fiat and the National Institute of Industry. Its first car was completed in 1953, and in 1969 it built its one millionth. The BL Spanish plant was taken over in 1975, INI took over Fiat's holding in 1981, and in 1982 there was an agreement with VW, which became the major shareholder in 1986. Early cars were in effect Fiats, and so was the 133 that was claimed to be exclusive in 1974; the Ibiza (1984) and Malaga (1985) were originals, in a decade that saw SEAT become a major European manufacturer.

Singer (GB) Built its first car in 1905, and in the 1920s its small cars were very successful, so that late in the decade Singer gave best only to Austin and Morris in British production terms. It was fading when Rootes took over in 1956, and survived to 1970 only with badge-engineered Hillmans.

Standard (GB) The name was well-intentioned, suggesting a uniform level of production in its first cars (from 1903), but unfortunate in that in some countries it meant 'basic'. Early Standards were competent, the Flying Standards of the late 1930s were eye-catching, and a one-model Vanguard range was essayed from 1948. It rescued Triumph after World War II, and that marque outlived it in the BL group – Standard was dropped in 1963.

Studebaker (USA) Built carriages and wagons in mass-production quantities from 1854, including many 'Prairie Schooners', a batch of electric cars in 1902, petrol cars from 1904 – and horse carriages until 1919. It seemed to flourish after World War I, but was bankrupt in 1928. The receiver sold it in 1933, and there was a sluggish recovery. There was promise in the post-World War II models styled by the Loewy studios, but by 1964 only Studebaker's Canadian plant was operating, and production ended in 1966.

Subaru (J) This company in the Fuji Heavy Industries group built its first micro car in 1958, its first full-size model in 1966, and the world's first mass-production 4-wd car in 1972. That pointed to a range that was to become increasingly sophisticated.

Sunbeam (GB) Another bicycle manufacturer, which built its first car – an odd device – in 1899. There was little outstanding about the following models; some notable racing cars came, especially in 1912 and 1923, when Sunbeam produced the first British car to win a Grand Prix. On the production side, the Sunbeam-Talbot-Darracq combine was unhappy. Rootes picked up some pieces in 1936, established the Sunbeam-Talbot marque. The Sunbeam name was revived in 1953, used on some nice sporting cars, and then badge-engineered cars through to 1976.

Talbot (GB/F) The first Talbots were Anglo-French (Clément-Talbots) in 1903, but by 1906 the company was building its own British designs. Some high-quality sporting cars were built between the wars, despite the problems of the STD combine, then under Rootes ownership the Talbot name was linked to Sunbeam. Meanwhile, a French Talbot company emerged in 1920, marketing its cars as Darracqs in Britain. It was given new life as Talbot-Lago from 1935, then faded away in the 1950s, the last car being built in 1959. However, Peugeot revived the name in 1979, for cars built at one-time Chrysler factories in Europe, but that lasted for only five years.

Tatra (CS) This Czech company built cars to Hans Ledwinka's highly original designs from 1923, culminating in big cars with rear-mounted V8s. This theme was picked up after World War II, and production continued in small numbers through the communist period and on into the 1990s.

Toyota (J) The first car built under Kiichiro Toyoda's direction in 1935 followed Chrysler Airflow lines, and 'aerodynamic' models were produced before and after World War II (from 1937 with the Toyota name). A conventional range was expanded from the 1950s, and in 1980 Toyota built more cars than Chevrolet. Soon there were joint manufacturing agreements with Chevrolet, and on through the 1980s Toyota production kept rising, then a European factory was opened in Britain.

Triumph (GB) A move into car manufacture came in 1923, and through the next 15 years Triumph grew with a semi-sporting image, before the company folded in 1939. It was resurrected by Standard in 1945, to build sports cars on largely 'traditional' lines until 1981 and saloons until 1984.

Vauxhall (GB) Early Vauxhalls ranged from the first runabout in 1903 to forerunners of the sports car in the years before World War I. General Motors took over in 1925, but did not immediately impose American practices. Vauxhall built the first British unitary-construction saloons in 1938. GM influences were more obvious after World War II, and from the 1970s Vauxhalls tended to follow Opel designs.

Volkswagen (D) One of the most familiar shapes on the world's roads for many years was the rear-engined Beetle, which had its origins in German 'people's car' projects from 1931, but did not reach production until 1945 – under British military control. The ten millionth Beetle was built in 1965; long after it had been set aside in Germany, production continued in Mexico and Brazil. The K70 of 1970, originally an NSU design which came under VW control with Audi, was the first front-wheel drive VW with a water-cooled engine. That pattern was to spread through the range, with the Golf being the principal model in the late 1970s and 1980s, and built in several countries.

Volvo (S) Prototype Volvos appeared in 1926 and modest production started in 1927. After World War II Volvo marketing efforts spread more widely, and safety was to be increasingly emphasised. Jensen built some Volvo bodies in the 1960s, in the next decade Volvo took over the Dutch Daf company, while there were collaborative efforts with Renault (although a merger with the French company failed to go through in the early 1990s). For a generation, Volvos were widely regarded as staid and safe medium/large cars, and perhaps in an effort to change this image the company entered racing in 1994.

Wolseley (GB) Another of the once-prominent British pioneering companies that eventually fell victim to mergers. Wolseley built its first car in 1899, to a design by Herbert Austin. Ironically, Austin's rival Morris acquired Wolseley in 1927. A wide range was maintained, including models with small six-cylinder engines. After World War II there were increasing interchanges with other Morris models, then BMC models, then British Leyland models, until 1976.

Volkswagen 'Beetle' production passed a landmark in 1982, when this car came off the production line in Mexico (an original production car, with its 'Pope's nose' number plate light, is in the foreground). In 1993 'Beetle' production restarted in Brazil.

MILESTONES

MARQUES

■ The most successful early steam car was the Locomobile. The Locomobile Co. bought the patent and manufacturing rights in the Stanley steam car in April 1899 for $250 000. The early popularity of the frail little Locomobile soon waned and the Stanley twins bought back the ailing business in May 1901 for just $20 000. Though their Stanley Motor Carriage Company carried on business in Newton, Massachusetts, until 1924, its peak annual output in 1912 was just 650 cars.

■ Long before Henry Ford devised mass-production, the idea of interchangeable parts was conceived in the Connecticut clock trade and brought to maturity by the American small-arms industry. Henry Leland (who had worked for Colt) and Ransom Olds in America, De Dion-Bouton in France and Lanchester in England all based their car production on fully interchangeable machined components with little or no hand fitting several years before Ford perfected the moving production line (which was inspired by the 'disassembly' lines used by the Chicago meat industry).

■ The first American to ride in a petrol car was piano maker William Steinway of New York, who met Gottlieb Daimler in Cannstatt on a visit to Europe in 1888, took a short trip aboard a 'road motor car' and secured American rights to the Daimler engine, which was built under licence in Hartford, Connecticut from 1891. Complete cars of German Daimler design were not made in the US until 1905, when 45-hp and 70-hp Mercedes were built in Long Island by the successors to Steinway's Daimler Motor Company.

■ Studebaker of South Bend, Indiana, were America's biggest carriage builders long before they became car manufacturers and made many of the 'Prairie Schooners' used by American settlers heading West in the 19th century. They built horse carriages until 1919.

■ The first time that a production car was given a distinctive model name occurred in 1893 when Carl Benz called his first four-wheeled car 'Viktoria' because he was delighted over 'the victory of a happy idea'. It was also the first of hundreds of cars named after girls.

■ One of the earliest and most famous car names is 'Mercedes', originally given in 1901 to the epochal new 35-hp Cannstatt Daimler. Emil Jellinek, a Daimler director and agent for the marque in Nice, agreed to take a series of 36 of the new model, provided it was named after his 11-year-old daughter Mercédès. The story goes that the Austrian affiliate of the Daimler company later adopted the name of her sister, Maja, as a marque name. It's a pretty tale but, sadly, Mercédès' baby sister was called Andrée.

■ American pioneer car builder Charles Duryea was a devout Trinitarian and the cars he built from 1900 to 1907 when he was active in Reading, Pennsylvania, exemplified his religious beliefs, for they had three wheels and three cylinders, while the elaborately-carved body sides were a representation of the Christian fish symbol.

■ America was the spiritual and temporal home of the steam car. Not only did it house the most successful makes – White, Stanley and Locomobile – but it also spawned some 380 other marques, most of them stunningly ephemeral. Many of them burned paraffin (kerosene), but some early marques (including Stanley) used high-volatility petrol. Wonderful to drive and possessing amazing acceleration, an early steamer is not for the faint hearted. The writer drove a borrowed Stanley to Brighton in the early 1980s and made his quickest-ever run despite catching fire twice. Seeing flames licking up between your knees is not a happy sight.

■ The maker of the Pierce-Arrow, one of America's finest luxury cars, the George N. Pierce Company of Buffalo, New York, began in 1865 by making cages for birds and pet squirrels. It also made ice boxes, the Victorian predecessor of the refrigerator.

■ Peerless, another of the 'three Ps' of the American luxury car world (the third was Packard), began by making clothes wringers. By 1900 it was making bicycles, too, and turned to automobiles that year. After car production ended in 1931 the company again changed direction and survives to this day as the brewers of Carling Black Label beer.

■ Peugeot, which built its first (steam-powered) car as long ago as 1889, began with the water-mill operated by Jean-Jacques Peugeot in the early 18th century. From 1832 the firm has been famous as a manufacturer of hardware such as tools, coffee grinders and pepper mills and – from 1885 – bicycles. Among its more bizarre products have been steel crinoline stays and dentures.

■ 'American' was popular as a marque name: seven different makers used it between 1896 and 1924 (and over 50 hopeful manufacturers said they were going to – and didn't). More than 50 makers used the adjective 'American' as part of their marque name.

■ Though Cadillac is one of America's leading marques, the man after whom it was named – Le Sieur Antoine de la Mothe Cadillac, Knight of the Royal & Military Order of St Louis, who founded the city of Detroit in 1701 – was, it seems, an imposter. Studies in the 1940s suggested that he was a humbly born French adventurer named Antoine Laumet who adopted the name of the defunct Chevalier de la Mothe (killed by Indians in 1690) after his arrival in the New World; the addition of 'Cadillac' to imply ownership of a town in the Bordeaux wine region was another fiction.

■ The Walter car built in New York between 1902 and 1906 was the product of the American Chocolate Machinery Company of Manhattan, whose principal business was the manufacture of chocolate-making equipment.

■ The most popular name for aspiring car manufacturers in the early days was 'Standard'. Apart from the well-known Coventry company, which lasted 60 years (1903–63), there were two Italian, one German, one Indian and 15 American companies who produced cars under this name – and 35 more US companies who announced their intention to build a car under this marque name (but probably didn't).

■ The first reinforced concrete building erected for motor car manufacture was the Packard factory constructed in Detroit in 1903 and designed by architect Albert Kahn, who was to become the leading designer of car factories for the American motor industry.

■ David Dunbar Buick, founder of the company bearing his name in 1903, made the money which enabled him to become a motor manufacturer (the original company name was 'Buick Auto-Vim & Power Company') by inventing a patent process for porcelain-enamelling cast iron bathtubs. An incompetent businessman, he was out of the Buick company by 1908 and died in poverty 21 years later.

■ The first car to be offered with a 'perpetual guarantee' was the 1904 Acme, from Reading, Pennsylvania. Perpetuity in this case was disturbingly finite: Acme closed down in 1911.

■ The origins of some companies were bizarre. They include pipe organs (Crawford 1904 and Dagmar 1922), radios and refrigerators (Crosley 1939), photographic plates (Stanley 1897), shirt collars (Dormandy 1903), typewriters and guns (Remington 1900), sewing machines (Swift 1898, Opel 1898 and White 1900), clocks and watches (Elgin 1916), barrel staves (Elmore 1899), pianos (Foster 1900 and Heine-Velox 1906), sheep-shearing machinery (Wolseley 1896), popcorn roasters (Glide 1903), football pools (Gordon 1954) and merry-go-rounds (Herschell-Spillman 1905).

■ The famous Vauxhall bonnet flutes that were such a prominent feature of the marque for many years from 1905 were inspired by the design of a company executive's wardrobe. The Vauxhall Griffin logo was the crest of the medieval nobleman Fulk le Bréant, whose London seat ('Fulk's Hall') was the origin of Vauxhall, where the company was founded as an ironworks in Victorian times. Coincidentally, Fulk had earlier lived at Luton, where the company moved in 1905.

■ Chevrolet's distinctive 'bow-tie' emblem was taken from the pattern on the wallpaper in a French hotel.

■ The famous Ford script emblem is not, as legend has it, based on Henry Ford's signature; it was taken from the type in a home printing outfit which Ford engineer Childe Harold Wills had used as a teenager to make pin-money, printing visiting cards.

■ Legros & Knowles of Willesden, London, expected their clients to have a sound classical education when they chose the name 'Iris' for their new marque in 1905. 'Iris' was the 'speedy messenger of the gods' in Greek mythology. That message having fallen on deaf ears, some bright spark coined the acronym 'It Runs In Silence', which was more ingenious than truthful.

■ The smallest four-wheeled 'automobiles' ever built were the motorised roller skates announced by Herdtlé & Bruneau of Paris in 1905. Each four-wheeled skate was 20 inches long and had a tiny petrol engine. It was claimed that it was capable of 40 mph. But what happened if one skate engine stopped at that speed?

■ The American-built Ariel of 1905–7 (which occupied no fewer than five factories during its brief life) offered not only one of the first overhead camshaft engines but also the choice of water-cooling for summer and air-cooling for winter.

■ The leading European make of steam car was the Serpollet (or Gardner-Serpollet). Léon Serpollet patented the first practicable 'flash' boiler, or instantaneous generator, in 1889. His early death in 1907 robbed the steam car of one of its most ingenious designers. The business was taken over by Darracq, but Darracq-Serpollet made steam buses for a few years and discontinued the private cars.

■ The only car to be fitted with two starting handles was the Carter Two-Engine of 1907. The idea of having two independent engines was purely a failsafe for the car (whose badge was two interlinked hearts) would run happily on one.

■ The American industry grew rapidly after the introduction of the Model T Ford in October 1908. During 1909, 10 607 Model Ts (cars or light commercial vehicles) were built, and in 1923 the peak was reached at 2 033 071 units. In addition to the parent factories in the USA, there were assembly plants on every inhabited continent, the principal ones being in Canada and England. When production of the Model T stopped in 1927 the grand total was around 16 million (though historians are still arguing about the precise total). This record was subsequently beaten by the VW 'Beetle' – over 20 million of these cars have been produced (over a far longer period) but no car has ever beaten – or is likely to – the Model T's 56.5 per cent share of world registrations set in 1921 or its 50.4 per cent of world car production, recorded in 1918 when the output of Model Ts reached 642 750 units out of a world total of 1 275 324 vehicles.

■ Acronyms and initials are fraught with peril for the unwary: when Messrs Everitt, Metzger and Flan-ders combined to build the EMF car in 1908, wags stated that the initials stood for 'Every Morning Fixit', 'Every Mechanical Fault' or 'Eternally Missing Fire'; Kenneth Krittenden's KRIT marque name was said to stand for 'Keeps Right In Town'.

■ In similar vein, De Dions became 'Ding-Dongs', Hispano-Suiza was dubbed 'Banana-Squeezer' and Pierce-Arrow (appropriately, because of its origins) was transmuted into 'Fierce-Sparrow'. The owner of the sole surviving 1899 Bégot-Mazurie obviously spoke from bitter experience when he dubbed this obscure veteran marque 'Bag o' Misery'.

■ The first company to be incorporated specifically to build taxicabs was the Gary Taxicab Company of Chicago, incorporated in 1909. More significant, though, was Yellow Cab, also of Chicago, founded in 1915 under the management of former newspaper boy and boxing manager John Hertz, who from 1908 had been converting second-hand cars into taxis. The Yellow Cab – sold on a form of franchise – was amazingly successful and the company became part of General Motors in 1925. John Hertz then went on to build cars for his next scheme, a car rental company, but found it was more profitable to buy cars built by other manufacturers. The corporate yellow colour scheme of Hertz Car Rental is a memento of the Yellow Cab.

■ It used to be possible to buy an automobile by mail order in the United States. Motor buggies were offered by the great Chicago mail order house Sears, Roebuck from 1908 to 1912. Sears, Roebuck's great rival, Montgomery Ward, offered the Modoc (named after an Indian tribe) from 1912 to 1914. Two Chicago makes – Birch (1916–23) and Bush (1916–25) – were sold exclusively by direct mail and Sears, Roebuck had a second try in 1952 with their Allstate, a special version of the Kaiser. It lasted only two seasons.

■ What's in a name? Not a lot, decided the promoters of marques such as the 'Car without a Name' (Chicago 1909), 'Nameless' (Hendon 1908), 'No Name' (Horley 1904) and 'Mystery Car' (Chicago 1925). Other makes whose promoters seemed a mite naïve were the Hazard (Rochester NY 1914), Blood (Kalamazoo 1903), Anger (Milwaukee 1913), Luck Utility (Cleburne TX 1911), Amusement (Pittsburgh 1906), Average Man's Runabout (Hiawatha KS 1906), Duck (Jackson MI 1913), Fish (Bloomington IL 1906), Bugmobile (Chicago 1909), Crock (New York 1920) and Seven Little Buffaloes (Buffalo NY 1909). All these models were remarkably unsuccessful.

■ The Carhartt company of Detroit were quite truthful when they spoke of their 28 years' experience when they launched into car production in 1911. But the experience lay in making overalls. Their involvement in cars proved to be more than 26 years less.

■ The first known product recall in the history of the automobile occurred in 1911 when the Morse company of South Eason, Massachusetts, recalled a number of its luxury cars because castings from an outside contractor had proved defective.

■ Peru, Indiana, birthplace of Cole Porter and Circus Capital of the World, gave birth in 1911 to a car

The predecessor of Skoda was the Laurin & Klement: two Type FC runabouts in Moscow c. 1913.

rejoicing in the name of 'Izzer', so-called because it was up-to-date. Only three Izzers were built.

■ The first car exclusively designed by women was probably the 1912 K-D from Brookline, Massachusetts, the work of Margaret Knight and Beatrice Davidson. Powered by a 90-hp slide valve engine designed by Miss Knight, the car proved short-lived. Margaret Knight had 40 years earlier devised a machine to make the sort of square-bottomed brown paper bag that is still widely used by US food and liquor stores.

■ Continuous conveyor belts bringing parts to the assembly lines were first installed in 1912, at Ford's new Highland Park, Detroit, factory. Component assembly lines were in operation there in the summer of 1913.

Since 1900, the British Royal family has bought more than a hundred Daimlers: 'A-3179' was a 45-hp model delivered to Queen Mary in 1913.

■ The first experimental moving chassis assembly line using ropes and windlasses was installed at Highland Park in late 1913 to prevent the chassis assemblers being overwhelmed by parts from the feeder lines like sorcerers' apprentices. It cut chassis assembly time from 12 h 30 min to 2 h 40 min. The first endless chain line was installed on 14 January 1914 but replaced by a new moving line built on rails and moving at 6 ft/min on 27 February.

■ The largest-engined private car ever catalogued was the 200 hp Benz of 1913–14. Its British price was £1800 in chassis form, nearly twice as much as a Rolls-Royce. Its four-cylinder engine had a bore and stroke of 185 × 200 mm, giving a swept volume of 21 504 cc.

■ Henry Ford's famous dictum that 'Any customer can have a car painted any colour that he wants so long as it is black' was a by-product of the speed-up of production due to his introduction of the moving production line in 1914. Cars were being built so fast that the only paint then available that would dry quickly enough was black japan enamel. Before the moving production line was installed, Ford cars came in a choice of colours, and did so again from 1926 when paint technology had at last caught up with production methods.

■ Henry Ford created industrial relations history at the beginning of 1914 by announcing that all his hourly paid employees over the age of 22 would receive a minimum daily wage of $5.00 and fixing the working day at 8 hours (instead of $2.34 for 9 hours). The Detroit Ford plant was besieged by 10 000 men seeking work.

■ On 15 August 1915 Henry Ford sent special $50 cheques to everyone in the USA who had purchased a Model T between August 1914 and August 1915 to honour a promise that he would make a rebate to purchasers if sales in that year exceeded 300 000 cars: they sold 308 213.

■ Ford became the first-ever manufacturer to build a million of any model when the 1 000 000th Model T left the production line on 10 December 1915.

■ The first woman automobile stylist is claimed to have been Miriam Warren Hubbard, a banker's daughter from Maryland, who suggested the vee radiator and other features of the 1915 Biddle built in Philadelphia.

■ The growing popularity of touring by automobile was shown by the launch in 1915 of the Spaulding 'Sleeping Car' with fold-down front seats which converted into beds; air mattresses and reading lights were included in the factory price of $1730.

■ The first country in the world in which automobile production exceeded a million units in a year was the USA in 1916. Amazingly, Model T Fords represented 585 388 (or 36.2 per cent) of the grand total of 1 617 708. No other country passed the million mark until 1954, when UK output reached 1 037 879.

■ The acronym Fiat not only stands for 'Fabbrica Italiana Automobili Torino' but also means 'let it be' in Latin. When the Italian firm opened an aircraft department in 1916 they showed rare wit by calling it 'Società Italiana Aeronautica' whose acronym 'SIA' was the Italian equivalent of the Latin 'fiat'.

■ Among the more curious car brands have been the 'Phianna' (Newark, New Jersey, 1917) named after Phyllis and Anna, the daughters of one of the company's backers, and the 'Windora' (1905), an imported 1905 Ariès christened in honour of its agent Stephen A. Marples' aunts Winifred and Dora.

■ The 'hybrid' car promoted by Volkswagen in 1991 is nothing new: the Woods Dual-Power built in Chicago in 1917 was powered by a small internal-combustion engine which drove an electric generator supplying current to the car's batteries, greatly extending its range. The car could be operated 'as a straight gasoline vehicle, as a straight electric vehicle, or as a combination gasoline-electric vehicle'.

■ Before the rise of Hollywood, the world's largest film distributing company was the Ford Motor Company, whose weekly 'Ford Animated Newsreels', distributed to 4000 picture palaces across America, reached an audience of five million in 1918.

■ The most remarkable compliment paid to a make of car was the naming of a town near Shreveport, Louisiana, 'Velie' to reflect local satisfaction with this Illinois-built marque around 1918. On the other hand, the 1913 creation of the village of Ford, Canada, merely indicated that it abutted Ford's Windsor factory.

■ The flying stork mascot of the Hispano-Suiza from 1919 was based on the squadron badge of France's World War I 'Ace of Aces' Georges Guynemer, whose SPAD biplane was powered by a Hispano-Suiza V8 engine. Other marques to use the insignia of the *Escadrille Cicogne* were Bignan-Sport and Bucciali.

■ Though various amateurs had built trailer caravans before World War I, the first trailer caravan to go into series production was the Eccles, built by J. M. Riley of Gosta Green, Birmingham, first produced in 1919

■ The double-chevron badge of the Citroën car is a link with the ill-fated liner *Titanic*. It commemorates the tooth-formation of the silent bevel gears which André Citroën made and supplied to rolling mills and shipbuilders (including the builders of the 'unsinkable' *Titanic*) before he established a car company under his own name in 1919 in his wartime munitions factory. From 1908 he also headed the board of Mors.

■ One of the most morbid business ventures in the American auto industry was A. O. Dunk's Puritan Machine Company of Detroit, which specialised in buying up the remaining assets of car companies immediately after they had gone out of business. Thus Mr Dunk could continue to supply owners of these 'orphan marques' with spares. By 1919 he had 149 companies on his books. In 1916 company manager H. G. Gremel built a car incorporating parts from 102 of them.

■ The largest number of different makes of car ever exhibited at a London Motor Show was 174, in 1920. That show (and the two following) was so large that two separate venues – Olympia and the White City – had to be used, linked by a free service of 'big-capacity motor coaches'. There were 97 makes on show at Olympia and 77 at the White City. In contrast, the 1993 London Motor Show, held in Earls Court, had 48 makes on show.

■ The first European car to be guaranteed for life was the Dutch Spyker C4 of 1920. Its German Maybach power unit was built by the firm which made Zeppelin engines during World War I. Despite the car's obvious quality and the patronage of Queen Wilhelmina of the Netherlands, only 150 C4s were sold before Spyker's factory closed in 1925.

■ Even in the 1920s it was usual to have to swing a starting handle on most cars, but the Horstman car had an ingenious mechanical kick starter operated from the driving seat which acted on a 'quick-threaded' Archimedes screw shaft to turn the engine. It beat getting out in the rain when the engine stalled.

■ The first woman to manage an automobile factory was Miss Dorothée Pullinger, daughter of T. C. Pullinger (head of Arrol-Johnston). Her factory, Galloway Motors, of Tongland, Kirkcudbrightshire, was also largely staffed by women and built the 10.5-hp Galloway between 1921 and 1922, when the works was closed down 'for the sake of economy' and production transferred to Arrol-Johnston.

■ The first manufacturer to exceed a million units in one year was Ford, which built 1 003 054 Model Ts in 1921 in its North American and British plants.

■ *Lèse-majesté* was a fault of at least two American marques: Dagmar (1922) carried the Danish royal emblem on its radiator and Windsor (1929) used the Prince of Wales' feathers on its badge, both without permission. Both removed these Royal coats of arms from their badges after representations from the appropriate embassies.

■ The most embarrassing product recall of the 1920s was the 'Copper-Cooled' Chevrolet, an air-cooled model intended to beat the Model T Ford. The idea was that all the 400 000 or so Chevrolets built annually should be 'copper-cooled' by July–October 1923, but the new power unit proved to lose power badly when hot. Only three months after production had begun in February 1923, all the 500 or so air-cooled Chevrolets that had been shipped were recalled and either scrapped or dumped in Lake Erie, N. America.

■ Ford US introduced a weekly purchase plan in 1923 under which customers were issued with savings books and made minimum payments of $5.00 to their dealers against the issue of stick-in coupons. When the book was full, it could be exchanged for a new car. Some 300 000 cars had been delivered under this scheme after two years. The idea was later borrowed by the Third Reich to sell its 'Strength through Joy' People's Car (or 'Volkswagen').

■ Opened in 1923, Fiat's new Lingotto factory in Turin boasted a 3600-ft/1097-m banked test track 53 ft/16 m wide on its roof, five floors above the ground.

■ An early attempt to produce a car for export to Japan, the 1923 Sekine from New York had all-round independent suspension by twin transverse springs but only drove to one rear wheel and braked on the other. It probably never got past the prototype stage, after which the Sekine company concentrated on importing toilet brushes.

■ Ford built its 10 millionth car – a Model T tourer – on 24 June 1924.

■ 'MG' stands for 'Morris Garages', W. R. Morris's original retail and repair business in Longwall Street, Oxford. The first MG cars were specially bodied Morris chassis built by Cecil Kimber, the Oxford Garages' manager, in 1924. MG's Oxford telephone number was '251' and that was also the first chassis number in any new series. When the factory moved to Abingdon, its phone number was Abingdon 251.

■ 'Just-in-time' or 'lean' production are the latest industry buzzwords for increased efficiency but the concept dates back – like so much else – to Henry Ford and the Model T. In 1924 Ford boasted that a boat-load of iron ore arriving at the Rouge Plant at 8 a.m. on Monday would be a complete car by 9 a.m. on Wednesday and in the hands of the dealer by noon – 'a conversion of raw material to cash in approximately 33 hours'.

■ The first transfer machine used in car production was installed at Cowley, Oxfordshire, by Morris Motors around 1924.

■ The first regular transportation of automobile parts by aeroplane took place on 13 April 1925 when the Stout All-Metal Monoplane *Maiden Dearborn* made the inaugural flight of the Ford Air Transport Service carrying a cargo which included 782 lb/355 kg of 'auto machine parts' from Detroit to Chicago.

■ Henry Ford's mass-production methods meant that the Model T got cheaper over the years: the lowest price was $260 (equivalent to £58) for a roadster in 1925.

■ Japan's first moving production line for car assembly went into action in a rented corrugated-iron shed on Yokohama Docks in 1925, building Model T Fords for the local market.

■ Forget the Skoda jokes: the famed armament company's first model, introduced in 1925, was a licence-built version of one of the world's finest luxury cars, the H6 Hispano-Suiza. In Czechoslovakia this splendid car went under the designation 25/100 KS.

■ The first Japanese cars to be exported were three Otomos (out of a total production of 150) shipped to Shanghai in 1925. Serious exports did not begin until well after World War II, though a few Datsuns were shipped overseas in the late 1930s. In contrast, Japan exported 4 408 884 cars out of a total production of 9 378 694 in 1992.

■ The first year in which closed cars became more popular in America than open models was 1925, in which 56.5 per cent of all cars built were sedans (or saloons) and 43.5 per cent were open two- and four-seaters, almost exactly reversing the proportions of the previous year. By the time that America entered World War II, only 0.2 per cent of new cars had open bodywork.

■ The term 'mass production' was first used in an article attributed to Henry Ford in the 13th (1926) edition of the *Encyclopædia Britannica*.

■ The concept of an annual model change to boost sales was formalised at a General Motors sales committee meeting on 29 July 1925, though GM had in fact been introducing new models on an annual basis since 1923.

■ Though the prototype straight-eight Bugatti Royale was built in 1926–7 with a 14.7-litre engine, production did not begin until 1930, in 12.8-litre form. Just five 'production' cars were built after the prototype and only three were actually sold to customers: despite the model name, not one was bought by a member of a Royal family.

■ The most eagerly awaited new model in history was the Model A Ford. Within a week of its unveiling on 2 December 1927, some 25 million people had flocked to showrooms to look at the car and two weeks after its launch some 400 000 orders had been taken. The millionth Model A left the production lines on 4 February 1929, a record 'first million' that would not be broken until the launch of Ford's first 'world' Escort in 1980 knocked three months off the 51-year-old figure.

■ MG did not use its famed octagon badge on a car before the 1928 model 14/40. Previous MGs used a round badge based on that of the 'donor marque' Morris and carrying the words 'MG Super Sports'. The octagon, used in advertising as early as 1924, was inspired by the shape of MG founder Cecil Kimber's dining table.

■ Until the late 1920s, no European quality car worth its salt had left-hand drive, irrespective of its national rule of the road. Delage offered the option from about 1922, but few had the lack of taste to take it up. The original Bugatti firm never built a left-hand drive car. Lancia, which retained right-hand drive until the mid-1950s before succumbing to popular fashion, ironically withdrew from right-hand drive markets in 1993 because of lack of demand. In those sporting cars right-hand drive suited most race circuits, where races are run clockwise; it was preferred by many luxury car manufacturers as a convenience for chauffeurs, who had to get out to open the passenger door.

■ Graham-Paige installed the first true transfer machines in their Dearborn factory during 1929; two years later, they created a transfer machine system using jigs and fixtures.

■ Needled by media misinterpretation of his 'history is more or less bunk' statement – he meant that text-book history failed to record the achievements of ordinary people – Henry Ford built one of the world's great museums. It is estimated that buying exhibits for the Henry Ford Museum, which opened in 1929, cost him over $30 million.

■ The famed World War II Jeep originated in the 1930 American Austin, a Pennsylvania-built version of the Austin Seven whose styling fully justified the adjective 'cute'. When – inevitably – this venture foundered in 1932, it was kept alive by Roy Evans, who ultimately reworked the moribund American Austin into the American Bantam in 1938. Two years later, American Bantam built the first Jeep. Did the 'Jeep' name come from 'GP' for 'General Purpose' or from cartoon character Popeye's magical little helper Jeep? The argument continues.

■ Probably the only power unit designed by an ordained minister of the church was the unorthodox Lever engine designed by the Rev. Alvah H. Powell and fitted in various limited-production chassis, notably Elcar, in the early 1930s.

■ The first £100 four-cylinder car to be sold in Britain was the side-valve 847-cc Morris Minor open two-seater, launched as the chimes of midnight rang in the New Year 1931. Britain's first (and only) £100 four-seat saloon was the 8-hp Model Y Ford Popular announced in October 1935.

■ One of the biggest confidence tricks played on the technical press was the '16-cylinder' Bucciali Double-Huit exhibited at the 1931 Paris Salon. Its V16 power unit was described in detail by journalists as being made up of two straight-eights mounted side by side and driving the front wheels but when, after years of immobility in France this grandiose Bucciali chassis was acquired by an American collection and dismantled for restoration, it was found that the magnificent engine was just a hollow shell stuffed with old French newspapers. Presumably the Bucciali brothers would only have developed this bold design further had someone actually paid the enormous asking price of 187 000 francs.

■ The shortest time taken from concept to production was the less than four months it took for Henry Ford to put his revolutionary V8 on the market. The go-ahead was given in December 1931 and the car was on the market on 31 March 1932.

■ Audi's four-ring badge commemorates the four German firms which amalgamated to form the Auto Union group in 1932 – Audi, DKW, Horch and Wanderer.

■ Carrying his passion for American Football too far, Albert Erskine of Studebaker named the company's new low-priced car range for 1932 'Rockne' after local hero Knute Rockne, coach of South Bend's Notre Dame university football team. But Rockne was killed when the wooden structure of the Fokker Monoplane, in which he was a passenger, failed before Rockne production began; the marque only survived from February 1932 to Easter 1933.

■ The performance of the Ford V8, launched in 1932, was so far above the norm that Henry Ford received two of the most unusual testimonials ever addressed to a motor manufacturer. They came from 'Public Enemy No. 1' John Dillinger and Clyde Barrow (of 'Bonnie and Clyde' fame). Both criminals wrote personal letters to the motoring magnate to tell him that they always stole a Ford V8 as a getaway car in preference to any other model.

■ When the Rolls-Royce emblem changed from red to black during 1933, it had no connection with the death of Sir Henry Royce that April. The Board felt that black was more appropriate to the firm's image.

■ The cheapest full-size American car of the 1930s was neither a Ford nor a Chevrolet, but the 1933 Continental Beacon roadster, which undercut them both at $335.

■ The first engine exchange scheme to be offered by a British manufacturer was announced by Ford of Dagenham, London in July 1934. Prices – inclusive of labour charges – were £9 10s for an 8-hp unit and £11 10s for the 14.9-hp and 24-hp types.

■ Three-abreast seating has been featured on some cars, like the Type 77 Tatra of 1935, the 1973 Matra-Simca Bagheera and the bizarre 1937 sleeve-valve Panhard Dynamic, which boasted a 'Panoramique' windscreen with curved corner pieces (and three wiper blades) and a steering wheel set just off-centre to leave room for a thin passenger on the driver's right and a fat one on his left . . .

■ The elegant Jaguar mascot was designed by *The Autocar* artist Frederick Gordon Crosby in 1936 after company chief William Lyons had complained that the original mascot for the new SS car looked 'like a cat shot off a fence'. Originally an optional extra, the leaping jaguar was banished from the bonnet of home-market cars in 1970 by petty-minded 'safety' regulations outlawing mascots on new cars (Rolls-Royce got round this by turning their flying lady into a species of Jill-in-the-Box which retracted into the dummy radiator cap if it was struck).

■ With the appointment of Sir Malcolm Campbell to its board in 1937, Ford of Britain became the only motor car company ever to have two land speed record holders on its board, for Henry Ford had set a world record speed in 1904 with his monstrous 999 racer. Moreover, the personal emblem of both men was the blue bird of happiness, whose image appeared on Campbell's record-breaking cars and boats and on Ford's private yacht *Sialia* and the flagship of his freight fleet.

■ The nearest that a flying car came to series production was in 1937, when Studebaker expressed an interest in selling the Waterman Arrowbile designed by 'famous flyer' Waldo Waterman. Sadly, he flunked his big opportunity by crashing the prototype while demonstrating it to a national convention of Studebaker dealers. Though he built five more Arrowbiles, Waldo could not convince anyone else to back him.

■ The Volkswagen was originally publicised in 1938 as the KdF-Wagen ('Kraft durch Freude', or 'Strength through Joy', was the slogan of the Nazi Labour Front). Although military derivatives were built during World War II, production of the familiar Beetle did not get under way until 1945. Then, for a quarter of a century, VW was almost invariably associated with cars which had rear-mounted air-cooled engines. However, it had run front-wheel drive prototypes in the mid-1950s.

■ The first Russian car to be imported into Great Britain was the official ZIS eight-cylinder limousine of Ivan Maisky, Soviet Ambassador to the Court of St James's in 1938.

■ The first British manufacturer to build a million cars was Morris, which reached this milestone in June 1939. Ford built its millionth British vehicle in 1942 and Austin reached its first million in June 1946.

■ In October 1946 a new Morris was flown to a Guernsey dealer from Reading Airport, probably the first delivery of a car by air in the United Kingdom.

■ The Jaguar XK120 sports car was originally intended as a 200-off limited production run to publicise the stunning new XK twin overhead camshaft

'Australia's Own Car' – the first Holden, built in 1948, was the 48/215.

six-cylinder engine. However, it proved to be the star of the 1948 London Motor Show and was put into quantity production. Timed at almost 133 mph/214 kph in 1949, the XK120 was then the fastest production car in the world.

■ The world's largest manufacturer of station wagons in 1948 was Crosley of Cincinnati, Ohio, maker of the Hotshot minicar. Out of the 28 000 cars sold that year, 23 000 were station wagons. Production collapsed thereafter and ended in 1952.

■ The first member of the British Royal Family to be actively engaged in the motor industry was the Hon. Gerald Lascelles, younger son of the Princess Royal, who worked for Ford from 1950 to 1951 and Aston Martin Lagonda from 1952 to 1954.

■ The first car made in China was a prototype produced for the Mao Tse-tung government in 1951 and referred to simply as 'the People's Car'.

■ The first fully-automated automobile plant was Ford's Cleveland engine plant, which went into production in September 1951. Its 1545-ft/470-m long production line incorporated 42 automatic machines linked by transfer devices which automatically moved the engine blocks from station to station. This 'first' was particularly appropriate because the word 'automation' had been coined by Ford manufacturing vice-president Delmar S. Harder.

■ The Daimler Conquest saloon of 1953–8 was so-called because its price before British purchase tax was originally £1066.

■ The first installation of fully automated body welding and final assembly was made in stages between 1953 and 1966 at the Volkswagen plant at Wolfsburg, Germany.

■ The first transfer machines automatically controlled by punched or magnetic tape were in action in 1954–5.

■ The first Australian-built car to be exported commercially was the Holden; the first shipments went to New Zealand in 1954.

■ Europe's first manufacturer to produce over a million units of a single model was Volkswagen, whose millionth Beetle was delivered during August 1955.

■ The car with the most outstanding export record was the 1955 MGA: 94 per cent of the 101 000 cars built before production ended in 1962 were exported.

■ The first year that British car production exceeded a million was 1958, when 1 051 551 cars were built (but new registrations were only 566 319). The first year that British registrations exceeded home production was 1977, when 1 327 820 cars were built and 1 335 311 were registered.

■ Ford lost an estimated $450 million on the 1958 Edsel, intended to plug the gap between the low-priced Ford range and the medium-priced Mercury range. But the gap vanished before the Edsel went on sale and it was withdrawn at the start of 1960, leaving the useful legacy of extra production capacity which gave Ford a head start when demand for more conventional cars picked up. Named after Henry Ford's only son (who died in 1943) the Edsel incorporated novel ideas like gears electrically selected by 'Teletouch' buttons on the steering wheel. It also had a speedometer that turned red when the car went too fast!

Before the Edsel name was chosen, the car was code-named 'Ventura'; poetess Marianne Moore, commissioned to dream up names for the new car, came up with such gems as 'Utopian Turtletop' and 'Bullet Cloisonné'.

■ Ford built its 50 millionth vehicle on 29 April 1959.

■ The first British model to sell over a million units was the Issigonis-designed Morris Minor, between October 1948 and January 1961.

■ 'Car Ahoy' was the curious slogan of the 1961–8 Amphicar, the only amphibious car ever seriously marketed. It was the creation of the German Hans Trippel, who designed his first amphibian in 1932 and during World War II built military amphibians in the occupied Bugatti factory. The Amphicar was neither a good car nor a good boat; in 1965, two British soldiers crossed the English Channel in two Amphicars at a cost of £4 in fuel. However, one Amphicar broke down and was towed by the other. The crossing took 7 h 20 min: it would have been 5 hours quicker by ferry.

(Opposite) The first Israeli-built production car was the 1961 Sabra, designed by Reliant.

(Above) A prototype for Sir Alec Issigonis's immortal Mini bears an Austin A35 radiator grille.

■ The first European manufacturer to produce a million private cars a year was Volkswagen in 1962.

■ On 2 July 1962 Ford built its 30 millionth V8 engine.

■ During 1964 Chevrolet became the first marque to build over three million vehicles in a year.

■ MG claimed that its Air Pollution Control Centre opened at Abingdon was the first such facility in the world for testing emissions of cars destined for export.

Ledwinka's legacy: the unorthodox Tatra layout, with a rear-mounted V8 engine in an aerodynamic body, dated back to the 1930s. This is a 1961 example.

■ On 16 March 1966 General Motors was the world's first manufacturing group to produce 100 million vehicles. The actual car was an Oldsmobile Toronado produced in the Lansing, Michigan, plant.

■ On 21 April 1967 General Motors became the first automotive group to produce 100 million vehicles in

(Above) Launched in 1962 and styled by Raymond Loewy, the Avanti was once-mighty Studebaker's last fling – the design outlived the company.

(Below) The first-ever production car with a Wankel rotary engine was the NSU Spider of 1963.

the USA. The 15 millionth had been built in January 1940, and the 50 millionth on 23 November 1954. All three 'landmark' cars were Chevrolets.

■ The first British manufacturer to produce over a million units in a year was the British Leyland Motor Corporation in 1968: 807 067 were private cars, with the best-selling model the front-wheel-drive Austin/Morris 1100/1300 range.

■ In January 1978 the last German-built VW Beetle, a 1200, came off the line; production continued at overseas factories and the 20 millionth (also a 1200) was completed in Mexico in May 1980.

■ 'Pacific Rim' nations where automotive companies were set up in the shadow of the formidable Japanese industry included South Korea, where the first Hyundai saloons were built in 1974, and Malaysia, where Mitsubishi-based Protons appeared in 1986.

■ At the end of 1992 production of the Toyota Corolla passed the 20 million mark, but as this was the seventh type to carry the name since 1966 (to honour a marketing system whereby some Japanese dealer franchises were allotted to model lines rather than marques), this was hardly a record.

■ A detail of the sweeping changes in the world industry in the 1990s came in two 1992 estate car announcements – the Mitsubishi Sigma estate was to be built in Australia for European and North American markets, and the Toyota Camry estate was to be built in Kentucky for Europe and Japan as well as the American market (while the Camry saloons were still built in Japan).

■ A breach in the wall of traditional Japanese 'jobs-for-life' employment practice was made when Toyota announced on 21 January 1994 that it was introducing one-year contracts for its 25 000 salaried employees.

(Left top) One of Ferrari's most beautiful coupés, the four-cam V12 GTB4 was current between 1966 and 1968.

(Left) Another styling sensation from Jaguar: the E-Type roadster – this is a 1968 model – represented an unbeatable combination of keen pricing and 150-mph performance.

The end of the line for DeLorean: having consumed millions of pounds of UK taxpayers' money, the Belfast factory went into receivership in 1982.

BODYWORK AND ACCESSORIES

■ Probably the first all-metal body in America was used on the 1898 Eastman steam car. The fact that it was lined with asbestos was probably an awful warning to prospective purchasers.

■ Though 'motor hot-water bottles' (upholstered to match the interior trim) were available as accessories in the early years of the 20th century, a primitive hot-water foot-warmer fed from the car's cooling system was used on some 1897–1900 Cannstatt Daimlers.

■ The first 'wheelchair-accessible' motor car was a specially built 6-hp touring phaeton produced by Fritz Scheibler of Aix-la-Chapelle in 1901 to the order of E. Le Pierre of Wiesbaden, Germany, who

had been paralysed in a riding accident. The rear end of the car could be lowered to form a ramp up which Herr Le Pierre's wheelchair was winched into the vehicle and fastened in place.

■ Seat belts were first fitted in a motor vehicle in the 1902 Baker Electric streamlined racer – just as well, as it crashed at around 100 mph during a record attempt on Staten Island. It was also the first car with a body developed by airflow testing (strictly, it was the result of hydrodynamic tests in a water tank, for America's only wind tunnel at the time was in the Wright Brothers' cycle shop in Dayton, Ohio).

■ Aluminium became widely available at the dawn of the motor age, and was being used to cast crankcases and other components in the 1890s. Its weight-saving, non-rusting properties soon attracted the attention of coachbuilders. Leading Paris *carrossier* Rothschild & Cie introduced aluminium panelling around 1901 and by 1905 was making all-aluminium four-seat bodywork. The first production-model Lanchesters (1900–5) had in-house bodywork with aluminium mudguards and other parts integral with a composite steel and aluminium chassis.

■ The first patent for seat belts was taken out in Paris in 1903 by inventor Gustave Lebeau, who described 'protective suspenders for automobiles and other vehicles'.

■ The first known use of the term 'convertible' was to describe the 1904 Thomas Flyer which had a removable hardtop.

■ One of the more bizarre ideas in the early part of the century was that of Lieutenant Walter G. Windham RN, whose 'sliding detachable bodies' were available from about 1905. By fitting the chassis frame with a special sliding track, several bodies (which had a retractable 'undercarriage' to enable them to be wheeled about) could be used on a single chassis. Windham suggested that a single chassis could be used for 'brougham, tonneau, business landaulette, racing, luggage and station bodies' (where you stored five spare bodies when your car was in use was your problem . . .).

■ The earliest known use of built-in direction indicators is on the 1905 Hedag electric, built by the Hamburg Elektro Droschken AG, on which indicators fitted on the front wings unfolded to the accompaniment of an electric horn.

■ The first bumpers were designed by Frederick R. Simms and fitted to his Simms-Welbeck cars in 1905. Unusually they were pneumatic, to absorb shocks. A couple of years earlier, the American Grout steamer had been offered with a locomotive-type cowcatcher.

■ Hand-operated windscreen wipers appeared in France early in 1907; the first wiper fitted to a British car was installed on a Daimler in 1910. Wipers became standard equipment on a number of American cars during 1916.

■ German inventor Richard Radke took out a US patent for spring-loaded safety belts in 1908.

■ When the English pioneer motorist Dorothy Levitt wrote a little book called *The Woman and the Car* in 1909 she advised the 'woman motoriste' to carry a mirror with a handle in the side pocket of the car. This was not only essential to repair the complexion after a drive, but would be handy, she wrote, 'to occasionally hold up to see what is behind you'. Miss Levitt also recommended 'motoristes' to carry a small revolver if they drove alone: 'I have an automatic Colt and find it very easy to handle.'

■ All-metal body construction without wood framing was used on lightweight 'racing shells' soon after the turn of the century. However, the real pioneer of all-steel bodywork was the American engineer Edward Gowan Budd, born in Delaware in 1870, who learned his craft with a company building all-steel railway carriages for the Pullman Company. He established links with Hupmobile as early as 1909 and resigned to set up on his own to make all-steel car bodies in 1912. The real breakthrough came when the Dodge brothers severed their association with Ford and began making Dodge cars in Detroit in November 1914, using welded all-steel Budd bodywork. The first cars were all open tourers but by 1916 a 'permanent steel hard top' had been devised and in 1917 Budd began making the first all-steel saloon bodywork for Dodge. Budd also collaborated with the English manufacturer William Morris in the setting up of the Pressed Steel Company in Oxford in 1925 and with André Citroën in France from 1924, and this relationship was to prove vital to the development of the 1934 Traction Avant.

■ The first cars had no windscreens at all but these became increasingly popular as cars began to go faster (though they were also a potential danger since they were made of plate glass). Another hazard was visibility in bad weather: on a rainy day pioneer motorists either kept dry and couldn't see where they were going, or opened the screen and got drenched to the skin. An early solution was Hall's Motor Flap, devised c. 1912, which was a small circular or oblong 'port-hole' cut in the screen glass in the driver's line of vision to give limited clear vision. It was probably better than the alternative methods of wiping the screen with a freshly cut apple or potato to repel the rainwater.

■ Before dynamos came into general use from 1912 (and indeed for many years thereafter), most cars had bulb horns – ranging from simple bugle horns to elaborate hooters shaped like serpent's heads and multi-note Testophones – but other 'non-electric' warning devices were used, too. These included warning bells, exhaust whistles and sirens. Most

Edward Gowan Budd pioneered welded all-steel bodywork on cars. Citroën was one of the companies to build bodies under Budd patent, here in the Javel factory in 1925.

complex was the Gabriel Horn, which operated like an organ pipe blown from the exhaust. The simpler models played a single chord, but there were multi-pipe versions with four or eight pipes and an in-car keyboard on which bugle calls and simple tunes could be played.

■ The first sliding sunshine roof was fitted to a 40/50-hp Rolls-Royce 'Prince Jacques' limousine built by Labourdette of Paris in 1913.

■ Fixed driving mirrors did not come into general use before 1914, though they had been available in horse-carriage days. In 1869 the magazine *English Mechanic* printed a drawing of Faber's 'new road locomotive', equipped with a rear-view mirror. Mirrors were also fitted to many turn-of-the-century steamers, though the purpose was to keep an eye on the boiler level gauge rather than watch out for following traffic.

(Above) This 1912 Itala was fitted with a remarkable transformable body: the rear section folded out to make an extra pair of seats.

(Below) One of the strangest fashions in bodywork was for cars that looked like 18th-century stage-coaches, like this 1910 Grégoire.

■ Early car bodies were panelled in wood, subsequently metal panelling was used – but the 1915 Briscoe cloverleaf roadster had a body panelled in papier-mâché, a novel constructional method used in more modern form on the East German Trabant from its launch in 1958 to its demise after the fall of the Berlin Wall in 1990. Initially resin-reinforced papier-mâché was used, but in the late Trabis plastics resin reinforced with fibres including cotton waste was employed (and the body construction was just one reason for the Trabi's notoriety, as for most of its life it was also under-powered with a two-stroke engine that produced a most noxious exhaust). Some competition Hanomags of the mid-1920s raced with wicker bodies.

■ The first horn button to be mounted in the centre of the steering wheel was fitted to the Scripps-Booth Model C launched in February 1915 by James Scripps-Booth, who had built Detroit's first V8 engine in 1912 to power his amazing car-on-two-wheels, the 'Bi-Autogo', a $25 000 6.3-litre 'one-off', capable of 75 mph. Another first seen on the Model C Scripps-Booth were electrically-operated door latches. These proved troublesome on open cars and were soon replaced by conventional locks on all but the coupé model. Winston Churchill owned one.

■ The first standard production model to store its spare wheel in the boot was the 1915 Franklin Six-30 Roadster built in Syracuse, New York. Britain's first production car with a concealed spare was the 1919 Austin Twenty.

■ The first 'pillarless' saloon – a four-door body with no central 'B' pillar, giving maximum access to the interior – was built on a 1916 Morris Cowley chassis by Hollick & Pratt of Coventry.

■ William Folberth of Cleveland, Ohio, tested the first practical mechanical windscreen wiper, driven by suction from the inlet manifold, in 1916. Folberth automatic windscreen wipers first went on the market in the US in September 1919. The first month's sales were just $208; by 1922 they had risen to $394 000.

■ Heaters were first seen on a number of closed cars exhibited at the New York National Automobile Show in 1917. Early heaters tended to be rather alarming devices which took their warmth from a sleeve around the exhaust pipe, which accounts for the reluctance to make them universal!

■ The first wind-up window mechanism (the 'Perfect') was introduced on 1919 model Packard and Pierce-Arrow cars. Before that, railway carriage-type leather strap window lifts were used.

■ The first aerodynamic production car was the Rumpler built in Berlin from 1921 to 1925 and powered by a rear-mounted two-row radial six-cylinder. Modern wind-tunnel tests have shown how efficient Rumpler streamlining was: the problem was that the cars looked so odd.

■ The first British manufacturer to produce a special left-hand drive export model was Lanchester, which shipped a 40-hp model to America with this specification in 1921. Only one (which survives) was built.

■ The first British cars to include a (hand-operated) windscreen wiper as standard were the 1922 Humber 11.4-hp coupé and saloon and 15.9-hp saloon de luxe.

■ The first average speed indicator was shown at the 1922 Paris Salon by Jaeger. Two needles indicated time and distance and average speed was shown on a central scale at the intersection of the two needles.

■ The first electrically-heated windscreen was the 1922 British-made 'Mistproof Plate', a 15½ in/39.4 cm-wide glass panel with 'practically invisible' resistance wires stretched across its surface which was attached to the main screen and heated by current from the car battery to clear fog, mist and snow.

■ Pioneer aviator and accessory manufacturer Charles Torres Weymann devised a lightweight construction method using a flexibly jointed wood-framing covered in leathercloth. The first production car with a Weymann fabric body was the French Darracq in 1922.

■ Tartan fabric body covering enjoyed a mercifully brief vogue in the 1920s. Among the manufacturers who succumbed were Voisin, on a 'Conduite Intérieure Ecossaise' in 1922, and Willys-Knight on their 1930 'Plaidside' roadster. The organisers of the 1912 Franch Grand Prix had prescribed blue plus the Gordon tartan to be the national colours for the Scottish Arrol-Johnston entry.

■ The first British car fitted with an automatic wiper was an Angus-Sanderson tourer belonging to H. C. Lafone of *The Autocar*, in February 1923. Automatic wipers were first fitted as standard to 1924 models of Sunbeam and Daimler.

■ The first electric windscreen wiper was the Berkshire, first seen in England in May 1923.

■ Though credit for the first production station

Austrian-born aviation pioneer Edmund Rumpler employed his aerodynamic skills to create the revolutionary 'Tropfenwagen' ('Tear-drop car') in 1921.

Four aspects of streamlining: the aerodynamic Bugatti 'Tank' (top) and Voisin 'Laboratoire' (above) which ran in the 1923 French Grand Prix at Tours; an Isotta-Fraschini shown in Berlin in 1937 (opposite top); the V12 Pierce 'Silver Arrow' of 1933 (opposite bottom).

The 1924 season Star was the world's first production station wagon.

wagon is usually given to Ford, which announced a station wagon version of the Model A Ford on 25 April 1929, a similar vehicle had been offered by Billy Durant's Star company of Elizabeth, NJ, as early as 1924.

■ Duco pyroxylin (cellulose) finish was first standardised on Oakland cars in 1924. Standard colour was 'True Blue'. The first British manufacturer to offer cellulose was AC in 1925. Cellulose dried so rapidly that Ford was once again able to offer a (limited) choice of colours on its American cars from the 1926 model year. Colours other than black had been seen earlier on Fords built outside North America. The Ford plant in Bordeaux offered a colour choice in 1923 and Trafford Park (Manchester) in 1924.

■ Chromium plating made its debut in mid-1925 on the Oldsmobile six-cylinder Model 30-C.

■ The first production car with a full-width aerodynamic body was the Chenard & Walcker 'Tank' of 1925. With an unsupercharged engine of only 1100 cc, it was capable of over 90 mph/145 kph.

■ The earliest recorded use of an oil pressure warning light was on the 1925 Fiat 509.

■ Arrow-type direction indicators on either side of the rear number plate were first seen in Britain on the 14–45-hp Talbot in 1926, though indicators had been available as accessories from around 1922. Indicators were commonplace by 1932, when the first flashing indicators were offered by Scintilla, but flashers were subsequently declared illegal. A macabre device of 1932 was the Birglow indicator, a light-up articulated hand mounted by the windscreen pillars and operated by a Bowden cable. The 1933 Morris cars were fitted with three-colour direction signals like miniature traffic lights. These were complex in operation and were also declared illegal. By early 1933 they had been supplanted by pop-up semaphore signals.

■ Safety-glass was first fitted as factory equipment on Stutz and Rickenbacker cars in 1926.

■ The first popular car with safety glass as standard equipment was the Model A Ford launched on 2 December 1927.

■ Even in the 1920s parking in city streets was becoming a problem but a resourceful inventor from Illinois named Villor P. Williams thought he had the answer. His 'Parkmobile' of 1927 was a hydraulically operated retractable wheeled undercarriage which could be deployed so that the car could be pushed sideways into a parking space. How you got it out again if the road was steeply cambered was not explained. A few were fitted to the obscure New York Six (or Davis Six) built in Richmond, Indiana, in 1928 but the idea did not last the year out.

■ The first on-board computer was fitted to the Model J Duesenberg launched at the end of 1928. Mechanical rather than electric, it controlled the automatic chassis lubrication and switched on warning lights to warn the driver to change the engine oil and check the battery at pre-determined intervals.

■ Integral screw jacks lifting two wheels at a time were introduced by Stevensons in 1926, followed in 1929 by the Smith's 'Jackall' four-wheel hydraulic jacking system. First fitted as factory equipment to Star cars in 1931 (the Star company closed down in 1932), Jackalls were fitted to quality cars until the beginning of the 1950s, when the separate chassis and beam axles for which they had been designed were supplanted by integral construction and independent suspension.

■ The 1930 American Austin was the first recorded car to have its battery concealed beneath the bonnet.

■ Before metallic paint became widely available, iridescent colour schemes had been obtained by laborious methods, like covering the bodywork in fish scales under a coat of clear lacquer. A 'pearlescent' finish on a Graham-Paige derived from fish scale pigment was a sensation of the 1930 New York Show.

■ Doors opening into the roof were pioneered on a custom saloon body built on a Duesenberg Model J chassis in 1930 by Murphy of Pasadena. Their first use on a series production body was on the Riley Falcon saloon introduced in 1933.

■ The first built-in demister, ducting warm air on to the windscreen through scuttle vents, was introduced by Horch in Germany in 1931.

■ Motorists of the writer's generation will clearly remember the light-up oval radiator emblem fitted by Wolseley cars from 1931, for from the 1930s Wolseley supplied many cars to the police forces of Britain. The sight of a lighted oval radiator badge in the rear-view mirror was a sign to drive carefully at night. However, the 13.5-litre American Fageol luxury car of 1916 also had an illuminated radiator badge (but made of ivory rather than plastic).

■ The Mathis cars shown at the 1931 Paris Salon were equipped with a 'pistomètre' which recorded the distance covered by the pistons.

■ Illuminated ignition keyholes were first used on American cars in 1932.

■ Rear-view mirrors became compulsory on motor cars in Great Britain on 1 January 1932.

■ The 'skirted fenders' of the 1932 Graham Blue Streak styled by Amos Northrup and built in Dearborn, Michigan, were widely copied and a Tootsietoy diecast model of the car sold by the million. But despite the full-sized car's influence on the rest of the industry, its sales were poor. The Graham company gave up cars in 1940, eventually became an investment company and today forms an important part of Gulf + Western as the Madison Square Garden Corporation.

■ The first British car with the battery under the bonnet was the Austin 10/4 introduced during 1932.

■ The first cars to be offered with an integral fire extinguishing system were the 'special models' of the 1933 Standard Big Nine and Sixteen. The conventional extinguisher under the scuttle was plumbed into the engine compartment to prevent carburetter or electrical fires.

■ One of the first attempts to provide fresh air inside saloon bodywork was the Fisher 'No-Draft Ventilation' offered on 1933 GM bodies.

■ To eliminate a separate starter pedal, some 1933 American cars featured a starter actuated by depressing the accelerator pedal when the engine was stationary. This idea was also marketed in England the same year by Lucas as the 'Pedomatic'.

■ The first self-cancelling indicators were fitted to the Singer Fourteen in 1933.

■ A curved windscreen without a central divider was fitted to the flagship Imperial Custom models of the 1934 Chrysler Airflow range.

■ The first powered convertible to go into production was Peugeot's 1934 décapotable électrique, with a retracting mechanism adapted from a dustcart tipping gear. This car's metal 'hard-top' foreshadowed the legendary Ford 1957 Sunliner of which 48 394 were sold in America during a three-season run.

■ Devices for the washing of car windscreens were first fitted as factory equipment on Standard and Triumph cars in 1935.

■ The only car to have its styling patented was the 1935 Cord 810 designed by Gordon Buehrig. In its 'new, original and ornamental design', a stream-lined nose with wraparound louvres replaced the conventional radiator grille. This earned it the nick-name 'Coffin-nose Cord'. It was the first mass-pro-duced American car to combine front-wheel drive with independent front suspension: its electrically controlled transmission featured overdrive fourth speed. It was also fitted with retractable headlamps, which were modified Stinson aircraft landing lights.

■ The first production saloon with fully recessed door handles was the 1935 Fiat 1500.

■ Built-in defrosters were first seen on many US models in 1936.

■ Electric divisions were first used in limousines by British specialist coachbuilders in 1937. Among the firms which exhibited them at the 1937 London Motor Show were Hooper, Park Ward and Thrupp & Maberly.

■ Safety padding was offered on the front seat back of the 1937 Chrysler, which also pioneered front seats that adjusted up and down as well as fore and aft.

■ Electric windows were occasionally fitted to be-spoke luxury car bodies before World War II – a surviving 1937 Rolls-Royce Phantom III with May-fair coupé bodywork has them – and were first seen on series-production cars in 1948 on the American Cadillac and Lincoln, and the British Daimler DE36 straight eight.

■ Metallic paint first became generally available on 1939 model American cars. It had been offered on custom bodies since the late 1920s, when it had been invented by chance, after a ball-bearing broke up inside a paint-grinding machine.

■ The first dashboard-operated bonnet release was probably that on the 1939 Hudson.

■ The first mass-produced American car with a uni-tary-construction body was the 1940 Nash 600.

■ Air conditioning was first offered on the 1940 model Packard Super-8 One-Sixty ('cooled by mechanical refrigeration') launched in August 1939. Nash's much-publicised 1938 'Weather-Eye' system was merely controlled heating and ventilation of filtered air, even though Nash had just purchased the Kelvinator refrigerator company.

■ The first mass-production car with retractable headlamps was the 1942 De Soto, launched in Au-gust 1941. The doors of the 'Airfoil' lamps retracted upwards and the lights went on when a knob under the instrument panel was pulled.

■ The US Government banned chrome plating on new private cars as a wartime emergency measure from 1 January 1942 until the construction of civilian vehicles ended five weeks later.

■ The first foam-filled seats were used on the 1942 De Soto range and the Chrysler Windsor models.

■ Radio telephones were first used in 1946 American cars, earlier British experiments having come to nothing.

■ Power-operated seats were first used on the 1947 Packards.

■ The first production key start system was stand-ardised on 1949 Chryslers (though the 1932 British Lucas 'Startix' self-started the engine if it stalled when the ignition key was turned to 'automatic').

■ Probably the first popular make of car to be offered with seat belts was the 1950 Nash Rambler (though the idea was to stop passengers rolling out of the reclining seat while asleep).

■ Tinted non-glare glass was introduced on the 1950 Buick model line.

■ Gullwing doors were first used on the Mercedes-Benz 300SL, unveiled in 1951 and put into produc-tion in 1954. They were necessitated by the high sill resulting from the car's space-frame construction.

■ Ford was almost certainly the world pioneer in crash-testing vehicles. Tests started in 1951 by its Engineering Research Department in America re-sulted in such benefits as anti-burst door locks. First made public in 1955 was Ford's programme of crash testing, using naturalistic dummies fitted with elec-tronic instrumentation.

■ In 1953 the Radio Corporation of America (RCA) announced that it was developing electronic brake and steering controls to stop or divert a car if an obstacle was in its path.

■ Singer was the first British manufacturer to put a car with a moulded plastic body into production, with the SMX roadster.

■ A seven-point attached safety harness was briefly an option in the 1953 Kaiser.

■ An average-speed calculator was standard equipment on the 1953 Fiat 1900.

■ Curved side windows were first seen in production on the 1954 Cadillac El Camino.

■ The 1954 air-cooled Dyna 54 Panhard had a catalytic-type petrol heater mounted on the engine bulkhead and fed from the fuel tank. It was claimed that this device worked at a low enough temperature to eliminate fire risk, but was soon replaced by a more conventional system, drawing hot air from the engine.

■ The radiator air intake on the 1954 Bristol 404 was a copy of the intakes for the turboprop engines of the ill-fated Bristol Brabazon airliner.

■ The first European car maker to offer seat belts was Ford-Britain, in 1955.

■ Electrically-controlled door locks were fitted to 1955 Packards.

■ The first boot-lid lock controlled from the driver's seat was fitted to 1955 Cadillacs.

■ Acrylic lacquers were first used on car bodies in the mid-1950s.

■ Anti-burst door locks were standardised on most American cars in 1955.

■ The 1956 American Ford range featured 'Life Guard' safety design with seat belts and a padded dash.

■ A retractable rear window, controlled from the dash, was featured on the 1956 Mercury.

Pioneer people-mover: the Fiat 600 'Multipla' of 1955 with forward control and seating for six.

The 1958 Oldsmobile 88 Holiday Coupé is typical of an era when the stylist was king.

■ The 1957 Volvo range had front seat belts as standard.

■ The biggest unit-construction bodyshell was fitted to the 1958 Lincoln.

■ The first production car with a unitary glass fibre body was the Lotus Elite of 1958. The first series-production model with a glass fibre body was the Chevrolet Corvette of 1953, which was also the first 'dream car' to become a production model.

■ Four-light emergency flashers were first fitted to Chryslers in 1959.

■ An electric boot release, controlled from the driving seat, was first offered on 1959 Fords. A vacuum-controlled remote boot release was fitted to 1960 model Oldsmobiles.

■ The 1959 Chryslers had electronically actuated interior mirrors which automatically 'dipped' when hit by the headlamp beam of a following car.

■ Exterior mirrors, adjustable from inside the car, were fitted on a number of US makes in 1959.

■ Separately adjustable reclining seats were fitted to the 1959 Rambler.

■ Most 1960 model Chryslers had vacuum safety door locks.

■ Front seat belts were compulsory to be fitted, not worn, on all new cars registered in Great Britain from 19 April 1961. In the USA, Wisconsin became the first state to require the fitting of front seat belts the same year.

■ The 1962 Ford Cortina was the very first car with a body designed for maximum strength and lightness on the same mathematical principles as an aircraft fuselage. It was the forerunner of today's finite element analysis method of body design. Though Ford had been the first company in the motor industry to use a computer in 1957, it did not use computers in its vehicle safety work until 1963, and Dennis Roberts, the former Bristol Aeroplanes stressman who did the work on the Cortina, covered hundreds of sheets of paper with his calculations.

■ From 1964 Ford was the first manufacturer to adopt the new Electrocoat total immersion method of applying primer to bodyshells.

■ The pioneering Aeroflow ventilation and air extraction system introduced by Ford in 1964 was developed by engineer Ken Teesdale who used old tin cans to build the first prototype. The Triumph TR4, introduced in 1961, had face-level ventilation, with controllable vents at each end of the facia.

■ Concealed windscreen wipers were pioneered on the 1967 American General Motors range.

■ In 1967 Chrysler and Dodge fitted rear-window wash/wipe on their station wagons.

■ With the launch of the 1967 Ford Executive, Ford-Britain was almost certainly the first maker to fit inertia reel seat belts as standard to all four seats of a catalogue model.

■ As a thief-deterrent, in 1967 General Motors introduced a warning buzzer that operated if the driver attempted to leave the car with the keys still in the ignition.

■ The first experiments with air bags which inflated on impact to cushion the occupants of a car were made in the USA during 1968.

■ Windscreen wipers controlled from the indicator stalk made their debut on the 1970 GM models announced during 1969.

■ The first electric sunroof appeared on Cadillacs in 1969.

■ In 1970 Victoria became the first Australian state to make the wearing of safety belts compulsory.

■ A sad little victory for the grey legislators came on 1 August 1973 when multi-tone, or musical, horns were banned on cars registered in Britain for the first time. It was claimed that this was to prevent confusion with the American-style electronic sirens which had replaced the readily identifiable bells on emergency service vehicles, but when did you last hear a police siren playing *Colonel Bogey*? Other popular tunes in the 'repertoire' of Fiamm, leading Italian musical horn maker of the 1960s, were the *Marseillaise, California Here I Come, Yankee Doodle, In my Merry Oldsmobile, Here Comes the Bride* and *Things Go Better with Coca Cola* . . .

■ The first production cars offering the option of air bags were produced by General Motors in 1973. The same year American cars were compelled to incorporate side impact protection beams.

■ The first car with fully electronic instrumentation was the Lagonda sports limousine, unveiled at the 1976 London Motor Show. Planned by Aston Martin chief engineer Mike Loasby in conjunction with Fotherby Willis of Leeds, the instrument display featured black translucent panels behind which digital and bar-chart displays lit up when the ignition was on. Only one of the 600-odd Lagondas built in its 13-year run had 'normal' analogue instruments.

■ The first production car with stainless steel external panelling was the ill-starred DeLorean of 1981–2: there has hardly been a rush to produce the second.

■ The first official testing of air bags began when Ford-US equipped a fleet of 5000 government-owned Tempos with them in 1985.

■ American car makers had to begin equipping their cars with automatic occupant restraint systems from 1987.

■ At the 1993 Detroit Auto Show, Chrysler announced that it was to produce a car without an ashtray as a 'step to help the health of Americans'.

BRAKES

■ Front wheel brakes were demonstrated at the 1903 Paris Salon by steam car makers Weyher & Richemond and front wheel brakes were first seen on some makes of tricar c. 1903. The first petrol car to have braking on the front wheels was the 1903 Spyker (which was also the first four-wheel drive car – the front brake was actually on the transmission – and the first car with a six-cylinder engine). It still survives in Holland. The first patent for front wheel braking was taken out in England by P. L. Renouf in 1904. Brakes built to this specification were available from Allen-Liversedge of London the following year. In 1906 Mercedes tested a front wheel braking system but it was not until 1909 that front brakes became available on a production car, when they were standardised on the 15.9-hp Arrol-Johnston (and dropped after 18 months due to lack of customer interest). Isotta-Fraschini of Italy and Argyll of Scotland standardised front brakes in 1910.

■ The Tincher car shown at the Chicago Show in February 1903 pioneered air braking. A small pump not only compressed the air for the brakes but also blew the whistle and could be used to pump up the tyres.

■ The first disc brakes were fitted to the transmission of 1903 Lanchesters but this 'reserve' brake design was dropped because adequate brake lining material was not then available. AC adopted a disc brake on the back axle in 1919.

■ Water-cooled brakes were found on some early Mercedes models, c. 1904. These had an arrangement to dribble water from a small tank on to the brake drum when the pedal was pressed; but the 1911 Locomobile and the 20/24 and 40-hp Hispano-Suizas of 1907–10 had a more elaborate system with hollow cast-aluminium brake shoes through which water circulated. Briggs Cunningham used a similar system on his Le Mans racers 50 years later.

■ Brake linings of woven or bonded asbestos were developed by Herbert Frood of Chapel-en-le-Frith (hence the trade-name 'Ferodo') c. 1905. Before that, leather, wood, compressed fibre, or woven camel-hair were used for brake lining; these were short-lived and easily burnt out. 'Metal-on-metal' brakes were used on many cars; these were durable and could not burn out, but were often noisy and snatched badly when hot.

■ The Chevrolet 490 of 1916 was the first car to incorporate a pedal-operated parking brake. The modern foot-operated type, now commonplace on American cars, was first standardised by Buick in 1942.

■ Most braking systems of the pre-World War I period (and quite a few in the 1920s) had a pedal brake acting on a drum on the transmission, and the hand brake (or 'side brake') operating the rear-wheel brake drums. Most motorists normally 'drove on the side brake' and kept the foot brake in reserve for emergencies. While it was more powerful, the foot brake imposed a great strain on the transmission.

■ The first car in the world to use servo-assistance to increase braking power was the overhead camshaft Hispano-Suiza H6B launched in 1919. It had four-wheel brakes when these were still uncommon. Rolls-Royce fitted the Hispano-Suiza braking system under licence for many years.

■ The first successful hydraulic brakes were developed by Californian Malcolm Loughead and were first fitted to production cars in 1920. Fearful that the customers might not be able to pronounce his name, Loughead used its phonetic form 'Lockheed'.

■ The first production car to fit Lockheed hydraulic brakes was the 1920 Duesenberg, which was also America's first car with a straight-eight engine. Until 1927 Lockheed brakes used external contracting brake bands but were then adapted to drum brakes. The first European production car with hydraulic brakes was the 1922 Rolland-Pilain 18CV Type CRK built in

Tours, France. The first American mass-produced car with hydraulic brakes was the Chrysler 70 of 1924 and the first British use was on 1925 Horstman and Triumph models.

■ Self-adjusting brakes first appeared on the 1925 Cole Series 890 from Indianapolis but J. J. Cole liquidated his company soon after it was introduced.

■ Vacuum servo-assisted braking was first used on the 1926 Pierce-Arrow, using the B-K system developed by racing driver Caleb Bragg and Victor Kliesrath.

■ The Walex disc brake produced by Auto-Produkt GmbH of Berlin in 1932 worked in the same way as modern disc brakes except that the disc was fabric faced. Poor heat dissipation seems to have been a problem, as the disc was enclosed within a drum.

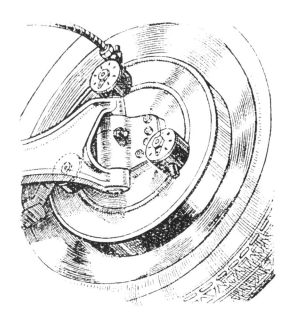

The Walex disc brake was offered by a Berlin component maker in 1932.

■ Dual-circuit brakes were first used on the 1936 Hudson. A separate reserve system went into action if the primary brakes failed.

■ The most expensive 1949 Chrysler models had hydraulic discs on all four wheels. In the same year they were also briefly tried on another American make, the Crosley Hotshot minicar.

The most technically advanced car in the world when it was introduced in 1955, the Citroën DS19 was the first to combine hydropneumatic suspension, hydraulic control of clutch, steering, gearbox and braking, and the first disc brakes fitted to a European series-production car. The streamlined body designed by Flaminio Bertoni was a masterpiece of applied aerodynamics. Early cars had a moulded polyester roof panel. On the day of its launch at the Paris Salon, 12 000 orders were taken and 1 250 000 D Series Citroëns were built before production ended in 1975.

The first British mass-production car to have disc brakes as a standard fitting (on the front wheels) was the Triumph TR3 from the autumn of 1956.

The first low-priced family car to be fitted with disc brakes was the 1962 Ford Classic.

The first ventilated disc brakes fitted to a production car were on the 1967 Porsche 911SC.

Electronic computer-controlled anti-skid braking was first offered as an extra during 1968 on the Ford Thunderbird and Lincoln Continental.

Ford's 1985 Scorpio was the first car range to be fitted, across the board, with anti-lock braking.

The option of anti-lock brakes on the 1989 Fiesta made Ford the first manufacturer to offer this important safety aid on every car line in its range.

CHASSIS, TYRES AND WHEELS

The first electric starter was experimentally fitted by a Mr Dowsing to his Arnold-Benz car in 1896, and electric starting was first fitted as standard to the 1909 Standard GE built in Philadelphia. The first firm to fit electric starting and lighting as standard equipment was Cadillac, whose electric starter had been devised by Charles F. Kettering of the Dayton Engineering Laboratories Company (Delco). It was first fitted to Cadillacs in 1912.

The first car to be fitted with a dynamo was the 1897 Mors, which used it as part of the electric ignition system.

Pneumatic starters were popular on luxury cars before Cadillac popularised electric starting. The pioneer American firm of Winton fitted them, as did Delaunay-Belleville in France, Minerva in Belgium, and Wolseley in England.

Tubeless tyres were essayed without much success on motorcycles and American light cars in the 1890s. The idea was 'reinvented' by the American Goodrich firm in 1948.

The first petrol vehicle designed from the start to run on pneumatic tyres was the 1894 De Dion-Bouton

The 1905 Rover was the first car with a backbone frame cast from aluminium.

tricycle. The first pneumatic-tyred four-wheeled car was a Peugeot – known as *L'Eclair* ('Lightning') from its propensity for travelling in a zig-zag path – which the Michelin brothers entered for the Paris–Bordeaux–Paris Race in July 1895. They used up their stock of 22 spare inner tubes and then spent so much time mending punctures and bursts that they gave up after 90 hours. Levassor, who won the race in 48 h 48 min, said the air-filled tyre would obviously never be of the slightest use for motor cars.

■ The car which set the pattern for car design for the next 90 years, the 1892 Panhard & Levassor, combined front-mounted vertical engine, foot-operated friction clutch and sliding pinion change-speed gear (it could hardly be called a 'gearbox' as the mechanism was not enclosed). Designer Emile Levassor said frankly that this gear system was *'brusque et brutal – mais ça marche!'*

■ Every Franklin car built between the start of production in 1902 and 1928 had a wooden chassis, tubular axles and full-elliptic springing. The idiosyncratic axles and springs persisted until 1932, when they were dropped at the insistence of the shortsighted banking syndicate that had assumed control of the company.

■ Six-wheeled cars have generally been adaptations of commercial or military vehicles, but the 1903 Pullman built in Pennsylvania and the 1905 Borderel-Cail from Denain, Northern France, were purpose-built cars whose outer axles steered and centre axle drove. De Dietrich also built a car of this type in 1903 to the order of an ostentatious nobleman, Baron Eckhardstein. At the 1930 London Motor Show, Crossley exhibited a six-wheel limousine with a 3.8-litre six-cylinder engine. It did not go into production. In the same period Morris Commercial Cars of Birmingham made a small number of six-wheeled (four driven) executive limousines with six-cylinder engines.

■ The first American manufacturer to use a pressed-steel chassis was Peerless in 1903.

■ Power steering was first seen in 1903 on a Columbia Electric Motor Truck, with the power provided by a separate electric motor.

■ Interchangeable wheels or rims were late on the scene. Quick-demountable rims were first seen at America's Fourth National Automobile Show in mid-January 1904 but were not available in Europe before 1905. Leaking or damaged tyres had to be repaired or replaced by the roadside with the wheels *in situ*. Then came the Stepney spare rim which clamped beside the rim of the deflated tyre and allowed the car to be driven home slowly. The Captain, the Warland and other types of detachable wheel rims followed soon after and the famous Rudge centre-lock wire wheel appeared in 1908.

■ The 1907 Brush Runabout from Detroit had not only a wooden chassis but also wooden axles mounted on coil springs. It inspired the unkind jingle: 'Wooden chassis, wooden wheels, wooden axles, wooden run . . .'.

■ In more than 80 years of car manufacture, Morgan has never sold a car with anything but 'sliding-pillar' independent front suspension. The system devised by company founder H. F. S. Morgan for his first three-wheeler in 1909 is still used on today's Morgan four-wheelers (though other systems have, admittedly, been tried on prototypes).

■ Probably the only car to possess eight wheels was the Reeves Octoauto built in Columbus, Indiana, in 1911, based on a 1910 Oldsmobile chassis. Milton O. Reeves thought that the more wheels a car had, the more comfortable it would be, but though he offered Octoautos for sale, it is doubtful whether any were sold. Probably the thought of parking a car with a 20 ft 8 in/6.30 m overall length and 15-ft/4.57-m wheelbase deterred any potential customers in those pre-power steering days. Undeterred, Milton Reeves then offered the six-wheeled Sextoauto, but only two were ever completed.

■ Self-levelling air suspension was first used on the Cowey car, built in Kew from 1913 to 1915.

■ The Bendix quick-thread starter drive was introduced on the 1914 Chevrolet 'Baby Grand'.

■ The first production car with all-round independent suspension was the 1914 Cornelian, whose name was a gemmy pun on the name of its constructors, the Blood Brothers of Kalamazoo, Michigan. It also pioneered unit body-chassis construction.

■ Three-wheelers have usually been built with either two front wheels and one rear or vice versa, but the 1915 Holden from Texas had its wheels in a triangular formation, two on the left (the front one steered, the back one drove) and one on the right. Four years later the British designer Alfred Angas Scott resigned from the motorcycle company bearing his name and built his Sociable, with a similar

(Above) In the days before detachable wheels, changing tyres was a job for he-men!

(Below) Henry Ford was the first in America to use a strong vanadium steel chassis to ensure that his Model T was – relatively – crashproof.

Independent front suspension featured on cars as varied as the 1907 Sizaire-Naudin (top), and all Morgans –
H. F. S. Morgan driving an early Morgan three-wheeler (above).

(Above) The first four-wheeled car with pneumatic tyres was this 1894 Peugeot entered in the 1895 Paris–Bordeaux race by the Michelin brothers.

(Below) Designed as an emergency treatment for punctured tyres, the Barnfather Patent Tyre Sustaining Pump was announced in 1915.

(Above) An engine-driven compressor provided air for the pneumatic springs of the 1913 Cowey light car.

(Below) The integral chassis-body of the 1920 Black Prince cyclecar was basically two planks.

wheel layout, though this time it drove on the single left wheel. Try as they might to convince people that this was the most comfortable layout for a tricar, neither company could persuade the public to buy a car that looked as though a wheel had fallen off.

■ Fully automatic chassis and engine lubrication was pioneered on the 1915 Fergus 'owner-driver' car built in Belfast but World War I curtailed the project.

■ Few cars – understandably – have been made with five wheels. The most successful five-wheeler was the Smith Flyer (1916–19), an American buckboard with a springless chassis made up of six parallel wooden slats. Its rear-mounted fifth wheel incorporated a small air-cooled engine and had originally been designed in England to power push bikes. Priced at $125 fob Milwaukee, the Smith Flyer could reach 25 mph/40 kph and was also available with ski runners for use on snow. The Flyer was later made by Briggs & Stratton (1919–23) and Red Bug (1924–39) and was so popular that today there is an owners' club for surviving Flyers!

■ Detachable steel artillery or wire wheels were almost universal on European cars by 1920, but fixed wood wheels with demountable rims survived on many American makes until 1932, as it was claimed they made it easier for a woman to cope with a flat tyre.

The 1913 Lagonda pioneered unit construction of body and chassis.

■ The first car with swing-axle rear suspension was the rear-engined Rumpler of 1921.

■ The first tyres with a guaranteed life were announced by F. Lionel Rapson at the end of 1921. He offered his 'unpuncturable tyres' with an optional guarantee that they would cover 5000 or 10 000 miles. The guarantee cost a penny a mile and covered 'everything that happens on the road'. If the tyres failed before the end of the guarantee, an allowance of a penny a mile was made against new covers; if they exceeded the guaranteed mileage, then the owner kept on paying ('which seems only fair').

■ All-wood integral construction was used in prototype cars by Frederick and George Lanchester in 1921–3, and by Marks-Moir in 1923. The Marks-Moir system of integral wooden body/chassis construction was designed to resist the 'colonial conditions' in its constructors' native Australia. The first production application of this system was on the 1933–4 Southern Cross, sponsored by Sir Charles Kingsford-Smith, the famous Australian aviator. Made in Sydney, the Southern Cross was named after his record-breaking Fokker Trimotor. Finance was short, only a few were built and the project ended when 'Smithy' went missing in another record-breaking aeroplane, *Lady Southern Cross*, in 1935.

■ Self-levelling front and rear suspension by interlinked horizontal coil springs was pioneered on the short-lived Gwalia built in Cardiff in 1922 and reappeared on the 2CV Citroën tested before World War II and announced at the 1948 Paris Salon.

■ Large-section 'balloon' tyres were pioneered by Firestone in America in 1923 and first offered later in the year by Cole. The first car to be designed specifically for balloon tyres was the Chrysler 70 of 1924.

■ The cast spoked aluminium wheel was patented by Edwin Birch in 1899 for his 'motor wheel' single-cylinder power pack (and used on Singer two- and three-wheelers from 1900 to 1904), but the first practical cast aluminium wheels on a motor car were those introduced on the Type 35 Bugatti Grand Prix car of 1924; the brake drums were cast integral with the wheel so that the brake shoes could be inspected and, if necessary, changed during a routine pit stop.

■ The first production car with all-round independent suspension, backbone chassis and rear-mounted four-cylinder engine was the 750-cc San Giusto of 1924–6. The output of this Milanese firm was limited but the prototype survives in the Biscaretti Museum in Turin.

■ Hypoid rear axles allowing the transmission line to be lowered were first seen on the 1926 Packard range. Their first European application was on the 1928 Mathis.

■ The first car to combine front-wheel drive and all-independent suspension was the 12/75 Alvis sports-car introduced in 1928.

■ The last new car to be catalogued with solid tyres was the Type XL Trojan of 1929 whose 'wonder-springs', claimed its optimistic British makers, made pneumatics unnecessary.

■ Centre accelerator pedals were widely used by European makers – particularly of sporting cars – until the early 1930s. Like right-hand gear and brake levers, they had a certain upper-crust cachet. Nevertheless, Bullnose Morrises had central accelerators but their MG counterparts used a right-hand throttle pedal.

■ Stainless steel wire wheels were first seen on Sir Malcolm Campbell's 1931 Rolls-Royce Phantom II saloon.

■ Pull-out 'umbrella-handle' brake levers under the dash were first seen on American cars – including Cadillac – in 1934.

■ The first popular car with monocoque body/chassis construction was the Opel Olympia from General Motors' German factory, unveiled at the 1935 Berlin Motor Show. Their 10-hp Vauxhall of October 1937 was the first British mass-market monocoque.

■ The last car catalogued with wood wheels as factory equipment was the Mercedes-Benz 'Nürburg' of 1939.

■ An international agreement standardising threads on screws, nuts and bolts was signed by the United Kingdom, USA and Canada in 1948.

■ Ford-Britain's Mark One Consul/Zephyr series launched in 1950 was the first in the world to use the new Macpherson strut independent front suspension system, invented by Ford's US vice-president of engineering, Earle Macpherson.

■ Goodyear offered 'puncture-sealing' tubeless tyres in 1950.

■ Full power steering was first offered by Chrysler on their 1951 Imperial models.

■ Suspended pedals were first seen on the 1952 Ford and Lincoln ranges.

■ The first successful radial ply tyre was the 1953 Michelin 'X'.

■ Dunlop introduced tubeless tyres to Britain in 1953 after much experiment.

■ Hydropneumatic suspension (on the rear wheels only) was first seen as an option on Citroën's 1954 six-cylinder Traction Avant, and was fitted to all four wheels of the 1956 DS.

■ Electrically controlled self-levelling suspension was used on 1955 Packards.

■ The first all-round independently suspended British family car was the 1959 Triumph Herald.

■ The first postwar American car with all-round independent suspension was the Chevrolet Corvair of 1960; the unpredictability of its swing-axle rear end inspired Ralph Nader's 'Unsafe at any Speed' anti-automobile campaign.

■ Two-ply tyres appeared on 1961 US compact cars in place of four-ply tyres.

■ Single-leaf rear suspension springs were introduced by Chevrolet and Dodge on their 1961 models.

■ 'Run-flat' tyres containing an inner air-chamber

on which the car could be driven for up to 100 miles after a puncture were introduced by Goodyear in the USA during 1963.

■ At the start of 1970, every new American car was fitted with radial tyres at the factory.

■ Continental Tyres introduced a novel tyre design called the AquaContact in 1991 which improved wet weather grip by ducting water through a central channel between two tread bands to simulate the behaviour of twin tyres.

■ The first car to have a stainless-steel chassis is the AC Ace launched at the 1992 London Motor Show. This advance was only made possible by the development of a new stainless steel alloy that could be formed and welded.

UNDER THE BONNET

■ The first car to be fitted with automatic ignition advance was the 1900 Model B Packard (the Packard brothers were in the electric lighting business before branching out into car manufacture). Centrifugal fly-weights varied the ignition timing in relation to engine speed, a principle which was universally used into the electronic era.

■ The in-line four-cylinder engine made its debut in 1896 when a four-cylinder Panhard & Levassor won the 1063-mile/1710-km Paris–Marseilles–Paris Race at an average speed of 15.7 mph/25.3 kph. The 80 × 120 mm 2413-cc engine was rated at only 8 hp. The Mors firm brought out the first V4 engine the following year.

■ Early motor cars were hardly efficient. In 1896 the slow-running Benz engines developed about 2 bhp/litre; the Panhard & Levassor (Daimler) developed 4 bhp/litre, while the new high-speed De Dion-Bouton engine achieved 7 bhp/litre. As late as 1914 average touring car engines developed about 10 bhp/litre.

■ A primitive form of fuel injection was used on the 1896 Pennington, which also had 'long-mingling spark' ignition. Though 'Airship' Pennington was an accomplished con man and his designs were universally outlandish, the few vehicles that he built did mostly seem to run quite well (but see p. 28).

■ The most hopeful idea for propelling a car was that proposed by Henry Silvester of St Louis, Missouri, in 1897. His automobile was supposed to be driven by air compressed by the up-and-down motion of the suspension. One shudders to think how sufficient suspension movement was to be obtained.

■ Though the use of rubber engine mounts is often credited to Chrysler in 1925, in fact they had been used on the French Mors as early as 1897.

■ Before fuel injection, multiple carburetter installations were the hallmark of a powerful car. The first factory-fitted quad carburetter installation was on 1901 Mercedes cars.

■ The concept of a transverse engine with the transmission in the sump was not the invention of Alec Issigonis on his 1959 Mini but was first seen in 1901 on the twin-cylinder Schaudel car designed by a former military gunsmith with workshops in Bordeaux. Sold in England as the 'British Ideal', M Schaudel's design was the sensation of the 1901 Paris Salon; production was taken over in 1902 by Emile Dombret under the name 'Motobloc'. Nor was the combination of front-wheel drive and transverse engine new to the Mini: these features were found on twin-cylinder DKWs as early as 1931.

■ The first in-line eight-cylinder car engine was produced in 1902 by Charron, Girardot & Voigt of Paris, but was not very successful; nor were straight-eight racing cars made in America soon afterwards by Winton, Franklin and Buffum, whose engines, made by coupling two fours together, were long and unwieldy. The first British straight eight, if the rather fanciful drawings in the firm's advertising is to be believed, was the 1905 Leader ('almost as elastic as steam') built in Nottingham, offered in 9425-cc 60-hp or 15 978-cc 90-hp form. The bonnet actually made up half the overall length of the car.

■ Hot air was proposed as a motive power for the 1902 Caloric built in Chicago. To start the car, its cylinder head had to be brought to red heat by a blow torch. Since it could also run on petrol, this seems to have been a somewhat chancy business.

■ Variable valve timing is promoted as the latest technical advance, but it actually dates back to the turn-of-the-century De Dion-Bouton. Thousands of engines with variable exhaust valve timing controlled by the decelerator pedal – another De Dion speciality – were produced in De Dion's Puteaux factory. Altering the exhaust valve lift slowed the car down; the final part of the pedal travel applied the transmission brake. Experience with the writer's 1903 De Dion shows that it is actually a very logical

(Above) Electric carriages were highly fashionable in Edwardian days: Countess Gladys de Grey paid her visits in this 1902 City & Suburban Grand Victoria.

(Right) The Winton 'Bullet' team for the 1903 Gordon Bennett Race: the left-hand car, driven by Winton himself, had a horizontal 16 862-cc eight-cylinder engine.

method of driving. By 1905 other makes like Horbick were also using variable valve timing.

■ The first successful six-cylinder cars were built by Napier of Acton, England, whose first 'six' was announced in 1903 and on the market early in 1904.

■ The first production car to use high-pressure lubrication was the four-cylinder Lanchester launched at the end of 1904, with big ends that were lubricated at 40–45 psi. Many cars then (and for 25 years afterwards) had crude unpressurised splash lubrication systems.

■ In an attempt to increase the efficiency of the early petrol engine, D. F. Graham of Middletown,

Connecticut, devised a 'dual-expansion' three-cylinder power unit in which the exhaust gases from the two outer cylinders drove the piston in the middle cylinder, rather like a compound steam engine. Engineer John Eisenhuth marketed cars using this engine under various marques, of which the 1904 'Compound' was the most successful.

■ The first eight-cylinder car offered for sale in America was the 1904 Buffum Model G Greyhound, powered by a horizontal 80-hp engine; in 1907 Buffum listed a 40-hp V8, which, along with the contemporary Hewitt V8, is a contender for the first of this archetypal American power unit configuration to go into production.

■ The V8 engine is actually European in origin. The first V8 was a 1903 Ader racer, and V8s were built in small numbers by several makers, including Rolls-Royce and Adams, between 1905 and 1909.

■ The first car with an overhead camshaft operating inclined valves in hemispherical combustion chambers was the 1905 Welch 30/35 hp; in 1906 the 8.7-litre 50/60-hp Pungs-Finch Limited built in Detroit also boasted this feature.

■ Electrically controlled valves were used on the 1905 Gas-au-Lec from Peabody, Massachusetts. The timing could, it was said, be altered by the driver and there was no camshaft. An electric motor geared to the drive shaft for slow running and hill climbing doubled as a starter. Sadly, the concept was too far ahead of 1905 technology.

■ A novel starting system was used on the 1906 Harrison from Grand Rapids, Michigan, which used an air pump to send a charge of acetylene into whichever cylinder was in the correct position to fire. The fact that the 'Car without a Crank' failed to survive two years in production speaks volumes about the viability of the system.

■ The first V12 car seems to have been the one-off Schebler built in Indianapolis in 1908–9 by carburetter maker George Schebler, using an engine designed by Philip Schmoll which could be operated either as a six or a twelve.

■ The first supercharged car to be available to the public was the 1908 Great Chadwick Six designed by Lee Sherman Chadwick of Pottstown, Pennsylvania. First seen on the firm's racing car in 1907, the belt-driven supercharger was available as a $375 option on the 11.6-litre Great Chadwick Six runabout.

*The remarkable power unit of the 1908 40/50-hp
Adams car was a V8 Antoinette aero engine.*

■ Mechanical complexity was no deterrent to manufacturers seeking smooth running: the ultimate version of the Gobron-Brillié opposed-piston engine of 1898–1914 was the 11.4-litre six-cylinder 70–90 hp with two crankshafts, 12 pistons and 12 conrods, but this was surpassed by the 1909 20-hp two-stroke Cooper (built by a maker of 'steam diggers' from King's Lynn in Norfolk) which had two crankshafts and 12 pistons for just four cylinders. . . . It also had adjustable rear springing operated by a large wing nut behind the rear number plate, six speeds forward (and two reverse) and was described as 'a triumph of inaccessibility'; typically, the body had to be taken off before the rear cylinder block could be removed.

■ Pneumatic bliss was paramount on the early Winton cars built in Cleveland, Ohio. Pneumatic

valve lifters were used early this century. They also had a pneumatically operated throttle control and – from 1909 – a pneumatic starter.

■ The first series-production V8 was the Model CL De Dion-Bouton of 1910, which was copied and improved by Cadillac to create their 1914 V8.

■ The first hydraulic tappets were seen on the 30-hp 1910 Type E built by Amédée Bollée *fils*, who in 1903 had designed a fuel injection system.

■ The Adams-Farwell car built in Dubuque, Iowa, between 1905 and 1913 featured three- and five-cylinder rotary engines and the curiously disturbing slogan 'It spins like a top'. Other idiosyncratic features of the marque included pedals and steering interchangeable between front and back seats and a 'side sliding steering wheel', enabling the car to be driven from either front seat (what happened if the pedals were operated from the back and the steering from the front was not made clear).

■ The first British car fitted with a dip stick to check the oil level in the sump was probably the 1915 Morris Cowley.

■ The first production V12 car was the 1915 Packard Twin-Six, which is also claimed as the first production car with aluminium pistons. But its engine was inspired by that of the 1913 British-built 9-litre Sunbeam racer *Toodles V* which raced in America after the outbreak of war in 1914. The Twin-Six was made until 1923. Twin-Sixes seen on World War I duty in his native Italy inspired Enzo Ferrari to adopt the V12 engine when he started building cars under his own name in 1946.

■ The first thermostatic radiator shutters were invented by Frederick Furber and featured on the 1917 Columbia Six built in Detroit: a thermostat mounted above the fan automatically opened the radiator shutters as the temperature rose. The first British car with thermostatically controlled radiator shutters was the 1920 Straker-Squire.

■ The first light car with an overhead-camshaft engine was the 1327-cc Type 13 Bugatti, first marketed in 1910 (Ettore Bugatti had started work on the prototype in 1908). Though the Bugatti is regarded as a French make, its factory was in Molsheim in Alsace, which was German territory between 1871 and 1919.

■ The first American production cars to combine a straight-eight engine and four-wheel brakes were the Model A Duesenberg and the Kenworthy Line-O-Eight, both launched in the closing weeks of 1920.

■ Leaded petrol was first successfully demonstrated on 9 December 1921 by the American scientist Dr Thomas Midgley Jr. It was first marketed on 2 February 1923 under the name 'Ethyl' in Dayton, Ohio, by General Motors Research Corporation. In 1924 GM collaborated with Standard Oil to form the Ethyl Corporation to market leaded petrol.

■ The first twin-overhead camshaft engine to be offered to the public was the Ballot 2LS, a French super-sports car introduced during 1921. The following year the 1200-cc 10–15-hp Salmson brought the twin-cam engine to a less exclusive clientele.

■ Europe's first supercharged production cars were the 6/25/40 PS and 10/40/65 PS Mercedes exhibited at the 1921 Berlin Motor Show. The first supercharged British car to be catalogued was the 12/80-hp Alvis of 1926, but the first one with a blower to be series-built was the S Type Lea-Francis of October 1927.

■ The first British car fitted with hydraulically servo-assisted four-wheel brakes was the 1924 Lanchester Forty; the servo was hydraulic, though the braking linkage was mechanical.

■ The first engine to use 14-mm spark plugs appears to have been the 1100-cc ohv Mathis Six launched at the 1922 Paris Salon.

■ The first car to be fitted with a replaceable cartridge oil filter was the 1924 Chrysler. The DI Delage of the same period had a full-flow filter gauze 'cartridge' which could be removed for cleaning.

■ Electric fuel pumps were first used on the 1924 Wills St Claire. The first British car so equipped was the 2-litre Arab of 1927.

■ The first road-going cars with oil coolers were the 1925 Renault 9.1-litre Model NM 45cv, and the 1925 California designed by Harry Miller and built in Los Angeles. The oil cooler for its overhead valve six-cylinder engine was built into the base of the radiator.

■ The Octane rating system for petrol was devised in 1926 by the American scientist Dr Graham Edgar.

■ Possibly only one straight-nine car has ever been built and that was the 1927 Willis from Maywood, Illinois. A car and a truck were fitted with this unusual power unit but though a range of cars was proposed, nothing more came of the venture.

■ The first mid-engined car with a transverse straight-eight power unit and integral body/chassis construction was the one-off Anderson Special built in Newton Mearns, near Glasgow, in 1926–7. Its power unit consisted of two Austin Seven engines bolted end-to-end on a fluid flywheel housing.

■ Perhaps the greatest technical triumph in the long history of General Motors was the introduction of the world's first production V16 car, the Cadillac Model 452 in January 1930. It was exceptionally silent, thanks to the first successful series-production use of hydraulic valve lifters. The only sound audible at tickover was the slight snap of the spark at the contact breaker points. The car could cruise at 70 mph and open V16s could reach 100 mph/160 kph.

■ Only three 16-cylinder private cars have ever been marketed, and two of those were American, the 1930–40 Cadillac and Marmon in 1931–3. Bugatti's Type 47 of 1930 was never made in series. Harry Miller built a one-off V16 Speedster in 1930. The 1931–2 prototypes by Bucciali and Peerless came to nothing; also stillborn was a plan to develop a super-sports coupé out of the original 1934 Grand Prix Auto Union.

■ In 1931 a straight-ten was proposed by the Nacional Pescara company of Barcelona but it seems to have remained at the project stage. The Marqués de Pescara subsequently moved to Switzerland, where he built three V16 SLM-Pescara luxury cars in 1935–6.

■ The last steam car to be catalogued was the 1931 Model E Doble, a four-cylinder machine with 'flash' generator. It weighed over 2 tons, had electrically ignited burners, cost up to $11 200 and could exceed 90 mph/145 mph. But this exclusive marque was killed by the Depression before the new Model F could go into production. Howard Hughes was a keen Doble owner.

■ As the amount of electrical equipment used on cars increased, high-output generators used in conjunction with voltage regulators became necessary. The first such installation was on the 1934 Cadillac.

■ The highest claimed specific power output achieved by any prewar car engine was the 113 bhp of the 1934 supercharged 750-cc MG Q-Type Midget, equivalent to 151 bhp/litre.

■ Though Voisin announced a straight-twelve range – the 6-litre V12L 'Ailée' and long wheelbase V12LL

'Croisière' – for 1937, only one prototype was ever built. The engine was so long that the two rear cylinders intruded into the cockpit.

■ The first diesel-engined private car to go into series production was the Mercedes 260D of 1936. Vibration problems had prevented the company launching a diesel car in 1934. Citroën had earlier built an experimental batch of cars with Ricardo diesels.

■ The 'Silent Knight' double sleeve-valve engine was designed to eliminate the problems experienced with early poppet valves. It combined ghostly silence with a tendency to smoke from the exhaust, thanks to the amount of oil needed to lubricate the sliding, slotted sleeves which replaced conventional valves. Its greatest exponent was Daimler (1908–35) but the last car to be fitted with a double-sleeve-valve engine was the six-cylinder Panhard of 1939. Single-sleeve-valve engines were also made, and the last were the Scottish Argyll and Arrol-Aster, discontinued in 1931. Slide-valve engines (in which only a section of the cylinder wall slid up and down) were used by Impéria of Belgium until 1934.

Gas turbine cars are an exclusive breed: the first was the 1950 Rover 'JET 1' developed by Gordon Bell and Spen King . . .

... and Austin fitted a 125-bhp unit into a modified Austin Sheerline limousine in 1954 ...

... while Chrysler put 50 experimental gas-turbine cars into the hands of selected private owners in 1964 ...

... and in 1965 Rover entered this neat two-seat coupé for the Le Mans 24-hour Race. It was based on a 1963 open car and was driven into 10th place by Graham Hill and Jackie Stewart, and later used on the road.

■ The world's first turbine-powered private car was the prototype Rover two-seater 'JET 1' developed by Gordon Bell and Spen King and first demonstrated on the MIRA test track at Lindley in March 1950. In 1952 it set speed records at 151.965 mph/244.56 kph on the Jabbeke motorway in Belgium.

■ The first production V6 engine was the 1950 Lancia Aurelia. However, as early as 1905 Howard Marmon of Indianapolis had built an experimental V6, having previously built a vee-twin and a V4. The following season he built a V8, but his production models were all in-line fours, sixes and eights until, in November 1930 Marmon unveiled a superlative V16, which remained in production until Marmon closed down in 1933. Right at the end an amazing backbone-chassis V12 prototype was built.

■ The first road-going car equipped with fuel injection as standard equipment was the Mercedes-Benz 300SL of 1954. The first American cars with fuel injection available as an extra were the 1956 Rambler, Pontiac and Chrysler. The first American car on which fuel injection was offered as standard was the Chevrolet Corvette of 1957, while Britain's first fuel-injected car was the Triumph TR5 announced in October 1967.

■ The first British diesel car was a version of the Phase II Standard Vanguard of 1954.

■ The first (and so far only) jet-engined private car to be series-built was the 1954 Chrysler Turbo Dart. Fifty were loaned to selected customers for appraisal but subsequently recalled. Turbine engines suffer from throttle lag and are therefore more suited to truck use, but truck makers have only built prototypes so far.

■ Mass-producers are constantly seeking the Holy Grail of a viable alternative to the conventional internal combustion engine. Millions have been spent on such projects but to little perceptible effect. In 1956, for instance, General Motors unveiled a 'free-piston' engine which could run on any fuel from high octane petrol to whale oil or peanut oil. In 1974 it was Ford's turn in the peanut barrel when it announced its work on the Stirling 'hot air' engine which could also run on peanut oil. Other bright ideas which lost their sparkle include the Polimotor plastic engine, the stratified charge engine, the variable compression engine, the ceramic engine, the miniature atomic pile and the fuel cell. In 1992 Ford was running tests on the Orbital two-stroke engine which its progenitors

claim overcomes the traditional disadvantages of the two-stroke cycle. Time will tell.

■ The last production straight eight was the Russian ZIL (formerly ZIS) of 1959 which was basically a 1942 Packard (the body dies were sold to Russia in 1943) powered by a 5.6-litre development of the 1936 Buick Master Eight.

■ The somewhat dubious concept of a 'sealed for life' cooling system was pioneered in 1961 on Renault's 750-cc and 850-cc R4 models. The first American marque with this feature was Cadillac, in 1968.

■ The first attempt to reduce emissions from petrol engines came with the fitting of a pipe which diverted crankcase vapours into the inlet manifold on 1961 US models sold in California.

■ Camshaft drive by cogged belt was first seen on the German Glas S1004 of 1961.

■ The first production car with a Wankel rotary-type engine was the NSU Wankel Spyder, displayed at the Frankfurt Motor Show in September 1963. Deliveries started a year later and the advanced Ro80 saloon was new in 1968. The NSU marque disappeared in 1977 following a merger with Audi who did not persist with the rotary. Today, Wankel rotary engines are only used by the Japanese Mazda firm, which introduced them in 1967.

■ Every domestic American-made car was fitted with an exhaust emission control system as standard in 1967.

■ From 1970 all US engines were redesigned to run on unleaded fuel.

■ Electronic ignition was standardised on 1973 Chryslers. Electronic control of spark advance followed three years later.

■ The first private car with an in-line five-cylinder engine was the 3-litre Mercedes-Benz 300D diesel saloon announced in 1974.

■ Bosch introduced the 'Lambda sensor' oxygen-sensing equipment in 1976 to control the air-fuel mixture and thus monitor exhaust emissions.

(Above) The world's first production turbocharged car was the 1974 BMW 2002 Turbo, good for 132 mph from a 2-litre engine.

(Below) The most consistent (and now the only) user of the Wankel rotary engine is Mazda: this is the 1993 RX-7 Turbo.

Solar powered electrics are not yet viable for normal motoring, but have shown stamina in a long-distance Australian contest. This is a 1993 endurance racer built by Kia of South Korea.

■ The first production turbocharged petrol car was the 1974 BMW 2002 Turbo and the first turbo diesel model was produced by Mercedes-Benz in 1978.

■ Audi offered the first five-cylinder petrol engined cars in 1977.

■ In 1984 Diahatsu launched the Charade Turbo, claimed to be the first 1-litre turbocharged production model.

■ The battery cover used on the Audi 80 from October 1990 was the first plastic part on any car in the world 100 per cent made of plastic recycled from old cars.

■ V10 engines are only slightly more common than hens' teeth – a prototype ohc V10 built for Henry Ford in the 1920s survives in store in the Ford Museum – but the 1992 Dodge Viper 8.0-litre sports car is the most successful application of this configuration outside the specialised world of racing.

TRANSMISSIONS

■ Described in *Horseless Age* in 1895, the Caffrey steam carriage built in Camden, New Jersey, had an independent steam engine for each wheel. When they were all running, this must have been the first four-wheel drive American car. Another early 4 × 4 steamer, the 1901 Cotta, led to the formation in 1904 of the Four-Wheel Drive company which built mostly petrol trucks (though some seem to have been fitted with car bodies).

■ Front-wheel drive is nothing new: the 1769 Cugnot had it. Various small turn-of-the-century cars like the Victoria Combination had front-drive, simply achieved by using the rear end of a De Dion tricycle as a pivoting power pack. But the first real exponent of front-wheel drive was Walter Christie, whose 1904 racer had a transverse 30-hp engine with the wheels driven directly off the ends of the crankshaft. Another racer had a similar set-up at both ends of the car and a total of 120 hp. Christie's 1907 Grand Prix car had a V4 of almost 20 litres and was 'near uncontrollable'. Production (limited) began in 1906 but most of Christie's output consisted of conversion kits to motorise horse-drawn fire engines.

■ An 'H'-pattern gate gear shift was installed on the first Packard automobile shortly after its maiden run in 1899.

■ Early motorists had problems changing gear on conventional sliding-pinion gearboxes: De Dion-Bouton light cars of the 1899–1910 period had an ingenious constant-mesh gear in which a rack running through the gearbox expanded clutches to engage each speed.

■ The earliest attempt to make automatic or semi-automatic transmissions were the Barber progressively variable hydraulic gearbox fitted to a Hutton car in 1903, and the Fouillaron belt and expanding pulley system (similar in principle to the modern Ford CTX transmission, but manually operated) of the same period. Numerous American examples include the Entz electro-magnetic system used on Owen-Magnetic and Crown-Magnetic cars. The Lentz hydraulic transmission was fitted to a few Charron cars in 1912.

■ A three-speed pneumatic gear shift operated by air compressed by the two-cylinder engine was featured on the short-lived 1904 Country Club car from Boston, Massachusetts.

■ Airscrew drive was tried in 1904 by J. B. MacDuff of Brooklyn and the French aviation pioneer Captain Ferber (1906) but the only propellor-driven vehicle to go into any semblance of production was the Leyat, built spasmodically between 1913 and 1927 by Marcel Leyat of Paris. Like a wingless aeroplane, the Leyat had a fabric-covered fuselage with a front-mounted light aeroplane engine, was started by swinging the propellor and steered by its rear 'undercarriage'. Amazingly, in view of their in-built risk factor, several Leyats survive.

■ The first production car with automatic transmission was the Sturtevant from Boston, Massachusetts. A prototype built in 1904 had a two-speed centrifugally operated transmission (and air brakes) while the production 'Automatic Sturtevant' model launched in 1905 had a three-speed transmission

This 1900 Eureka voiturette was one of the earliest front-wheel driven cars on the market.

In the 1920s this airscrew-driven Leyat was driven all over France by author Gustave Coureau; small-scale production included saloons and vans. The rear wheels steered!

(plus a conventional sliding gear reverse). Production only lasted until 1907.

■ America's first purpose-built four-wheel-drive petrol car appears to have been the 1905 Van Winkle made in San Joaquin, California. It looked remarkably like a converted 1903 Ford or Cadillac and only one demonstration model was built. Of greater significance was the 1910–12 FWD, for this Wisconsin marque decided to concentrate on 4 × 4 trucks and became one of America's best-known names in this field.

■ Friction drive was common in the early days. It offered simplicity of construction and ease of gear changing – moving the friction wheel at right angles across the face of the driving disc gave an infinite variety of speeds – but was prone to slip and wear.

Most successful of the friction-drive marques were the GWK from Maidenhead, which offered 'a gear for every gradient' between 1911 and 1931, and the Metz from Waltham, Massachusetts, which was probably the only marque literally sold on the instalment plan. Metz owners bought the car in 14 'groups' of mechanical components which cost $25 each for home assembly.

■ Strange indeed was the mysterious Airmobile from California: the Rotary Air Brake Company of Los Angeles claimed in 1914 to be making a car with 'combined frictionless rotary air motor and brake' driving each wheel. The drawings looked fun, anyway.

■ Overdrive was first offered on the 1914 Cadillac range, which had electrically selected alternative final drive ratios of 4.04 or 2.5:1 and was awarded the Dewar Trophy for this feature. Gearboxes with an overdrive top were not uncommon before World War I; the 40/50-hp Rolls-Royce had such a 'sprinting gear' from 1907 to 1909.

■ Between 3 July and 1 August 1916, a 12-cylinder Pathfinder car fitted with only top and reverse gears made an officially observed crossing of the USA from San Diego, California, to New York, a distance of 4889 miles/7866 km. It then covered a flying mile at over 60 mph/95 kph to prove that it was not ridiculously low-geared.

■ The first production cars with an electrically selected transmission were the 1916 Pullman 32 hp from York, Pennsylvania and the 1918 Premier built in Indianapolis. They were fitted with the Cutler-Hammer transmission in which the ratios were selected by a lever on the steering wheel.

■ The first light car with an automatic expanding pulley belt transmission was the 8-hp RTC cyclecar of 1922: the pulleys were opened and closed by a centrifugal governor.

■ The concept of four-wheel drive plus four-wheel steer goes back to steam carriage days and was seen on commercial vehicles just before World War I. In 1923 a 4WD/4WS prototype called the Holverter was demonstrated in England, but the first 4WD/

Bugatti's 1932 Type 53 was a four-wheel drive racing car: with 300 bhp on tap, it was tricky to control.

4WS car to see any kind of production was the SABA, of which a few were built in Italy in 1927–8. In 1899 T.H. Parker of London demonstrated an electric car with rear-wheel drive and four-wheel 'turntable' steering giving a 7-ft/2-m turning circle.

■ The Wilson 'self-changing' transmission (best known of the pre-selective systems) was tried experimentally by Vauxhall in 1927 and first catalogued as an option on the 1929 Armstrong-Siddeley range. The German ZF-Soden preselector gearbox was fitted to several ephemeral makes (Fadag, Lindcar, Szawe) in 1923.

■ The first cars to be fitted with a synchromesh gearbox were the 1929 Cadillac and LaSalle. Mercedes, Mathis, Maybach and Horch fitted synchromesh in 1931. The first British makers to adopt synchromesh were Vauxhall, Ford and Rolls-Royce in 1932. All had unsynchronised first speeds.

■ Bendix introduced an automatic clutch in 1931.

■ The first gearbox with synchromesh on all speeds was announced by ZF ('Zahnrad-Fabrik') of Germany in 1931, but the first car fitted with such a gearbox as standard was the British Alvis Speed Twenty in October 1933.

■ Dual-ratio transmissions have become common in recent years, but the first dual-ratio four-speed transmission was the Maybach *Doppelschnellgang* ('dual overdrive box') of 1931–9, which also offered four reverses. This package was offered on the 1932 Lagonda 3-litre 'Selector Special' but there were few takers.

■ An automatic overdrive was offered on 1934 Chrysler and De Soto Airflow models.

■ Announced at the 1933 Olympia Show was an 18-hp Austin fitted with the Hayes infinitely variable gear, but it cost £40 and only a few people were interested. The first British automatic to be standardised was the Brockhouse Turbo-Transmitter used on the Invicta Black Prince of 1946–50.

■ Some turn-of-the-century cars had two gear levers – usually a separate lever engaged reverse – but on French cars with the Cotal electrically selected gearbox introduced in 1931 a fingertip column selector moving in a tiny gate was used in conjunction with a floor-mounted forward/reverse lever, so four speeds could be obtained in either direction. Cotal-equipped marques included Delage, Delahaye, Salmson and Voisin. It could be used in conjunction with the Fleischel automatic selector, which changed gears as revolutions fell when the engine came under load.

■ Though Reo had offered a primitive automatic transmission in 1934, and 1937 Buicks and Oldsmobiles were available with Automatic Safety Transmissions, the first 'modern-generation' automatic transmission was the General Motors Hydramatic, sold as a $100 option on the Oldsmobile during the 1940 season. The Cadillac got Hydramatic the next year but it cost $25 extra. The Dynaflow hydraulic convertor transmission was introduced on 1948 Buicks.

■ A limited-slip differential was fitted to 1955 Packards.

■ Because of American safety legislation the standard selector positions on automatic-transmission quadrants, which used to be arranged P-N-D-L-R (Park-Neutral-Drive-Low-Reverse), were amended to the safer P-R-N-D-L during 1964.

LIGHTING

■ Before electric lighting became practicable, cars usually carried oil-burning side and tail lamps (although some of the real pioneers ventured out at night by the light of candle-burning carriage lamps). Headlamps burning acetylene gas came into use about 1898; many of these were large, heavy, elaborate and expensive. Louis Blériot, who in 1909 made the first crossing of the English Channel by aeroplane, amassed the fortune that allowed him to become an aircraft constructor by making some of the best acetylene lamps.

■ The first stop light was the 'Sonolux', available in France in 1908. It was a metal case which contained a lamp – oil, acetylene or electric – which not only lit up the number plate at night but also illuminated a red 'Attention' sign covered by a flap which flew open when the driver trod on the brake pedal.

■ Headlamps set into the wings were a Pierce-Arrow trademark as early as 1913, though it was possible even in 1930 to specify a conventional mounting. The first British production model with headlamps fully faired into the wings was the Series-E Morris Eight of 1939.

■ Dipping headlamps were introduced on the 1915 Cadillac.

■ Stop lights were first fitted to American cars in 1915.

■ The Barker dipping headlamp system, in which the bodies of the lamps were physically dipped by a hand-lever and rod mechanism, appeared in 1921. It was standardised on a number of British cars, among them Alvis and Morris. The same year Lionel Rapson introduced a similar system at a basic cost of £5.

■ An automatic reversing lamp was first fitted to the 1921 Wills St Claire.

■ The first dual headlamp installation was made on a 16/40-hp Sunbeam in 1922. These 'anti-dazzle' lamps were the invention of Cooke and Lindsell of Tottenham and consisted of a conventional (direct beam) portion with a crescent-shaped (dipped) lamp superimposed. The upper and lower sections had independent reflectors and bulbs.

■ The first twin-filament bulbs, allowing headlamps to be dipped electrically rather than mechanically, were introduced in the USA in 1924.

■ The first purpose-designed fog lamp was offered

The first stop lamp – the 1908 'Sonolux' – was also the first number plate with integral illumination.

by Desmo of Birmingham in 1928. Before that (since 1925) accessory manufacturers had made yellow celluloid 'fog-discs' which fitted over the headlamps.

■ Headlamp flashers were first used on the 1935 Fiat 1500.

■ Sealed-beam headlamps were adopted for the 1940 model year by most American makers.

■ A single central spotlamp was featured on the Rover 75 from 1950 to 1952 but the basic idea was nothing new. Central headlamps had been tried on at least three American cars nearly 40 years earlier: the Garford (1913), the Wells (1914) and the Briscoe (1915). Since single headlamps were illegal in many states, this seemed like false economy.

■ The 1952 Oldsmobiles were fitted with automatic headlamp dimmers.

■ The first post-war use of dual headlamps, still fitted on luxury cars like the Jaguar, was on the 1954 Cadillac El Camino. Lincoln followed suit in 1957,

though the last Pierce Arrows of 1936–8 (and the more expensive 1937 Packards) featured auxiliary headlamps intended for use as pass lights.

■ Sealed-beam headlamps were standardised on all new American cars by mid-1955.

■ The first car fitted with an alternator instead of a direct current dynamo was the 1960 Plymouth Valiant.

■ Headlamps which automatically came on when it got dark were offered on some 1960 model American cars, while headlamps that automatically turned on at dusk and off at dawn when the ignition was on were introduced in 1963 by Cadillac under the name 'Twilight Sentinel'. They were presumably intended for blind drivers.

■ Amber front turn indicators were adopted across the American industry in 1962 after tests proved they were more clearly visible than white signals.

■ Push-button operated pop-up headlamps were introduced on the 1963 Chevrolet Corvette.

■ Headlamps turning with the wheels (illegal in Britain) were first seen as regular equipment on the 1967 Citroëns, but the American Tucker Torpedo of 1946 had a swivelling, centrally mounted Cyclops-eye spotlight. As early as 1928–9, Tilt-Ray swivelling headlamps marketed by an American accessory firm were fitted to luxury models in the Cadillac-Lincoln class.

■ Quartz halogen spot lamps appear to have first been available on a production model on 1969 Chryslers.

IN-CAR ENTERTAINMENT

■ The first recorded car fitted with a radio was the 1912 Model T Ford tourer belonging to Alan M. Thomas, an electrical engineering student at Toronto, Canada, who carried out experiments on 'radio communication from automobiles' in 1914. Equipped with an aerial which looked more like a multiple clothes line, the car had to be stationary (and earthed) in order to receive radio signals, but Thomas was able to hear clearly the government station at Toronto Island and 'amateurs throughout the city' while the VBC station at Midland, some 180 miles north, could be faintly distinguished.

■ The first wireless communication from a moving car was a Morse transmission made by S. F. Edge's riding mechanic during a 'double-12' record at Brooklands on 20 July 1922 while their Spyker was travelling at 80 mph.

■ The first successful radio communication from an automobile in the USA was made from a Dodge belonging to Edward Dallin, who broadcast 10-mile transmissions during 1922.

■ The first recorded use of a radio receiver in a private car in the UK was in August 1922, when the Cardiff & South Wales Wireless Society installed a set in a touring car (which may well have been the first car to receive a wireless programme while 'travelling at touring speeds'). In September 1922, a Burndept two-valve wireless set was fitted to a new Cadillac coupé for Mrs Geoffrey Duveen of London:

the car had to be stationary with its 50-ft aerial slung in a tree before broadcasts could be received.

■ The first air-to-car communication took place in August 1922, when the pilots of aeroplanes fitted with radio telephones to monitor a threatened strike in Paris spoke with the Prefect of Police in his car.

■ The first factory-installed wireless set was a Marconi unit fitted in a 45-hp Daimler limousine shown at Olympia in October 1922. It could receive broadcasts while the car was in motion.

■ The first private car fitted with an independent radio telephone was an AC two-seater carrying an Electrical Disposals Syndicate set on its passenger seat, with a microphone clipped to the body side. A three-wire aerial was mounted in the dickey seat. It was successfully tested at Brooklands on 23 November 1922, the receiving station being set up on the Test Hill. The call sign '5HX' was allocated to radio experiments at Brooklands.

■ America's first factory-fitted radio sets were the 1922 'Motoradio' from Van Nuys, California, and a set offered by the Springfield Body Company in 1923.

■ The Philadelphia Storage Battery Company introduced the first commercially available car radio – the Philco – in 1927.

■ Radios were offered as optional equipment on many 1929 American cars. That autumn a New York dealer sold 1930-model Dodge Seniors fitted with Automobile Radio Corporation wireless sets as a special promotion. The first cars actually to incorporate aerials and wiring to enable radios to be fitted after purchase were the 1930 Cadillac, Chrysler, Dodge, LaSalle, Marmon and Roosevelt ranges.

■ The advance of car radio in the USA was so rapid that by mid-1933 Philco was selling 50 000 sets a month to US car makers. By 1935 some three million cars were fitted with radio sets.

■ The first popular British car radio was the six-valve HMV Super-het receiver announced in October 1933, priced at 17 guineas. The first British car with a factory-installed radio set as standard was the 1934 Hillman 'Melody Minx', which had a mascot in the shape of a human harp. The radio was a specially designed Philco.

■ The first in-car record player was an experimental installation in the 1936 Ford V8 of Donald Mattheson in the USA.

■ Delco in the US introduced the first multi-button car radio tuner in 1939.

■ Delco offered the first production signal-seeking car radio set, the Model R-705, during 1947.

■ An all-transistor radio was first offered on 1955 Chrysler models.

■ CD disc players may be commonplace on modern cars but in 1956 Chrysler offered a built-in gramophone as an extra. The 'Highway Hi Fi Record Player' played special 16-rpm extended play vinyl discs. Marilyn Monroe had one in her Dodge. Also available on Chrysler's 1959 Crown Imperial was a foot-controlled transistor radio.

■ Available on 1960 model Chryslers, the RCA Ultra-Fi record player could play up to 14 45-rpm records.

■ The first cassette player for car installation was the 1964 Autostereo MC-8, another 'first' from Van Nuys, California. It played pre-recorded four-track tape cartridges.

■ The first car with the radio aerial embedded in the windscreen was the 1969 model Pontiac Grand Prix.

■ The first American car to offer a compact cassette tape player was the 1971 Pontiac.

■ CD players became available on American cars in 1985.

The first car radio was this clumsy installation fitted to a Model T Ford in 1914.

MEN OF MOTORING

Gianni Agnelli, Italian (b. 1921). Grandson of Fiat's founder who has made the already mighty group mightier yet, to the point where it controls virtually all of Italy's motor industry – and much more of the country's business and financial institutions.

Giovanni Agnelli, Italian (1866–1945). Former cavalry officer who was a co-founder of Fiat and built it up into a powerful industrial empire, not unaided by his friendship with a right-wing journalist and rising politician named Mussolini. His great monument is the Fiat factory at Lingotto, with its rooftop test track, whose construction marked the transition of Fiat into a mass-market giant.

W. O. Bentley in the first Bentley car.

Edgar Apperson, American (1870–1959) and **Elmer** (1861–1920). Two Indiana brothers who collaborated with Elwood Haynes to build one of America's first cars in 1894, then formed the Haynes-Apperson company. When they split with Haynes, they started the Apperson Brothers Motor Car Company.

Herbert Austin, British (1866–1947). Born in the Chilterns, Austin sought his fortune in Australia where he perfected a mechanical sheep shearer for the Wolseley Sheep-Shearing Company. He returned to England to build the first Wolseley car in 1895 but left 10 years later to found his own company. Milestone Austin designs included the Seven, Twenty and Twelve-Four. Knighted in 1917, he became Lord Austin in 1936.

John Barnard, British (b. 1946). Leading racing car designer, with Parnelli and Chaparral before joining McLaren. Responsible for the innovative cars that

restored the marque to the Grand Prix forefront in the early 1980s. Then, as racing technical director, he set up Ferrari's advanced design bureau in Britain, and some time after that was closed down he was called on to re-establish it. Meanwhile he had been technical director of the Benetton team.

Walter Owen Bentley, British (1888–1971). Trained as a railway engineer, but soon turned to cars and pioneered the use of aluminium pistons in 1914 on the DFP car for which he was agent. Designed rotary aero engines during World War I and launched the Bentley car in 1919. Despite sporting success, his company failed in 1931 and was acquired by Rolls-Royce. He eventually joined Lagonda: his V12 was one of the outstanding cars of the 1930s.

Carl Benz, German (1844–1929). Gas engine pioneer who in 1885–6 built the first successful petrol car designed from first principles. But though he was first to offer petrol cars for sale, Benz found it difficult to progress far beyond his first basic concept of a low-speed engine mounted in the tail of a belt-drive carriage.

Marc Birkigt, Swiss (1878–1953). This gifted engineer moved from Switzerland to Spain to work on water towers but soon entered the new motor car industry, and created Hispano-Suiza cars and aero engines.

Sir John Black, British (1895–1965). Aggressive tycoon behind Standard-Triumph. Knighted for wartime aircraft production at Standard; brought out the Standard Vanguard in 1947.

Amédée Bollée *fils*, French (1867–1926). Followed his father's lead in steam carriages but built advanced petrol cars from 1896. His 1899 streamlined racer had underslung chassis and four-cylinder engine with hemispherical combustion chambers and twin carburetters. Patented the hydraulic tappet in April 1910.

Amédée Bollée *père*, French (1844–1916). From a long line of Le Mans bell founders, he pioneered independent front suspension and other advanced technical features on his steam carriages in the 1870s.

Léon Bollée, French (1870–1913). Teenage inventor of an advanced mechanical computer who devised a sporting tandem-seat voiturette (1895) and built refined, silent quality cars from 1903.

Benjamin Briscoe, American (1869–1945). Founder in 1910 of the United States Motor Company, combining some 130 firms, which folded in 1912. Began building cars under his own name from 1913 and – with his brother **Frank** (1875–1954) – built light cars in France and America.

Eric Broadley, British (b. 1928). Self-taught racing car designer, whose Lola company became one of the most successful specialist constructors, notably with sports/racing cars and Indycars.

Sir David Brown, British (1904–93). Heir to the David Brown engineering empire who bought Aston Martin and Lagonda in 1947 and created the immortal 'DB' Aston Martins. Sold his interest in the company in 1972 but was appointed 'chairman for life' in the 1990s.

Ettore Bugatti, Italian (1881–1947). Born in Milan, he moved to Alsace where he designed cars for De Dietrich before he was 21. He later joined Mathis, then in 1910 built his first Bugatti car. This eccentric genius ruled his factory at Molsheim (Alsace) in feudal splendour.

David Dunbar Buick, British (1855–1929). His invention of the enamelled bathtub provided the money to found the Buick Motor Car Company (with backing from the Briscoe brothers) in 1903 but he was bought out by Billy Durant in 1904.

Lee Sherman Chadwick, American (1875–1958). Built his first car in 1899, joined Searchmont in 1900 and founded the Chadwick company in 1903. His racing cars were first to use superchargers. After his company closed in 1916 he headed a stove company.

Roy Chapin, American (1880–1936). First worked with Oldsmobile, then helped found Thomas-Detroit in 1906 and Hudson in 1909. He campaigned for better roads for America.

Colin Chapman, British (1928–82). Gifted – and often controversial – designer/constructor of Lotus sports and racing cars. Among his specialities were

Colin Chapman

light and compact construction, advanced suspension and aerodynamics, and unitary construction in fibreglass, while he introduced the monocoque concept to modern single seaters.

Fernand Charron, French (1866–1928). French cycle and car racer invested his profits from the motor trade in building (with Girardot and Voigt) the CGV car and later worked for his father-in-law, Adolphe Clément. After they split up, Charron built the 'Alda' car.

Louis Chevrolet, Swiss (1878–1941). Inventor who emigrated to the USA in 1900 to promote a wine pump of his own design. He raced for Buick and – with Etienne Planche – designed the first Chevrolet Six in 1911. He later founded Frontenac to build racing cars and tuning equipment for Model T Fords.

John Walter Christie, American (1886–1944). Pioneered front-wheel drive in the USA and even entered his fwd racer in the French Grand Prix (where his racing number 'WC-1' provoked considerable mirth). He later produced front-wheel drive tractor units for fire appliances; built an advanced tank in the 1930s.

Walter Percy Chrysler, American (1875–1940). Locomotive engineer who joined Buick in 1911 and eventually became its president – and the first vice-president of General Motors. He joined Willys in 1920 and saved it – and Maxwell-Chalmers – from bankruptcy. Maxwell was the origin of the Chrysler Corporation. Chrysler had a well-deserved reputation for mechanical innovation.

André Citroën, French (1878–1935). This French production genius founded his own company in 1919 and attempted to emulate Henry Ford by producing 'people's cars'. His soaring ambition prompted the development of a magnificent new factory and the mould-breaking Citroën Traction Avant – but the effort killed him.

Adolphe Clément, French (1855–1928). Cycle manufacturer who made a fortune out of pneumatic tyres before entering the motor car industry. After selling manufacturing rights to his 'Clément' car, he changed his name to 'Clément-Bayard' to sidestep an embargo on using the 'Clément' trademark on cars. Also pioneered aeroplane and airship manufacture.

Louis Coatalen, French (1879–1962). Born in Brittany, this gifted engineer came to England in 1900 to work in the motor industry. His greatest designs were achieved at Sunbeam, where he became managing director. He built the first V12 racing car in 1913 and also pioneered the use of twin-cam engines.

Gioacchino Colombo, Italian (1903–77). Gifted designer for three decades from the mid-1920s, responsible for Alfa Romeos – especially the all-conquering 158 GP car – the first Ferrari V12s, Maserati world championship cars, and a notable failure, the last Grand Prix Bugatti.

Erret Lobban Cord, American (1894–1974). Dynamic entrepreneur whose Auburn-Duesenberg-Cord combine was only part of his complex business empire, which also included Lycoming engines, American Airlines, Stinson Aircraft and New York Shipbuilding.

Gottlieb Daimler, German (1834–1900). Became interested in gas engines in the 1860s and helped develop the Otto gas engine. His 1800s quest for a 'universal power source' led to the development of a light petrol engine in collaboration with Wilhelm Maybach. This engine was fitted into a carriage in 1886 to create the first Daimler car.

Alexandre Darracq, French (1855–1931). Entered the cycle industry in 1891, making the popular 'Gladiator' cycles. Sold Gladiator in 1896 to begin building Darracq cars in his aptly named 'Perfecta' works. Never drove a car himself, did not particularly like riding in cars and hated being driven fast. Retired in 1912 to concentrate on his casino at Deauville and the Hotel Negresco in Nice, as his only interest in cars had been the money he made out of them.

Albert de Dion, French (1856–1946). Noted duellist, lover and gambler, the young Comte de Dion sponsored the brothers-in-law, Bouton and Trépardoux, in the manufacture of steam carriages and thus created the world's first motor car company. Bouton developed the first practicable De Dion-Bouton petrol engine in 1894 and these compact power units were the catalyst which really established the French motor industry. De Dion became a Marquis in 1901.

Louis Delage, French (1877–1947). One-eyed autocrat who began making Delage cars in 1905. The golden days of the Delage company came after World War I, when it built some of France's finest and most beautiful sports and luxury cars. Delage's extravagant lifestyle came home to roost in 1935 when he lost control of his company and he died in poverty.

Abner Doble, American (1890–1961). Obsessive

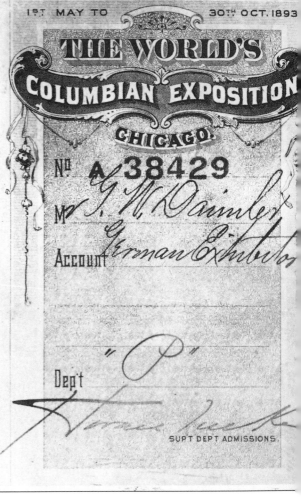

advocate of steam power who built his first steam car in 1906. He drove a prototype to Detroit in 1914 in search of backing. Production began in San Francisco in 1920, and though his output was limited, his cars represented the peak of steam car design and engineering.

John Dodge, American (1864–1920) and **Horace** (1868–1920). The rough and tough Dodge brothers were machinists and cycle makers who built transmissions for Oldsmobile (1901–2) and then produced chassis and engines for Henry Ford in exchange for a one-tenth share in his company. They sold their Ford shares for $25 million to found the Dodge Brothers marque, whose motto was 'dependability'.

(Above) Gottlieb Daimler's admission pass for the 1893 Chicago World's Fair.

(Opposite) Albert de Dion (right) and Georges Bouton.

Keith Duckworth, British (b. 1933). Intuitive engineer, co-founder of Cosworth, and the designer behind a series of outstanding racing engines, notably the DFV Grand Prix V8. His increasingly sophisticated company undertook development work for industry majors, such as Mercedes-Benz, although by the 1990s Duckworth was no longer so active.

Frederick Duesenberg, American (1877–1932). Of German immigrant stock, Fred Duesenberg designed his first car in 1904. In 1913 he set up the Duesenberg Motor Company to build engines. Fred and his brother **August** built the Duesenberg luxury cars from 1920, though E. L. Cord was owner of the company from 1927. Fred Duesenberg died as a result of crashing a Duesenberg car.

William Crapo Durant, American (1861–1947). A major force in the carriage-building industry, Billy Durant took over Buick in 1904, then, in 1908, founded the General Motors group but was ousted in 1910. He took over once more in 1915 but was forced out again when shares crashed in 1920. Established a 'Second Empire' which survived until the Depression. Ended up running a shop and bowling alley.

Charles Duryea, American (1861–1939) and **Frank** (1870–1967). After building their first prototype in 1893, founded the Duryea Motor Power Wagon Company (1896), America's first company to build cars for sale.

Harley Earl, American (1893–1969). Designed custom cars for well-heeled Californians in the early 1920s before becoming head of GM's new 'Art and Colour' studio in 1927. The father of mass-production styling, 'Misterl' gave the world vast chrome grilles and tail fins.

Selwyn Francis Edge, Australian (1868–1940). Came to England and became a well-known racing cyclist. Entering the car trade, he was the sales genius behind the Napier car. His notable racing victories included the only British victory in the Gordon Bennett Cup series (1902). After a spell as a pig farmer, he backed AC and Cubitt cars in the 1920s.

Virgil Exner, American (1909–73). Stylist who created Chrysler's 'Forward Look', with its prominent tailfins and long bonnet line.

Enzo Ferrari, Italian (1898–1989). A moderately successful racing driver who managed Alfa Romeo's racing operations from 1929–39 and then turned to manufacture, creating some of the world's most glamorous sports and racing cars. His prancing horse badge was originally the emblem of Italian World War I air ace Francesco Baracca, given to Ferrari by the Contessa Baracca in memory of her son.

Enzo Ferrari (right) and Nicola Romeo (centre) at Monza in 1923.

Walter Flanders, American (1871–1923). Among the US automobile industry's first mass-production experts, he was hired as production manager by Ford in 1908. He resigned in 1909 to found the EMF company and subsequently established the United States Motor Company group.

Edsel Ford, American (1893–1943). Tragically overshadowed by his father, he was an intuitive designer whose influence on Ford styling was vital to its sales success from 1928 on. The monument to this 'perfect gentleman' is the Model A, which was everything the Model T was not.

Henry Ford, American (1863–1947). Son of an immigrant Irish farmer, Henry Ford – 'the boy with wheels in his head' – became an engineer in Detroit, where he built his first car in 1896. After walking out on two companies (one of which became Cadillac), he founded the Ford Motor Company on 16 June 1903. His resistance to the ALAM group freed the American automobile industry from the shadow of monopoly.

Henry Ford II, American (1917–87). Grandson of the first Henry who succeeded his grandfather in 1945 and transformed the Ford Motor Company into a modern organisation after it had gone into seemingly terminal decline, losing $10 million a month.

Mauro Forghieri, Italian (b. 1935). Presiding over the design and technology of Ferrari racing teams for a quarter of a century, Forghieri combined automotive talent with Latin fire, in one of the less easy jobs in racing. During one of Ferrari's periodic upheavals he was moved to an R & D role in 1985, but soon left and designed Lamborghini's racing engines and transmissions.

Herbert Franklin, American (1867–1956). Newspaper proprietor, pioneer of die casting, advocate of air-cooling, put the first Franklin car on the market in 1902.

Joseph W. Frazer, American (1894–1973). After working for Packard, GM and Pierce-Arrow, became president of Willys-Overland in 1939. With Henry Kaiser, founded Kaiser-Frazer in 1946. Their attempt to break the monopoly of the 'Big Three' over the popular car market was a noble failure.

Henry Ford

Dante Giacosa, Italian (b. 1905). Fiat designer who specialised in small cars. The 'Topolino' ('Little Mouse') (1935) and the front-wheel-drive '128' (1969) were outstanding examples of his work.

Eugene Gregorie, American (b. 1908). Naval architect who switched to automotive design and created the Ford 8-hp Model Y ('Popular') and V8 of the 1930s, establishing Ford's first in-house design department which he headed until he retired in 1948.

Sir George Harriman, British (1908–73). Engineer and protegé of Leonard Lord who became deputy chairman of BMC in 1956 and chairman in 1961 but lacked the financial discipline necessary to make the group a financial success.

Elwood G. Haynes, American (1857–1925). Metallurgist (he invented stainless steel) from Kokomo, Indiana, who built his first car in 1894 aided by the Apperson Brothers. Founded the Haynes Automobile Company in 1898.

Patrick Head, British (b. 1947). One of the outstanding designers of the modern era, responsible for Williams Grand Prix cars from the late 1970s into the 1990s.

Donald Healey, Irish (1898–1988). World War I pilot, leading rally driver – he won the Monte Carlo Rally in 1931 – technical director of Triumph in the 1930s, set up the Healey company in 1946. Known for his sports cars from that period, above all for the 100 that became the first Austin-Healey.

Sir Patrick Hennessy, British (1898–1981). Dynamic chairman of Ford of Britain who started as a foundryman in the Ford-Ireland factory at Cork in 1920 'to build up my muscles for Rugby football'. A close friend of the Ford family – Henry Ford II called him 'Uncle Pat' – he was the inspiration behind the record-breaking Cortina of 1962.

Soichiro Honda, Japanese (1906–91). Started his business in 1946, producing auxiliary engines for bicycles, developed the largest motorcycle company in the world, moved into the automotive industry in the 1960s, built modestly successful Grand Prix cars and immensely successful engines. Preferred engineering to business, yet was an outstanding entrepreneur.

Lido Iacocca, American (b. 1924). Super-salesman who fathered the Ford Mustang but fell out with Henry Ford II and was 'retired' in 1978. He then joined the Chrysler board and dramatically turned the ailing company around.

Sir Alec Issigonis, British (1906–88). Autocratic Turkish-born 'loose-cannon' designer of Morris Minor (1948), Mini-Minor (1959) and other front-wheel-drive British Motor Corporation cars. His apt retirement present was a No. 10 Meccano set.

Vittorio Jano, Italian (1891–1965). Designer for Fiat, Alfa Romeo and Lancia; created some of the finest sports and racing cars of all time.

Thomas B. Jeffery, British (1845–1910). He emigrated to the USA at the age of 18. He began manufacturing 'Rambler' bicycles in 1879, invented a 'clincher' tyre in 1891, built his first successful automobile in 1900 and began production of Rambler cars in 1902.

Claude Johnson, British (1864–1926). First Secretary of the ACGBI (later the Royal Automobile Club) who subsequently became the first managing director of Rolls-Royce and dictated company policy.

Edward Jordan, American (1882–1958). Journalist who became advertising manager for Rambler and left to found the Jordan Motor Car Company in 1916. Better known for his purple advertising prose ('Somewhere West of Laramie' was his most famous) than for his automobiles.

Charles F. Kettering, American (1876–1958). 'Boss Ket' organised the Dayton Electrical Company ('Delco') laboratories to develop electrical ignition and then evolved an electric self-starter for the 1911 Cadillac. In 1920 he became head of GM's research laboratories.

Cecil Kimber, British (1888–1945). Sales manager of Morris Garages in the early 1920s, Kimber was responsible for special-bodied Morris Oxfords and Cowleys, and the first MGs. From 1929 he built up the MG company at Abingdon, left in 1941.

Charles Brady King, American (1868–1957). Built the first motor vehicle to run in Detroit (1896). Later designed the 'Silent Northern' and 'King 8' cars before turning to aero engines in 1916.

Antonio Lago, Italian (1893–60). Clever and charming businessman, equally at home in England, France, or his native Italy, who took over the ailing Automobiles Talbot of Paris and turned it into one of the great marques of the late 1930s and '40s.

Frederick Lanchester, British (1868–1946). Built his first car in 1895. Made substantial contributions to English automobile engineering and aeronautical science. Founded Lanchester in 1899 and later acted as consultant to Daimler.

George Lanchester, British (1874–1970). Succeeded his elder brother as Daimler designer in 1909 and also designed post-1910 Lanchesters.

Vincenzo Lancia, Italian (1881–1937). Brilliantly innovative designer and one of the best racing drivers of his day. His masterpiece was the Lambda, one of the first cars with unit constructed chassis/body plus independent front suspension.

Sir Alec Issigonis

Harry J. Lawson, British (1852–1925). 'Father of the British Motor Industry' who attempted from 1896 to form a patent monopoly and floated several over-capitalised companies – notably Daimler of Coventry, which survived the collapse of his empire in the early 1900s.

Hans Ledwinka, Czech (1878–1967). Brilliant Bohemian designer who worked for Nesselsdorf, Steyr and Tatra, where his brilliant designs featured backbone chassis, all-independent suspension and air-cooled engines – including rear-mounted V8s.

Henry M. Leland, American (1847–1931). 'Master of Precision' who learned his art in the arms industry (and also invented the mechanical hair-clipper). His Leland & Faulconer built engines for some of the earliest companies. He reorganised the Henry Ford Company as 'Cadillac' after Ford left in 1902 and subsequently left to found Lincoln.

J.-J. Etienne Lenoir, Belgian (1811–1900). Inventor who built a horseless carriage in Paris in 1862.

Emile Levassor, French (1844–97). The engineering brains of Panhard-Levassor who devised the 'Système Panhard', in which an engine at the front under a bonnet drove the rear wheels through a sliding pinion gearbox.

Sir Leonard Lord, British (1896–1967). Outstanding production engineer who became managing director of Morris Motors in 1932 but left in 1936 after a clash of personalities with Sir William Morris and later joined Austin, becoming chairman in 1945. Architect of the Austin-Morris merger that formed the British Motor Corporation in 1952. Became Lord Lambury.

Sir William Lyons, British (1901–85). The Swallow Sidecar Company he founded in Blackpool in 1922 grew into Jaguar of Coventry via special bodywork for popular chassis like the Austin Seven. His rare talent for design produced many best sellers.

Siegfried Markus, Austrian (1831–98). Inventor who built internal combustion-engined test-benches from 1868. His first true car, once thought to date from 1875, was built in the late 1880s.

Jonathan Dixon Maxwell, American (1864–1928). Co-founder in 1903 of the Maxwell-Briscoe Motor Company which eventually became Chrysler.

Wilhelm Maybach, German (1846–1929). Daimler's brilliant protegé who combined all the most advanced elements to create the original Mercedes in 1901. Later famed for aero engines and mammoth 'Zeppelin' luxury cars, built under his own name.

André Michelin, French (1853–1931) and **Edouard** (1859–1940). From backgrounds in heavy industry and as an artist, the Michelin brothers came together to develop a major automotive company. Among early innovations were demountable bolt-on tyres,

Sir William Lyons

then tyres in which steel and rubber were bonded, and much later their company pioneered radial tyres. In the 1930s a Michelin take over kept Citroën in existence.

Harry Miller, American (1875–1943). Natural engineering genius best known for his twin-cam engines and front-wheel drive racers.

William Mitchell, American (1912–88). Succeeded Harley Earl as head of design at GM; created such designs as the Cadillac 60 Special, Corvette Sting Ray and the controversial Corvair.

H. F. S. Morgan, British (1881–1959). Intuitive engineer whose three-wheeler was the most successful cyclecar (1909–52). The company began producing four-wheelers in 1935 and still uses the sliding pillar independent front suspension devised by H. F. S. in 1909.

William Morris, British (1871–1963). Cycle and motor agent who built his first Morris Oxford light car in 1912, and dominated the British motor industry from 1924. A renowned philanthropist, he became Lord Nuffield in 1934.

Gordon Murray, South African (b. 1947). Designer, responsible for a succession of notable Brabham and McLaren racing cars, later for the exemplary McLaren F1 'supercar'.

Montagu Napier, British (1870–1931). Member of a family with a rare engineering tradition, launched company building high-quality cars, in partnership with S. F. Edge. Built early straight sixes, and the outstanding Lion aero engine, but allowed the car side of the business to decline after Edge left in 1912.

Charles W. Nash, American (1864–1948). Former farm labourer who joined the Durant-Dort carriage company, then moved to Buick and became its president in 1910, and of the whole General Motors group in 1912. He then took over Jeffery and transformed it into the Nash Motor Company.

Ransom Eli Olds, American (1864–1950). Built his first steam car in 1896, and his first petrol car in 1894. Success came with the 1901 Curved-Dash Oldsmobile. Later founded Reo and also invented an early motor mower.

Edmund Joel Pennington, American (1858–1911). 'Mechanical charlatan' whose crazy automobiles defied rational mechanical laws (but appeared to work).

Sir Percival Perry, British (1878–1956). Worked for Lawson in 1896 and was present when the first Ford to reach England was uncrated in 1904. Headed the Ford interests in Britain 1904–19 and 1928–48 and became a close friend of Henry Ford. Oversaw the building of Dagenham. Became Lord Perry in 1938.

Armand Peugeot, French (1849–1915). Translated the family ironmongery firm's expertise in making steel rods to replace whalebone in crinoline skirts into the manufacture of cycles. In 1889 the Peugeot company built a steam car designed by Serpollet, but then constructed tubular-framed Daimler-engined cars, France's first production cars.

Battista Pininfarina, Italian (1893–1966). Born 'Farina', he affixed his childhood nickname of 'Pinin' to his surname to differentiate it from the family coachbuilding business when he set up his own *carrozzeria* in 1930. One of the great Italian stylists, the company is closely identified with Ferrari coachwork and also with mass producers like BMC.

Albert Augustus Pope, American (1843–1909). Colonel Pope founded a successful cycle manufacturing group in 1879; his complex automobile empire started with electric vehicle manufacture as early as 1896 but was dragged down by the collapse of cycle sales.

Ferdinand Porsche, Austrian (1875–1951). Gifted designer who worked for Steyr, Austro-Daimler, Mercedes, Auto-Union and Cisitalia. He founded his own design bureau in the 1930s and created the Volkswagen. After World War II was involved in the first cars of the Porsche marque, although most credit in this is due to his son Ferry.

Finley Robertson Porter, American (1871–1964). Designer of America's first sports car, the Mercer Raceabout. Later created FRP and Porter cars before becoming chief engineer of Curtiss Aircraft in 1919.

Louis Renault, French (1877–1944). Button maker's son, Louis Renault converted his De Dion tricycle into a shaft-driven voiturette in the garden shed when he was 21. He got so many orders that he went into production and by 1900 had become one of France's leading makers, building 350 cars a year. His range of cars was complex but popular, ranging from cheap runabouts to huge luxury cars. He died mysteriously in prison, accused of collaborating with the Nazis during the Occupation of France.

Georges Roesch, Swiss (1891–1969). Brilliant engineer who became chief engineer of Talbot (London) aged only 25. His high speed tourers possessed great mechanical refinement.

The Hon. Charles Stuart Rolls, British (1877–1910). Lord Llangattock's youngest son was a pioneer motorist who became a racing driver and upper-crust motor trader. He joined with the engineer Royce in 1904 to build a car with their Rs on the badge. Rolls was also a leading aviator who became the first man to fly the English Channel both ways. Killed in a stupid flying accident at the Bournemouth Centenary Fêtes meeting.

Sir William Rootes, British (1894–1964). Son of a cycle shop owner who entered the motor trade in 1919 and built up an industrial empire by snapping up car companies which were in financial difficulties during the Depression – Sunbeam, Talbot, Humber, Hillman, Singer – but its success drained away in the 1960s. Knighted in 1942, Rootes became a peer in 1959. Ford nearly bought the Rootes Group in 1964: Chrysler did buy it – and soon regretted it!

Sir Henry Royce, British (1863–1933). Engineer who overcame childhood poverty to establish a successful electrical business. Trying to achieve perfection in car design, he built a twin-cylinder car in 1904. In conjunction with Rolls, he created the 'best car in the world' – the 'Silver Ghost' – just two years later. His aero engines made aviation history and led directly to the Merlin of World War II.

George Baldwin Selden, American (1846–1932). A patent attorney who filed a patent for a self-propelled vehicle in 1879. The patent was ultimately granted in 1895, retrospective to 1877, and sold to Columbia on a royalty basis in 1899. It was used to set up the Association of Licensed Automobile Manufacturers monopoly.

Léon Serpollet, French (1858–1907). Inventor of a flash steam boiler who built a steam tricycle in 1887. Steam three-wheelers of a more solid nature followed from 1889 but serious production had to wait until he was backed by the American Frank Gardner at the turn of the century. His sprint racers set new speed records, but his quest for a steamer that matched a petrol vehicle for ease of control was ended when he died prematurely from consumption.

Frederick R. Simms, British (1863–1944). Introduced Daimler engines into Britain in 1891 to power motor launches on the Thames. Formed the Daimler Motor Syndicate in 1893, which was reformed under Lawson in 1896. He founded the Automobile Club of Great Britain & Ireland (later the Royal Automobile Club) and the Society of Motor Manufacturers & Traders. He later built Simms and Simms-Welbeck cars.

Alfred P. Sloan, American (1875–1966). Former roller-bearing salesman who sold his Hyatt business to Billy Durant in return for a substantial stake in the newly formed United Motors Corporation of accessory manufacturers, of which he became president. It then became part of General Motors and Sloan became a GM director. He reorganised the GM corporate structure and was its president from 1923–1936.

Charles Sorensen, Danish (1881–1968). Brilliant pattern-maker whose metal-casting skills made the Model T Ford and mass-production possible. Joined Ford 1904 and left in 1944 when he was president to join Willys-Overland.

Francis E. Stanley, American (1849–1918) and **Freelan O.** (1849–1940). Twins who used the money from selling their photographic dry-plate business to develop a steam car, whose rights were bought for $250 000 to create Locomobile. The Stanleys then developed an improved design, and built steamers well into the 1920s.

Harry C. Stutz, American (1871–1930). Transmission designer who engineered Marion and American Underslung cars before starting manufacture of Stutz cars in 1911. An early Stutz did well enough at Indianapolis to justify the slogan 'The Car that Made Good in a Day'. Harry Stutz (who was also a talented saxophonist) resigned in 1919 and subsequently built the HCS.

Edwin Ross Thomas, American (1850–1936). Another famous car maker who could not drive, he built the Thomas Flyer in Buffalo, New York. It achieved its greatest fame by winning the 1908 New York–Paris Race.

John Tjaarda, Dutch (1897–1962). English-educated designer who worked in the USA. He created the Lincoln Zephyr and claimed to have inspired Porsche's design for the Volkswagen.

Preston Tucker, American (1903–56). Super-salesman who built the postwar Tucker Torpedo, a

revolutionary rear-engined car combining advanced engineering and styling with many safety features. But a government watchdog body accused Tucker of fraud: though he was eventually acquitted, the project died at birth and just 51 cars were built.

Gabriel Voisin, French (1880–1973). Aviation pioneer and renowned lover who built advanced but unorthodox sleeve-valve cars.

Felix Wankel, German (1902–88). 'Father of the rotary engine', his preoccupation from his first studies in the early 1920s to production types in the 1960s.

Windsor White, American (1866–1958), **Rollin** (1872–1968) and **Walter** (1876–1929). Sewing machine makers Rollin and Windsor built their first White Steamer in 1900 and sent Walter to London in 1901 to develop the European market. After becoming the most successful steam car makers, the Whites turned to petrol in 1910, abandoning steam altogether the following year. Rollin left the White Company in 1914 to build Cleveland tractors, launching the Rollin car in 1923.

Childe Harold Wills, American (1878–1940). Brilliant metallurgist who assisted Henry Ford in his early days and also created the 'Ford' script logo. He became chief engineer of the Ford Motor Company and developed vanadium and molybdenum steel. When he left Ford, he used his $1.6 million separation pay to found the highly acclaimed (but ultimately unsuccessful) Wills Sainte Claire company. Became chief metallurgist for Chrysler in 1933.

John North Willys, American (1875–1933). Super-salesman who unloaded the entire 1906 output of Overland, then saved the company when it was in difficulty the following year. He moved the firm to Toledo where in 1915 he increased Overland production to 95 000 units – second only to Ford.

Charles Wilson, American (1890–1961). GM chief executive renowned for his statement, 'What's good for General Motors is good for America and vice versa', which he put into practice by becoming US Secretary of Defense (1953–7), and was thus the only man in history to administer both the world's largest private corporation and its biggest public agency.

Alexander Winton, British (1860–1932). Marine engineer who sought his fortune in America where he became a bicycle producer. Built a prototype car in 1896 and set up the Winton Motor Carriage Company in 1897. His designs featured pneumatic controls. Car production ended in 1924 but his company became the GM diesel engine division in 1930.

RACING AND RECORDS

■ A contest between road locomotives in Wisconsin in July 1878 was more akin to a modern rally than a race but included a road race (as well as categories such as ploughing) in its 201 miles/323.4 km; a steam Oshkosh was the only entry to complete the course, in 33 h 27 min. Doubtless there were other unrecorded local trials of strength and speed between owners of early traction engines.

M Fossier of *Le Vélocipède* tried to organise a genuine race in Paris in 1887. Only the Comte de Dion came to the start, but at least he completed the distance on his De Dion steam quadricycle.

■ The Paris–Rouen Reliability Trial was the forerunner of rallies and races; 25 vehicles started the 78.75-mile/126.7-km run, a De Dion stream tractor with a semi-articulated passenger trailer set the pace, averaging 11.6 mph/18.7 kph, but as it did not meet the regulations or the spirit of the contest first prize was awarded jointly to a Panhard and a Peugeot.

■ The first true motor race, the Paris–Bordeaux–Paris over 732 miles/1178 km was contested by 22 starters in June 1895. Nine finished, led by Emile Levassor in a Panhard. He completed the course in 48 h 48 min (15 mph/24.1 kph).

■ Late in 1895 the Chicago *Times-Herald* contest was the first motoring competition in the USA, comprising a race and tests for efficiency. A Duryea won – the first car to compete and win on pneumatic tyres (André Michelin had used pneumatic tyres on his Peugeot in the Paris–Bordeaux–Paris, but failed to complete the course).

Emile Levassor, moral winner of the first true race, the 1895 Paris–Bordeaux–Paris that set the pattern for the great city-to-city races. He drove the twin-cylinder Panhard throughout, his longest stop lasting for 22 minutes, and he finished almost 6 hours ahead of Rigoulot, who was the official winner as his Peugeot had four seats.

■ A committee set up to organise the 1895 Paris–Bordeaux race was the basis of the Automobile Club de France – the first motor sports club in the world.

■ The start of the 1896 Paris–Marseilles–Paris race was actually in Versailles, and it saw the first recorded racing accident involving a spectator. The driver of a Fisson, Ferté, could not avoid a man in the Avenue de Paris – as so often in the early city-to-city races, the public had little perception of car speeds. That spectator was only slightly injured. During this race an unrecorded number of competitors were injured; the most serious casualty was one Noblesse, thrown out of Villefranche's Panhard.

■ The 149-mile/239.7-km Marseilles–Nice–la Turbie

(Opposite top) By an extraordinary coincidence, the first true race in America was also won by a car carrying the number 5. Frank Duryea drove one of his own cars to win this Chicago–Evanston–Chicago race, run on a bitterly cold day at the end of November 1895.

(Opposite bottom) The atmosphere of early road racing is captured in this shot of Marcel Renault in the 1903 Paris–Madrid, before his fatal crash.

race in 1897 saw the only road race victory to be gained by a steam vehicle, a De Dion driven by the Comte de Chasseloup-Laubat (average 19.2 mph/ 30.89 kph). This event showed that automobile sport could exist in January on the Riviera and it was split into special stages; in these respects it foreshadowed the Monte Carlo Rally.

■ 'Streamlined' bodies were introduced on a Panhard with a 'wind-cutting' nose driven by Charron in the 1897 Paris–Trouville race, on Bollées with underslung chassis and pointed tails as well as noses in 1899, and a Vallée run in the 1899 Tour de France with a 'wedge' nose. The value of these bodies was questionable, as they were mounted above cumbersome running gear.

■ The first hill climb was run over a short course at Chanteloup in 1898 and won by Camille Jenatzy in an electric car (a hill climb had been run in 1897, but only as part of the Marseilles–Nice race). At the first organised sprint meeting, at Achères, the Comte de Chasseloup-Laubat set the fastest time in a Jeantaud electric vehicle, which became the first speed record. The most famous of the early sprint meeting were the Nice Speed Trials, run from 1899 until 1904, when Rigolly covered the flying kilometre in 23.6 seconds (94.78 mph/152.50 kph). The nearest British equivalent was the sprint meeting organised at Bexhill-on-Sea, 1902–7 and again in the 1920s.

■ Notable racing 'firsts' in 1898 included the first races in Germany and in Belgium, the first marque race (for Mors cars), the first massed-start race (Paris–Bordeaux), the first fatal race accident (in the Circuit de Perigueux, when the Marquis de Montaignac and his mechanic were killed as their Landry et Beyroux rolled), and the first of the great city-to-city races to cross frontiers. This was the 889-mile/1430-km Paris–Amsterdam–Paris, won by Charron on a Panhard at 26.9 mph/43.3 kph. The equivalent principal events in the succeeding years were: 1899, Tour de France over 1350 miles/2172.5 km, won by René de Knyff (Panhard) at 30.2 mph/48.6 kph; 1900, Paris–Toulouse–Paris, won by Levegh (Mors) at 40.2 mph/64.6 kph; 1901, Paris–Berlin over 687 miles/1105.5 km, won by Fournier (Mors) at 44.1 mph/70.9 kph; 1902, Paris–Vienna over 615 miles/989.7 km, won by Farman (Panhard) at 38.4 mph/61.7 kph; 1903, Paris–Madrid, stopped short at Bordeaux after a succession of accidents, when Gabriel (Mors) was declared the winner, having averaged 65.3 mph/105.06 kph over the 342 miles/550 km.

■ The first lady to race in a car was a Madame Laumaille, driving a De Dion tricycle in the 1898 Marseilles–Nice race (she finished fourth in class, beating her husband!).

■ A world speed record, forerunner of the Land Speed Record, was established by the Comte Gaston de Chasseloup-Laubat in 1898, driving a Jeantaud electric car at Achères near Paris to record 39.24 mph/63.14 kph. Until 1964 only vehicles powered through the wheels were eligible, but the doors were then opened to jet- and rocket-propelled vehicles and speeds increased dramatically. Since 1964 there have been a separate record category for wheel-driven automobiles. In a record attempt two runs have to be made, in opposite directions, over a flying kilometre or mile course; this stipulation came into effect in 1911 and has ruled out some spectacular 'one-way' speeds. The record holders are:

	Driver	Car	Venue	Speed (mph/kph)
1898	G. de Chasseloup-Laubat	Jeantaud	A	39.24/63.14
1899	C. Jenatzy	Jenatzy	A	41.42/66.64
	G. de Chasseloup-Laubat	Jeantaud	A	43.69/70.29
	C. Jenatzy	Jenatzy	A	49.92/80.32
	G. de Chasseloup-Laubat	Jeantaud	A	57.60/92.68
	C. Jenatzy	Jenatzy	A	65.79/105.85
1902	L. Serpollet	Serpollet	N	75.06/120.77

	Driver	Car	Venue	Speed (mph/kph)
	W. K. Vanderbilt, Junior	Mors	Ab	76.08/122.41
	H. Fournier	Mors	D	76.60/123.25
	M. Augières	Mors	D	77.13/124.10
1903	A. Duray	Gobron-Brillié	O	83.47/134.30
	A. Duray	Gobron-Brillié	D	84.73/136.33
1904	H. Ford	Ford	SC	91.37/147.01*
	W. K. Vanderbilt, Junior	Mercedes	Da	92.30/148.51
	L. E. Rigolly	Gobron-Brillié	N	94.78/152.50
	P. de Caters	Mercedes	O	97.25/156.47
	L. E. Rigolly	Gobron-Brillié	O	103.55/166.61
	P. Baras	Darracq	O	104.52/168.17
1905	A. Macdonald	Napier	Da	104.65/168.38*
	V. Héméry	Darracq	A-S	109.65/176.43
1906	F. H. Marriott	Stanley	Da	121.57/195.61
1909	V. Héméry	Benz	B	125.95/202.65
1910	B. Oldfield	Benz	Da	131.27/211.19*
1911	R. Burman	Benz	Da	141.37/227.46*
1914	L. G. Hornsted	Benz	B	124.10/200.17**
1919	R. de Palma	Packard	Da	148.87/241.15*
1920	T. Milton	Duesenberg	Da	156.03/251.05*
1922	K. L. Guinness	Sunbeam	B	133.75/215.20
1924	R. Thomas	Delage	Ar	143.31/230.58
	E. Eldridge	Fiat	Ar	146.01/234.93
	M. Campbell	Sunbeam	P	146.16/235.17
1925	M. Campbell	Sunbeam	P	150.76/242.57
1926	H. O. D. Segrave	Sunbeam	S	152.33/245.09
	J. G. P. Thomas	Thomas Special	P	169.30/272.40
	J. G. P. Thomas	Thomas Special	P	171.02/275.17
1927	M. Campbell	Napier-Campbell	P	174.88/281.38
	H. O. D. Segrave	Sunbeam	Da	203.79/327.89
1928	M. Campbell	Napier-Campbell	Da	206.95/332.98
	R. Keech	White-Triplex	Da	207.55/333.95
1929	H. O. D. Segrave	Irving-Napier	Da	231.44/372.38
1931	M. Campbell	Napier-Campbell	Da	246.09/395.96
1932	Sir M. Campbell	Napier-Campbell	Da	253.97/408.64
1933	Sir M. Campbell	R-R Campbell	Da	272.46/438.39
1935	Sir M. Campbell	R-R Campbell	Da	276.82/445.40
	Sir M. Campbell	R-R Campbell	Bon	301.13/484.52
1937	G. E. T. Eyston	Thunderbolt	Bon	312.00/502.11
1938	G. E. T. Eyston	Thunderbolt	Bon	345.50/555.91
	J. R. Cobb	Railton-Mobil	Bon	350.20/563.47
	G. E. T. Eyston	Thunderbolt	Bon	357.50/575.22
1939	J. R. Cobb	Railton-Mobil	Bon	369.70/594.85
1947	J. R. Cobb	Railton-Mobil	Bon	394.20/634.27
1963	C. Breedlove	Spirit of America (3)	Bon	407.45/655.59*
1964	D. Campbell	Proteus-Bluebird (W-D)	E	403.10/648.59
	T. E. Green	Wingfoot Express	Bon	413.20/664.84
	A. Arfons	Green Monster	Bon	434.02/698.34

	Driver	Car	Venue	Speed (mph/kph)
	C. Breedlove	Spirit of America (3)	Bon	468.72/754.17
	C. Breedlove	Spirit of America (3)	Bon	526.28/846.78
	A. Arfons	Green Monster	Bon	536.71/863.57
1965	C. Breedlove	Spirit of America Sonic I	Bon	555.583/893.933
	A. Arfons	Green Monster	Bon	576.553/927.673
	R. Summers	Goldenrod (W-D)	Bon	409.277/658.526
	C. Breedlove	Spirit of America Sonic I	Bon	600.601/966.367
1970	G. Gabelich	The Blue Flame	Bon	630.388/1014.294
1983	R. Noble	Thrust 2	BR	633.46/1019.237

* Not recognized by the AIACR (the international governing body).
** AIACR two-way runs requirement met.
Cars: (3), three-wheeler; (W-D), wheel-driven.
Courses: A, Achères (F); Ab, Ablis (F); A-S, Arles-Salon (F); Ar, Arpajon (F); B, Brooklands (GB); Bon, Bonneville (USA); BR, Black Rock (USA); D, Dourdan (F); Da, Daytona (USA); E, Lake Eyre (AUS); N, Nice (F); O, Ostend (B); P, Pendine (GB); S, Southport (GB); SC, Lake St Clair (USA).

Camille Jenatzy on his electric 'Jamais Contente', decorated after one of his successful 1899 record attempts.

Malcolm Campbell's 'Bluebird' in its 1935 form, with a 36.5-litre Rolls-Royce V12, twin rear wheels and full-width bodywork, at Daytona when he lifted the LSR above 300 mph (top). Craig Breedlove drove 'Spirit of America' to lift the record above 500 mph in 1964; this three-wheeler had a General Electric jet engine (above). Gary Gabelich set the record above 1000 kmh with the rocket-powered 'Blue Flame' in 1970 (opposite top). Richard Noble's 'Thrust 2', driven from a cockpit to the left of its Rolls-Royce Avon jet engine, ran on solid aluminium wheels when he broke the record in 1983 (right).

■ The first mass start came during the 1898 Paris–Bordeaux–Paris race, actually as a restart after a neutralised section. There was a true mass start for the Paris–Ostend race in 1899; this ended in a dead heat, Girardot (Mors) and Levegh (Panhard) completing the 201 miles/323 km in 6 h 11 min and crossing the finish line together.

■ The first British hill climb was a 325-yard/297-m ascent of Petersham Hill, as one of a series of tests around Richmond. The driver of a Barrière tricycle was fastest, at about 14 mph/22.5 kph.

■ Bollée and Decauville built the first racing cars with independent front suspension in 1899.

■ Flag signals were first used by race marshals in 1899, yellow for 'caution' and red for 'stop'. These still have the same meanings.

■ The first successful attempt to climb the road up Mount Washington, New Hampshire, was made by F. O. Stanley in a Stanley Steamer in 1899. It took him some 2 h 3 min. In 1904 the hill climb became an organised event and was won by Harry Harkness in a 60-hp Mercedes with a time of 24 min 37.4 s and second fastest was F. E. Stanley (twin brother of F. O.) in a Stanley Steamer.

■ The first circuit race, the Course du Catalogue, was run over two laps of a triangle of roads at Melun on 18 February 1900, and won by Girardot (Panhard).

■ A sprint meeting in Welbeck Park was part of the 1900 Thousand Miles Trial. It was the second of its type in Britain – effectively the first as a competitive event, as an 1899 sprint at Colchester attracted only one entry! The Hon. Charles Rolls was fastest at Welbeck, averaging 37.64/mph/60.57 kph in a Panhard.

■ A ladies' race was run at the Ranelagh Club near London in 1900, Miss Thea Weblyn (Daimler) beating three other ladies 'most skilfully and gracefully'.

■ The Gordon Bennett Trophy race series between teams representing nations was run 1900–5, the first from Paris to Lyons and contested by three French Panhards, a Belgian Bolide and a Winton (the first US car to compete in Europe). Two Panhards were the only finishers. For this event, national racing colours were first allotted – blue for France, yellow for Belgium, red (originally black) for Italy. Others, such as white for Germany and, in 1902, green for Britain followed, and blue and white (originally red) became the American colours. The requirement that cars be painted in the colours of their entrants, irrespective of the nationality of driver or country where the car was built, fell into disuse as sponsorship became widespread and today only Ferraris, predominantly red, are a reminder of that detail of Grands Prix past.

French interests meant that the Gordon Bennett races were superseded by the Grand Prix. Meanwhile it had seen an international race victory for a British car: the Napier driven by S. F. Edge in 1902. The triumph was rather hollow for Edge was 16th overall in the concurrent Paris–Vienna and there were no other Gordon Bennett finishers!

■ The first race in Italy, later to become one of the pre-eminent motor sport nations, was the 1900 Brescia–Cremona–Brescia, won by Panhard driver Franchetti. An earlier reliability trial had been organised over a Turin–Asti–Turin route in 1895.

■ The first race to carry the title 'Grand Prix' was run at Pau, as part of a 1901 motor sport week. The race, over 206 miles/331 km, was won by Farman (Panhard). It was a secondary event (the title Grand Prix had little motor racing significance before 1906) and on various Pau circuits second-line races were run intermittently through to the 1980s. From 1933 the title Pau Grand Prix was picked up, although the long break undermines claims that this is the oldest motor race. Since the 1970s the principal Pau race has been a Formula 2 (until 1984) or Formula 3000 event, on a street circuit used from 1933 (the Pau circuit used for the 1930 French GP was outside the town).

■ A 1-mile race on the cycle track at London's Crystal Palace on 8 April 1901 was won by Charles Jarrott, driving a Panhard.

■ The first race which could be considered a sponsored event in the modern sense was the 1902 Circuit du Nord, backed by the French Ministry of Agriculture to promote the use of alcohol fuel. Contemporary reports suggest that competitors used it as little as possible – challenging the scrutineers is by no means a modern pastime – and that curious odours lingered behind the cars. Winner of the 537-mile/864-km race was Panhard driver Maurice Farman. Full race sponsorship did not come to the Grand Prix world until 1971, when the British event was backed by the International Wool Secretariat, incorporating 'Woolmark' in its title.

■ The first circuit race to rank as a major international event, the 318-mile/512-km Circuit des Ardennes in July 1902, was also the first significant race to be won by a British driver, Charles Jarrott (driving a Panhard).

■ The Mont Ventoux hill climb in France was the longest in Europe from 1902 until 1973, at 13.48 miles/21.69 km, save for an interlude 1925–30, when the Cuneo–Colle della Maddelena (41.5 miles/70.25 km) supplanted it. The fastest Ventoux climb in 1902 was made by Panhard driver Chauchard at 29.65 mph/47.76 kph; in 1973 Mieusset climbed it in a March at 88.41 mph/142.28 kph.

■ The Gordon Bennett Trophy was the first major race run in the British Isles, and an Act of Parliament was necessary before it could be organised on remote country roads near Ballyshannon in Ireland. Racing on public roads was assumed to have been impossible on the mainland of Great Britain, although legislative bodies in Ulster (as well as Eire), Jersey and the Isle of Man allowed it, even encouraging it as a tourist attraction. That 328-mile/528-km Gordon Bennett race in 1903 was won by Mercedes driver Camille Jenatzy at 49.2 mph/79.2 kph. Motor racing returned to public roads in mainland Great Britain when a Birmingham Grand Prix was run for Formula 3000 cars on a street circuit, 1986–90.

■ Gobron-Brillié used opposed-piston engines in competition cars from 1903 until 1907 with little success in racing, although one of these machines was the first piston-engined car to exceed 100 mph/ 161 km.

■ Clément Ader in France and Alexander Winton in the USA built eight-cylinder racing engines; two years later Franklin built an air-cooled racing straight-8.

■ Daytona Beach in Florida was used for speed trials for the first time in 1903. Alexander Winton was fastest in one of his own Bullet cars, covering the flying-start mile at 69.0 mph/111 kph. The Beach was to be the venue for numerous Land Speed Record attempts.

■ Association Internationale des Automobile Clubs Reconnus (AIACR), the first international governing body of motor sport, was formed in 1904 after wrangles over French proposals to change the Gordon Bennett rules. It was reconstituted as the Fédération Internationale de l'Automobile in 1946. From 1922 until 1978 sporting matters were delegated to the Commission Sportive Internationale (CSI), which was succeeded by the Fédération Internationale du Sport Automobile (FISA). Its last president was Max Mosley (1991–3), and late in 1993 FISA was absorbed into the FIA, with a parallel FIA Motor Sports Council and an FIA Council for tourism and the automobile.

■ The first international race in the USA, the 1904 Vanderbilt Cup, was run on a Long Island circuit and won by George Heath (Panhard). Five more Cup races were run on that circuit, then from 1911 until 1916 on circuits from Savannah to Santa Monica. The G. Vanderbilt Cup run at Roosevelt Field in 1936–7 attracted leading European teams (the winners were Nuvolari and Rosemeyer); then America turned its back on this style of racing until after World War II.

■ Louis Rigolly became the first driver to achieve 100 mph/161 kph over an accurately measured distance, a kilometre at Ostend, actually recording 103.55 mph/166.61 kph in a 16.7-litre Gobron-Brillié in 1904. In 1953 John Cooper reached the magic 100 mph in a Cooper with a 341 cc engine (at Montlhery, when he was timed at 105.71 mph/170.11 kph).

■ Walter Christie raced his first front-wheel drive racing car in the eliminating trials for the 1905 Vanderbilt Cup. Two years later he won a Daytona Beach event in a front-wheel drive car, and introduced this layout to Grand Prix racing.

■ The RAC Tourist Trophy was first run in 1905, for standard touring cars on a 52-mile/84-km Isle of Man circuit (won by J. S. Napier driving an Arrol-Johnston, at 33.9 mph/54.54 kph). The last Manx race was run in 1922; subsequent events have been run at Ards (9), Donington (2), Dundrod (5), Goodwood (7), Oulton Park (5) and Silverstone (18). For many years (1928–54) it was a sports car race, and a handicap event, but at Silverstone reverted to its origins in that it became a touring car (saloon) race and a round in the European Touring Car Championship, before lapsing again after the 1988 race.

■ The first hill climb was run at Shelsley Walsh, the oldest surviving hill climb venue in Europe. The 1905 event was won by E. M. C. Instone, driving a Daimler. Narrow and sinuous and by international standards ludicrously short at 1000 yd/914 m, Shelsley Walsh has a firm place in the affections of many British enthusiasts.

■ American short tracks saw two notable 24-hour achievements in 1905. The Seule brothers won a 24-hour race at Columbus in a Pope-Toledo, covering 828 miles/1332 km; late in the year Clemens and Merz covered more than 1000 miles in 24 hours, driving a National on a track at Indianapolis (actual distance 1095 miles/1764 km).

■ The Brighton Speed Trials was first run over a standing-start mile, on the lines of events at several British seaside towns including Bexhill and Blackpool; unlike those, the Brighton event is still run. Its history was fragmented, lapsing after that first running in 1905 until 1923–4, then again until 1932–8. From 1946 it was run over a standing-start kilometre, from 1980 over a half-mile run (in the 1990s terminal speeds reached 180 mph/290 kph).

■ The Targa Florio was first run in 1906, over the 'Great Madonie' circuit of 92.48 miles/148.82 km of challenging Sicilian roads, and won by Itala driver Cagno, who averaged 29.07 mph/46.78 kph over the three laps. Jealously guarded by its patron, Vincenzo Florio, the event was occasionally run within the Tours of Sicily and from 1937 until 1940 was run on the relatively sophisticated Palermo circuit, but usually it was run on one of the Madonie circuits of roads climbing into the mountains, from 1932 on the 44.74-mile/72-km 'Short Madonie'. The 57th Targa Florio, in 1973, was the last to count in the sports car cham-

pionship (World Championship of Makes by that time), although the title was carried by a national Italian rally after that, then as an historic quasi-race. The first race on the Short Madonie was won by Nuvolari in an Alfa Romeo at 49.27 mph/79.27 kph, the 1973 race by Gijs van Lennep and Herbert Müller in a Porsche RSR at 71.27 mph/115.39 kph.

■ The first French Grand Prix – the Grand Prix de l'Automobile Club de France and the first of all national Grands Prix – was run on two days and over 770 miles/1239 km at Le Mans, and won by Szisz

(Renault) at 63 mph/101 kph in June 1906. Until 1921 it remained unique; then an Italian Grand Prix was run. In an effort to maintain its status, only manufacturers' entries were accepted until 1924, when a 'semi-works' Miller was allowed to start. The event had a chequered history, usually being a Formula race but sometimes a sports car event.

Winners of the world championship French GPs: 1950 (R) Fangio (Alfa Romeo); 1951 (R) Fangio and Fagioli (Alfa Romeo); 1952 (Ro) Ascari (Ferrari); 1953 (R) Hawthorn (Ferrari); 1954 (R) Fangio (Mercedes-Benz); 1956 (R) Collins (Ferrari); 1957 (Ro) Fangio (Maserati); 1958 (R) Hawthorn (Ferrari); 1959 (R) Brooks (Ferrari); 1960 (R) Brabham (Cooper); 1961 (R) Baghetti (Ferrari); 1962 (Ro) Gurney (Porsche); 1963 (R) Clark (Lotus); 1964 (Ro) Gurney (Brabham); 1965 (C) Clark (Lotus); 1966 (R) Brabham (Brabham); 1967 (LM) Brabham (Brabham); 1968 (Ro) Ickx (Ferrari); 1969 (C) Stewart (Matra); 1970 (C) Rindt (Lotus); 1971 (PR) Stewart (Tyrrell); 1972 (C) Stewart (Tyrrell); 1973 (PR) Peterson (Lotus); 1974 (D) Peterson (Lotus); 1975 (PR) Lauda (Ferrari); 1976 (PR) Hunt (McLaren); 1977 (D) Andretti (Lotus); 1978 (PR) Andretti (Lotus); 1979 (D) Jabouille (Renault); 1980 (PR) Jones (Williams); 1981 (D) Prost (Renault); 1982 (PR) Arnoux (Renault); 1983 (PR) Prost (Renault); 1984 (D) Lauda (McLaren); 1985 (PR) Piquet (Brabham); 1986 (PR) Mansell (Williams); 1987 (PR) Mansell (Williams); 1988 (PR) Prost (McLaren); 1989 (PR) Prost (McLaren); 1990 (PR) Prost (Ferrari); 1991 (MC) Mansell (Williams); 1992 (MC) Mansell (Williams); 1993 (MC) Prost (Williams).

Circuits: C, Clermont-Ferrand; D, Dijon–Prenois; LM, Le Mans; MC, Magny-Cours; PR, Paul Ricard (le Castellet); R, Reims; Ro, Rouen.

■ During the formative period of Grand Prix racing, the principal regulations were based on weights until 1914, when an engine capacity limit (that has been the basis of all subsequent successful sets of rules) was introduced:

1906 Maximum car weight, 1000 kg/2204 lb.
1907 Maximum fuel allowance, 231 litres/50.8 gallons for the 477½ mile/770 km race (allowing a consumption of 30 litres/100 km or about 9.4 mpg).

Ferenc Szisz waiting to start in the first Grand Prix, the French race at Le Mans in June 1906. He won the two-day 770-mile race by half an hour from Felice Nazzaro's FIAT.

1908 Minimum weight, 1100 kg/2425 lb; cylinder bores restricted.
1912 Maximum body width, 175 cm/69 in.
1913 Weight limits 800–1100 kg/1763–2425 lb; fuel allowance 20 litres/100 km (14.12 mpg).
1914 Maximum engine capacity 4.5 litres; maximum weight 1100 kg/2425 lb.

■ The first purpose-built circuit in Australia was opened at Aspendale (Victoria) in 1906. A 1-mile/1.6-km gravel track, it was soon abandoned, then reopened with a concrete surface in 1923 and used spasmodically through to the 1930s.

■ The fastest steam car ever was the boat-shaped Stanley in which Fred Marriott broke the land speed record at Daytona in 1906, at 121.57 mph/195.606 kph.

■ In 1907 the first British Grand Prix car, the Weigel straight-8, appeared. Two started in the French GP, both retired.

■ In 1907 the Brooklands Motor Course, the world's first purpose-built race circuit, opened at Weybridge. Built by Hugh Locke-King on his estate, it had a lap distance of 3¾ miles/6 km and featured two long banked curves; later variations were contrived. The fastest officially-recorded lap was set by John Cobb in the Napier-Railton in 1935, at 151.97 mph/244.52 kph. The Land Speed Record was broken at Brooklands before World War I, numerous class records were set at the track, and the first two RAC (British) Grands Prix were run on it. But although it was central to British motor sport for several years, the track was generally insignificant in international terms, and in the 1930s the most important races in Britain were being run on the road circuit at Donington. The last Brooklands meeting was held in August 1939, and in recent years part of the banking and the clubhouse complex have opened as a museum celebrating a long-past age of motor sport.

■ The 1907 Peking–Paris 'race' (in most respects it was more akin to a modern rally) was won by a crew captained by Prince Scipio Borghese. Using a 7.4-litre Itala, they completed the run in 44 days of driving. One more marathon international race, New York–Paris, was run in the following year and won by an American crew with a Thomas Flyer.

■ The St Petersburg–Moscow race, the only major race ever run in Russia, was run for the first time and won by Arthur Duray (Lorraine-Dietrich). It was run again in 1908, when Hémery won in a Benz.

■ The largest engine ever to be raced in a Grand Prix was the 19 891 cc V4 in American Walter Christie's entry in the 1907 French GP. This was also the first GP car to have a V4 (mounted transversely) and the first to have front-wheel drive. Later that year a Christie was the first front-wheel drive car to win a major race (a 250-mile/402-km event at Daytona Beach).

■ A Chadwick run in the 1908 Vanderbilt Cup and American Grand Prize races had an engine with forced induction, by means of a centrifugal forerunner of the supercharger.

■ 'Pit' became a racing term that has persisted in the face of inaccuracy – it owed its origin to the trench with a counter just above road level that was provided for team crews at the 1908 French GP. Ever since, a 'pit' has been a ground-level shelter, sometimes forming the ground floor of elaborate structures.

■ The only man ever to drive his very first race in the premier event of the year, and win it, was Christian Lautenschlager, in a Mercedes in the 1908 French GP.

■ The first fatal Grand Prix accident occurred in the 1908 French GP. Cissac and his riding mechanic Schaube were killed when their Panhard crashed after a tyre failure.

■ The first American Grand Prize race was run over 402 miles/647 km at Savannah in 1908 and won by Wagner (Fiat). That forerunner of the American Grand Prix was run seven times, for the last time at Santa Monica in 1916, and the first US Grand Prix was run for sports cars at Riverside in 1958 (won by Chuck Daigh in a Scarab). In the following year it was a world championship Formula 1 race, Bruce McLaren becoming the youngest driver (at 22) ever to win a Grand Prix when he took the flag at Sebring. For two decades it seemed to find a permanent home at Watkins Glen, effectively becoming the US Grand Prix East as the Long Beach race became established from 1976. 'The Glen' was abandoned by the Formula 1 circus after the 1980 GP, and from 1982 a race entitled United States Grand Prix (Detroit) effectively took its place, until 1988. Then its title became simply the United States Grand Prix again and it was run at Phoenix, on another featureless street circuit where it survived for three years. In 1984 a US Grand

Prix (Dallas) that mercifully proved to be a one-off event was run in great heat on a disintegrating street circuit, and won by Rosberg (Williams).

Winners of the world championship GPs: 1959 McLaren (Cooper); 1960 Moss (Lotus); 1961 Ireland (Lotus); 1962 Clark (Lotus); 1963 G. Hill (BRM); 1964 G. Hill (BRM); 1965 G. Hill (BRM); 1966 Clark (Lotus); 1967 Clark (Lotus); 1968 Stewart (Matra); 1969 Rindt (Lotus); 1970 Fittipaldi (Lotus); 1971 Cevert (Tyrrell); 1972 Stewart (Tyrrell); 1973 Peterson (Lotus); 1974 Reutemann (Brabham); 1975 Lauda (Ferrari); 1976 Hunt (McLaren); 1977 Hunt (McLaren); 1978 Reutemann (Ferrari); 1979 Villeneuve (Ferrari); 1980 Jones (Williams); 1982 Watson (McLaren); 1983 Alboreto (Tyrrell); 1984 Piquet (Brabham); 1985 Rosberg (Williams); 1986 Senna (Lotus); 1987 Senna (Lotus); 1988 Senna (McLaren); 1989 Prost (McLaren); 1990 Senna (McLaren); 1991 Senna (McLaren).

Early races took place at Watkins Glen, except 1959, Sebring, and 1960, Riverside; 1982–8 races were run at Detroit; 1989–91 races at Phoenix.

■ Indianapolis Speedway opened in 1909. Promoted by four local citizens, led by Carl G. Fisher, and designed by P. T. Andrews, this 2½-mile/4-km oval was to have a much longer life than any other main-line racing venue, despite its obvious limitations as speeds increased towards the 220-mph/350-kph-plus laps of the 1990s. At the first meeting the track surface broke up, so by the end of that first year it had been resurfaced with 3 200 000 bricks – hence 'The Brickyard'. The first race was a short sprint won by Louis Schwitzer (Stoddard-Dayton), and the first major event was a 250-mile/402-km race won by Bob Burman (Buick), but the opening meeting was marred by the first fatal accident at Indianapolis.

■ In 1910 the first board track was opened in the USA, at Playa del Rey. Steep bankings were a characteristic of these tracks (and a few similar concrete or asphalt tracks) and speeds were high. That first track had a lap of 1 mile/1.6 km, with later tracks tending to be of 1½ mile/2.4 km or 2 miles/3.2 km, and feature races of up to 500 miles/804 km were run on them. New tracks were built through to the mid-1920s, but maintenance costs were high so that by the end of that decade short-oval racing, on flat, loose-surfaced tracks, had taken over.

■ The Argentine Grand Prix of the Roads, first run in 1910 from Buenos Aires to Cordoba (475 miles/764 km), picked up the theme of open-road city-to-city races abandoned in Europe after the 1903 Paris–Madrid and as the Gran Premio Nacional was run

over various courses until 1933. It was revived in 1936; the outstanding driver in these late *turismo carretera* races was Juan Manuel Fangio.

■ The 500-Mile Sweepstakes at Indianapolis was first run in 1911. After a doubtful start at the track, Carl Fisher found a formula for success, and since then 'Indianapolis' has meant just one race, run on Memorial Day (30 May). It was run over 300 miles/483 km in 1916, outwardly as a gesture towards the war in Europe but in part because that meant few new machines (only 21 cars started, and the crowd was small), while it has occasionally been cut short by rain and in 1986 was postponed because of heavy rain on Memorial Day.

The first races were run to engine capacity regulations: 9.8 litres (600 in³) in 1911–12; 7.4 litres (450 in³) in 1913–14; and 4.9 litres (300 in³) in 1915–19. The limit was 3 litres until 1922, then 2 litres until 1925 and 1.5 litres to the end of the decade; various capacity and fuel-related rules were applied until 1938 when the then-current GP capacities of 4.5 litres for unsupercharged engines and 3 litres for a supercharged unit were adopted. These lasted through to 1956 when the familiar 4.2/2.8-litre (256/170-in³) rules for normally-aspirated or supercharged engines came in, with allowances for diesels and, in the 1960s, for steam engines, rotary engines and gas turbines (when the latter became competitive later in the decade, the rules were changed to handicap them out of contention). In the 1970s up to nine capacity categories were applied in attempts to cover a range from pure racing to stock-block engines, two- and four-strokes, overhead, the rather quaintly termed 'nonoverhead' camshaft types, and so on. Turbo-charger boost pressures were to be limited.

The race has always been the pinnacle of US motor sport, and frequently the largest single-day sporting event in the world in terms of spectator attendances. Technical changes have not always been welcomed by an organisation that has sometimes been extraordinarily reactionary, and this has diluted international interest, although in the last two decades the most significant technical changes have been influenced by European practices, for example the swing to rear-engined designs after Lotus' victory in 1965 and the supremacy of Cosworth engines in the first half of the 1980s. Chevrolet engines (actually Ilmor units built in England) took over in 1988.

The increase in race speeds has been inconsistent, as regulations changed or conditions were unusual, as in 1992 when the race was slowed by a cold track

and numerous accidents. The 200-mph lap speed was achieved by Tom Sneva on one 1977 practice lap, but his qualifying speed was just below the magic figure, which was first recorded as a pole speed by Bobby Unser in 1981; in 1989 Emerson Fittipaldi pushed it above 225 mph (225.301 mph/362.586 kph).

Incidentally, two ladies have started in the 500, Janet Guthrie in 1977 and 1978, when she was 29th and 9th respectively, and Lyn St James, classified 27th although actually retired in 1993.

Winners of the 500: 1911 Harroun/Patschke (Marmon) 74.59 mph/120.01 kph; 1912 Dawson (National) 78.72/126.66; 1913 Goux (Peugeot) 75.92/122.17; 1914 Thomas (Delage) 82.47/132.69; 1915 de Palma (Mercedes) 89.84/144.55; 1916 Resta (Peugeot) 84.00/135.15; 1919 Wilcox (Peugeot) 88.05/141.67; 1920 Chevrolet (Monroe) 88.62/142.59; 1921 Milton (Frontenac) 89.62/144.19; 1922 Murphy (Murphy

Famous photograph of Ray Harroun in the first Indianapolis 500. His Marmon Wasp had a straight six, at a time when successful main-line racing cars invariably had four-cylinder engines; it was a single-seater, hence the prominent rear-view mirror – normally drivers relied on their riding mechanic to advise them of overtaking cars.

Special, i.e. Duesenberg-Miller) 94.48/152.02; 1923 Milton (Miller) 90.95/146.34; 1924 Corum/Boyer (Duesenberg) 98.23/158.05; 1925 de Paolo (Duesenberg) 101.13/162.72; 1926 Lockhart (Miller) 95.91/154.32; 1927 Sounders (Duesenberg) 97.55/156.96; 1928 Meyer (Miller) 99.48/160.06; 1929 Keech (Miller) 97.58/157.01; 1930 Arnold (Miller) 100.45/161.62; 1931 Schneider (Miller) 96.63/155.47; 1932 Frame (Miller) 104.14–167.56; 1933 Meyer (Miller) 104.16/167.59; 1934 Cummings (Miller) 104.86/

168.72; 1935 Petillo (Miller) 106.24/170.94; 1936 Meyer (Miller) 109.07/175.49; 1937 Shaw (Gilmore) 113.58/182.75; 1938 Roberts (Miller) 117.20/188.57; 1939 Shaw (Maserati) 115.03/185.08; 1940 Shaw (Maserati) 114.27/183.86; 1941 Davis/Rose (Noc-Out Spl) 115.12/185.23; 1946 Robson (Thorne Spl) 114.82/184.74; 1947 Rose (Blue Crown Spl) 116.34/187.19; 1948 Rose (Blue Crown Spl) 119.81/192.77; 1949 Holland (Blue Crown Spl) 121.33/195.22; 1950 Parsons (Kurtis) 124.00/199.51; 1951 Wallard (Belanger Spl) 126.24/203.12; 1952 Ruttmann (Agajanian Spl) 128.92/207.43; 1953 Vukovich (Fuel Injection Spl) 128.74/207.14; 1954 Vukovich (Fuel Injection Spl) 130.84/210.52; 1955 Sweikert (John Zink Spl) 128.21/206.29; 1956 Flaherty (John Zink Spl) 128.49/206.74; 1957 Hanks (Belond Spl) 135.60/218.18; 1958 Bryan (Belond Spl) 133.79/215.27; 1959 Ward (Leader Card Spl) 135.86/218.59; 1960 Rathman (Ken-Paul Spl) 138.77/223.28; 1961 Foyt (Bowes Seal Fast Spl) 139.13/223.86; 1962 Ward (Leader Card Spl) 140.29/225.73; 1963 Jones (Agajanian Spl) 143.14/230.31; 1964 Foyt (Sheraton Thompson Spl) 147.35/237.08; 1965 Clark (Lotus) 150.69/242.46; 1966 G. Hill (Lola) 144.32/232.21; 1967 Foyt (Coyote) 151.21/243.29; 1968 B. Unser (Eagle) 152.88/245.98; 1969 Andretti (Hawk) 156.87/252.40; 1970 A. Unser (Colt) 155.75/250.60; 1971 A. Unser (Colt) 157.73/253.78; 1972 Donohue (McLaren) 162.96/262.20; 1973 Johncock (Eagle) 159.04/255.89; 1974 Rutherford (McLaren) 158.59/255.17; 1975 B. Unser (Eagle) 149.21/240.08; 1976 Rutherford (McLaren) 148.72/239.29; 1977 Foyt (Coyote) 161.33/259.58; 1978 A. Unser (Lola) 161.36/259.63; 1979 Mears (Penske) 158.69/255.33; 1980 Rutherford (Chaparral) 142.86/229.86; 1981 B. Unser (Penske) 139.08/223.78; 1982 Johncock (Wildcat) 162.02/260.69; 1983 Sneva (March) 162.11/260.83; 1984 Mears (March) 163.62/263.25; 1985 Sullivan (March) 152.982/246.200; 1986 Rahal (March) 170.722/274.691; 1987 A. Unser Sr (March) 162.17/260.99; 1988 Mears (Penske) 144.81/233.05; 1989 Luyendyk (Lola) 185.98/299.13; 1990 Fittipaldi (Penske) 167.58/269.69; 1991 Mears (Penske) 176.46/283.98; 1992 A. Unser Jr (Galmer) 134.48/216.42; 1993 Fittipaldi (Penske) 157.21/253.00.

■ The Grand Prix was run again in 1912, after a three-year lapse due to factors as diverse as a recession in the infant car industry and French intransigence because 'their' race had been won by foreign teams. The age of giant cars – comprising large-capacity engines in rudimentary chassis – was passing. In the French race, still the only Grand Prix, new standards were set by Peugeot with a four-valves-per-cylinder twin-overhead camshaft engine of 7.6 litres. One of them, driven by Georges Boillot, won the race ahead of a traditional 14.1-litre Fiat.

■ Sunbeam scored the first team 1–2–3 in a major race, in the 1912 Coupe de l'Auto.

■ The last Grand Prix cars fitted with chain drive were the Mercedes run in the 1913 Grand Prix de France at Le Mans (one placed third).

■ Isotta-Fraschini pioneered the use of brakes on all four wheels of racing cars in 1913, although these machines were not pure-bred but derived from sporting models. Cars with 10.6-litre engines were run, and a trio of 7.2-litre cars run in the Indianapolis 500, where all retired. In the following year Delage, Fiat, Peugeot and Piccard-Pictet built Grand Prix cars with four-wheel brakes.

■ The Spanish Grand Prix was first run in 1913, as a touring car race at Guadarrama (won by Salamanca in a Rolls-Royce). It was run as a Formula race in 1923 and 1927, then twice in the 1930s. It was revived on the Pedrables circuit at Barcelona in 1951, then lapsed until the late 1960s when it was run at the uninspiring Jarama autodrome. The Montjuich circuit in Barcelona's largest park was demanding and was discarded following an accident in which five spectators were killed in the 1975 GP. Financial uncertainties led to another interlude in the early 1980s, then there was another revival, the 1986 race at Jerez appropriately being sponsored by a sherry producer. A new Circuit de Catalunya near Barcelona has been used since 1991, when it was generally welcomed.

Winners of the world championship races: 1951 (P) Fangio (Alfa Romeo); 1954 (P) Hawthorn (Ferrari); 1968 (J) G. Hill (Lotus); 1969 (M) Stewart (Matra); 1970 (J) Stewart (March); 1971 (M) Stewart (Tyrrell); 1972 (J) Fittipaldi (Lotus); 1973 (M) Fittipaldi (Lotus); 1974 (J) Lauda (Ferrari); 1975 (M) Mass (McLaren); 1976 (J) Hunt (McLaren); 1977 (J) Andretti (Lotus); 1978 (J) Andretti (Lotus); 1979 (J) Depailler (Ligier); 1981 (J) Villeneuve (Ferrari); 1986 (Je) Senna (Lotus); 1987 (Je) Mansell (Williams); 1988 (Je) Prost (McLaren); 1989 (Je) Senna (McLaren); 1990 (Je) Prost (Ferrari); 1991 (B) Mansell (Williams); 1992 (B) Mansell (Williams); 1993 (B) Prost (Williams).

Circuits: B, Barcelona; J, Jarama; Je, Jerez; M, Montjuich; P, Pedrables.

■ The first time 100 miles were covered in one hour was in 1913, by Percy Lambert in a Talbot. In 1915 Dario Resta won a 100-mile race on a board

Hero of France. Georges Boillot at the Peugeot pits during the 1912 French GP. The car set new standards with a fast-revving twin-ohc 7.6-litre engine, and Boillot won the race by 13 minutes.

speedway at Maywood, near Chicago, in a Peugeot at 101.86 mph/163.92 kph.

■ The first Grand Prix winner to construct a GP car bearing his own name was Felice Nazzaro, who had won the 1907 French GP for Fiat. His Nazzaro cars appeared in the 1914 French GP (all three retiring), a year after he had driven a Nazzaro to win the Targa Florio. After World War I Nazzaro returned to Fiat, for whom he won the 1922 French GP.

■ The 1914 French Grand Prix over 468 miles/743 km of a circuit near Lyons was one of the great events of the first period of GP racing, contested by 37 cars representing six nations (France, Italy, Germany, Britain, Belgium and Switzerland). For the first time cars were started in pairs – hitherto, single cars had been started at intervals. The leading roles were played by Boillot, expected to win 'for France' in a Peugeot, and Mercedes drivers Sailer and Lautenschlager. Boillot and Sailer retired, Lautenschlager scored his second GP victory, and a month later Europe was at war.

■ The first racing car with a monocoque construction chassis/body was built in 1914 by the Blood Brothers Machine Co., and named Cornelian. It also featured independent suspension front and rear. Powered by modest 1.7- and 1.9-litre engines, the Cornelian showed considerable promise (before retiring, it ran 12th in the 1915 Indianapolis 500). The line was not developed after World War I.

■ The first Pike's Peak hill climb meeting was held in 1916, on the 12.42-mile/20-km road rising 1500 m/ 4918 ft above Colorado Springs. It was to become the only internationally known climb in the USA. Fastest time at that first meeting was 20 min 55.6 s, set by Rea Lentz in a Romano Eight Special; in the 63rd Pike's Peak Race to the Clouds (1985) a new record time of 11 min 25.39 s was set by Michele Mouton in an Audi Sport Quattro. However, in the following year the record was back in the hands of Bobby Unser, with an 11 min 9.22 s climb in a 500-bhp Audi Sport Quattro S1. Peugeot sent its redundant rally 405s to Pike's Peak in 1988, when Ari Vatanen knocked 0.53 seconds off that record. Robby Unser, son of Bobby, was to win in 1989, 1991 and 1992, bringing the Unser family total to 30. Until 1970 Pike's Peak had been a points-scoring event in the USAC Championship Trail, which also included the Indianapolis 500!

■ Two drivers in the 1916 Prest-O-Lite Maxwell team at Indianapolis, Eddie Rickenbacker and Pete Henderson, were the first to wear crash helmets. These were padded metal hats. Rickenbacker started favourite for a race cut to 300 miles, soon retired with steering failure, then took over the second Maxwell to finish sixth. The shortened race and thin field was rated 'dull', and one of the 'star' drivers was notably absent – Ralph de Palma demanded start money, and the Speedway authorities refused to open that floodgate. Dario Resta won in a Peugeot.

■ First of the classic races to be revived after the war was the Indianapolis 500 in 1919, run one day after its traditional Memorial Day date to avoid accusations of insults to the dead. For the first time, 100-mph/ 161-kph laps were recorded in qualifying, seven drivers exceeding the magic figure. Howdy Wilcox won in a Peugeot – the last victory for a European car for 20 years – while among novelties there was a V12 Packard which Ralph de Palma placed sixth, having led the early laps (this car inspired Enzo Ferrari's long love affair with the V12 layout).

■ The first European race of substance to be run after the war was the Targa Florio, late in November 1919. André Boillot won in a Peugeot. First of the 25 starters was Enzo Ferrari, whose CMN lasted to the third lap.

■ The first Bugatti victory was scored by Ernst Friderich in a Type 13 in the international voiturette (light car) race at Le Mans in 1920.

■ The Grand Prix regulations between the two World Wars varied and were not always acceptable to race organisers or entrants, for example in 1930 when only the Belgian GP was run to the ruling formula and most races were *formule libre* events. Sometimes the regulations did not work as the sport's administrators envisaged, most notoriously the 1934–7 maximum weight formula.

1921 Maximum engine capacity, 3 litres; minimum car weight, 800 kg/1763 lb.

1922–5 Maximum engine capacity, 2 litres; minimum car weight, 650 kg/1433 lb; riding mechanic not called for after 1924.

1926–7 Maximum engine capacity, 1.5 litres; minimum car weight, 700 kg/1543 lb.

1928 Car weight, 550–750 kg/1212–1653 lb.

1929–30 Minimum car weight, 900 kg/1980 lb; fuel *and* oil allowance, 14 kg per 100 km (approximating to 14.5 mpg).

1931 Minimum race duration, 10 hours.

1932 Race duration 5–10 hours; single-seater bodies permitted.

1933 Minimum race distance, 500 km/312 miles.

1934–7 Maximum car weight, 750 kg/1653 lb (without wheels and liquids); minimum body width at cockpit, 85 cm/33.5 in.

1938–9 Maximum engine capacities, 3 litres (supercharged) or 4.5 litres (unsupercharged); minimum weight of cars with engines to upper capacity limits, 850 kg/1874 lb.

■ The 1921 French Grand Prix at Le Mans saw the first American victory in a major European race, Jimmy Murphy driving a Duesenberg to win the 322-mile/518-km event at 78.10 mph/125.69 kph. This Duesenberg was the first GP car to have hydraulic brakes, to the front wheels only (a 1933 Maserati was the first racing car to have them on all four wheels).

■ The first Italian Grand Prix was run in 1921, at Brescia. It was won by Jules Goux driving a Ballot, at 89.94 mph/144.71 kph. In the following year it was moved to Monza, where with few exceptions (Leghorn, 1937; Turin, 1948; Milan, 1949; Imola, 1980)

Banked tracks seemed to have a real future in the 1920s, although the American board tracks were soon to fade away. Brooklands was notable for its concrete expanses, and the section in this photograph has been preserved (left, a mixed bunch of cars during a Double 12). Full-blown GP cars were seldom run on bankings by the 1930s, an exception being for races at Berlin's Avus circuit (below, Berndt Rosemeyer's rear-engined C-type Auto Union with wheel-enclosing streamlined bodywork for the 1937 Avusrennen).

it has been run ever since, although the circuits used at the Autodromo Nazionale outside Milan have varied. The first notable Italian GP was the 1923 race, the first Grand Prix to be won by a supercharged car (the Fiat 805 driven by Carlo Salamano); a combined road and banked track circuit at Monza was occasionally used in the 1950s, and for a Grand Prix for the last time in 1960 (when Phil Hill won in a Ferrari); the fastest race was run in 1971, Peter Gethin in a BRM winning in a four-car blanket finish at 150.76 mph/242.61 kph, before the road circuit was artificially slowed.

Winners of the world championship GPs: 1950 Farina (Alfa Romeo); 1951 Ascari (Ferrari); 1952 Ascari (Ferrari); 1953 Fangio (Maserati); 1954 Fangio (Mercedes-Benz); 1955 Fangio (Mercedes-Benz); 1956 Moss (Maserati); 1957 Moss (Vanwall); 1958 Brooks (Vanwall); 1959 Moss (Cooper); 1960 P. Hill (Ferrari); 1961 P. Hill (Ferrari); 1962 G. Hill (BRM); 1963 Clark (Lotus); 1964 Surtees (Ferrari); 1965 Stewart (BRM); 1966 Scarfiotti (Ferrari); 1967 Surtees (Honda); 1968 Hulme (McLaren); 1969 Stewart (Matra); 1970 Regazzoni (Ferrari); 1971 Gethin (BRM); 1972 Fittipaldi (Lotus); 1973 Peterson (Lotus); 1974 Peterson (Lotus); 1974 Peterson (Lotus); 1975 Regazzoni (Ferrari); 1976 Peterson (March); 1977 Andretti (Lotus); 1978 Lauda (Brabham); 1979 Scheckter (Ferrari); 1980 Piquet (Brabham); 1981 Prost (Renault); 1982 Arnoux (Renault); 1983 Piquet (Brabham); 1984 Lauda (McLaren); 1985 Prost (McLaren); 1986 Piquet (Williams); 1987 Piquet (Williams); 1988 Berger (Ferrari); 1989 Prost (McLaren); 1990 Senna (McLaren); 1991 Mansell (Williams); 1992 Senna (McLaren); 1993 D. Hill (Williams).

■ The Monza autodrome opened in 1922, in a royal park north of Milan, comprising a high-speed banked track and a road circuit (the two could be used in combination). The original banked track was demolished in 1939, and a new track built in 1955; neither was frequently used, whereas the road circuit has been the home of the Italian Grand Prix and other international events, notably for endurance and touring car championship races.

■ First massed-start Grand Prix, and the first to have a rolling start, was the 1922 French GP at Strasbourg.

■ Vauxhall built a team of 3-litre Grand Prix cars – for 1922 and the first season of racing under a 2-litre maximum capacity limit! The cars were raced only in the Tourist Trophy and national British events.

■ The first 24-hour road race to be run in Europe was the Bol d'Or at Saint Germain, won by André Morel in a 1.1-litre Amilcar at 37.54 mph/60.40 kph. The second race resulted in a tie between Salmson drivers Benoist and Desvaux. The race continued as a 1.3-litre event at Saint Germain until 1937 when it was run at Montlhéry, the first capacity increase (to 1.5 litres) coming in the following year. The race survived until 1955, and was a little odd in several ways, most notably in its regulation permitting only one driver, a rule which lasted until 1953.

■ Mercedes introduced the supercharger to European racing, running a pair of 1.5-litre cars in the 1922 Targa Florio, where one was placed a lowly 20th, overshadowed by Masetti's victory in an essentially pre-war Mercedes.

■ In 1923 Fiat introduced the supercharger to Grand Prix racing, on the 805. Fiat also scored the first race win for a supercharged racing car in Europe, with a car driven to victory in the Gran Premio Vetturette at Brescia.

■ Delage built the first V12-engined Grand Prix car. Designed by Charles Planchon, it was built in only four months, although it was not fully raceworthy until 1924. Its 1923 failure cost Planchon his job, although he was Louis Delâge's cousin and the engine 'came good' with development.

■ Voisin built Grand Prix cars on semi-monocoque lines, which were raced in the 1923 French GP. Lack of power from what were essentially production engines was a handicap, but in principle these cars anticipated the true monocoque in GP racing by 29 years.

■ Benz built the first Grand Prix car with its engine mounted behind the cockpit. The team achieved encouraging results in its only Grand Prix (the 1923 Italian race) but lack of funds hampered development. Two were run as sports cars in German national events in 1924–5, but the programme was abandoned as Benz and Mercedes amalgamated in 1926.

■ The first British victory in a Grand Prix was scored by Henry Segrave, driving a Sunbeam in the French event at Tours in 1923.

■ The title 'European Grand Prix' was first used for the 1923 Italian race at Monza. It was an additional title for one national Grand Prix each year through to the 1960s, adding nothing save supposed extra status. Then in 1983 the title was revived and occasionally applied to a second championship race in one country.

Winners of the world championship European Grands Prix: 1983 (Brands Hatch) Piquet (Brabham); 1984 (Nürburgring) Prost (McLaren); 1985 (Brands Hatch) Mansell (Williams); 1993 (Donington Park) Senna (McLaren).

■ For the first time since the first '500' single-seaters were admitted to the Indianapolis race. Engines were smaller (122 in³/2 litres) and cars were lighter, so speeds were a little lower and drivers complained bitterly about the pounding inflicted by stiff suspension on the far-from-smooth brick track. This 1923 race saw the first spectator fatality, when a youth who was watching through a hole in a fence where Alley crashed was killed. Riding mechanics were back in 1930.

■ The first Le Mans 24-hour Race was run at the end of May 1923. Conceived as a test for touring cars, it was the first international event to be run for such a duration and its 'inventors', Charles Faroux, Emile Coquille and Georges Durand, intended that the emphasis should be on endurance rather than speed. It was to become the pre-eminent sports car race – sometimes the most widely publicised of all road races – and its fortunes have not necessarily reflected the ups and downs of sports car racing, for through the 24-hour race its organisers, the Automobile Club de l'Ouest, have been able to influence change in the category.

The race has survived several crises: the most sombre coming in the aftermath of racing's worst accident, at Le Mans in 1955 when 83 spectators and Mercedes driver 'Pierre Levegh' (Bouillon) were killed; the most worrying for its future as crowds fell sharply in the 1980s. However, later in that decade its stature increased as the importance of the international sports car championship declined and it stood alone as there was no international series in 1993.

Throughout, the race has been run on the same basic circuit, although this has several times been modified, most drastically after the 1931 race. In 1990 two chicanes were introduced on the 3.5-mile/5.7-km Mulsanne straight, and this meant that low-drag 'slippery' car bodies were no longer all-important to fast lap times and Le Mans entrants turned to cars with more aerodynamic downforce. The regulations have been complex, and contests such as fuel efficiency 'indices' within the race have been very important; in recent years the regulations generally followed world endurance championship and IMSA

rules (incidentally, no driver may drive for more than 4 hours in a stint, or 14 hours in total). The 1993 race was the last to admit out-and-out (Group C) sports-racing cars, and that year these were run by only two top teams with the bulk of the field made up of GT cars that may have been less spectacular but in spirit were nearer to the early races.

Le Mans 24-hour Race winners (starters/finishers in parentheses):
10.726-mile/17.258-km circuit: 1923 (33/30) Lagache/ Leonard (Chenard et Walcker) 57.205 mph/92.065 kph; 1924 (40/14) Duff/Clement (Bentley) 53.782

mph/86.555 kph; 1925 (49/16) de Courcelles/ Rossignol (La Lorraine) 57.838 mph/93.082 kph; 1926 (41/13) Bloch/Rossignol (La Lorraine) 66.082 mph/ 106.350 kph; 1927(22/7) Benjafield/Davis (Bentley) 61.354 mph/98.740 kph; 1928 (33/17) Barnato/Rubin (Bentley) 69.108 mph/111.218 kph.

10.153-mile/16.336-km circuit: 1929 (25/10) Barnato/ Birkin (Bentley) 73.627 mph/118.492 kph; 1930 (17/ 9) Barnato/Kidston (Bentley) 75.876 mph/122.111 kph; 1931 (26/6) Howe/Birkin (Alfa Romeo) 78.127 mph/123.735 kph.

8.475-mile/13.636-km circuit: 1932 (26/9) Sommer/ Chinetti (Alfa Romeo) 76.840 mph/123.084 kph; 1933 (29/13) Sommer/Nuvolari (Alfa Romeo) 81.400 mph.131.001 kph; 1934 (44/23) Chinetti/Etancelin (Alfa Romeo) 74.743 mph/120.289 kph; 1935 (58/28) Hindmarsh/Fontès (Lagonda) 77.847 mph/125.283

Sports car racing flourished in the 1920s, with the most durable of all sports car events, the Le Mans 24-hour Race, inaugurated in 1923. Until 1927 cars had to run through the opening phase with hoods erected, as on this Bentley trio leading away in 1927.

kph; 1937 (48/17) Wimille/Benoist (Bugatti) 85.125 mph/136.997 kph; 1938 (42/15) Chaboud/Trémoulet (Delahaye) 82.335 mph/132.539 kph; 1939 (42/20) Wimille/Veyron (Bugatti) 86.855 mph/139.781 kph; 1949 (49/19) Chinetti/Selsdon (Ferrari) 82.281 mph/132.420 kph; 1950 (60/29) Rosier/Rosier (Talbot) 89.713 mph/144.380 kph; 1951 (60/30) Walker/Whitehead (Jaguar) 93.495 mph/159.466 kph; 1952 (57/17) Lang/Reiss (Mercedes-Benz) 96.699 mph/155.575 kph; 1953 (60/26) Rolt/Hamilton (Jaguar) 105.841 mph/170.336 kph; 1954 (57/18) Gonzalez/Trintignant (Ferrari) 105.145 mph/169.215 kph; 1955 (60/21) Hawthorn/Bueb (Jaguar) 107.067 mph/172.308 kph.

8.364-mile/13.457-km circuit: 1956 (49/14) Flockhart/Sanderson (Jaguar) 104.465 mph/168.122 kph; 1957 (54.20) Flockhart/Bueb (Jaguar) 113.845 mph/183.217 kph; 1958 (55.20) Gendebien/P. Hill (Ferrari) 106.200 mph/170.914 kph; 1959 (53/13) Shelby/Salvadori (Aston Martin) 112.569 mph/181.163 kph; 1960 (55/20) Gendebien/Frère (Ferrari) 109.193 mph/175.730 kph; 1961 (55/22) Gendebien/P. Hill (Ferrari) 115.902 mph/186.527 kph; 1962 (55.18) Gendebien/P. Hill (Ferrari) 115.244 mph/185.469 kph; 1963 (49/12) Scarfiotti/Bandini (Ferrari) 118.104 mph/190.071 kph; 1964 (55.24) Guichet/Vaccarella (Ferrari) 121.563 mph/195.638 kph; 1965 (51/14) Rindt/Gregory (Ferrari) 121.092 mph/194.880 kph; 1966 (55/15) Amon/McLaren (Ford) 125.389 mph/210.795 kph; 1967 (54/16) Gurney/Foyt (Ford) 135.488 mph/218.038 kph.

8.369-mile/13.465-km circuit: 1968 (54/15) Rodriguez/Bianchi (Ford) 115.286 mph/185.536 kph; 1969 (45/14) Ickx/Oliver (Ford) 129.400 mph/208.250 kph; 1970 (51/7) Herrmann/Attwood (Porsche) 119.298 mph/191.992 kph; 1971 (49/13) Marko/van Lennep (Porsche) 138.133 mph/222.304 kph.

8.475-mile/13.636-km circuit: 1972 (55/18) Pescarolo/G. Hill (Matra) 121.450 mph/195.472 kph; 1973 (55/21) Pescarolo/Larrousse (Matra) 126.670 mph/202.247 kph; 1974 (49/19) Pescarolo/Larrousse (Matra) 119.265 mph/191.940 kph; 1975 (55/31) Ickx/Bell (Mirage) 118.981 mph/191.482 kph; 1976 (55/27) Ickx/van Lennep (Porsche) 123.494 mph/198.746 kph; 1977 (55/21) Ickx/Barth/Haywood (Porsche) 120.950 mph/194.651 kph; 1978 (55/17) Jaussaud/Pironi (Renault) 130.604 mph/210.188 kph.

8.467-mile/13.623-km circuit: 1979 (55/22) Ludwig/Whittington/Whittington (Porsche) 108.100 mph/173.913 kph; 1980 (55/25) Jaussaud/Rondeau (Rondeau) 119.225 mph/192.000 kph; 1981 (55/21) Ickx/Bell (Porsche) 124.930 mph/201.056 kph; 1982

(55/18) Ickx/Bell (Porsche) 126.389 mph/204.128 kph; 1983 (55/21) Schuppan/Haywood/Holbert (Porsche) 130.699 mph/210.295 kph; 1984 (53/22) Ludwig/Pescarolo (Porsche) 126.880 mph/204.149 kph; 1985 (49/24) Ludwig/Barilla/'Winter' (Porsche) 131.749 mph/212.021 kph.

8.406-mile/13.528-km circuit: 1986 (52/19) Stuck/Bell/Holbert (Porsche) 128.72 mph/207.197 kph.

8.411-mile/13.535-km circuit: 1987 (47/12) Bell/Stuck/Holbert (Porsche) 124.06 mph/199.65 kph; 1988 (49/25) Lammers/Dumfries/Wallace (Jaguar) 137.74 mph/221.665 kph; 1989 (55/19) Mass/Reuter/Dickens (Sauber) 136.701 mph/220.000 kph.

8.451-mile/13.599-km circuit: 1990 (48.29) Brundle/Nielsen/Cobb (Jaguar) 126.781 mph/204.034 kph; 1991 (38/15) Weidler/Herbert/Gachot (Mazda) 127.588 mph/205.333 kph; 1992 (28/17) Warwick/Dalmas/Blundell (Peugeot) 123.864 mph/199.340 kph; 1993 (47/31) Hélary/Bouchut/G. Brabham (Peugeot) 132.574 mph/213.358 kph.

■ The Montlhéry autodrome, longest-lived of European tracks, was opened in 1924. Designed by Raymond Jamin on an estate on the Orléans road some 15 miles/24 km south of Paris, it included a symmetrical banked *piste de vitesse* and roads which could be used to make up six circuits. It was extensively used for racing and record-breaking through to the 1960s; in the following decades it saw minor races and historic events, then in the 1990s reconstruction was proposed.

■ Duesenberg followed the Grand Prix lead and built supercharged racing engines, and won the Indianapolis 500 with one in 1924. For the first time two drivers shared the winning car, as Fred Duesenberg called Lora L. Corum in soon after half distance and put renowned lead foot Joe Boyer in the car (he climbed from fifth to win, Corum collecting the prize money!). Three months later, Boyer died in a crash at Altoona speedway. Later in 1924, Jimmy Murphy became the first posthumous American champion, for he was killed at the Syracuse board speedway after he had clinched the AAA title.

■ The Spa-Francorchamps circuit was also inaugurated in 1924. A fast, demanding circuit, it was made up of roads linking Francorchamps, Malmédy and Stavelot in the Ardennes, and came to be regarded as a classic Grand Prix circuit. However, controversy about safety aspects led to the Belgian GP being run at other venues after 1970. The Grand Prix returned to a shorter Spa circuit, which cleverly incorporated stretches of the original, in 1983 (lap length 4.318 miles/6.949 km).

■ The first Spa 24-hour Race was run in 1924, for touring cars (won by Springuel and Becquet in a Bignan at 48.70 mph/78.38 kph). It was run 11 more times before World War II, then occasionally as a sports car race, before it was positively revived as a touring car event in 1966. It has become established as one of the premier saloon races in Europe.

■ The first Pescara Grand Prix (Coppa Acerbo) in 1923 was won by Enzo Ferrari, driving an Alfa Romeo. Races for Formula or sports cars were run on this long circuit of public roads for many years, and the 1957 event was a world championship race, won by Stirling Moss in a Vanwall.

■ The first race of any consequence in Switzerland was the run for voiturettes at Geneva in 1924. The Talbot pair Kenelm Lee Guinness and Dario Resta placed first and second. Before the year was out both had died in racing accidents.

■ Alfa Romeo introduced the first of its classic Grand Prix cars, the P2 designed by Vittorio Jano to take the place of the unsuccessful (and unraced) P1. Antonio Ascari drove a P2 to a debut victory at Cremona in 1924.

■ The first Belgian Grand Prix was run at Spa, which was to be the venue for the 28 races run 1925–70. After that the circuit in the Ardennes was abandoned by Formula 1 until the Belgian GP was once again run at Spa in 1983, albeit on a shorter circuit. The first race was won by Antonio Ascari (Alfa Romeo P2) at 74.56 mph/119.96 kph, while Pedro Rodriguez set a Grand Prix record speed by winning the 1970 race at 149.95 mph/241.31 kph in a BRM P153; Damon Hill's winning speed in a Williams FW15C in 1993 was 135.331 mph/217.705 kph.

Winners of the world championship Belgian GPs: 1950 Fangio (Alfa Romeo); 1951 Farina (Alfa Romeo); 1952 Alberto Ascari (Ferrari); 1953 Alberto Ascari (Ferrari); 1954 Fangio (Maserati); 1955 Fangio (Mercedes-Benz); 1956 Collins (Ferrari); 1958 Brooks (Vanwall); 1960 Brabham (Cooper); 1961 P. Hill (Ferrari); 1962 Clark (Lotus); 1963 Clark (Lotus); 1964 Clark (Lotus); 1965 Clark (Lotus); 1966 Surtees (Ferrari); 1967 Gurney (Eagle); 1968 McLaren (McLaren); 1970 Rodriguez (BRM); 1972 (N) Fittipaldi (Lotus); 1973 (Z) Stewart (Tyrrell); 1974 (N) Fittipaldi (McLaren); 1975 (Z) Lauda (Ferrari); 1976 (Z) Lauda (Ferrari); 1977 (Z) Nilsson (Lotus); 1978 (Z) Andretti (Lotus); 1979 (Z) Scheckter (Ferrari); 1980 (Z) Pironi (Ligier); 1981 (Z) Reutemann (Williams); 1982 (Z) Watson (McLaren); 1983 Prost (Renault); 1984 (Z) Alboreto (Ferrari); 1985 Senna (Lotus); 1986 Mansell (Williams); 1987 Prost (McLaren); 1988 Senna (McLaren); 1989 Senna (McLaren); 1990 Senna (McLaren); 1991 Senna (McLaren); 1992 Schumacher (Benetton); 1993 D. Hill (Williams).

All races took place at Spa, except as noted: N, Nivelles-Baulers; Z, Zolder.

■ The first Moroccan Grand Prix was run in 1925, as a touring car race at Casablanca, and won by de Vaugelas in a Delage. Run as a non-championship Formula 1 race on the Ain-Diab circuit in 1957 (won by Jean Behra in a Maserati), and for the only time as a championship race in 1958, when it was won by Stirling Moss in a Vanwall.

■ The 100-mph/160-kph barrier was broken at Indianapolis in 1925, Peter de Paolo winning the '500' at 101.13 mph/162.72 kph in a Duesenberg.

■ Riding mechanics, whose role had been reduced to that of heroic passengers in the 1920s, were barred from the Grands Prix from 1925 (although cars still had to have two seats!).

■ Classic Reims-Gueux circuit on the sweeping roads of the Marne was first used in 1925. It had a lap length of 4.85 miles/7.814 km, revised in the 1950s to 5.18 miles/8.347 km. It was the scene of very fast and often memorable French GPs, such as the races that saw Mike Hawthorn's narrow victory over Fangio in 1953 or Jack Brabham's first GP win in a car bearing his name in 1966. Major sports car races were also run at the circuit. In the second half of the 1960s, the organising club (the AC de Champagne) was in decline, and so was the circuit. By the end of the decade the last race had been run on it.

■ The British Grand Prix, or the RAC Grand Prix as it was then, was run for the first time in 1926, on a pseudo-road circuit at Brooklands and won by Sénéchal and Wagner, sharing a Delage, at 71.61 mph/115.22 kph. It was the first race to count towards the newly-instituted world championship in

1950; and it is one of only two races that have counted towards every championship.

The winners since 1950: 1950 (S) Farina (Alfa Romeo); 1951 (S) Gonzalez (Ferrari); 1952 (S) Ascari (Ferrari); 1953 (S) Ascari (Ferrari); 1954 (S) Gonzalez (Ferrari); 1955 (A) Moss (Mercedes-Benz); 1956 (S) Fangio (Ferrari); 1957 (A) Brooks/Moss (Vanwall); 1958 (S) Collins (Ferrari); 1959 (A) Brabham (Cooper); 1960 (S) Brabham (Cooper); 1961 (A) von Trips (Ferrari); 1962 (A) Clark (Lotus); 1963 (S) Clark (Lotus); 1964 (B) Clark (Lotus); 1965 (S) Clark (Lotus); 1966 (B) Brabham (Brabham); 1967 (S) Clark (Lotus); 1968 (B) Siffert (Lotus); 1969 (S) Stewart (Matra); 1970 (B) Rindt (Lotus); 1971 (S) Stewart (Tyrrell); 1972 (B) Fittipaldi (Lotus); 1973 (S) Revson (McLaren); 1974 (B) Scheckter (Tyrrell); 1975 (S) Fittipaldi (McLaren); 1976 (B) Lauda (Ferrari); 1977 (S) Hunt (McLaren); 1978 (B) Reutemann (Ferrari); 1979 (S) Regazzoni (Williams); 1980 (B) Jones (Williams); 1981 (S) Watson (McLaren); 1982 (B) Lauda (McLaren); 1983 (S) Prost (Renault); 1984 (B) Lauda (McLaren); 1985 (S) Prost (McLaren); 1986 (B) Mansell (Williams); 1987 (S) Mansell (Williams); 1988 (S) Senna (McLaren); 1989 (S) Prost (McLaren); 1990 (S) Prost (Ferrari); 1991 (S) Mansell (Williams); 1992 (S) Mansell (Williams); 1993 (S) Prost (Williams).

Circuits: A, Aintree; B, Brands Hatch; S, Silverstone.

■ The German Grand Prix was first run as a sports car race at Avus (Berlin) in 1926. The following year it was run over the full 17.58-mile/28.28-km Nürburgring, then from 1931 over the Nordschleife or North Nürburgring circuit, which was to become familiar as *the* Nürburgring. It was first run there as a world championship race in 1951, was run at Avus in 1959 and at Hockenheim in 1970 before finding a semi-permanent home at that featureless circuit from 1977. In 1985 the race was run at the Nürburgring again, albeit on the little-loved new autodrome-style circuit.

Winners of the world championship German GPs: 1951 Alberto Ascari (Ferrari); 1952 Alberto Ascari (Ferrari); 1953 Farina (Ferrari); 1954 Fangio (Mercedes-Benz); 1956 Fangio (Ferrari); 1957 Fangio (Maserati); 1958 Brooks (Vanwall); 1959 Brooks (Ferrari); 1961 Moss (Lotus); 1962 G. Hill (BRM); 1963 Surtees (Ferrari); 1964 Surtees (Ferrari); 1965 Clark (Lotus); 1966 Brabham (Brabham); 1967 Hulme (Brabham); 1968 Stewart (Matra); 1969 Ickx (Brabham); 1970 Rindt (Lotus); 1971 Stewart (Tyrrell); 1972 Ickx (Ferrari); 1973 Stewart (Tyrrell); 1974 Regazzoni (Ferrari); 1975 Reutemann (Brabham);

1976 Hunt (McLaren); 1977 Lauda (Ferrari); 1978 Andretti (Lotus); 1979 Jones (Williams); 1980 Laffite (Ligier); 1981 Piquet (Brabham); 1982 Tambay (Ferrari); 1983 Arnoux (Ferrari); 1984 Prost (McLaren); 1985 Alboreto (Ferrari); 1986 Piquet (Williams); 1987 Piquet (Williams); 1988 Senna (McLaren); 1989 Senna (McLaren); 1990 Senna (McLaren); 1991 Mansell (Williams); 1992 Mansell (Williams); 1993 Prost (Williams).

■ The smallest Grand Prix field ever appeared for the 1926 French race at the Miramas autodrome near Marseilles – three Bugattis, of which one completed the full distance, one ran for 85 of the 100 laps, one retired. This was the first race of a new Formula, no other teams had cars ready, the organisers neglected to include a clause allowing for cancellation if a specified number of cars did not appear . . .

■ The first Maserati Grand Prix car was built in 1926. A straight-8, it followed the lines of the 1925 GP Diatto, which had been designed by Alfieri and Ernesto Maserati.

■ The first single-seater built for road racing in Europe was the Itala Type 11, which appeared in 1926, 15 years after a single-seater had won at Indianapolis. The Itala never started in a race.

■ The first running of the Mille Miglia, the 1000-mile/1600-km road race from Brescia south to the outskirts of Rome, then looping back north over the Apennines to finish at Brescia, took place in 1927. It was to become one of the great sports car races, although it perhaps survived beyond its time into the 1950s; accidents in the 1957 race sealed its fate, but the spirit of the event has been recalled by commemorative runs in the 1980s. The first race was won by Minoia and Morandi in an OM at 47.99 mph/ 77.21 kph, the last by Taruffi in a Ferrari at 94.84 mph/152.59 kph, while the fastest race was driven by Moss and Jenkinson in a Mercedes in 1955 (97.96 mph/157.62 kph). Only one other non-Italian driver, Caracciola in 1931, won the full Mille Miglia. In the 1990s the Mille Miglia has been a popular 'retrospective' event for historic cars.

■ The Nürburgring circuit in the Eifel mountains was opened in 1927, some 20 years after the idea of a permanent German circuit in this region had been mooted. It was eventually built under the aegis of Konrad Adenauer, then mayor of Cologne, as a means of alleviating unemployment. The north circuit, best known of the variants, was 14.17 miles/ 22.799 km long, with 176 bends or corners and numerous changes of gradient. It changed little from 1927 until 1976 when the last Grand Prix was run on it. A bland new circuit utilising a fraction of the old came into use in 1984, when it was the venue for the European GP.

■ The last Grand Prix Fiat, a very advanced 1.5-litre twin-6, was completed and raced just once, to win the 1927 Milan GP. This marked the end of a distinguished line, which as far as the Grands Prix were concerned stretched back to the first event and in the 1920s had produced some innovative cars. Fiats continued to be seen in other types of motor sport and from 1963, when the company took a controlling interest in Ferrari, it has underwritten the Ferrari GP programme.

■ The first Australian Grand Prix was run on a 6.46-mile/10.4-km circuit of loose-surfaced roads on Phillip Island off Victoria in 1928, as road racing was not permitted on the mainland. Winner was A. C. R. Waite (Austin 750). As the 1980s opened the race was run for Formula 1 cars, and won by Australian Alan Jones in a Williams; then for four years it was a Formula Pacific race. The 1981 and 1983–4 races fell to Roberto Moreno, the 1982 race to Alain Prost (the winning car was a Ralt RT4 in each race). Since 1985 the Australian Grand Prix has been the final event in

the world championship, run on a 2.35-mile/3.78-km street circuit in Adelaide, which has attracted universal praise. It also saw the shortest championship race, when the 1991 Grand Prix was abandoned after 14 laps (33 miles/53 km) in atrocious weather.

Winners of the world championship Australian GPs: 1985 Rosberg (Williams); 1986 Prost (McLaren); 1987 Berger (Ferrari); 1988 Prost (McLaren); 1989 Boutsen (Williams); 1990 Piquet (Benetton); 1991 Senna (McLaren); 1992 Berger (McLaren); 1993 Senna (McLaren).

■ The first Grand Prix accident involving a number of spectators occurred at Monza in 1928, when a Talbot driven by Materassi crashed into the crowd, killing 23 people.

■ The first Monaco Grand Prix – the original 'round-the-houses' race – was run in April 1929 and won by Bugatti driver 'Williams' at 49.83 mph/80.17 kph. The best-known circuit in the world remained

First Grand Prix start at Monaco, with tram track still in place. Bugattis dominate – in 1929 there were no other works teams, and few other cars for private entrants – with winner 'Williams' in a Type 35B starting from the middle of the second row.

virtually unchanged until 1972, when modifications to the stretch alongside the harbour extended the lap from 1.9 miles/3.06 km to 2.037 miles/3.28 km. Although this introduced more tight, slow corners, it did not greatly affect speeds; the first driver to exceed 80 mph/129 kph was Graham Hill in 1969, when he scored his fifth victory in the race. A new chicane extended the lap to 2.08 miles/3.35 km in 1986; Nigel Mansell set the lap record for this version of the classic – if outmoded – street circuit at 91.234 mph/148.827 kph in 1992. Ayrton Senna's six victories included a run of five from 1989.

Winners of the world championship Monaco GPs: 1950 Fangio (Alfa Romeo); 1955 Trintignant (Ferrari); 1956 Moss (Maserati); 1957 Fangio (Maserati); 1958 Trintignant (Cooper); 1959 Brabham (Cooper); 1960 Moss (Lotus); 1961 Moss (Lotus); 1962 McLaren (Cooper); 1963 G. Hill (BRM); 1964 G. Hill (BRM); 1965 G. Hill (BRM); 1966 Stewart (BRM); 1967 Hulme (Brabham); 1968 G. Hill (Lotus); 1969 G. Hill (Lotus); 1970 Rindt (Lotus); 1971 Stewart (Tyrrell); 1972 Beltoise (BRM); 1973 Stewart (Tyrrell); 1974 Peterson (Lotus); 1975 Lauda (Ferrari); 1976 Lauda (Ferrari); 1977 Scheckter (Wolf); 1978 Depailler (Tyrrell); 1979 Scheckter (Ferrari); 1980 Reutemann (Williams); 1981 Villeneuve (Ferrari); 1982 Patrese (Brabham); 1983 Rosberg (Williams); 1984 Prost (McLaren); 1985 Prost (McLaren); 1986 Prost (McLaren); 1987 Senna (Lotus); 1988 Prost (McLaren); 1989 Senna (McLaren); 1990 Senna (McLaren); 1991 Senna (McLaren); 1992 Senna (McLaren); 1993 Senna (McLaren).

■ Maserati built a twin-engined car for road races. This 1929 Sedici Cilindri appeared conventional as its two-in-line engines were mounted side by side ahead of the driver. Two years later Alfa Romeo built the Type A on the same lines. Both cars were modestly successful.

■ The Irish Grand Prix was a handicap sports car race which took into account the results of the unlimited Eireann Cup and 1.5-litre Saorstat Cup. Venue was Dublin's Phoenix Park, where races were still run in the 1980s, albeit not for significant categories (it is doubtful if such events would have been sanctioned on a circuit that was primitive by contemporary standards).

Winners of the three Irish GPs were: 1929 Ivanowski (Alfa Romeo); 1939 Caracciola (Mercedes-Benz); 1931 Black (MG).

■ The JCC Double Twelve was a worthy attempt to run a 24-hour race at Brooklands, necessarily in two parts to circumvent track usage restrictions – night racing has seldom been possible on any British circuits, although recently a national-level 24-hour saloon race has become established at Snetterton.

Winners of the three sports handicap Double Twelves were: 1929 Ramponi (Alfa Romeo); 1930 Barnato/Clement (Bentley); 1931 Earl of March/ Staniland (MG).

■ The first Czech Grand Prix run on the 18-mile/30-km Masaryk circuit at Brno in 1930, von Morgen and Prince zu Leiningen sharing the winning Bugatti. The race was run six more times in the 1930s, and effectively once after World War II in 1947, when Whitehead won in a Ferrari.

■ In 1930 Woolf Barnato became the first driver to win three successive Le Mans 24-hour Races. Other drivers to achieve the 24-hour hat trick have been Olivier Gendebien (1960–2), Henry Pescarolo (1972–4) and Jacky Ickx (1975–7). Ickx came within 64 seconds of a second hat trick when he finished second in 1983.

■ As the Grand Prix regulation requiring two-seater bodywork was dropped, Alfa Romeo introduced the Type B (P3), the first true monoposto Grand Prix car, in 1932. The Type B set new standards, which were not surpassed until Mercedes-Benz and Auto Union introduced a new generation of GP cars in 1934.

■ Bugatti introduced a four-wheel drive car, the T53, which was intended for Grands Prix but in fact appeared in practice for only one race, in 1932. It was relegated to hill climbs. The first four-wheel drive car actually to compete against GP cars was a Miller driven by Peter de Paolo in the 1934 Tripoli GP.

■ The first Grand Prix starting grid to be determined by lap times in practice formed up at Monaco in 1933.

■ Midget racing became formalised in the USA in 1933, leading to American Automobile Association control in the following year, although a national championship did not come until 1948.

■ A Citroën named 'La Petite Rosalie' droned round Montlhéry for 133 days in 1933 (with a break while the French Grand Prix was run) to cover 180 000 miles/289 600 km at an average speed of 58 mph/ 93.32 kph.

■ The 1933 Tripoli Grand Prix was rigged, according to Piero Taruffi, the holders of the winning tickets in the State lottery run in conjunction with the race apparently sharing their profits with the leading drivers! After that the lottery arrangements were changed (and there have been no other known incidents of rigging).

■ The first Swiss Grand Prix was run in 1934 on the challenging Bremgarten circuit at Berne, and won by Hans Stuck with an Auto Union. The race was run annually until 1939, and then from 1947 until 1954, when all racing was banned in Switzerland. The title was then applied to a non-championship race run at Dijon in 1975 (won by Clay Regazzoni in a Ferrari), then to a one-off championship event at this French circuit in 1982.

Winners of the world championship Swiss GPs: 1950 Farina (Alfa Romeo); 1951 Fangio (Alfa Romeo); 1952 Taruffi (Ferrari); 1953 Ascari (Ferrari); 1954 Fangio (Mercedes-Benz); 1982 Rosberg (Williams).

■ Fatal accidents at Indianapolis in 1933 – two in qualifying for the 500, three in the race, when 42 drivers managed the 100 mph average for 10 laps to qualify – led to a limit of 33 cars for the 1934 race, and every subsequent race. The familiar cry 'cars too fast' came after the 1933 finish, when the first six finishers had all exceeded 100 mph.

■ The first South African Grand Prix was run in 1934, as a handicap event at East London. After World War II it was revived as a *formule libre* race in 1960 and became a world championship race in 1962, being run three times at East London and, since 1967, at Kyalami. After a lapse, a greatly revised Kyalami circuit was used for a one-year revival in 1992. One thing did not change – Nigel Mansell in a Williams won the 1985 and 1992 South African GPs.

Winners of the world championship races: 1962 G. Hill (BRM); 1963 Clark (Lotus); 1965 Clark (Lotus); 1967 Rodriguez (Cooper); 1968 Clark (Lotus); 1969 Stewart (Matra); 1970 Brabham (Brabham); 1971 Andretti (Ferrari); 1972 Hulme (McLaren); 1973 Stewart (Tyrrell); 1974 Reutemann (Brabham); 1975 Scheckter (Tyrrell); 1976 Lauda (Ferrari); 1977 Lauda (Ferrari); 1978 Peterson (Lotus); 1979 Villeneuve (Ferrari); 1980 Arnoux (Renault); 1982 Prost (Renault); 1983 Patrese (Brabham); 1984 Lauda (McLaren); 1985 Mansell (Williams); 1992 Mansell (Williams).

■ The 1934 season was the first year of the Grand Prix formula that became known by its principal stipulation, a maximum car weight of 750 kg/1653 lb, and which saw all cars following the then-established practice outmoded by the summer. Two German teams, encouraged by rabid nationalism, introduced cars which set new technical and technological standards. Mercedes-Benz and Auto Union were to sweep all before them in the following years, their occasional defeats at the hands of the Italian teams coming completely against the trend.

The Mercedes-Benz W25 at least appeared conventional although, as it featured 'novelties' such as all-independent suspension, this was far from so. The Auto Union was designed by Dr Ferdinand Porsche for a team representing the combination of the Audi, DKW, Horch and Wanderer companies, and had its V16 engine mounted behind the cockpit.

The Mercedes won the Eifel race at the Nürburgring (thus becoming the first 'all-independent' Grand Prix car to win a race), while Hans Stuck's victory in the German GP was the first in a race of that stature for a rear-engined car.

■ A 1934 race meeting at Mines Field, California, has some claim to be the forerunner of airfield-circuit road racing.

■ Tazio Nuvolari scored a remarkable victory for the old order in Grand Prix racing when he drove an Alfa Romeo P3 to defeat the mighty German teams in their 'home' Grand Prix at the Nürburgring in 1935.

■ Luigi Bazzi conceived the Bimotore Alfa Romeo for Scuderia Ferrari; Alfa approved and seconded designer Arnaldo Rossi to the project. This was an attempt to match the power of contemporary German GP cars with two Tipo B engines (one ahead of the cockpit, one behind it); the two 1935 cars were the first built by Scuderia Ferrari, and the first to carry the prancing horse badge adopted by Enzo Ferrari. The Bimotore showed flashes of speed – it was intended for record attempts as well as racing – but was never a practical circuit car. The Donington Collection has restored one car.

■ In 1935 top-flight driver Count Carlo Trossi built an experimental Grand Prix car with a supercharged two-stroke air-cooled radial engine mounted ahead of the front wheels, and driving through them. It was never raced.

■ Crash helmets became obligatory at Indianapolis in 1935.

■ A Donington Grand Prix was first run in 1935. The circuit in parkland between Nottingham and Derby

Scuderia Ferrari's line-up of supremely elegant Alfa Romeos before the 1934 French GP. The Tipo B ('P3') was all too soon to be outmoded by new German cars. Drivers, left to right, were Achille Varzi, race winner Louis Chiron, and Count Felice Trossi.

was the first true road-racing venue on the British mainland, opened for motor-cycle racing in 1931 and made suitable for car racing in 1933. It closed in 1939, but was acquired by local builder and enthusiast Tom Wheatcroft in 1971; he built a new track, with lavish facilities, where racing started again in 1977 and where an extension to a length (2.5 miles/4 km) suitable for Grands Prix was opened in 1985.

Winners of the Donington Grands Prix: 1935 Shuttleworth (Alfa Romeo); 1936 Ruesch/Seaman (Alfa Romeo); 1937 Rosemeyer (Auto Union); 1938 Nuvolari (Auto Union). In 1993 the European Grand Prix brought a full GP field to the new Donington circuit.

■ The outer circuit record at Brooklands was set in 1935 by John Cobb in the Napier-Railton of 1 min 0.41 s; 143.55 mph/230.79 kph was never beaten.

■ The only Thai driver to make a mark in international racing, Prince Birabongse of Siam, started competing in 1935. In the second half of the 1930s he scored seven international race victories with ERAs. (Out of a total of 24 ERA victories in second-level single-seater racing his seven was the greatest number achieved by a single driver.) Bira competed in Grands Prix after the war, in cars such as Gordinis and Connaughts. He died in London in 1985.

■ A Hungarian Grand Prix was run at Budapest in 1936, and won by Tazio Nuvolari (Alfa Romeo). Save for some Formula Junior races in the early 1960s, the only postwar Hungarian events that could be regarded as 'international' were for East European championships. Then in 1985 the Formula 1

Constructors' Association signed a deal for a championship Grand Prix to be run on the new 2.4-mile/3.8-km Hungaroring circuit 9 miles/15 km outside Budapest, with a first race in 1986.

Winners of the world championship Hungarian GPs: 1986 Piquet (Williams); 1987 Piquet (Williams); 1988 Senna (McLaren); 1989 Mansell (Ferrari); 1990 Boutsen (Williams); 1991 Senna (McLaren); 1992 Senna (McLaren); 1993 D. Hill (Williams).

■ Another lap record destined to stand for all time was set by Auto Union driver Bernd Rosemeyer in the 1936 Swiss GP. He lapped Berne's Bremgarten circuit in 2 min 34.5 s (105.40 mph/169.59 kph) and, although this was improved on in practice sessions, it was never broken in a race before the circuit closed in 1954.

■ The Vanderbilt Cup races at Roosevelt Field attracted mainline European teams to the USA for the only time in the 1930s. The 1936 race was won by Nuvolari (Alfa Romeo); the 1937 winner was Rosemeyer (Auto Union).

■ The first Brazilian races to attract front-rank European entrants were run on circuits at São Paulo and Rio de Janeiro (Gavea) in 1936. Carlo Mario Pintacuda drove an Alfa Romeo to a rare victory over one of the dominant German teams (Auto Union) on the sinuous Gavea circuit in 1937.

■ The four-cylinder Offenhauser engine powered the winning car (Shaw's Gilmore Special) at Indianapolis for the first time in 1936. Based on a marine engine designed by Harry Miller in 1926, this strong beefy power unit was prominent in USAC racing until the second half of the 1970s, its position through almost 40 years being threatened only occasionally, for example by the Maserati victories at Indianapolis in 1939–40 or the Ford triumphs in the 1960s. In the next decade the Cosworth DFX decisively ended the reign of the Offy, which powered the Indianapolis 500 winner for the last time in 1976. The last top placing for an Offenhauser-powered car in the 500 was Bettenhausen's third with a Wildcat in 1980.

■ The 1937 Mercedes-Benz W125 was long regarded as the most powerful Grand Prix car ever built, its supercharged 5.66-litre straight-8 producing 600 bhp (646 bhp was recorded with a record-car 'sprint' version). In racing outputs of 550–600 bhp were normal. Save for the ineffectual BRM V16, this output was not approached in road-racing cars until the

late 1960s, in CanAm sports-racing cars. The most powerful of these was the turbocharged Porsche 917-30 unit, a 5374 cc flat-12 engine which produced up to 1100 bhp. By the mid-1980s, 1.5 litre turbocharged Grand Prix engines had potential power outputs (in 'qualifying' boost trim) equalling that of the Porsche, and exceeding that of the Mercedes in race trim (the turbocharged era in Grand Prix racing ended in 1988).

■ Riding mechanics appeared for the last time at Indianapolis in 1936, the 500 thereafter falling into line with international racing practice. There was irony in this late adoption of a single-seater requirement, as the very first 500 had been won by a monoposto car . . .

■ Crystal Palace circuit opened in south London in 1936, the only one in Britain controlled by a local authority and, until Donington was rebuilt, the only one to be used before and after World War II. Its major events were Formula 2 races. The circuit was closed in 1972.

■ The only important Formula race to be run in Eire was the 1938 Cork Grand Prix, won by René Dreyfus in a Delahaye.

■ The first racing car to have disc brakes was a rear-engined Miller built for the 1938 Indianapolis 500. These were in effect pressure plates working on one face of a disc; the first racing cars to use the now-familiar disc-and-calliper type were BRMs and the Thinwall Special Ferrari in 1952.

■ The Bathurst circuit was first used, for the 1938 Australian Grand Prix (won by Peter Whitehead in an ERA at 66.1 mph/106.35 kph). This is a rare circuit on public roads, which survives into the 1990s and has become internationally known as the venue for an outstanding touring car race.

■ Kurtis Kraft was founded in 1938, on the basis of Frank Kurtis' existing race-car shop where short-track midget cars had been built since the mid-1930s. More than 1000 Kurtis midgets were to be sold (some in 'kit' form), and after World War II Kurtis twice started small-scale sports car production. However, the marque became best known for its Indianapolis roadsters – 58 were built, including five winners of the 500 and such famous cars as the Novis, before Kurtis turned away from race-car construction in the early 1960s.

■ Prescott hill climb was first used in 1938, as a

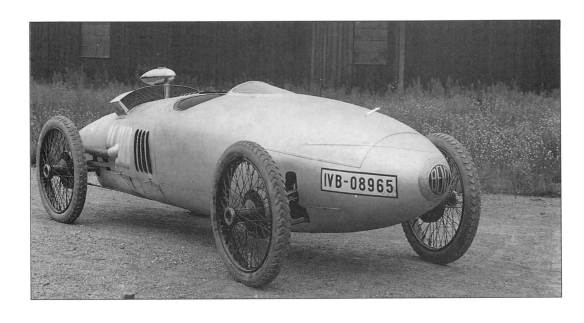

The mid-engined racing car layout did not become universal until the 1960s. Benz's efforts with the Tropfenwagen (opposite top) designed by Dr Edmund Rumpler in 1923 were under-funded. Auto Union enjoyed Grand Prix success in the 1930s (opposite, Nuvolari driving a D-type in the 1938 Donington Grand Prix). The American Gulf-Miller of 1939 (top) never completed a race. Eventually, Cooper proved the layout with essentially simple cars; Stirling Moss scored Cooper's first World Championship victory in this Rob Walker-entered car in the 1958 Argentine GP (above).

venue developed by the Bugatti Owners' Club. This is a typical British hill climb, in that it is very short and the atmosphere is very friendly. The original climb was only 880 yd/805 m, lengthened to 1127 yd/1030 m in 1960.

■ In 1939 the Indianapolis 500 fell to a European car for the first time since 1919, Wilbur Shaw winning in a Maserati 8CTF ('Boyle Special'). This was Shaw's second 500 victory and in the following year he became the first driver to win three times at Indianapolis (he drove the same Maserati again in 1940). He became president and general manager of the Speedway after World War II.

■ The last races at Brooklands, on the Outer, Mountain and Campbell circuits, were run in August 1939. Respective winners were Baker (Grahame-Paige), Cotton (ERA) and Mays (ERA). Recently non-competitive demonstrations have been run on the airfield and on a part of the banking that has been renovated by members of the Brooklands Society.

■ The first, and as it transpired only, Yugoslav Grand Prix was run on a circuit at Belgrade. It started 6 hours after Britain and France declared war on Germany, on 3 September 1939. Nuvolari won the race in an Auto Union, scoring the last victory for that marque.

■ The last races in Europe before World War II became a widespread conflict were the first Gran Premio Brescia della Mille Miglia – a substitute for the Mille Miglia as that race was banned, but generally considered to be the 13th Mille Miglia – and the Targa Florio, run on the closed Favorita circuit at Palermo. The 'Mille Miglia', over nine laps of a 109-mile Brescia–Cremona–Mantua–Brescia circuit, was won by von Hanstein and Baumer (BMW) and the Targa Florio by Villoresi (Maserati). There was one

Racing continued into the first year of World War II, when BMW won the 1940 'substitute' Mille Miglia with this forward-looking 328 coupé.

more 'European' race in 1940, the last Tripoli Grand Prix, won by Farina (Alfa Romeo).

■ The first car to be built by Ferrari as an independent constructor appeared in 1940. It was built under the name Auto Avio Costruzioni, as Ferrari's agreement with Alfa Romeo then precluded the use of his own name. This Vettura 815 was a 1.5-litre straight-8 sports car, largely built around Fiat components. Two ran in the 1940 Mille Miglia; both led their class, both retired.

■ Also in 1940, Alfa Romeo laid down the Type 512, in which designer Wilfredo Ricart followed Auto Union lines in mounting the engine (a supercharged flat-12) behind the cockpit. Two were built, and tested in 1942–3. One was destroyed in a fatal test accident; the other survives as a curiosity. Auto Union also prepared a car for the 1.5-litre formula that had been due to come into effect in 1941: it is intriguing to speculate that if races had been run to these regulations in the early 1940s, rear engined Grand Prix cars might have become the norm some 15 years before they did. As it was, Cooper set the trend in the second half of the 1950s.

■ The last competitive event in America before the country entered World War II was the 1941 Pike's Peak hill climb, won by Louis Unser in a Maserati. He had first won the climb in 1934 (the first victory for a member of the Unser family), scored his ninth win in 1953, and continued to compete until 1966, when he was 70 years old.

■ The Sports Car Club of America (SCCA) was formed in 1944. In its early years this was an amateur organisation for amateur drivers, but early in the 1960s it took on the responsibility for running FIA championship events in the USA, and later such professional series as CanAm.

■ The first postwar race meeting in Europe took place in the Bois de Boulogne, Paris, on 9 September 1945. The first race was won by Amédée Gordini, the 1.5-litre Coupe de la Libération was won by Louveau (Maserati), while the main event, the 74-mile/119-km Coupe de Paris was won by Jean-Pierre Wimille (Bugatti).

■ A round-the-houses circuit at Geneva used for the first of three Grands Prix des Nations, this 1946 event marking the true revival of front-line racing (Farina won the 86-mile/138-km race in an Alfa Romeo at 64.10 mph/103.16 kph). Earlier Geneva races were insignificant, run on the Mayrin circuit outside the city.

■ There was a season of racing on the mainland of Europe in 1946, largely contested by Italian and French cars from the 1930s. Outstanding among these were the Alfa Romeo 158s, voiturettes before the war and destined to become outstanding Grand Prix cars under regulations which came into effect in 1948. These cars had been hidden through the war and were brought out to be raced four times in 1946. They failed at their first outing but in the Grand Prix des Nations at Geneva started a run of 31 victories.

■ The first postwar race in Britain, the 1946 Ulster Trophy at Ballyclare, was won by Bira (ERA).

■ The first British airfield circuit was opened at Gransden Lodge in 1946.

■ NASCAR (National Association for Stock Car Racing) was formed by Bill France in 1947, and was soon to become the most important organisation in this field. France's immediate objective was to move Daytona racing away from its beach-and-road circuit to a proper track, and out of this ambition came the Darlington banked oval. This was followed by other banked tracks, above all of course at Daytona.

■ Four of the classic Grands Prix were revived in 1947, the Swiss, Belgian, Italian and French.

■ The first race for 500-cc cars was run at Gransden Lodge in 1947, and won by Eric Brandon in a Cooper. This was to provide the basis for the first international Formula 3, which was to be dominated by rear-engined Cooper cars, usually powered by Norton engines.

■ The first Ferrari as such was the 125 sports-racing car, which made its competition debut in a sports car race at Piacenza in May 1947 (two were entered, one failed to start, the other retired in the race). In May Cortese drove one to score Ferrari's first victory, in a minor event at Rome's Caracella circuit. The first significant victory for the marque was scored by Raymond Sommer at Turin's Valentine circuit in October 1947. The 125 was a stubby little car with a 1.5-litre V12 engine, run with cycle wings or fully enveloping bodywork in 1947.

■ Silverstone circuit was opened in 1948 on an airfield that had been used by an RAF Operational Training Unit. Initially it was leased by the RAC, and the first official meeting was the RAC Grand Prix. The circuit used the runways, and the erstwhile perimeter track layout for the Grand Prix circuit was adopted in 1949. Essentially, it remained unchanged for a quarter of a century, although corners were reprofiled and the pits rebuilt. Concern about the speed of cars through the last corner before the start/finish line, Woodcote, led to a chicane in 1975 and a new double corner on the approach to Woodcote in 1987. Meanwhile, elaborate new pits had taken shape for 1988.

More elaborate modifications came for 1991 – a sequence of bends replacing the old second and third corners, a completely new stretch of track incorporating two new 'slowing' bends at the south end of the circuit, and a complex of corners before Woodcote. This increased the lap length to 3.247 miles/5.225 km, and that year GP speeds were down to 135 mph/217 kph, whereas they had been close to 160 mph/260 kph in the mid-1980s. A shorter National circuit was modified, and a South Circuit contrived (these two could be operated independently). This major centre of British motor sport continues to develop.

■ Goodwood circuit was also opened in 1948, on another disused airfield (Westhampnett). This never achieved the status of Silverstone, although in the 1950s it was the venue for championship sports car races. Seemingly racing ended in 1966, although the circuit survived for testing and demonstrations, but following a very successful Goodwood Festival of Speed in the nearby Park in 1993, moves to revive it for historic racing got under way.

■ Zandvoort circuit opened in 1948, with a meeting organised by the British Racing Drivers Club. It too has changed little although, like Silverstone, the increase in its lap speeds was curbed with artificial corners. It saw its last GP in 1985, but survived threats from an anti-racing faction as secondary events were run into the 1990s, most notably a prestigious Formula 3 meeting.

■ In 1948 the first postwar road race in the USA was organised on a 6.6-mile/10.6-km circuit which ran through the main street of Watkins Glen, a tourist village near Lake Seneca. An accident in 1952 spelled the end for that 'European-style' circuit. An alternative outside the village was used 1953–5, then a 2.3-mile/3.7-km permanent circuit was built. This was the venue for 20 US Grands Prix (1961–80).

■ The first drag strip opened at the Santa Barbara airport in Goleta, California, in 1948.

■ The first Formula 2 as such was introduced in 1948, although the idea of a secondary class was almost as old as racing, going back to the light cars that ran in the city-to-city races of the early 1900s. Throughout, a second category never meant 'second rate'; for example in the second half of the 1930s the leading cars included ERAs and the Alfa Romeo 158s that were to set the pace in the early world championship Grands Prix. The idea grew up that Formula 2 was a final stepping stone on a driver's path to Grand Prix racing, although to some it became an end in itself.

The 1948 regulations allowed for cars with engines up to 2 litres or 500 cc supercharged; it ran until 1953 and, as Formula 1 virtually collapsed when Alfa Romeo withdrew at the end of 1951, the world championship races were run for Formula 2 cars in 1952–3 (Ferrari winning all save one of the championship races). A 1.5-litre Formula 2 was current from 1957 until 1960, when, to all intents and purposes, it became the Grand Prix formula. A 1000-cc Formula 2 ran from 1964 until 1966, and for 1967 it was succeeded by 1.6-litre rules. In 1972 the capacity limit was raised to 2 litres, for production-based engines, and this limit applied when 'pure' racing engines were admitted in 1976. The European Formula 2 championship was run until 1984 (the last Formula 2 race being run at Brands Hatch), when it was succeeded by Formula 3000. While Formula 2 withered in Europe, its flourishing equivalent in Japan was that country's premier racing class until 1986. Then it too gave way to Formula 3000.

■ During the recovery period after World War II, races were run to free formula regulations, but in 1948 a new set of regulations governing the Grands Prix came into force, soon to be universally known as

There seemed to be few signs of coming British supremacy through to the early 1950s. But the 500-cc Formula 3 (opposite top, a trio of Coopers at Silverstone) provided an invaluable grounding for drivers and constructors. And young Colin Chapman had built his first Lotus cars (opposite, driving a Lotus 2 in a 1949 trial) – in the 1960s and 1970s he was to become a most innovative GP car constructor.

Formula 1. World Championship races have been run to these rules since 1950, except for the 1952–3 seasons when negligible support from teams promised poor racing and organisers turned to Formula 2.

The regulations have not always worked as the sport's administrators intended, for many racing car

The principal regulations governing Grands Prix since 1948.	
1948–51	Maximum engine capacities 1.5 litres (supercharged) or 4.5 litres (normally aspirated)
1952–3	Formula 2 regulations applied – maximum engine capacities 500 cc (supercharged) or 2 litres (normally aspirated)
1954–60	Maximum engine capacities 750 cc (supercharged) or 2.5 litres (normally aspirated). 'Commercial' fuel obligatory from 1958
1961–5	Maximum capacity 1.5 litres (minimum 1.3 litres); minimum weight 450 kg/990 lb
1966–85	Maximum engine capacities 3 litres (normally aspirated) or 1.5 litres (with forced induction – originally intended to admit supercharged engines, but applied to turbocharged units). Initial minimum weight 500 kg/1102 lb, increased by 585 kg/1287 lb by 1981, then reduced to 540 kg/1188 lb in 1983. Many subsidiary regulations introduced: for example to ban engines with more than 12 cylinders from 1971; to ban excessive aerofoils ('wings') and high engine air intake airboxes; to rule out space frames (by banning bag fuel tanks), ground effects (including sliding 'skirts') and the lowering of suspension systems by stipulating flat-bottom cars; to ban more than four wheels; and so on. Among positive requirements with safety in mind, culminating in 'survival cell cockpit' (1982), were on-board fire extinguisher systems, deformable fuel tanks, then single fuel cells. Fuel consumption was effectively introduced in 1984 as the allowance per car for a race was cut from 250 litres to 220 litres/48.4 imp. gallons/58.1 US gallons, then progressively reduced to 150 litres/33 imp. gallons/39.6 US gallons for the last turbo cars in 1988
1986	Turbocharged engines only (capacity 1.5 litres), with chassis requirements following preceding years, and fuel allowance 195 litres/43 imp. gallons
1987–8	Maximum capacities 3.5 litres (normally aspirated) or 1.5 litres (turbocharged). Multi-stage and liquid-cooled intercoolers banned, along with other turbo refinements; turbo boost restricted by 'pop-off' valves; and a weight penalty (540 kg to 500 kg/1188 lb to 1102 lb) in favour of cars with normally aspirated engines. These regulations were intended to achieve power equality over two seasons
1989–	Normally-aspirated engines only, maximum capacity 3.5 litres. Race distances 305 km/199 miles or 2 hours, whichever was shorter. Components such as 'active suspension' banned from 1993, and refuelling during races reintroduced. Additional regulations aimed at increased safety were progressively introduced after the accidents at the San Marino Grand Prix meeting in 1994

designers have been infinitely more talented than bureaucrats, especially bureaucrats with oblique motivations, and these designers have been able to exploit loopholes. Thus FISA worked hard towards the goal of all-turbo Grands Prix in the mid-1980s, only to find as it was achieved that costs and performance potential were soaring out of control; the goalposts were therefore moved, and turbos eventually barred.

The principal restriction has been on engine capacities, but attempts to legislate equivalencies between normally aspirated power units and forced-induction types have generally failed. Other requirements have been subsidiary; for example, concerning race distances or durations, types of fuel, car and tyre dimensions, and aerodynamic devices (where rule-makers were flat-footed by designers). Many changes have been made in the interests of safety, and more recently in the hope that racing would become closer, as advanced technology was rated secondary to TV and other marketing interests.

■ Ferrari's first Grand Prix victory was scored by Alberto Ascari in the 1949 Swiss GP, driving a single-stage supercharged 125. Late in the year Peter Whitehead drove a single-stage car to win the Czechoslovak GP, the first British driver to win an event of such status since World War II. In the same year Ferrari gained the first of nine victories in the Le Mans 24-hour Race, which was to include a six-race sequence of wins, 1960–5.

■ The extraordinarily advanced Cisitalia GP car (Porsche Type 360) was completed in 1949, with a horizontally opposed 12-cylinder supercharged engine mounted behind the cockpit, four-wheel drive, a space frame chassis and all-independent suspension. This car was never seriously raced (its only competitive appearance was in Argentina, as the Autoar) as the Cisitalia company failed.

■ The Silverstone International Trophy race was first run in 1948 (and won by Alberto Ascari in a Ferrari). This was eventually to have the longest history of all non-championship Formula 1 races, through to 1978 as a 'mainline' Formula 1 race. Then it was run for Formula 2 cars until, in 1985, it became the first race for the Formula 3000 category (won by Mike Thackwell driving a Ralt).

■ The World Championship of Drivers was first contested in 1950. Overall placings are decided on a points basis, and scores in varying numbers of races have counted, for example four in the earliest seasons, or 11 through the 1980s, until from 1991 all points scored counted towards a driver's total.

Until 1959 the first five finishers in a race scored 8, 6, 4, 3 and 2 points, with a point for the fastest race lap. In 1960 sixth place earned a single point. From 1961 until 1990 the first six places scored 9, 6, 4, 3, 2 and 1; since 1991 the points awarded have been 10, 6, 4, 3, 2 and 1. Half points were awarded for shared drives until 1957, and for shortened races such as the 1975 Spanish and Austrian GPs or the 1991 Australian GP.

Grands Prix in 22 countries have been scoring events, plus the Indianapolis 500 until 1960. Circumstances led to a second race being run in Italy in 1957, at Pescara, and more recently the San Marino GP has been run on an Italian circuit, while the Grand Prix of Europe has meant occasional second races in Britain, and in 1984 in Germany. There were three championship races in the USA in 1982 (at Long Beach, Detroit and Las Vegas). Only the British and Italian Grands Prix have been run in every World Championship season.

World Champion Drivers (the number of championship races in a season is given in brackets after the date, and, where applicable, the champions' net/gross points scores after their names): 1950 (7) Giuseppe Farina (I), Alfa Romeo (30); 1951 (8) Juan Manuel Fangio (RA), Alfa Romeo (31/37); 1952 (8) Alberto Ascari (I), Ferrari (36/52½); 1953 (9) Alberto Ascari (I), Ferrari (34½/46½); 1954 (9) Juan Manuel Fangio (RA), Maserati and Mercedes-Benz (42/57); 1955 (7) Juan Manuel Fangio (RA), Mercedes-Benz (40/41); 1956 (8) Juan Manuel Fangio (RA), Ferrari (30/33); 1957 (8) Juan Manuel Fangio (RA), Maserati (40/46); 1958 (11) Mike Hawthorn (GB), Ferrari (42/49); 1959 (9) Jack Brabham (AUS), Cooper (31/34); 1960 (10) Jack Brabham (AUS), Cooper (43); 1961 (8) Phil Hill (USA), Ferrari (34/38); 1962 (9) Graham Hill (GB), BRM (42/52); 1963 (10) Jim Clark (GB), Lotus (54/73); 1964 (10) John Surtees (GB), Ferrari (40); 1965 (10) Jim Clark (GB), Lotus (54); 1966 (9) Jack Brabham (AUS), Brabham (42/45); 1967 (11) Denis

Hulme (NZ), Brabham (51); 1968 (12) Graham Hill (GB), Lotus (48); 1969 (11) Jackie Stewart (GB), Matra (63); 1970 (13) Jochen Rindt (A), Lotus (45); 1971 (11) Jackie Stewart (GB), Tyrrell (62); 1972 (12) Emerson Fittipaldi (BR), Lotus (61); 1973 (15) Jackie Stewart (GB), Tyrrell (71); 1974 (15) Emerson Fittipaldi (BR), McLaren (55); 1975 (14) Niki Lauda (A), Ferrari (64½); 1976 (16) James Hunt (GB), McLaren (69); 1977 (17) Niki Lauda (A), Ferrari (72); 1978 (16) Mario Andretti (USA), Lotus (64); 1979 (15) Jody Scheckter (ZA), Ferrari (51/60); 1980 (14) Alan Jones (AUS), Williams (67/71); 1981 (15) Nelson Piquet (BR), Brabham (50); 1982 (16) Keke Rosberg (SF), Williams (44); 1983 (15) Nelson Piquet (BR), Brabham (59); 1984 (16) Niki Lauda (A), McLaren (72); 1985 (16) Alain Prost (F), McLaren (73/76); 1986 Alain Prost (F), McLaren (72); 1987 (16) Nelson Piquet (BR), Williams; 1988 (16) Ayrton Senna (BR), McLaren; 1989 (16) Alain Prost (F), McLaren; 1990 (16) Ayrton Senna (BR), McLaren; 1991 (16) Ayrton Senna (BR), McLaren; 1992 (16) Nigel Mansell (GB), Williams; 1993 (16) Alain Prost (F), Williams.

■ Formula 3 was adopted as the third-level international racing category in 1950, for cars with unsupercharged 500-cc engines. It was in force until 1960 and, although its effectiveness was diluted by Cooper domination, it provided an excellent schooling category for many drivers. After a five-year period of Formula Junior racing at this level, a 1-litre Formula 3 ran from 1964 until 1970, and this was followed by regulations admitting cars with 1.6-litre engines which had their power outputs restricted by a limit on air supply. The capacity limit was raised to 2 litres from 1974, and in the early 1980s the most prominent engines were Toyota, Alfa Romeo and Volkswagen units, race-prepared by specialists such as Novamotor and Judd. A major change came in 1985 when 'flat-bottom' cars were required, but sensibly the regulations have remained stable. Into the 1990s the most successful chassis were built by Dallara in Italy and Reynard in Britain, while basic engines came from Alfa Romeo, Fiat, Honda (Mugen), Toyota, Vauxhall and others.

■ Brands Hatch car racing circuit was opened in 1950, with a lap of 1 mile/1.6 km. It followed the lines of a slightly shorter motor-cycle grass track that had been in use since 1928 (which in turn followed the lines of a 1926 cycle racing track). It was extended to 1.24 miles/2 km in 1954, and the 2.69-mile/4.33-km Grand Prix circuit was opened in 1960. The basic circuit did not change greatly in the next three decades, although several corners were realigned and this reduced the lap to 2.60 miles/4.18 km (and the short Indy circuit to 1.20 miles/1.94 km), while safety features were uprated. For more than 20 years it was the accepted alternate venue for the British GP (run at Brands Hatch 12 times, 1964–86) and also staged two European GPs and numerous events in international championship series, from sports cars to the British Rallycross GP. However, in the late 1980s and on into the 1990s its international significance dwindled.

■ The first BRM started in a race in 1950. This was an extremely complex Grand Prix car, with a 1.5-litre supercharged V16 engine, which stretched the resources of the small BRM team to the limit. The car had a very long gestation period, was never developed to raceworthiness as a Grand Prix contender (its only placings in championship races were a fifth and a seventh in the 1951 British race) but lingered in second-line racing until 1955. Power output of its V16 was claimed to be 485 bhp at 12 000 rpm, although this has been questioned. 'Respectability' came to BRM much later, with a first Grand Prix victory in Holland in 1959, and when Graham Hill gained the world championship with the team in 1962. The team was in decline in the mid-1970s and was wound up in 1979. BRMs started in 197 Grands Prix and won 17.

■ Sebring circuit was first used in 1950, showing fast-growing interest in road racing in the USA. This Florida track had considerable shortcomings (the airfield on which it was contrived remained operational), but it became the venue for the sports car championship 12-hour race, first run in 1952, and for the first US Grand Prix to be a world championship event, in 1959.

■ The first Carrera Panamericana was run in 1951, over 2178 miles/3504 km across Mexico, and won by Hershel McGriff in an Oldsmobile at 77.43 mph/ 124.58 kph. The next four races attracted top European teams, to race over a 1934-mile/3112-km course on normal roads. Ferrari won 1953–4, Mercedes-Benz 1952 and Lancia 1953. The race was an anachronism in the 1950s and was discontinued; a historic 'revival' event has been organised in recent years.

■ Alfa Romeo won the first world championship race in which its team competed, although this was on a technicality as its 158s had been raced before that 1950 British GP. Only two other marques have achieved such a notable 'first'; Mercedes-Benz in 1954 (French GP) and Wolf in 1977 (Argentine GP). The Alfa Romeo team's record of six successive victories in that season has been bettered only in years when there were more championship races on the calendar (by Ferrari in 1952–3, McLaren in 1984, 1988 and Williams in 1987, 1993).

■ The first Netherlands Grand Prix was run in 1951 on the challenging circuit among the seaside dunes at Zandvoort that was used for all subsequent Dutch GPs. The race became a world championship round in 1952, was run fairly regularly until 1985, then was dropped from the calendar in 1986.

Winners of the world championship races: 1952 Ascari (Ferrari); 1953 Ascari (Ferrari); 1955 Fangio (Mercedes-Benz); 1958 Moss (Vanwall); 1959 Bonnier (BRM); 1960 Brabham (Cooper); 1961 von Trips (Ferrari); 1962 G. Hill (BRM); 1963 Clark (Lotus); 1964 Clark (Lotus); 1965 Clark (Lotus); 1966 Brabham (Brabham); 1967 Clark (Lotus); 1968 Stewart (Matra); 1969 Stewart (Matra); 1970 Rindt (Lotus); 1971 Ickx (Ferrari); 1973 Stewart (Tyrrell); 1974 Lauda (Ferrari); 1975 Hunt (Hesketh); 1976 Hunt (McLaren); 1977 Lauda (Ferrari); 1978 Andretti (Lotus); 1979 Jones (Williams); 1980 Piquet (Brabham); 1981 Prost (Renault); 1982 Pironi (Ferrari); 1983 Arnoux (Ferrari); 1984 Prost (McLaren); 1985 Lauda (McLaren).

■ In 1950 Louis and Jean-Louis Rosier in a Lago-Talbot became the only father-and-son team to win the Le Mans 24-hour Race. Mario Andretti, cherishing an ambition to emulate the French pair, was third with his son Michael in 1983 (Alliot shared their Porsche 956) and Mario, his nephew John and Michael formed the first three-member family team in 1988, when they were sixth in a Porsche.

■ At the end of 1951 Alfa Romeo withdrew the Type 158/159 from racing, where it had dominated the Grands Prix in 1946–8 and 1950–1, gaining 31 victories from 35 starts. This car had been designed for prewar voiturette racing, and turned out to be the last effective Grand Prix car with a supercharged engine.

(Opposite) Long-distance races on normal roads had outlived their time by the 1950s. The Carrera Panamericana was a stage race across Mexico, which attracted entries from major companies. This Mercedes-Benz 300SL was driven to win the 1952 race by Kling and Klenk.

■ The longest Grand Prix ever to count for the world championship was the French event in 1951, run at Reims over 77 laps of the classic circuit running through the hamlet of Gueux (total distance was 374 miles/601.8 km).

■ Jaguar won the Le Mans 24-hour Race for the first time in 1951, with the XK120C ('C-type') derivative of the XK120. In 1953 a 'C' won again, then its D-type successor won three successive Le Mans races, 1955–7.

■ National Hot Rod Association was formed in Los Angeles by Wally Parks in 1951, in parallel with the American Hot Rod Association, to control the fast-expanding but then irresponsible sport of drag racing. It was quickly moved off the highways and on to disused airstrips, and towards its development as one of the most important of all motor sports. At that time 17 seconds was a good time for the ¼-mile/402-metre acceleration contest that is the heart of the sport. Four decades later the record was down to 4.779 seconds, set by Eddie Hill at Pomona in 1992 – appropriately, as that had been the first 'legal' drag strip. Meanwhile, Don Garlits ('Big Daddy', a pace-setter through the first two decades of organised drag racing) had been the first to achieve a 250 mph/402 kph terminal speed in a Top Fuel dragster, in 1975. Then, early in 1992, Kenny Bernstein was the first to clock a 300 mph speed (his 301.70 mph/485.44 kph was soon beaten by Pat Austin, who achieved 303.64 mph/488.66 kph at Atlanta).

■ The first Portuguese Grand Prix was run in 1951, as a sports car race at Oporto. It was first run for Formula 1 cars in 1958, over a street circuit at Oporto. After 1960 it lapsed, to be revived in 1984 at the Estoril autodrome.

Winners of the Formula 1 races: 1958 (O) Moss (Vanwall); 1959 (L) Moss (Cooper); 1960 (O) Brabham (Cooper); 1984 (E) Prost (McLaren); 1985 (E) Senna (Lotus); 1986 (E) Mansell (Williams); 1987 (E) Prost (McLaren); 1988 (E) Prost (McLaren); 1989 (E) Berger (Ferrari); 1990 (E) Mansell (Ferrari); 1991 (E) Patrese (Williams); 1992 (E) Mansell (Williams); 1993 (E) Schumacher (Benetton).

Circuits: E, Estoril; L, Lisbon; O, Oporto.

■ Crash helmets became compulsory in FIA-governed events in 1951, road racing thus falling into line with Indianapolis.

■ Disc brakes were fitted to formula and sports cars in 1952, on the BRMs and Thinwall Special Ferrari, which complied with Formula 1 regulations but were raced only in *formule libre* races, and the C-type Jaguar. In the following year disc brakes were fitted to the Cooper-Alta driven by Stirling Moss in non-championship Formula 2 races and the French GP.

■ The world championship Grands Prix were run to the 2-litre Formula 2 regulations in 1952–3, and in both seasons Ferrari achieved unbroken runs of seven successive victories. This remained unequalled until 1984, when the dominant McLaren team scored seven successive victories; then McLaren won 11 successive races in 1988.

■ 'Pierre Levegh' (Pierre Bouillon) was the last driver to attempt to drive single-handed through the Le Mans 24-hour Race. He was leading with 1½ hours to go when the engine of his Talbot failed. Thereafter such efforts were ruled out.

■ The first Cooper to race in Grands Prix was the Bristol-engined 2-litre T20 in 1952–3. Ironically, in view of the contemporary success of rear-engined Formula 3 Coopers and the imminence of the reintroduction of this layout to Grand Prix racing by Cooper, these T20s were front-engined. The first rear-engined Cooper to appear in Grands Prix was the T40 raced by Brabham in 1955.

■ Confederation of Australian Motor Sport (CAMS) took over control of motor sport from the Australian Automobile Association in 1952.

■ The first Argentine Grand Prix was run in 1953, at the Buenos Aires autodrome where, spasmodically, all subsequent races counting for the world championship were held.

Winners: 1953 Ascari (Ferrari); 1954 Fangio (Maserati); 1955 Fangio (Mercedes-Benz); 1956 Musso and Fangio (Ferrari); 1957 Fangio (Maserati); 1958 Moss (Cooper); 1960 McLaren (Cooper); 1972 Stewart (Tyrrell); 1973 Fittipaldi (Lotus); 1974 Hulme (McLaren); 1975 Fittipaldi (McLaren); 1977 Scheckter (Wolf); 1978 Andretti (Lotus); 1979 Laffite (Ligier); 1980 Jones (Williams); 1981 Piquet (Brabham).

■ Oulton Park circuit was opened in attractive parkland near Chester in 1953. As another indication of the spread of British interest in racing, this circuit seemed to have a bright future and for many years front-line teams were attracted to its non-championship Formula 1 events, and the Gold Cup attained considerable status. This withered in the 1970s when, for car racing, the long circuit was abandoned; its revival in the 1980s did not bring an increase to the stature of Oulton Park, or its races.

■ World Sports Car Championship was inaugurated in 1953. In effect this continued through to the 1990s, although it lacked the continuity – and indeed the popular appeal – of the Grand Prix championships for drivers and constructors, in part because it was subject to the whims of the sport's administrators and politicians.

The original championship ran until 1961, when it was superseded by parallel 'GT' and 'Prototype' championships. The first reflected a move to kill off sports-racing cars, the second the failure of that move! In 1968 a Manufacturers' Championship – a sports car championship in all but title – was introduced, the title 'World Championship of Makes' being used through the 1970s. Then in 1981 came the World Endurance Championship of Makes and the World Endurance Championship for Drivers; confusingly, these were not parallel, there being more races counting for the drivers' title than for the constructors! This partly came about because there were more American races in the drivers' championship, as the administrators were incapable of closing the very narrow gap between the regulations for 'European-style' sports car racing and the increasingly important IMSA series in the USA. Moreover, the two capacity classes in the constructors' championship scored equally, so the overall champion marque could – and did in the early 1980s – come from the ranks of the small-engine category. The final phase saw title changes, to the FIA Sports-Car (or Sports-Prototype) Championship, but this did not bring a sports car revival or even arrest declining spectator interest.

The IMSA GT championship in the USA remained relatively healthy, and so did a Japanese series, while Le Mans was strong enough to stand alone, albeit the organisers had to admit very mixed fields. But the international championship was abandoned after the 1992 season.

World Sports Car Championship winners: 1953 Ferrari; 1954 Ferrari; 1955 Mercedes-Benz; 1956 Ferrari; 1957 Ferrari; 1958 Ferrari; 1959 Aston Martin; 1960 Ferrari; 1961 Ferrari.

GT Championship winners: 1962 Ferrari; 1963 Ferrari; 1964 Porsche; 1965 Ferrari; 1966 Porsche; 1967 Ferrari.

Prototype Championship winners: 1962 Ferrari; 1963 Ferrari; 1964 Ferrari; 1965 Shelby; 1966 Porsche; 1967 Porsche.

World Championship of Makes winners: 1968 Ford; 1969 Porsche; 1970 Porsche; 1971 Porsche; 1972 Ferrari; 1973 Matra; 1974 Matra; 1975 Alfa Romeo; 1976 Porsche; 1977 Porsche; 1978 Porsche; 1979 Porsche; 1980 Lancia.

World Endurance Championship of Makes winners: 1981 Lancia; 1982 Porsche; 1983 Porsche; 1984 Porsche; 1985 Porsche.

FIA Sports-Car Championship winners: 1986 Porsche (Brun Motorsport); 1987 TWR Jaguar; 1988 TWR Jaguar; 1989 Sauber; 1990 Sauber; 1991 Jaguar; 1992 Peugeot.

■ Mike Hawthorn became the first British driver to win a World Championship Grand Prix, when he beat Fangio by the narrowest of margins in the 1953 French GP at Reims, driving a Ferrari. Previous world championship races (except the Indianapolis 500) had all been won by Italian or Argentine drivers; Maurice Trintignant was to be the first Frenchman to win a championship GP (at Monaco in 1955), and the next 'national firsts' were: Australia (Jack Brabham at Monaco in 1959); Sweden (Jo Bonnier in Holland in 1959); New Zealand (Bruce McLaren in the 1959 US Grand Prix); the USA (Phil Hill in Italy in 1960); Germany (Wolfgang von Trips in Holland in 1961); Mexico (Pedro Rodriguez in South Africa in 1967); Belgium (Jacky Ickx in France in 1968); Switzerland

(Jo Siffert in Britain in 1968); Austria (Jochen Rindt in the USA in 1969); Brazil (Emerson Fittipaldi in the USA in 1970); South Africa (Jody Scheckter in Sweden in 1974); Canada (Gilles Villeneuve in Canada in 1978); Finland (Keke Rosberg in the 1982 Swiss GP).

■ The first World Championship race accident involving spectators occurred in Argentina, nine being killed when Farina crashed in a Ferrari during the 1953 Grand Prix.

■ The New Zealand Grand Prix was first run in 1951, as a *formula libre* race at Ardmore (where it was to be run until 1962, when it was moved to Pukekohe). Stan Jones won that first race in a Maybach Special; Moss won three of the Ardmore GPs, as did Brabham.

■ Buenos Aires 1000-km race in 1954 was the first sports car championship event to be run in South America, won by Farina/Maglioli driving a Ferrari. It was run at the Buenos Aires autodrome, which became the usual venue for the event (in 1957 it was run at Costanera). However, the race had an erratic history and was run for the last time in 1972.

■ Aintree circuit was inaugurated in 1954, using the facilities of a horse-race course; consequently it was fairly flat and dull and, initially, a rare 'anti-clockwise' circuit. It was the venue for five British Grands Prix (the first in 1955, the last in 1962), and secondary Formula 1 events were also run on the 3-mile/4.8-km Grand Prix circuit. This fell into disuse, but valiant local efforts kept the shorter club circuit in being.

■ Mercedes-Benz returned to Grand Prix racing in 1954 with the W196. This car had a straight-8 engine with desmodromic (mechanical) valve gear, which had been seen in a Grand Prix car as early as 1914 on a Delage, was first successfully applied in this Mercedes, yet has not featured subsequently. It also had inboard, shaft-driven front brakes (featured again in 1970 on a Lotus) and full-width bodywork. This was soon abandoned in favour of conventional open-wheel bodies. Much of the team's 1954 success was owed to Juan Manuel Fangio, but its superiority in 1955 was more clear cut as Stirling Moss backed up the great Argentine driver.

■ Lancia entered the Grand Prix lists in late 1954 with a highly original car designed by Vittorio Jano. It had a tubular frame and the engine was used as a load-bearing member, more than a dozen years before this practice became widespread. Its appearance was unusual, too, with outrigged sponsons carrying fuel and oil. It showed great promise in its GP debut, but as a Lancia this D50 design was never developed to full raceworthiness – the company was in serious financial trouble, and part of the Fiat-underwritten cost of survival was to hand over the GP equipment to Ferrari.

■ The first Vanwall appeared in 1954, with a 2-litre engine as it had been intended for the Formula 2 GPs of 1953. Larger engines were developed, and the team survived a difficult period, which continued as a striking low-drag bodywork was introduced in 1956. That year Moss drove a Vanwall to win the International Trophy at Silverstone, and in the following year the team won Grands Prix – the Vanwall driven to victory in the British race by Tony Brooks and Stirling Moss was the first British car ever to win a World Championship race.

■ Argentine driver Onofre Marimon was the first driver to be killed in an accident at a World Championship meeting, in practice for the 1954 German GP. The first driver to be killed during a championship race was Bill Vukovich, at Indianapolis in 1955 (the 500 was then a championship event). In the first four decades of World Championship racing, 25 drivers were fatally injured in accidents at GP or Indianapolis 500 meetings.

■ Every car in the 1954 Indianapolis 500 had an Offenhauser four-cylinder engine – a 'first' – and two thirds of the chassis were built by Kurtis-Kraft. Winner was Bill Vukovich, the 'mad Russian'. He became the 50th person to die in a Speedway accident, going for his third victory in a row in 1955.

■ The worst accident in racing history occurred towards the end of the third hour of the 1955 Le Mans 24-hour Race, when a Mercedes-Benz 300SLR driven by 'Pierre Levegh' (Bouillon) touched an Austin Healey and was deflected into a public enclosure, a safety bank failing to contain it. Levegh and 83 spectators were killed.

■ In 1955 DB built a Grand Prix car using the power unit alternative to a 2.5-litre normally aspirated engine permitted by the Formula – a 750-cc supercharged engine, using it to drive the front wheels. The car was quite uncompetitive at its only race appearance.

■ A Connaught driven by Tony Brooks won the non-championship 1955 Syracuse GP in Sicily – the first British car to win a Grand Prix since 1924. This led to the B-type Connaught being named 'Syracuse'. The Connaught team scored some good GP placings with their 2.5-litre cars, but it was sadly underfinanced and ceased operating in 1957.

■ The United States Auto Club (USAC) was formed in 1956 to take over the control of the four premier categories of racing in the USA, as the American Automobile Association withdrew from its sporting role. At the time the Indianapolis-based USAC seemed forward-looking; little more than a decade later its resistance to overseas influences and technical advances made it appear reactionary and led to conflict with organisations such as CART in the 1970s.

■ The first Lola car built by Eric Broadley in 1956 was an 1172-cc Formula sports-racing car, for club events. Two years later the Mk 1 became the first Lola to be produced in some numbers (35 were built) and win at an international level. Lola subsequently built cars for most single-seater and sports-racing categories, producing their 1000th car in 1975. Production reached 2565 in 1993.

■ First Lotus single-seater was the 1956 Type 12 Formula 2 car, with a front-mounted Coventry Climax engine. It made its debut in the Easter Monday meeting at Goodwood. Driven by Cliff Allison, it retired, thus accurately foreshadowing the performances of Colin Chapman's clever little front-engined single-seaters.

■ The Cuban Grand Prix was inaugurated at Havana in 1957, where it enjoyed a brief life as a sports car championship race. First winner was Fangio, Moss won the next two events (one very short, as it was stopped after a fifth-lap accident), then such frivolous entertainments became alien to the island.

■ Race of the Two Worlds, run over the banked track at Monza in 1957, was billed as a confrontation between the then very different worlds of European and US track racing. It failed to live up to its billing primarily because it received little support from European entrants, the principal opposition to the track roadsters coming from Ecurie Ecosse Jaguar sports cars. In 1958 the European response was stronger, and a Ferrari was placed third. That was not enough encouragement for the organisers to repeat the event, and Indianapolis cars were not seriously raced in Europe again until 1978, when USAC National Championship races were run at Silverstone and Brands Hatch. Winners of the

1957–8 Monza races (each over 499 miles/803 km) were Jimmy Bryan (160.06 mph/257.53 kph) and Jim Rathmann (166.72 mph/268.25 kph).

■ The last European race in the spirit of the old city-to-city events, the Mille Miglia was run in 1957 – a crash which cost the lives of Ferrari driver the Marquis de Portago, his co-driver and 12 spectators and led the Italian government to restrict racing. The title was used by a rally, and later the 'retrospective' Mille Miglia was a popular and successful historic event.

■ Riverside International Raceway was opened in 1957, in the mountains some 60 miles/95 km from Los Angeles. It offered alternative circuits, and was the venue for races as diverse as a United States Grand Prix (in 1960) and NASCAR events. The circuit flourished through to the end of the 1960s, then slipped into a decline.

■ The first permanent racing drivers' school (as distinct from occasional, short-lived courses) was established by Jim Russell at Snetterton in 1957.

■ The first British car to win a World Championship race was a Vanwall, driven by Tony Brooks and Stirling Moss in the 1957 British Grand Prix at Aintree.

■ The European Hill-Climb Championship was revived in 1957, in effect as a successor to the Mountain Championship of the 1930s. It has been made up of between six and twelve rounds, sometimes including an international motor sport event in Andorra as well as the only one in Switzerland since 1955 (the St Ursanne–Les Rangiers climb). The series was open to 2-litre sports cars, saloons and GT cars, and more recently to production cars (saloons) and 'racing cars' (mainly 2-litre sports-racers).

■ The Formula 1 Constructors' Championship was introduced in 1958, with a points scoring system generally following the more widely publicised Drivers' Championship: 8, 6, 4, 3, 2 in 1958–9; 8, 6, 4, 3, 2, 1 in 1960; 9, 6, 4, 3, 2, 1 from 1960 until 1990; 10, 6, 4, 3, 2, 1 since 1991. Only the highest-placed car of a marque scored in the first 21 seasons, since 1979 all points scored by cars in the first six in a race have counted, save that until 1980 only the best results in specified numbers of GPs have scored (e.g. the best five in each 'half-season' in 1980). Recently all points have counted, as in the drivers' scoring.

■ Winners of the Constructors' Championships: 1958 Vanwall (GB); 1959 Cooper (GB); 1960 Cooper (GB); 1961 Ferrari (I); 1962 BRM (GB); 1963 Lotus (GB); 1964 Ferrari (I); 1965 Lotus (GB); 1966 Brabham (GB); 1967 Brabham (GB); 1968 Lotus (GB); 1969 Matra (F); 1970 Lotus (GB); 1971 Tyrrell (GB); 1972 Tyrrell (GB); 1973 Lotus (GB); 1974 McLaren (GB); 1975 Ferrari (I); 1976 Ferrari (I); 1977 Ferrari (I); 1978 Lotus (GB); 1979 Ferrari (I); 1980 Williams (GB); 1981 Williams (GB); 1982 Ferrari (I); 1983 Ferrari (I); 1984 McLaren (GB); 1985 McLaren (GB); 1986 Williams (GB); 1987 Williams (GB); 1988 McLaren (GB); 1989 McLaren (GB); 1990 McLaren (GB); 1991 McLaren (GB); 1992 Williams (GB); 1993 Williams (GB).

During those first 36 years of the Constructors' Championship, McLaren won 104 GPs, Lotus 79 and Ferrari 78. Over the longer period of the world championship, 1951–93, Ferrari was the top-scoring team until 1993, with 103 victories; in the last race of 1993, the Australian GP, Senna's win for McLaren took that team ahead of Ferrari, with 104 victories.

■ The first victory for a rear-engined car in a World Championship race was scored by Stirling Moss, driving Rob Walker's Cooper Climax in the 1958 Argentine Grand Prix. The first championship race in Europe to fall to a rear-engined car was the Monaco GP, won by Maurice Trintignant in Walker's Cooper.

■ Diminutive Maria Teresa de Fillipis was the first lady driver to enter World Championship races, in 1958.

■ The first Lotus Grand Prix car was the slim front-engined 16 of 1958, complicated and unreliable, and consequently unsuccessful.

■ Formula Junior was introduced in Italy in 1958, as a national class. In the following year it became an international formula, effectively taking the place of Formula 3 for a period and also attracting entrants from the small-capacity sports car classes. It admitted single-seaters with production-based engines up to 1000 cc or 1100 cc, according to the weight of the car. Within a year of its upgrading to an international category, the front-engined cars on 'traditional' lines had been swept away by rear-engined British cars, above all by Cooper and Lotus, while the dominant power units were basically BMC and Ford engines. Formula Junior proved to be an excellent *ab initio* class, drivers of the calibre of Clark, Stewart and Surtees cutting their single-seater teeth on it.

■ The first Zeltweg circuit came into use, and was to be the venue for the early Austrian GPs, from 1963. It was extemporised on an operational airfield and a new purpose-built circuit took shape nearby as the Österreichring, opened in 1969. This became established as one of the outstanding championship circuits of Europe, fast and demanding for drivers, set in a bowl in the hills to give spectators first-class viewing (lap length 3.692 miles/5.942 km); 18 world championship GPs were run at the Österreichring, 1970–87.

■ British Touring Car Championship was run for the first time in 1958, inspired by the success of saloon car events at race meetings through the decade. In time it became the RAC Touring Car Championship, still crowd-pleasing but not without problems as haggles over the minutiae of regulations became as intense as the races. In the 1990s it gained a new lease of life under Class 2 (2-litre) regulations, run by TOCA, attracting teams representing up to ten manufacturers, and giving exciting racing.

■ Daytona International Speedway opened, 4 miles/6.4 km from the historic Daytona Beach site (the last stock car race on the old combined beach and road circuit was run in 1958). Initially the emphasis was on stock car racing on the banked tri-oval; then, with a road circuit combining infield roads with the bankings, it became a venue for international sports-car championship events, including the only 24-hour race in the USA. The first Daytona 500 (for stock cars) was run in February 1959 and won by Lee Petty (Oldsmobile).

■ Bruce McLaren became the youngest driver to win a World Championship Grand Prix when he took the flag at the end of the 1959 United States GP at Sebring. He was 22 years 104 days old; Jacky Ickx was 22 years 188 days old when he won the 1968 French GP; Schumacher and Emerson Fittipaldi won GPs when they were 23; Hawthorn, Scheckter, de Angelis and Collins won when they were 24. Troy Ruttman, at 22 years and 80 days, was the youngest driver to win a world championship race, the 1952 Indianapolis 500 (he was also the youngest winner of that race).

■ The great period of transition in single-seater racing was almost completed in 1960 but, aside from the American tracks, there was one last victory for a front-engined car on classic lines when Phil Hill won the Italian Grand Prix in a Ferrari Dino 246. To the partisan Monza crowd it was of little account that this Ferrari victory was achieved against negligible opposition, as British teams chose to boycott the race. The last front-engined car on conventional lines had made its appearance in the Grands Prix of that year,

the Scarab built by Lance Reventlow's *équipe*, which had cut its teeth on sports-racing cars in the USA. Lessons could have been learned from the failure of the front-engined Aston Martin DBR4/250 in 1959, and the Scarab was so outclassed that the team was withdrawn in mid-season.

■ The first Canadian Grand Prix was run as a sports car race at Mosport Park in 1961. It became a Formula race, and a world championship event in 1967, and since 1978 has been run at Montreal's Île Notre Dame circuit, now named after Gilles Villeneuve, Canada's greatest driver.

Winners of the World Championship races: 1967 (M) Brabham (Brabham); 1968 (J) Hulme (McLaren); 1969 (M) Ickx (Brabham); 1970 (J) Ickx (Ferrari); 1971 (M) Stewart (Tyrrell); 1972 (M) Stewart (Tyrrell); 1973 (M) Revson (McLaren); 1974 (M) Fittipaldi (McLaren); 1975 (M) Hunt (McLaren); 1976 (M) Scheckter (Wolf); 1978 (ND) Villeneuve (Ferrari); 1979 (ND) Jones (Williams); 1980 (ND) Jones (Williams); 1981 (ND) Laffite (Ligier); 1982 (ND) Piquet (Brabham); 1983 (ND) Arnoux (Ferrari); 1984 (ND) Piquet (Brabham); 1985 (ND) Alboreto (Ferrari); 1986 (ND) Mansell (Williams); 1987 no race; 1988 (ND) Senna (McLaren); 1989 (ND) Boutsen (Williams); 1990 (ND) Senna (McLaren); 1991 (ND) Piquet (Benetton); 1992 (ND) Berger (McLaren); 1993 (ND) Prost (Williams).
Circuits: J. St Jovite; M, Mosport Park; ND, Île de Notre Dame.

■ Intercontinental Formula devised for 1961, for single-seaters with unsupercharged engines of 2–3 litres. This was an attempt by the British establishment to extend the life of the 2.5-litre Grand Prix formula, in a reaction against the new 1.5-litre GP regulations. The intent was misguided, the Intercontinental Formula short-lived.

■ Kyalami circuit opened in 1960 on a plateau 15 miles/24 km outside Johannesburg, some 5000 ft/1525 metres above sea level and the second highest circuit used for top-line racing (after Mexico City). It had a lap distance of 2.54 miles/4.08 km, with one long straight. Kyalami has been the venue of the South African Grand Prix since 1967, and was favoured by teams for winter testing. It was last used for a Grand Prix in that form in 1985. A revised and less daunting 2.647-mile/4.261-km circuit was used for the 1-year revival of the South African GP in 1992.

■ The Cooper team ran a T54 in the 1960 Indianapolis 500, following tests with an unmodified T53 Grand Prix car the previous year. The T54 had a Coventry

Climax FPF engine of 2.7 litres producing 270 bhp, which on paper was far from adequate, yet Jack Brabham drove it to ninth place in the 500. That was too easily dismissed by some observers, but the 'funny little car' signalled the end of the long reign of 'roadsters' in US track racing.

■ Mosport Park circuit opened, some 60 miles/100 km east of Toronto. In the 1960s this 2.46-mile/3.96-km circuit was considered more than adequate, but in the second half of the 1970s it fell out of favour. The Canadian Grand Prix was run at Mosport eight times between 1967 and 1976.

■ The 1961 Dutch Grand Prix was the only World Championship race in which no drivers retired and none made pit stops (15 cars started, eight of the 15 finishers were on the same lap as von Trips' winning Ferrari).

■ The Ferguson P99 was the first four-wheel drive car to win a Formula 1 race and, incidentally, the last front-engined car to be built to Formula 1 regulations (it also served as a test vehicle for Ferguson Research). The race victory came in the 1961 Oulton Park Gold Cup, when it was driven by Stirling Moss. Its only Grand Prix appearance was in the 1961 British race, when it was disqualified. The P99 was later run in Tasman races, and Peter Westbury used it to win the 1964 British Hill Climb Championship.

■ The first Brabham car made its debut in 1961, as an MRD – initials which combine unfortunately in French and were therefore discarded in favour of Brabham's name coupled with that of his partner, Ron Tauranac, in the model designation 'BT'. The name and designation sequence were carried through the last Brabham although Tauranac had no connection with the company after 1972. The MRD was a Formula Junior car, and the first Grand Prix Brabham (BT3) appeared in 1962.

■ Lola became a Grand Prix car constructor in 1962, but while it has enjoyed great success in other categories, notably sports cars and Indy cars, there has been little in Formula 1, in part as Eric Broadley has preferred his company to be a supplier and set his face against works teams. John Surtees was second in two GPs for the Bowmaker-Yeoman Credit Lola team in the mid-1960s, Graham Hill had little success with his T370s in the mid-1970s and the Beatrice Lolas in the mid-1980s achieved little. A joint venture with Gérard Larrousse from 1987 yielded just 17 championship points in four years, the 1993 cars

supplied to Scuderia Italia were sadly disappointing, and after that season Broadley at last looked to an exclusive Lola F1 programme.

■ The first Chaparral appeared in 1961. It was a conventional sports-racing car, unlike the innovative Chaparrals that were to follow it. The name derives from the sagebrush country commonly found in Texas.

■ Wolfgang von Trips, first German driver to win a World Championship race (the 1961 Dutch GP), crashed after colliding with Clark's Lotus in the 1961 Italian GP at Monza. Von Trips and 13 spectators were killed as his Ferrari left the track.

■ The Grand Prix Drivers' Association was formed in 1961. After occasional and largely inconsequential conflict with the constructors and some organisers it was merged with the Formula 1 Constructors' Association in 1976, then re-formed independently in 1979. In 1982 most of the Formula 1 drivers at Kyalami for the South African GP 'withdrew their labour' on the first day of practice, in protest against a licence system. The Professional Racing Drivers Association succeeded it in 1982, but was not active in a 'trade union' sense. The GPDA was revived in 1994.

■ The first Mexican Grand Prix was run in 1962 at Mexico City, at 7300 ft/2255 m above sea level the highest circuit ever used for championship racing. In the following year it became a championship race; undisciplined crowds were a major factor leading to the event being dropped 8 years later. The race was revived on the Ricardo Rodriguez circuit in 1986.

Winners of the World Championship GPs: 1963 Clark (Lotus); 1964 Gurney (Brabham); 1965 Ginther (Honda); 1966 Surtees (Cooper); 1967 Clark (Lotus); 1968 G. Hill (Lotus); 1969 Hulme (McLaren); 1970 Ickx (Ferrari); 1986 Berger (Benetton); 1987 Mansell (Williams); 1988 Prost (McLaren).

■ Lotus introduced monocoque construction to Grand Prix cars with the 25 in 1962. This significant little machine had a 'bathtub' structure that was simple by modern standards, comprising twin side pontoons linked by bulkheads and the undertray, was light and stiff, and gave the driver more protection in an accident situation where a contemporary space frame chassis could 'fold' about the weak part, the cockpit. Eventually every other GP car constructor was to follow the Lotus lead.

■ The only World Championship victory for a car with an air-cooled engine was scored by Porsche,

Dan Gurney driving an 804 with a flat-8 engine to win the 1962 French GP at Rouen. Porsche also won a secondary race, but abandoned GP racing before the end of the 1962 season. An air-cooled DB had run in one 1955 race, when it was hopelessly outclassed; a Honda RA302 with a 3-litre air-cooled engine started in the 1968 French GP, but after its fatal crash the Japanese company abandoned the development.

■ The Tasman series of races in Australia and New Zealand originated in 1962, with regulations that were virtually carried over from the 2.5-litre GP formula. It thus extended the life of erstwhile GP cars, and made for a cohesive summer season in the southern hemisphere. It was later run for F5000 cars, but then the two countries went their own ways (in motor sporting matters).

■ Formula Vee was born in Florida in 1962, the first single-seater class built around standard components from one range of cars, the Volkswagen Beetle, to gain international acceptance. It performed its *ab initio* role admirably for several years, until generally overshadowed by classes such as Formula Ford, which in part was more attractive as its regulations made for cars more like 'proper' racers in their characteristics.

■ The 150-mph barrier was broken at Indianapolis in 1962, when Parnelli Jones qualified at 150.370 mph/241.945 kph in an Offenhauser-engined Watson. Rodger Ward won the race at 140.293 mph/225.731 kph, also a record. This race also saw the entry of a gas turbine-powered car by John Zink and, more significantly, the first car with a stock-block engine to qualify for the '500' since 1947 – and the Buick engine in that car, built by Mickey Thompson, was mounted behind the cockpit. Dan Gurney qualified it for the third row, and failed to finish the race, but he was to be instrumental in clinching the 'rear-engined revolution' on US tracks.

■ The first Austrian Grand Prix was run in 1963 as a non-championship race at Zeltweg airfield circuit, which had been in use for sports car, F2 and F1 races since 1958. After its second running it became a sports race until 1970, when it was run at the splendid Österreichring circuit, which continued as the venue until the race lapsed.

Winners of World Championship Austrian GPs: 1964 Bandini (Ferrari); 1970 Ickx (Ferrari); 1971 Siffert (BRM); 19762 Fittipaldi (Lotus); 1973 Peterson (Lotus); 1974 Reutemann (Brabham); 1975 Brambilla (March); 1976 Watson (Penske); 1977 Jones (Shadow);

1978 Peterson (Lotus); 1979 Jones (Williams); 1980 Jabouille (Renault); 1981 Laffite (Ligier); 1982 de Angelis (Lotus); 1983 Prost (Renault); 1984 Lauda (McLaren); 1985 Prost (McLaren); 1986 Prost (McLaren); 1987 Mansell (Williams).

■ Dragsters run by leading drivers such as Don Garlits appeared with 'wings' in 1963, the first cars actually to compete with such aerodynamic aids – surprisingly, in view of the demonstrated value of stub wings on devices like the Opel rocket car three decades earlier. The Swiss designer-engineer Michael May had fitted a very large wing to a Porsche 550 in 1956; this car was run in practice for two races, but was not permitted to race with a device that seemed potentially dangerous (it appeared only a year after the Mercedes-Benz 300SLR was run with its air brake at the rear). The first race use of high-mounted wing aerofoils, to provide downforce as an aid to road-holding, was on the Chaparral 2F sports-racing car in 1967. In 1968 high wings came into general use on road-racing single seaters, only to be precipitately restricted by regulations after dramatic accidents in 1969.

■ The first gas turbine-engined car to run in a classic road race was the Rover-BRM driven by Graham Hill and Richie Ginther in the 1963 Le Mans 24-hour Race. As a formula equating its power unit with a piston engine could not be agreed, it ran a 'time trial', covering a distance which would have classified it eighth overall. In 1965 it was run at Le Mans again, with a sleek coupé body, Hill and Jackie Stewart placing it tenth overall.

■ In 1963 the Suzuka circuit was opened in Japan with the first international race meeting in that country. This was dominated by invited drivers from overseas, Peter Warr winning in a Lotus 23. This 3.73-mile/6-km circuit had been constructed primarily as a Honda test facility, and Fuji was to take its place as Japan's premier circuit.

■ The first victory for a car powered by an American engine in an FIA championship, in this case the GT championship, came in the 1963 Bridgehampton Double 500, which Gurney won in a Ford-powered Shelby AC Cobra. In 1965 the Cobras won the GT championship in the names of Ford and Shelby – another American 'first', although the British origins of the chassis were conveniently forgotten.

■ Rallycross was born in 1963 out of the RAC Rally's misfortune. The first event was devised hastily and run at Brands Hatch to fill a TV slot when the RAC Rally had to be cancelled because of an outbreak of foot and mouth disease. It caught on, and a European series developed. In the 1980s, rallycross provided an opening for continued sporting use of the Group B rally 'supercars' when these were outlawed from the world rally championship.

■ Ford unveiled its challenge for international sports car honours early in 1964. The GT40 was a sleek GT coupé following 'European' lines, and indeed built in England. In some respects the venture was over-elaborate, but a MkII derivative did win at Le Mans in 1966, thus achieving the primary objective of the Ford programme, while a MkIV won in 1967. Remarkably, a GT40 run by the Gulf-JWA team then won the 24-hour race twice (1968–9).

■ St Jovite (Mont Tremblant) circuit was opened in French Canada in 1964. Picturesque, but less than adequate in some respects, this 2.65-mile/4.265-km circuit was used for the Canadian Grand Prix in 1968 and 1970.

■ The first Honda Grand Prix car appeared in 1964 and in the following year won its first race (and the last of the 1.5-litre GP formula), the Mexican GP. This was also the first GP with a transversely mounted 12-cylinder engine.

■ The first McLaren racing car completed, in 1964, was a space-frame sports-racing car. The first GP McLaren, the M2B, which had a novel stressed-skin hull formed of an aluminium-balsa wood-aluminium sandwich material, came in 1966.

■ In 1964 Watson provided the chassis for the Indianapolis winner for the fourth successive year (and this was the last roadster to win the 500).

■ The first British drag-race meeting was held at Blackbushe Airport in 1964, as one of a series of five events organised by Sydney Allard. It saw American Don Garlits record 8.28 seconds over the ¼ mile/402 metres. (In a 1963 demonstration, Dean Moon and Mickey Thompson had recorded 8.84 quarters, then the fastest standing-start ¼ miles run in Europe.) The sport slowly became established in Britain and Scandinavia, with venues such as Santa Pod, Avon Park and York Dragway, but modest resources meant that European Top Fuel times have never matched American times, for example the lowest elapsed time in 1992 (by Norwegian Liv Berstad) was 5.13 seconds, 0.35 seconds outside the best US time.

■ Zolder circuit was first used for an international meeting in 1965. With a lap distance of 2.6 miles/4.18 km it conformed to modern ideas of an artificial road circuit, almost flat but with an acceptable mix of corners and bends among the pine trees. It was first used for the Belgian GP in 1973, then for an unbroken sequence of Grands Prix, 1975–82. Practice for that 1982 race was marred by Gilles Villeneuve's fatal accident. The circuit was improved, but failed to win the Grand Prix back from Spa. It was a venue for secondary international events, such as a round in the German Touring Car Championship.

■ The first Matra racing cars appeared in 1965. The French aerospace company entered racing almost accidentally, for, as a principal creditor, it acquired the assets of the small specialist constructor René Bonnet when that company failed. The first Matra (MS1) was a Formula 3 car, which won one of the main F3 races of the year at Reims. This was immensely encouraging to an *équipe* which naturally adopted a leading role in the resurgence of French racing. Formula 2 cars followed, leading to a close association with Ken Tyrrell and Jackie Stewart, and to substantial backing for a French Grand Prix effort. In partnership with Tyrrell and Stewart this was successful, albeit with Ford-DFV engines (nine races fell to the team in 1968–9). From 1970 Matra pressed on with an all-French effort, less successfully.

■ Jim Clark won the 1965 Indianapolis 500 in a Lotus 38 with a 500-plus bhp Ford V8, the first win in the 500 for a British constructor and a British driver and, incidentally, the first at over 150 mph (150.686 mph/242.454 kph). This was the high point of a Ford-backed assault on the race, which had come close to success at the first attempt, when Clark drove a Lotus 29 into second place in 1963.

■ Fuji International Speedway was the venue for the first major international single-seater race to be run in Japan. This 1966 event was for USAC cars, and was won by Jackie Stewart in a Lola. Alternative circuits were available within the Speedway, which became the country's principal racing venue. The first two world championship Japanese Grands Prix were run at Fuji in 1976–7.

■ The first American car to win a major European sports-car race outright was a Chaparral 2D, driven in the 1966 Nürburgring 1000-km race by Phil Hill and Jo Bonnier. This was also the first major race victory for a car with automatic transmission. Within months, Ford scored the first American victory at Le

Mans, its Mk II being driven by New Zealanders Chris Amon and Bruce McLaren. This was the first car to cover more than 3000 miles (3009.5 miles/ 4843.1 km) in the 24-hour classic. In an attempt to stage a dead heat, another Mk 2 was alongside at the flag, but as it had started from nearer to the actual line it was credited with second place.

■ The new Hockenheim circuit was opened in 1966. Built with compensation funds received when an Autobahn was cut across the old circuit, which had been used for minor races before and after World War II, it comprised a twisting stadium section with two long fast legs linked by a fast and demanding curve. Chicanes were to be constructed on the fastest stretch. Hockenheim gained notoriety as the circuit where Jim Clark had his fatal accident in a 1968

Jim Clark in a Lotus 49 heads Denny Hulme in a Brabham BT20 in the 1967 Dutch GP. Clark scored a maiden race victory for the 49 and Ford's DFV engine in this race; the DFV was to power 153 championship race winners (and three more fell to its DFY derivative). Hulme was World Champion in 1967.

Formula 2 race. It was first used for the German Grand Prix in 1970, then from 1977 until 1984 while the new Nürburgring was built, and from 1986.

■ The Canadian-American Challenge Cup (CanAm) series was first run, for sports-racing cars. John Surtees won the first short 1966 series in a Lola, then came a period of McLaren domination with the classic M8s (McLarens won 31 races), followed in 1972 by Porsche invincibility with turbocharged 5- and 5.4-litre 917 Spyders. That in turn led to the adoption of F5000 until 1976. In the next season there was a reversion to sports-racing cars, or pseudo sports-racing cars as many were single seaters with full-width bodywork. It that form CanAm lost much of the significance it once had.

■ In 1966 Claude Ballot-Léna co-drove a Marcos into 15th place at Le Mans; in 1985 he became the first driver to contest 20 consecutive 24-hour races at the Sarthe circuit. He usually drove Porsches, placing as high as third (1977), or Ferraris, placing in the top six with the by-then rare Italian cars in 1972, 1973 and 1981.

■ The first lady to compete in an NHRA A-class dragster was Shirley Muldowney, who broke the local record on her debut at Englishtown in 1966. She became a leading Top Fuel competitor, winning three championships, and survived a very serious accident in 1984 to return to the sport in 1986.

■ In 1967 the Jarama circuit was opened, near Madrid, with a 2.1-mile/3.4-km sinuous lap that included only one straight. It was used for nine Spanish GPs between 1968 and 1981.

■ The BOAC 500 at Brands Hatch became the British round in the sports-car championship. The first race was won by Phil Hill and Mike Spence in a Chaparral 2F. The event became the BOAC 1000 in 1970, and then the British Airways 1000 in 1974. It was then abandoned, and the next endurance championship race (for the drivers' championship that had by then come into existence) to be run at Brands Hatch was the Flying Tigers 1000 in 1981 (won by Guy Edwards and Emilio de Villota in a Lola). This race became the Shell Oils 1000, then the Grand Prix International 1000 km, and in 1984 the British Aerospace 1000 km, before Shell resumed their sponsorship. Meanwhile, the British round in the principal championship, for Makes, was the Silverstone Six Hours (later a 1000-km event).

■ The most important Grand Prix engine of the late 1960s and the 1970s was the Ford-Cosworth DFV 3-litre V8, which appeared in 1967. Designed by Keith Duckworth to fulfil the second part of a commission from Ford (the first had been for a Formula 2 engine), the DFV (Double Four Valve) was exclusive to Team Lotus in 1967, when it powered the winning car in four Grands Prix.

It then became generally available, and was in the forefront through to 1983, powering 155 Grand Prix-winning cars of 12 different teams, as well as the winners of many non-championship and endurance events. From 1985 it was the mainstay power unit of Formula 3000 (the 400th DFV was delivered to an F3000 team in 1986). A variant, the DFY, came as the turbo era was firmly established, and that 155th victory was scored by Michele Alboreto in a Tyrrell in the 1983 Detroit GP.

Meanwhile, a turbocharged derivative built at the Cosworth plant in Northampton, the DFX, had started to make an impression on USAC/CART racing in North America in 1976, when Al Unser won three races in a Cosworth-powered Parnelli. Two years later the DFX was totally dominant in this form of racing, and was still firmly on top in its tenth anniversary season, after which it was displaced by Ilmor ('Chevrolet') engines.

■ The only Formula single-seater to have a chassis made largely of wood was the 1967 F2 Protos, which had a stressed-skin hull of laminated plywood designed by Frank Costin. Its best race placing was a second at Hockenheim.

■ The first Formula Ford race took place at Brands Hatch in 1967; 14 cars were entered, and five of these were delivered on the morning of the race. This soon proved to be an ideal low-budget category in which aspiring drivers could develop driving skills and gain racing experience, and by the 1980s was the most widely subscribed racing formula of all time, by which time it had also given rise to another successful category, Formula Ford 2000. Originally F Ford was built around the Ford Cortina 1.5-litre engine. Tight chassis regulations were aimed at simplicity, again to help keep costs low and exemplified in the first batch of Lotus 51 cars built in response to John Webb's order for 50 cars to get F Ford off the ground; 25 years later more than 9000 F Ford cars had been built. The regulations had been changed, partly to keep pace with changing Ford production components (notably engines) but the category remained essentially straightforward, and its popularity was maintained.

(Overleaf) Jaguar won the 1988 Sports Car Championship with the XJR–9, here driven by Martin Brundle.

■ A Lotus 56 came within 8 miles/13 km of victory in the 1967 Indianapolis 500 – the nearest a gas turbine-powered four-wheel-drive car has ever come to winning a race of such importance. Driven by Parnelli Jones, the dayglow-red car had dominated the race, leading 171 laps and was well ahead of the field with three laps to go when a gearbox bearing with an estimated value of $6 failed. That race was also the first '500' to be run over two days, being stopped by heavy rain after only 17 laps and re-started on 31 May. It had attracted the largest-ever entry, of 90 cars.

■ National Off-Road Racing Association (NORRA) was formed in 1967, primarily to run the first organised Mexican 1000 Rally, in effect the Baja desert race down the length of the lower California peninsula.

■ John Surtees joined the ranks of the driver-constructors, building his first car at the end of 1968, the TS5 for Formula 5000. His first GP car, the TS7, came in 1970. That year Surtees drove one to win the Oulton Park Gold Cup, but Grand Prix success proved elusive although the neat Surtees cars sometimes came close to victory (Mike Hailwood's second in the 1973 Italian GP in a TS9 was the best placing). Surtees abandoned racing car construction, and his team, in 1979.

■ Sponsorship came to Grand Prix racing in 1968, in the form of Lotus 49s painted in the colours of Players' Gold Leaf brand of cigarettes, and the entrant became Gold Leaf Team Lotus. Although the cost of racing was obviously increasing – albeit not then spiralling as it would a decade later – the governing bodies had tried to prevent this. Earlier efforts such as Jack Brabham's 'Redex Special' Cooper in the mid-1950s had been ruled out, but by the late 1960s attempts to restrain commercial decals within specified areas on cars were obviously pointless, and Formula racing inevitably followed the US track racing example. In the 1980s anti-smoking lobbies began to influence TV producers, and hence race organisers mindful of a major source of income, and while cars continued to be painted in the colours of cigarette packets actual brand names were removed in some countries. Oddly, the 1968 Lotus initiative was not imitated until 1970, when Yardley sponsored the BRM team.

■ A championship Grand Prix fell to an independent entrant for the last time, when Jo Siffert drove R. R. C. Walker's Lotus 49 to victory in the 1968 British race, at Brands Hatch.

■ The 1968 sports car championship was gained for Ford, ironically after the company had withdrawn its official teams. With Gulf sponsorship, the JWA team campaigned GT40s, 'obsolescent' according to Ford, but uprated under the direction of John Wyer to remain effective contenders. His JWA team clinched the championship in the last race of the series, at Le Mans.

■ The electric-powered vehicle speed record was raised to 138.862 mph/223.503 kph by Jerry Kugel, driving the Ford-Autolite 'Lead Wedge' at Bonneville in 1968.

■ Santa Pod, Britain's first permanent drag strip, was established in 1968 at the disused Poddington airfield.

■ Four-wheel drive enjoyed fleeting popularity among Grand Prix teams in 1969 – the British race was the first GP in which more than one such car started, no fewer than four coming to the grid. These were built by Matra, Lotus and McLaren. Significantly, BRM did not follow this 1969 trend, for it had experience which proved that weight and complexity outweighed the traction advantages (and these were in fact diminishing because of tyre improvements). Four-wheel drive reappeared only briefly, in 1971 as Lotus ran the 56B gas turbine car in a few Grands Prix.

■ A Ford GT40 (1075) run by the JWA team became the first car to win the Le Mans 24-hour Race in successive years. This was next achieved by the Joest team with a Porsche 956 (117) in 1985–6. Apart from an attempted dead heat in 1966, the JWA victory in 1969 was the closest in the 24-hour race – the GT40 driven by Jacky Ickx traded places with Hans Herrmann's Porsche 908 through the last lap, and the Ford won by roughly 100 yards.

■ The first March Grand Prix cars were built in 1970 by a company which had produced its very first racing car in the second half of the previous year. The 701 was a straightforward car, used by independent entrants as well as the works team, and in one of these Jackie Stewart scored the marque's first Grand Prix victory, in the 1970 Spanish GP. Only two more World Championship races fell to March, in the 230 contested (in 1991–2 under the Leyton House name). For several years March was dominant in Formula 2, building 327 cars and winning the European championship six times, 1971–82. Its Indycar successes included five Indianapolis 500 victories in the 1980s, and two World Series titles. The production company absorbed Ralt in 1988, but output declined in the 1990s; in 1989 the Formula 1 operation was sold, and a March team failed to appear in 1993.

■ The first Tyrrell Grand Prix car was built, in great secrecy. It appeared in time for the autumn 1970 races, showing potential in the hands of Stewart but failing to finish in four starts. Thereafter the Tyrrell team was enormously successful for three seasons, and reasonably successful for another ten, winning 23 championship events between 1971 and 1983. Ken Tyrrell was the last constructor to use the Ford-Cosworth DFV engine, turning to turbocharged units (Renault) only in 1985, and he was the first to take up the normally-aspirated option in 1987 with Ford-Cosworth DFZ engines for four seasons, with best championship placings in 1989 and 1990. Then Tyrrell turned to Honda engines for 1991, Ilmor engines in 1992 and Yamaha V10s in 1993, when for the first time the team failed to score World Championship points (although its 1984 score was annulled, because an 'illegal fuel additive' was detected after one race).

■ The first road racing car in which 'negative lift' was generated by means other than external aerodynamic devices was the 1970 Chaparral 2J sports-racing car, which used an auxiliary engine to exhaust underbody air and thus 'suck' it down on to the road. Flexible skirts partly sealed the underbody area. This car failed to win a CanAm race, but demonstrated potential (and drew designers' attention to the undersides of cars) before it was banned.

■ Bruce McLaren, a quiet New Zealander, winner of four Grands Prix, winner at Le Mans, twice CanAm champion, founder and inspiration of the racing car company that bears his name, was killed while testing a 1970 CanAm car at Goodwood.

■ Jochen Rindt became the first driver to be awarded the world championship posthumously. He died after an accident in practice for the 1970 Italian Grand Prix, but in the last three races of the season no other driver equalled the score of 45 points he had built up before the Italian race. Austrian Rindt was enormously successful in Formula 2 in the second half of the 1960s, won at Le Mans in 1965, contested 60 Grands Prix and won six.

■ The first British sprint championship, in 1970, was won by Patsy Burt. Driving a McLaren powered by a 4.4-litre Oldsmobile V8, she won the first six of the nine qualifying events which she entered. That year she was also first in the British hill climb championship, driving a Formula 2 Cooper.

■ Lotus raced the gas turbine-engined 56B in some 1971 Grands Prix, achieving little with this modified version of a design for the Indianapolis 500 – its best placing was eighth in the Italian GP.

■ In 1971 Goodyear introduced slick – treadless – tyres into GP racing.

■ The fastest World Championship Grand Prix was run at Monza in 1971, when Peter Gethin won the Italian GP in a BRM at 150.671 mph/242.615 kph. That race also saw a famous blanket finish, with 0.18 seconds covering the first four – Gethin, Peterson, Cevert and Hailwood. No other world championship races have been run at over 150 mph, although the 1970 Belgian GP speed was within a whisker, Pedro Rodriguez winning in a BRM at 149.95 mph/241.31 kph. Since then circuit changes have made races slower, usually for safety reasons.

■ The 1971 British Grand Prix was the first world championship race to incorporate the name of a sponsor ('Woolmark') in its title.

■ The Fittipaldi brothers, Emerson and Wilson, started in Gold Leaf Team Lotus cars in the 1971 Argentine GP, the first time brothers had raced together in a Formula 1 team.

■ Two 1971 Formula 2 races were run at Bogota, at 8000 ft/2440 m above sea level the highest circuit ever used for formula events (winners of the races were Siffert and Rollinson).

■ The IMSA GT championship was inaugurated in the USA in 1971. For the next 14 years it was dominated by Porsche cars. In 1984 the overall championship fell to March-Chevrolet, but in 1985 Porsche 962s won 16 of the 17 races in the series, the odd one falling to Jaguar. In the second half of the 1980s this championship attracted larger and more varied entries than World Series races, and it flourished through to 1992, then a well-intended effort to reduce high-cost advanced technology backfired and support fell away, and the series was dominated by one team, Dan Gurney's Toyotas.

■ The speed and distance records set in the 1971 Le Mans 24-hour Race have yet to be equalled, partly because very powerful cars were admitted that year, and partly because circuit modifications to slow speeds came for 1972. Driving a Porsche 917, Helmut Marko and Gijs van Lennep averaged 138.133 mph/ 222.304 kph through the 24 hours, covering 3315.36 miles/5335.13 km. The numerical dominance of Porsche in that race has never been equalled – the German company built 33 of the 49 starters at Le Mans in 1971.

■ The first Williams Grand Prix car appeared in 1972, albeit named 'Politoys' for its principal sponsor. A limited budget meant that it appeared late and ran only twice. Williams cars named Iso started 30 times in 1973–4, then in 1975 Frank Williams' cars were at last run as Williams. They were promising, and that promise was fulfilled in 1979 and the early 1980s (the Constructors' Championship fell to Williams in 1980–1). Frank Williams held out against turbocharging until 1983, when he linked with Honda in a Grand Prix racing partnership that was slow to mature but eventually gave GP victories to Rosberg, Mansell and Piquet, and the Constructors' Championship again in 1986–7. There was a lean year with Judd engines in 1988, but from 1989 Frank Williams developed an alliance with Renault, and his team gained its fifth and sixth Constructors' Championships in 1992–3. Through this period, Williams continued to control the team, despite a crippling road accident in 1986.

■ The first 200 mph/322 kph qualifying lap for a USAC race, was set by Bobby Unser in an Eagle during practice for the 1972 California 500.

■ The first Brazilian Grand Prix ranking as a World Championship event was run at the Interlagos autodrome, although races for Grand Prix cars had been run at Rio de Janeiro and São Paulo in the 1930s.
    Winners of the World Championship races: 1973 (I) Fittipaldi (Lotus); 1974 (I) Fittipaldi (McLaren); 1975 (I) Pace (Brabham); 1976 (I) Lauda (Ferrari); 1977 (I) Reutemann (Ferrari); 1978 (J) Reutemann (Ferrari); 1979 (I) Laffite (Ligier); 1980 (I) Arnoux (Renault); 1981 (J) Reutemann (Williams); 1982 (J) Prost (Renault); 1983 (J) Piquet (Brabham); 1984 (J) Prost (McLaren); 1985 (J) Prost (McLaren); 1986 (J) Piquet (Williams); 1987 (J) Prost (McLaren); 1988 (J) Prost (McLaren); 1989 (J) Mansell (Ferrari); 1990 (I) Prost (Ferrari); 1991 (I) Senna (McLaren); 1992 (I) Mansell (Williams); 1993 (I) Senna (McLaren).
    Circuits: I, Interlagos; J, Jacarepagua (Rio de Janeiro).

■ The Shadow Grand Prix team appeared in 1973, the UOP-backed DN1 cars showing considerable promise. This was sustained through to the second half of the decade – Alan Jones scored the team's only championship win in 104 starts in Austria in 1977. Then as key members of the team left in acrimonious circumstances to form the Arrows team, Shadow's fortunes went into a decline and 1979 was the team's last full season.

■ Adrian Reynard built his first car in 1973, and set up his Reynard company in 1974, when it completed one car; in 1984 it delivered 151 cars and another ten years on its total production had passed 1500. Most had been for third- and second-level classes, and most had been successful; a Grand Prix programme was stillborn, but for 1994 Reynard built its first Indycars – Michael Andretti drove this 941 to a debut race victory at Surfers Paradise, thus extending Reynard's first-race success record, in Formula 3 (1985) and Formula 3000 (1988).

■ First Hesketh F1 car built, following Lord Hesketh's extrovert little team's success with a March driven by James Hunt in 1973. Hunt drove the conventional 308B to victory in the 1974 Silverstone International Trophy, and in the following year won the Dutch GP. In the autumn of that year the original team collapsed, although an element of it remained to run cars for drivers with their own financial backing.

■ Roger Penske, successful racing driver and, towards the end of the 1960s, an entrant (in track and road racing), became a constructor, setting up a base at Poole. First car was the straightforward Cosworth-engined PC1 which made its debut in the 1974 Canadian GP. Two years later John Watson scored the team's only Grand Prix victory, in Austria. At the end of the 1976 season, after contesting 30 Grands Prix, the team concentrated on US racing, where Penske was a leading figure in the formation of CART. In 26 years in USAC/CART Indycar racing, the Penske team scored a record nine victories at Indianapolis, when Emerson Fittipaldi won the 500 in a PC22 in 1993, and it won pole ten times. By 1993 it had also scored a record number of victories (79) in this category and championships (8), some gained with March or McLaren cars but most with Penskes.

■ In a season when several valiant efforts, such as the Amon, the Lyncar and the Token, flitted across the Grand Prix stage, the Maki F101 stood out in 1974, simply because of its Japanese origins. It was in fact a 'Cosworth kit car' using such staple items as the DFV engine and Hewland gearbox and in its only circuit appearances was dismally uncompetitive.

■ Electric car records were set in 1974 over a two-way flying start kilometre and mile at Bonneville by Roger Hedlund in 'Battery Box', at 175.061 mph/281.673 kph.

■ In 1975 the first major race was run on a street circuit at Long Beach, for F5000 cars (won by Brian Redman in a Lola T332). This 'proved' the circuit, created (and dismantled) very quickly with concrete walls, tyre walls, debris catch fencing, etc., and a year later the race was a World Championship event. As such it was run until 1983, when a CART event took its place and title.

Winners of the World Championship Grands Prix of the United States (West): 1976 Regazzoni (Ferrari); 1977 Andretti (Lotus); 1978 Reutemann (Ferrari); 1979 Villeneuve (Ferrari); 1980 Piquet (Brabham); 1981 Jones (Williams); 1982 Lauda (McLaren); 1983 Watson (McLaren).

■ In 1975 Renault introduced a turbocharged version of the V6 engine used in their sports-racing car programme, the Garrett AiResearch turbocharged CHS unit producing around 500 bhp. In the A442 it won its first race, but the Renault team did not win another race until Le Mans in 1978, which was their last sports car event. By that time Renault had introduced the turbocharger to GP racing.

■ The Copersucar appeared, as the first Brazilian GP car, although Richard Divila's design was a 'Cosworth kit car' under its striking skin. The team entered 72 GPs under this name between 1975 and 1979, then its name was changed to Fittipaldi. Despite the work of Emerson Fittipaldi in the later years, it was a forlorn effort and after contesting a total of 104 GPs with little to show but 44 points, it was wound up.

■ Lella Lombardi became the first lady driver to score a world championship point, or more correctly a half point as she was sixth in the 1975 Spanish GP which was stopped prematurely because of an accident. Lombardi contested 12 GPs, but was more successful in small sports cars and touring cars. She died in 1992.

■ The first Ligier Grand Prix car, the Matra-engined JS5, made its debut in the 1976 Brazilian GP. First championship victory came in the 1977 Swedish GP, but the team's most successful seasons were 1979–80 when the JS11 was DFV-powered. A change of name to Talbot-Ligier meant a return to the Matra engine; a reversion to Ligier meant another spell with DFVs; then from 1984 the team used a variety of engines. With Renault turbo units it was fifth in the 1986 Constructors' Championship, then its fortunes slipped and it failed to score at all in 1990–1. Guy Ligier relinquished control and under Cyril de Rouvre the team's performances improved, and in 1993 it was again fifth in the championship.

■ Tyrrell caused a sensation in 1976 with the six-wheeled Project 34 Grand Prix car. Its four 10-in/25-cm front wheels were intended to reduce drag and give improved cornering and braking through the larger tyre 'contact patch'. It won only one race, driven by Scheckter in the 1976 Swedish GP. Partly because tyre development for the small wheels lagged behind that for conventional wheels, this striking car was less competitive in 1977 and was then abandoned. Later March and Williams tested cars with tandem rear wheels; neither was raced (although the March did appear in some hill climbs) and in 1983 cars were restricted to four wheels by the regulations.

■ The name Alfa Romeo returned to Grand Prix racing, as suppliers of sports-unit-based engines to the Brabham team in 1976.

■ Renault brought the turbocharged engine into Grand Prix racing, in the RS01 which made its debut at Silverstone in 1977. The team scored its first points at the end of the next season, and in 1979 was fully competitive with the RS11 – that year a Renault won the French GP. More victories followed – three in each of the next two years, four in 1982 and 1983 – but the championships that were so important to Renault never came. The turbo engine was made available to other teams, and this policy was continued after Renault's own GP team was wound up at the end of 1985. By then it had contested 123 Grands Prix and won 125, amassing 312 Constructors' Championship points.

■ The first Wolf Grand Prix car, WR1 designed by Harvey Postlethwaite, was driven to a debut race victory by Jody Scheckter in Argentina in 1977. Scheckter won two more GPs for Walter Wolf's team, but there were no victories after that year and Wolf

gave up at the end of 1979 when the team's assets were acquired by the Fittipaldi brothers.

■ Lotus introduced 'ground effects' aerodynamics to single-seater racing, in the type 78 of 1977. This utilised the airflow passing under a car, funnelling it through sidepods to venturi to generate downforce. 'Skirts' beneath the outer edges of the sidepods sealed most of the airflow under the car. A refined derivative of the 78, the Lotus 79, dominated the World Championship in 1978 when the black and gold cars won eight GPs.

■ In 1977 A. J. Foyt became the first driver to win the Indianapolis 500 four times.

■ Arrows was the newcomer of the year, with the A1. The team was formed by four ex-Shadow personnel in November 1977, and the A1 was completed in January 1978. In a High Court action in the summer of that year it was shown that the car had more than coincidental similarities to a Shadow design, and it had to be withdrawn.

The Arrows name derived from its founders' names – AR for Italian financier Franco Ambrosio, R for Alan Rees, O for Jackie Oliver, W for engineer Dave Wass and S for designer Tony Southgate. The team's achievements were modest, with just one pole position in its first 15 years (at Long Beach in 1981) and its highest championship placing fourth in 1988. Under Japanese ownership, its name was changed to Footwork in 1991 but in 1994 a return to the Arrows title was announced.

■ Brabham essayed a ground-effects system in which a large fan drew air from beneath the car, which was 'sealed' at the sides with 'skirts'. This BT46 was raced only once, in the Swedish GP in 1978, when Lauda drove it to a clear victory. That result had to stand, as it could not clearly be shown that the car breached the regulations. But these were rewritten and the BT46 was effectively banned.

■ Michelin introduced radial tyres into Grand Prix racing, and the first victory for a car fitted with them fell to Ferrari when Carlos Reutemann won the 1978 Brazilian GP.

■ The first races to count as scoring events in the USAC national championship to be run outside North America were held at Silverstone and Brands Hatch in 1978, being won by A. J. Foyt (Coyote) and Rick Mears (Penske) respectively.

■ Alfa Romeo returned to Grand Prix racing in its own right in 1979 (it continued to supply engines to Brabham, although at the end of the year that team returned to DFV engines). The Alfa Romeo raced was the 177, effectively a development car. In the following year the 179 was introduced for a serious effort. The results were disappointing, and were to be so through succeeding seasons. From 1983 until 1985 the Euroracing team ran the Alfa Romeos in Grands Prix, then Alfa Romeo withdrew its cars from racing, although engine development continued. Alfa Romeo withdrew from Formula 1 racing in 1987 to concentrate on saloon racing.

■ Championship Auto Racing Teams (CART), which had been formed in the previous year, ran its own race series in 1979, in direct opposition to the established USAC championship trail, thus bringing to the boil a conflict that had been simmering in top-flight American racing. There was no immediate victory, but in the following seasons the CART PPG series became dominant, while in the early 1980s the Indianapolis 500 was to become the only USAC-sanctioned Indycar race.

■ First driver to exceed 300 mph/483 kph on British soil was Sammy Miller, in a dragster at Santa Pod in 1979 (his terminal velocity was 307 mph/494 kph).

■ USAC introduced a sudden change in Indycar regulations in 1980, substantially reducing the turbo boost pressure permitted for six-cylinder racing engines. This seemed blatantly aimed at Porsche, developing a six-cylinder turbo unit for this class of racing – this engine, which was being track-tested as the change was announced, was rendered obsolete overnight. Effectively this seemed to rule out the entry of a European-style works team into USAC (and CART) racing, but Lotus did build the 96 for 1985 (financial arrangements fell through and the car never raced). Porsche adapted the 1980 engine for endurance racing, and it was used in the 936 that scored a stunning debut victory at Le Mans in 1981. Porsche built its own Indycar machine in 1987, with a turbocharged V8. In racing, this made no impression and it was abandoned.

■ Stan Barrett claimed to be the first man to exceed the speed of sound on land, driving the Budweiser Rocket tricycle at Rogers Dry Lake (formerly Muroc Dry Lake) in 1980. US Air Force readings showed the device reached Mach 1.0106, or 739.666 mph/1190.12 kph, on its single run. The simple fact that Barrett did not make a second, return, run meant that he could not claim an official speed record.

■ The youngest driver ever to qualify to start in a Grand Prix was New Zealander Mike Thackwell (born 1961), at the 1980 Canadian GP. An accident led to a restart, for which Thackwell had to hand over his car to Tyrrell team-mate Jean-Pierre Jarier, and as the restarted race was run for the full distance Thackwell did not actually *race* so the youngest driver distinction still belongs to another New Zealand driver, Chris Amon.

■ Jean Rondeau became the first man to win the Le Mans 24-hour Race in a car bearing his name, co-driving a Rondeau M379 to victory in 1980 with Jean-Pierre Jassaud. The first Rondeau sports car had been built in 1976. The M379 was the most successful type, some replicas being sold to other entrants. Its sports-racing successors were failures, and in 1984 Rondeau turned to building Reynard Formula Ford cars under licence.

■ The first 24-hour race to be run in Britain was organised in 1980 at Snetterton – the one circuit sufficiently remote from built-up areas to allow night racing (for that reason an earlier '24-hour' race had been split into two parts, as the Brooklands Double Twelve, run 1929–31). The Snetterton saloon event was a modest venture at national level, and as such it was a success.

■ Diesel car records were set at the Nardo track in Italy by the ARVW (Aerodynamic Research Volkswagen), which had a 2.4 litre turbocharged engine. In 1980 it achieved 215.405 mph/330.496 kph for the standing-start mile and averaged 219.89 mph/353.80 kph for an hour from a standing start.

■ Toleman entered Grand Prix racing in 1981 with the TG181, powered by a Hart turbo engine. The team did not qualify to start in its first nine attempts in Formula 1, but in the following seasons the Tolemans became more competitive, Senna placing one second at Monaco (and within an ace of victory) in 1984. For the 1986 season the team was taken over by its principal sponsor, Benetton.

■ McLaren International introduced the MP4/1. Designed by John Barnard, this was to become the outstanding Grand Prix car of the first half of the 1980s, winning 24 races in its first five seasons, driven by Lauda and Prost – who both gained World Championships with it – and Watson. Initially the MP4/1 was powered by Cosworth DFV engines, but it had been laid down in anticipation of the TAG Porsche turbo engine becoming exclusively available to the resurgent McLaren team, and was most successful with this sophisticated engine. Meanwhile, John Watson's victory in the 1981 British Grand Prix was the first for a car with a carbon-fibre monocoque chassis, which went some way to offset misgivings about this 'space-age material', which came into general use (by 1994 McLaren had extended its use to major suspension components).

■ In 1981 Lotus introduced the 'twin-chassis' 88, in which the outer chassis (primarily the bodywork) absorbed aerodynamic loadings, while the inner chassis (comprising monocoque, engine, gearbox and fuel tank) took loadings from the suspension. Through the first half of the season the innovative 88 was the subject of protests and intense study of the regulations by baffled race stewards. Eventually it was ruled out.

■ New turbocharged engines were introduced by BMW, initially exclusively for the Brabham F1 team (and then only usable in racing after many test and development failures, although eventually they were to be successful), and later in 1981 by Alfa Romeo.

■ In 1981 Ralt cars started on a sequence of victories in British F3 racing that was to run unbroken from May until the opening race of the 1985 season, when a Reynard won at Silverstone.

■ The San Marino Grand Prix was first run in 1981 at the superbly equipped Dino Ferrari autodrome near Imola. Initially the Italian Grand Prix was successfully run at this circuit in 1980, and the Imola organisers followed up its success by naming their race after the nearby independent republic in order to avoid the rule that two national Grands Prix should not be held in a season – this was thus deemed not to be a second Italian GP, at least in its title!

Winners of World Championship San Marino GPs: 1981 Piquet (Brabham); 1982 Pironi (Ferrari); 1983 Tambay (Ferrari); 1984 Prost (McLaren); 1985 de Angelis (Lotus); 1986 Prost (McLaren); 1987 Mansell (Williams); 1988 Senna (McLaren); 1989 Senna (McLaren); 1990 Patrese (Williams); 1991 Senna (McLaren); 1992 Mansell (Williams); 1993 Prost (Williams).

■ The Caesar's Palace Grand Prix was run on a sinuous circuit contrived on the car park of a Las Vegas hotel. It was a World Championship event twice, its place then being taken by a CART event. World championship GP winners: 1981 Jones (Williams); 1982 Alboreto (Tyrrell).

■ Bobby Unser took pole for the 1981 Indianapolis 500 in a Penske PC9 at 200.545 mph/322.677 kph – the first over 200 mph. He also won the race, but when the definitive result was posted on the following day had been penalised one lap (for passing cars during a 'hold station' period following accidents) so that Mario Andretti became winner, only for Unser to be reinstated five months later!

■ A. J. Foyt scored his 67th victory in a USAC championship race in the 1981 Pocono 500, a record unequalled in USAC or CART terms.

■ When he won the 1981 Belgian GP, Carlos Reutemann completed an unbroken run of 15 points-scoring finishes in World Championship races, that had started with third place in the 1980 Belgian race. This record-breaking run ended when he retired with gearbox failure in the Monaco GP.

■ World Endurance Championship for Drivers took in a confusing number of races (seven of the scoring events were run in North America) and was open to drivers in a confusing number of categories – the imbalance in both respects being intended to attract US interest in sports-car racing. The winner was American Bob Garretson.

Under changed regulations subsequent champion sports car drivers were: 1982–3 Jacky Ickx (B); 1984 Stefan Bellof (D); 1985 Hans Stuck (D) and Derek Bell (GB); 1986 Derek Bell; 1987 Raul Boesel (BR); 1988 Martin Brundle (GB); 1989 Jean-Louis Schlesser (F); 1990 Jean-Louis Schlesser and Mauro Baldi (I); 1991 Teo Fabi (I); 1992 Derek Warwick (GB) and Yannick Dalmas (F).

■ A driver cooling system devised by Denis Carlson was first used in Trans-Am events, then adopted by Indycar drivers in 1983, by some GP teams in 1984 after Williams drivers had proved its worth in the extremely hot Dallas GP, and by NASCAR drivers in the following year. The system involved a hood with many 'capillary tubes' through which cooling gel was pumped from a refrigerated cartridge. Later vests were developed on the same lines.

■ Seven United States Grands Prix (Detroit) were run on a 2.50-mile/4.02-km street circuit at Detroit.

This was bumpy, very hard on transmissions and ran between walls or guard rails for much of the lap, allowing little margin for driver error.

Winners of the World Championship GPs at Detroit: 1982 Watson (McLaren); 1983 Alboreto (Tyrrell); 1984 Piquet (Brabham); 1985 Rosberg (Williams); 1986 Senna (Lotus); 1987 Senna (Lotus); 1988 Senna (McLaren).

■ McLaren and TAG (Techniques d'Avant Garde, then one of Williams' sponsors) announced their funding of a Porsche-designed Grand Prix engine in 1982. This was to bring to the Porsche name Grand Prix success in an abundance denied the German company in its 1960s ventures.

■ Jaguar's return to major endurance races was foreshadowed when the XJR-5 coupé, built and raced by Group 44, made its debut at Elkhart Lake in 1982.

■ Grand Prix drivers staged a strike in protest against a new 'super-licence' form in 1982. In particular they objected to clauses regarding their contracts with teams which they were expected to sign. This action threatened the South African GP, but in the event final practice sessions and the race took place. There were no similar follow-up activities.

■ Most teams which were members of the Formula 1 Constructors' Association – which meant most Grand Prix teams – decided to boycott the 1982 San Marino GP, in protest against a ban on topping up the tanks for water-cooled brakes after a race. This practice exploited a possible loophole in the minimum weight regulations, especially welcomed by the teams running normally-aspirated engines, for any form of weight reduction helped them remain competitive with the turbo cars. Fourteen cars raced (the smallest GP field since there were 13 starters in the 1969 French and German GPs). Pressure from sponsors helped to ensure that there was no repetition of this incident.

■ The 1982 Monaco GP saw bewildering changes of fortune in its last two laps. Prost led in a Renault, but crashed; Patrese then led, and spun to a standstill just off the racing line on the damp track; Pironi took over the lead in a Ferrari, but coasted to a halt as his engine died because of an electrical fault; de Cesaris then led in an Alfa Romeo, which stopped as it ran out of fuel; Daly might have taken the lead in a Williams, but a little earlier he had smashed the gearbox casing and as the oil ran out it ceased to function. Meanwhile Patrese's Brabham had been pushed to a place of safety by a marshal, and that happened to get it into a position where it could run downhill; Patrese let it roll, the engine fired, he completed the lap . . . to win.

■ At Indianapolis the Wildcat-Cosworth driven by Gordon Johncock and the Penske-Cosworth driven by Rick Mears were side by side at the end of the 500. Johncock won by 16-hundredths of a second. This 1982 '500' was the first to have a purse exceeding $2m.

■ Jacky Ickx won the Le Mans 24-hour Race for the sixth time. His co-driver Derek Bell scored his third Le Mans victory in that 1982 race. Bell went on to score two more victories, in 1986–7 with Holbert and Stuck. Other multiple winners at Le Mans have been Gendebien and Pescarolo with four wins each.

■ The pit stop was reintroduced to Grand Prix racing as a strategy (rather than as a response to a mishap or mechanical failure) by Brabham in 1982. The advantages to be gained by running half a race on half a tank of fuel and relatively soft tyres, with a stop to refuel and change wheels, were such that other teams had to follow the example. Refuelling was to be banned in 1984, but reintroduced in 1994 despite misgivings among teams. Wheel-change stops remained a feature of GP racing; in the better-drilled stops during 1985 cars were at a standstill for less than 10 seconds while all wheels were changed and by the early 1990s this time had been halved.

■ Grand Prix cars were subject to a 'flat-bottom' rule, and most pundits agreed that sense prevailed as the ground-effects era ended. By 1985 flat bottoms were required in all international single-seater categories. However, Indycar regulations for 1984–7 allowed for side-pod ground effects, albeit with ground clearance stipulated.

■ Honda returned to GP racing, supplying the turbocharged RA 163-E for the Spirit team's solitary car – an arrangement whereby the V6 was race-tested in a conversion of a Formula 2 car in preparation for a full season with Williams in 1984 (when the Spirit team had to use Hart or Cosworth engines).

■ Team Lotus raced a Grand Prix car within five weeks of the decision to start design work. Early in the 1983 season it became only too obvious that the 93T was uncompetitive, so JPS Lotus' team manager determined to lay down a successor rather than spend further development time on it. The 94T was designed by Gerard Ducourage, two were built and performed well in their first race, the British GP.

■ The 128 dragsters in the Super Gas field at the US Nationals at Indy Raceway Park in 1983 were covered by 0.068 seconds after qualifying.

■ Richard Noble broke the 21-year US stranglehold on the Land Speed Record, when he reached 633.46 mph/1019.237 kph in Thrust 2 at the hitherto-unused Black Rock desert venue in the USA in 1983.

■ The first United States Grand Prix (Dallas) was run on a contrived 2.424-mile/3.901-km circuit which fell far short of the standards which should have been stipulated – even the requirement that an international race be run to 'prove' a circuit before a Grand Prix could be sanctioned was overlooked . . . However, the financial requirements were met. At the first meeting the track surface broke up, but the race was run. Winner was Keke Rosberg in a Williams.

■ The 1984 Austrian GP was an 'all-turbo' race, as the two cars with normally aspirated engines which practised did not qualify to start. The first race with an all-turbo entry was the 1985 Dutch Grand Prix.

■ The 1984 fuel allowance of 220 litres/48.4 imp. gallons for a Grand Prix led to the spectacle of 'economy runs' and to side effects, ranging from pre-chilling of fuel (which contracts as its temperature falls) to turbo engines burning pistons as mixtures were too lean.

■ McLaren won 12 Grands Prix in 1984, handsomely surpassing the previous best score of eight victories set by Lotus in 1978. Ferrari, Lotus and Tyrrell had earlier scored seven victories in single seasons. In 1988 McLaren was to win 15 Grands Prix. Ten victories in a season have been recorded by McLaren (1989) and Williams (1992–3).

■ The nine points which Niki Lauda scored in the 1984 South African Grand Prix in April lifted his overall points score above 400. At that time only two other drivers, Stewart and Reutemann, had ever scored more than 300 points in their careers. Lauda's total score of 420½ points in 11 seasons was to be overshadowed by Alain Prost and Ayrton Senna in the next ten years.

■ March enjoyed an astonishing numerical superiority at Indianapolis in 1984: 30 of the 33 cars which qualified for the start were built by March, 27 84Cs and three 83Cs. Moreover, every one of the 14 cars which finished in the 500 was a March – 13 84Cs and an 83C. The slowest qualifying speed had been 201.217 mph/323.758 kph, the fastest was 210.029 mph/

Touring car – saloon – racing reached one of its peaks in 1984, when Jaguar, BMW and Volvo were leading marques, top at Brno. The British 2-litre regulations of the 1990s did not allow high-cost development and *were widely adopted in Europe and beyond. Ten manufacturers contested the 1994 British series; above Alfa Romeo heads Ford, Vauxhall and BMW at Thruxton.*

337.937 kph, and the race was won by Rick Mears in a Cosworth-engined 84C at a record speed of 163.612 mph/263.252 kph.

■ Six weeks before the first race of the 1984 endurance championship the regulations were changed, the promulgated 15 per cent cut in the fuel allowance being abandoned as FISA endeavoured to bring the World Championship into line with the flourishing American IMSA series. One outcome was that Porsche withdrew its works team from Le Mans, where it had contested the 24-hour race every year since 1951 (except 1975). An independent Porsche won at Le Mans (heading six others), and a month later the governing body decided that the fuel allowance cut would be implemented in 1985.

■ A new 2.982-mile/4.54-km Nürburgring circuit was opened in the summer of 1984 and was the venue for the European GP in the autumn. Replacing the old 'Ring, it had a succession of constant-radius corners – safe but utterly bland.

■ The last international championship Formula 2 race was run at Brands Hatch, won by Philippe Streiff in an AGS. Between 1967 and 1984, 209 F2 championship races were run. The most successful chassis constructor was March (78 victories), followed by Ralt (22) and Brabham (18), while BMW engines powered 95 race-winning cars. Jochen Rindt won most races (12), closely followed by Bruno Giacomelli (11), Mike Thackwell and Jacques Laffite (8 each); Thackwell scored the highest number of points (164 in four seasons), followed by Brian Henton (126) and Patrick Depailler (119). Local F2 series continued until 1986 in Japan and in South America.

■ In 1985 Renault Sport developed a version of the EF15 GP engine with a pneumatic valve operation system, in which springs were replaced by pistons operated by compressed air. This obviated the age-old problem of 'valve-bounce', and raised the effective rev. limit of the engine by around 1500 rpm to 13 000 rpm. Renault also developed a substitute for the traditional distributor, comprising a low-tension electrical system distributed to cylinders by computer.

■ Formula 3000 was introduced in 1985 to take the place of Formula 2 and the European Formula 3 championship. Regulations stipulated normally aspirated 3-litre engines with an approved electronic rev. limiter which imposed a 9000 rpm rev. limit. Together with restrictions on tyres and other regulations, this was intended to contain car performances

at a level roughly midway between Formula 3 and Formula 1. Grids were modest in the international (i.e. European) series in 1985, but usually full after that, although the championship programmes were often uneven. From 1987 a Japanese series was successful, but a hoped-for South American 'mini-series' did not materialise. High costs meant that a British national series for obsolescent F3000 cars (known as Formula 2 from 1991) attracted small fields. Throughout, British constructors Lola and Reynard supplied most of the cars for all F3000 series.

■ Bill Elliot won the 1985 Winston 500 NASCAR Grand National race at Talladega (Alabama) at 186.288 mph/299.801 kph in a Ford Thunderbird. This was the fastest 500-mile race ever run.

■ The 1985 Australian GP winner Keke Rosberg made three pit stops, all for tyre changes. This had not happened in the modern era of championship racing, and had seldom occurred throughout the years of the 2.5-litre formula (although the winning Vanwall shared by Brooks and Moss in the 1957 British GP did stop three times), but the tactical advantages to be gained with quick tyre-change stops meant these became quite acceptable by the 1990s – for example, Senna stopped four times during his victorious drive in the 1993 European GP at Donington Park.

■ A second international championship was introduced into the endurance series in 1985, for Group C2 cars (700 kg/1540 lb minimum weight), which had been inaugurated two years earlier as a Junior class to fill grids. The first C2 championship fell to Spice Engineering's Tiga GC85 and its drivers Gordon Spice and Ray Bellm. Ecurie Ecosse won the title in 1986 with their MG Metro 6R4-engined car, Ray Mallock and Marc Duez driving it to clinch the championship at Fuji.

■ The first Malaysian race to be an international championship event was the Selangor 800 at Shah Alam, final race in the 1985 World Endurance Championship, won by Mass and Ickx in a works Porsche 962C from a Jaguar XJR-6.

■ Christian Danner became the first German driver to win an international single-seater championship since World War II when he clinched the 1985 European F3000 title in the final race of the series at Donington Park.

■ The Estonian constructor TARK completed its 1000th racing car in 1985, an Estonia 20M for the East

European 1.3-litre Formula Vostok. The first Estonia, an F3 car on Cooper lines, was built in 1958, and succeeding models followed West European patterns, although through to the second half of the 1980s all were space-frame designs. At the end of the decade an up-to-the-minute F3 TARK appeared, with a carbon-fibre monocoque made in Germany by Eufra, but lack of power from its VW-based engine meant it made little impression.

■ Van Diemen became the first constructor to complete 1000 cars for a single road-racing category, Formula Ford. Ralph Firman had formed Van Diemen in 1973, and through the next ten years his F Ford cars were consistently successful, a lapse in 1983 being followed by a rapid recovery.

■ Robert Barber reached 145.60 mph/234.33 kph in the steam-powered 'Steamin' Demon' at Bonneville in 1985.

■ Benetton was an active sponsor in Formula 1 from 1983, and after it took over Toleman the team was renamed . . . Benetton. Its cars were often in the forefront, there was a GP victory (in the 1986 Mexican GP) in its first season and at least one a year 1989–93. In the early 1990s it was the only team to break into the McLaren and Williams success runs, it was Ford's 'preferred team' and dedicated to a high-technology approach, yet the real breakthrough did not come until 1994.

■ The closest-ever Grand Prix finish came at the end of the revived Spanish event at Jerez in 1986, when Ayrton Senna in a Lotus won from Nigel Mansell in a Williams by an official 0.014 seconds, or 36.6 in/93 cm.

■ Brazilian 'government officials' attempted to hold the organisers of the 1986 GP to ransom, demanding extra free tickets, but achieved no more than delays to the first day's practice.

■ The 1986 Italian Grand Prix was started with neither of the fastest drivers in qualifying at the front of

Porsche ruled sports-car racing for much of the 1980s, with cars such as the Le Mans-winning 956 in 1982 (below). Mazda gained the victory several Japanese constructors had sought when its 787B won the Le Mans 24-hour Race in 1991 (opposite top). Peugeot took the championship in its final season, 1992, and Le Mans victories with the 905 in 1992 and 1993 (opposite bottom).

the grid. Teo Fabi (Benetton), who should have been on pole, started from the back after his engine 'died' before the parade lap, while Alain Prost abandoned his McLaren as its engine refused to fire and started in the spare car after the rest.

■ In 1986 the American Racing Series ('Mini-Indy') was launched under an SCCA sanction to fill the wide gap between F Ford and CART racing, with a ten-race series run as supporting events at CART oval-, road- and street-circuit meetings. In many respects this category was a parallel to the European F3000, but ARS was inaugurated as a one-model series, March building 25 86A cars for it. Derived from the F3000 85B, the 86A was powered by a Buick 4.2-litre V8, and was known as a Wildcat for US promotional purposes. It became the Indy Lights Championship in 1991, the Lola T93s were specified, still with Buick engines, and for 1994 there was a cumbersome new title: 'PPG-Firestone Indy Light Championship Powered by Buick'. There were 12 events in this Indycar Official Development Series, each around 75 miles/120 km. The Lola T93/20 was based on the F3000 design, and the specification frozen for three years; the V6 was rated at 425 bhp, and these engines were owned and maintained by ARS, sealed and leased to entrants.

■ In 1986 Rick Mears set a closed-circuit record at 233.934 mph/376.399 kph in a Penske Racing March 86C at the Michigan International Speedway, thus breaking Mark Donohue's 1975 record of 221.160 mph/355.846 kph set in a Porsche 917-30K at Talladega Speedway. These were both specially set-up attempts, but in 1993 Mario Andretti qualified at Michigan at 234.276 mph/377.030 kph.

■ The last-ever Formula 2 race was the final event in the All-Japan championship, run at Suzuka in 1986 and won by Kazuyoshi Hishino in a March-Honda.

■ The first street-circuit meeting on the British mainland in 1986 had the Halfords Birmingham Super Prix as its principal race, unhappily ruined by a downpour. It was won by Luis Sala, in an F3000 Ralt Cosworth.

■ Jaguar won its first victory in a world sports car championship race since 1957, when Derek Warwick and Eddie Cheever drove a factory-backed XJR-6 (built and run by Tom Walkinshaw Racing) to win the 1986 Silverstone 1000-km race at 129.08 mph/207.69 kph.

■ Lotus was the first team to race Grand Prix cars

with 'active suspension', and the first to win with it, when Ayrton Senna drove a 99T to victory in the 1987 Brazilian GP. After that season Lotus turned back to 'passive' suspension, but as Williams developed a reliable 'active' system for 1992, most other teams had to follow. The great advantages were in reducing the aerodynamic variations that came with changes in the ride height of cars with conventional suspension – the objective of the first Lotus experiments in 1983 – in consistency of weight distribution and maintaining an optimum tyre 'contact patch'.

■ Honda exhibited a V10 racing engine at the 1987 Tokyo Motor Show, refined versions were tested in McLaren chassis in the following year, and the Japanese V10 was developed to raceworthiness for the 1989 Grand Prix season. That year Renault also introduced a V10, which was used by the Williams team.

■ The Suzuka circuit was first used for a Japanese GP in 1987. Its basic figure of 8 configuration is unique in Grand Prix racing, with the sinuous outward leg passing under the principal straight. Built as a Honda test track, it has been developed as part of a leisure complex. There are physically testing changes of direction and elevation in its 3.644-mile/5.864-km lap.

■ The 1987 Indianapolis 500 saw the fifth successive victory for a March car. March had first appeared in the 500 in 1982 (best placing third), then came five victories, a second place in 1988, and the last top ten place (eighth) in the 1989 500.

■ Porsche scored its 12th victory in the Le Mans 24-hour Race in 1987, that win being the last of an unbroken run of seven, with the greatest triumph for the German marque coming in 1983, when Porsches filled the first eight places. Ferrari won the race nine times between 1949 and 1965, Jaguar had seven wins (the first in 1951, the latest in 1990), while Alfa Romeo and Ford each won the 24-hour race four times.

■ McLaren won 15 of the 16 Grands Prix in the 1988 World Championship series, an achievement without parallel in the history of the Constructors' Championship.

■ Bobby Allison won the 1988 Daytona 500 by two car lengths from his son Davey. Father drove a Buick, and his winning speed was 137.531 mph/221.334 kph; Davey drove a Ford. Later in the year, 51-year-old Bobby was seriously injured in another NASCAR race, at Pocono.

■ Ferrari introduced an electro-hydraulic semi-automatic transmission system on the 640 Grand Prix car in 1989. A clutch pedal was needed only at the start, thereafter gear changes were made with finger-tip levers on the steering wheel, clutch and gearbox being electrically actuated. Nigel Mansell drove a 640 to a debut win, in the Brazilian GP, but a period of teething troubles followed.

■ A Lamborghini V12 Grand Prix engine was introduced for 1989, when it was used by the Larrousse Lola team. Designed by one-time Ferrari technical supremo Mauro Forghieri, it was not notably successful in racing.

■ A long-running feud between top drivers Alain Prost and Ayrton Senna came to a head in the 1989 Japanese Grand Prix when they tangled as Senna attempted to pass his McLaren team-mate Prost. The Frenchman retired on the spot, Senna restarted but was later excluded. In the same race in 1990 they collided at the first corner, but at least they were driving for different teams in that race.

■ Ferrari and Williams experimented with traction control on their 1990 GP cars, and this was soon to be widely applied, primarily to eliminate wheelspin at the race start and in cornering. Wheel speeds were computer-monitored and when a tyre started to lose adhesion (or spin) as the rear wheels momentarily turned faster than the front wheels the engine was electronically cut for an instant – hence a car could sound distinctly unhealthy.

■ Ferrari became the first team to score 100 World Championship victories when Alain Prost won the 1990 French Grand Prix.

■ Mario Andretti, his sons Michael and Jeff and his nephew John all competed in an Indycar race at Milwaukee in 1990 (Mike was 5th, John 7th, Jeff 17th, Mario 21st). In 1991 they were the first four family members to start in the Indianapolis 500 (Michael 2nd, John 5th, Mario 7th, Jeff 15th). Michael and Mario were first and second in a 1992 race at Laguna Seca, their first as Indycar team-mates (but the fifth time they had taken first and second places in races).

■ In 1991 Max Mosley successfully challenged Jean-Marie Balestre for the Presidency of FISA. The autocratic Frenchman had a reputation for sometimes being arrogant, and given to whims or chauvinism; the younger Englishman had a background as a lawyer, racing driver and co-founder of March. His application of his talents to preparing motor sport for the 21st century, for example to containing costs and forwarding the commercial aspects that had become its life blood, did not meet with universal approval. In 1993 FISA ceased to exist, and Mosley became president of the Fédération Internationale de l'Automobile.

■ For many years the little Magny-Cours circuit near Nevers was best known for the Martini-Winfield racing school. Then with the not-inconsiderable patronage of politicians with local connections, François Mitterrand and his then-finance minister Pierre Beregovoy, it was developed as a generously equipped and bland venue for the French Grand Prix, run there from 1991.

■ The little Minardi Grand Prix team seemed to pull off a major coup when it obtained Ferrari engines for 1991. But like other Italian outfits, from the Castelotti Cooper T51s in 1960 to Scuderia Italia in 1992, it found that Ferrari engines did not constitute passports to racing success.

■ The 1991 Australian Grand Prix was the shortest World Championship race, stopped after 14 of the scheduled 81 laps (and less than 25 minutes' racing) in torrential rain at Adelaide. Half points were awarded to the six leading drivers.

■ Goodyear provided the tyres for a Grand Prix winner for the 250th time, on Ayrton Senna's McLaren MP4/6 in the 1991 Brazilian GP. The tyre company's first GP win had been the 1965 Mexican GP (Ginther's Honda RA272) and in the 1970s it became the principal supplier, sometimes the only tyre company involved in Formula 1 racing.

■ The Jaguarsport Intercontinental Challenge comprised short races for XJR-15 coupés at three GP meetings in 1991. At the end of the first two races, the owner of the winning car received an XJR-6; the only prize at the last was $1 million for the winner, which the owner split with driver Armin Hahne – for a 28-minute drive at Spa.

■ Al Teague set a new speed record for wheel-driven cars at Bonneville in 1991, achieving 409.986 mph/ 659.790 kph over the flying mile in 'Spirit of 76'.

■ Ferrari contested its 500th World Championship race in Hungary in 1992, but as one race had been the 1952 Indianapolis 500, the score was reached in Grand Prix terms at the Belgian GP.

■ Safety cars were introduced into Grand Prix racing in 1992; already familiar in other categories, a safety car is an alternative to stopping a race after a serious incident, as the race field circulates behind it until the track is cleared.

■ McLaren introduced an electronic throttle on its 1992 MP4/7, and this 'fly-by-wire' system was soon adopted by other leading teams, as part of a movement towards electronic sophistication that the sport's governing body was to rein back in 1994 together with other restrictions.

■ In 1992 Nigel Mansell won a record nine World Championship races, including five in succession; Senna won eight in 1988 (and seven in 1991), while Clark won seven in 1963 and Prost equalled that score in 1984, 1988 and 1993.

■ The once-powerful Brabham team faded away in 1992, victim of cash starvation. Its 399th and last Grand Prix came in Hungary, when Damon Hill finished 11th, and last.

■ The French anti-smoking lobby seemingly triumphed when a regional court 'fined' Williams and Renault a total of £4.2 million because their cars carrying cigarette advertising were shown on French TV in 1992. Somehow, that fine was not enforced. On the other hand, in 1993 the Larrousse team obtained a £3.5 million government grant to compensate it for sponsorship 'lost' as a result of anti-tobacco legislation.

■ In 1992 Al Unser Jr became the third member of the Unser family to win the Indianapolis 500, in the wheel tracks of father Al and uncle Bobby.

■ The significance of the Swiss Sauber team's arrival in Formula 1 in 1993 was not so much in its race placings – although sixth place in the Constructors' Championship was no mean achievement – but in the 'Concept by Mercedes-Benz' message on the engine covers of its C12s (components such as active suspension and ABS were developed by the German company). Its 1994 C13 was designated Sauber-Mercedes, for although the engine was still an Ilmor V10, Mercedes had acquired an interest in that British engine specialist. Sauber also had the first lady team manager in Formula 1, Carmen Ziegler.

■ ABS (anti-lock) braking came into use on GP cars in 1993, the principal objective being optimum braking on each wheel, rather than to prevent wheels locking, as with the ABS systems on road cars.

■ Benetton ran its B193B with four-wheel steering at the end of the 1993 season, albeit with very limited movement of the rear wheels.

■ Ferrari accepted Honda assistance in 1993 with its Formula 1 engine programme – a situation that would have been unthinkable in Enzo Ferrari's days, and was short-lived.

■ Riccardo Patrese started in his 250th World Championship race, in the 1993 German GP. His first was the 1977 Monaco GP. In a distinguished career he drove for six F1 teams and won six Grands Prix.

■ A Honda Indycar engine ran its track tests in the USA in the spring of 1993, and later that year Honda F1 'development cars' were tested in Japan.

■ Alain Prost was the first driver to score 500 World Championship points, the first to 600 and to 700 (in South Africa in 1993). At the end of 1993 Prost had started in 200 Grands Prix (only technically in the 1991 San Marino GP, when he slithered off on the wet parade lap), and scored 798½ points, while his great rival Senna had recorded 614.

■ Nigel Mansell was the first driver in Indycar history to take pole for his first race, and then win the event, at Surfer's Paradise in Australia in 1993. He went on to become the first 'rookie' to win the PPG Indycar title.

■ Mario Andretti became the oldest driver to win an Indycar race, 53 when he won at Phoenix in 1993. Later in the season he set a closed-circuit qualifying record at the Michigan Speedway, at 234.276 mph/377.030 kph.

■ Damon Hill was the first second-generation driver to win a World Championship Grand Prix, seeing the chequered flag first at the end of the 1993 Hungarian GP (his father, Graham, won 14 GPs).

■ All the drivers who scored points in the 1993 European Formula 3000 Championship drove Reynard cars.

■ When he retired at the end of the 1993 Grand Prix season, Alain Prost had won 51 World Championship races, ten more than Ayrton Senna. He had also recorded most fastest race laps (41), but achieved only 33 pole positions – the same as Jim Clark, and well behind Senna's 62.

■ In 1993 Ford scored its 200th victory in British Touring Car Championship races – 146 more than its nearest rival, Chevrolet.

■ Sentul circuit in Indonesia staged its first international race, a saloon-car event dominated by quasi-works BMWs.

■ Late in 1993 work started on the first permanent race circuit in China, at Zhu Hai near Hong Kong. This was to be completed to Grand Prix standards in 1994.

Three teams and three drivers dominated Grand Prix racing in the early 1990s, as high technology reached a zenith, before devices such as traction control were banned for 1994. Ayrton Senna scored most of his 41 Championship victories driving for McLaren (below left), here a Honda-powered MP4/7 in 1992, carrying the number 1 as he was reigning Champion. Nigel Mansell (below right) took the title in 1992, driving Frank Williams' advanced cars, before he turned to Indycar racing and won that title in 1993. Michael Schumacher won Grands Prix for Benetton from 1992. (Bottom) Schumacher driving a 1993 Ford-engined B193B.

RALLIES

■ Arguably the first competition to take place on public roads between mechanically propelled vehicles was an event held in Wisconsin, USA in July 1878. It received six entries from various steam-propelled vehicles but eventually only two took the start. In the course of the event they had to tackle special tests which comprised for the most part ploughing and weight hauling. The winners were Messrs Shomer and Farrand at the helm of an Oshkosh locomotive which averaged 6 mph/9.7 kph and took just over 33 hours to reach the finish in Madison and collect the $5000 first prize.

■ In November 1895 an event took place in the USA which modelled itself on the original Paris–Rouen. This was largely due to the reports of that event in the *New York Herald* from an intrepid young reporter who had followed part of it on a bicycle. The American event was sponsored by the *Chicago Times-Herald* and ran over a 94-mile/151-km course between Chicago and Waukegan. Like its European predecessor, it received over 100 entrants but on the start day, 2 November, only two turned up. The Duryea broke down and the Benz driven by Muller won the reduced first prize of $500 for finishing. The event was rescheduled for 28 November when six cars, four petrol and two electric, turned up. Because of snow, the route was shortened to 54 miles/87 km and the only two cars to get through to Evanston were Frank Duryea and the aforementioned Mr Muller. Duryea had covered the distance in 8 h 23 min to average 7 mph/11.3 kph. Perhaps the most remarkable aspect of his win was that he was serviced by his brother Charles who used a horse-drawn sleigh, surely the first example of a factory service car in rallying.

■ In 1897 the journal *The Engineer* organised a trial for motor vehicles to be held on 27–8 May. It had 70 entrants but on the day only six appeared to tackle the 200 miles/320 km and diverse tests. Regrettably, the judges saw fit to stop the contest in mid-song since none of the vehicles seemed to fulfil the conditions specified in the regulations.

■ The first Tour de France Automobile was held between 16 and 24 July 1899, in seven daily stages amounting to 1350 miles/2172 km. It saw the first appearance of the *parc fermé* that is so well known in modern rallying. Each night, the cars were put in a park where the driver had one hour to service his vehicle before withdrawing. He had another hour in the morning before the restart. Anyone arriving at the restart after they were due to leave – a common occurrence – was given 2 hours to work on his car. The event was won by the Chevalier René de Knyff in a 16-hp Panhard. His average speed for the whole event was just over 30 mph/48 kph.

■ The first 1000-Miles Trial was held in Britain in 1900. This precursor of the RAC Rally was organised by the Automobile Club of Great Britain and started from Hyde Park Corner in London on 23 April. It lasted 11 days and was tough enough with its special sections and a speed test on a private road to reduce the 65 starters to 23 at the finish. Best of these was the Hon. C. S. Rolls driving a Panhard, but the British team of Daimlers won the team prize. The event was perhaps a little too fast for public acceptance and lower average speeds were later set.

■ The Automobile Club of America held a trial from New York to Buffalo in 1901, which was distinguished because it had to be stopped when the news broke that President McKinley had been assassinated. Some 42 of the 80 starters were still running at Rochester when proceedings were halted.

■ The most successful of all the inter-city races of the early era, which were to be reincarnated as rallies in the 1930s, was the 1902 Paris–Vienna. It was won by

Marcel Renault in his 16-hp Renault. Because of problems encountered with recce-ing and practising of the route on the cancelled Nice–Abbazia race in April of the same year, recce-ing was forbidden on the Paris–Vienna to make the route authorisations easier to obtain.

■ The Scottish Automobile Club held its first trial in 1902, from Glasgow to London with a night halt in York. It attracted five entries and the winners were Stocks/Talbot-Crosbie in a De Dion.

■ The second 1000-Miles Trial was held in Britain in 1903. Centred on the Crystal Palace in South London, it comprised eight daily loops and the principal requirement was that the cars should not at any time stop during the day's run. A hundred of the starters failed to do that: only four managed to comply.

■ The first recorded motoring event to take place in India was organised by the Motor Union of West India to coincide with the 1904 Christmas holidays. It started from Delhi and finished in Bombay but was more of a treasure hunt than a serious motoring event. It was not for some 64 years that India was to see a major international rally, the 1968 London–Sydney, and another ten after that before creating its own very tough Himalayan Rally.

■ The first Herkomer Trophy was held in southern Germany in 1905 and was organised by the portrait

Early events that are recalled as races had some features that now seem to belong to rallies. This is René de Knyff's Panhard at a control during the 1903 Gordon Bennett race.

painter Sir Hubert von Herkomer, whose second love was the motor-car. The event started and finished in Munich and visited Baden-Baden, Regensburg and Nuremberg, lasting well over a week. Competitors had to keep to set average speeds which varied over the sections and there were numerous time controls. In those respects it resembled a modern rally. Despite its confusing calculations, it proved socially and internationally popular and a second event was held in 1906 in which there was a Royal participant, Prince Heinrich of Prussia, driving a 40-hp Benz. He liked the driving but he did not like the regulations or the wild cheating that went on. The event died on its feet when it was held for the final time in 1907 as a purely German event with no overseas entries.

■ Prince Heinrich lent his name and authority to the first Prinz Heinrich Fahrt and insisted that observers be carried in the cars to prevent rules going unobserved. The 1908 event was successful and attracted 130 starters who covered a route between Berlin and Frankfurt in just over a week. It was dominated by factory entries and won by Fritz Erle in a works 50-hp Benz.

■ In the year that the third Prinz Heinrich Fahrt was won by a chap called Ferdinand Porsche driving a Daimler, the Austrian Automobile Club organised its first International Alpenfahrt where much emphasis was placed on ascent of various passes. There was no outright winner in 1910 but cups were given for good performances. By 1912 it had expanded considerably and took seven days instead of the original three. Rolls-Royce entered and was defeated by the severity of the Austrian roads. They returned in 1913 and one of its team finished unpenalised in what was an unremarkable event. But in the 1914 Alpenfahrt, James Radley returned with a specially prepared Rolls-Royce and he had the distinction of gaining one of the 16 cups awarded for finishing with no penalties. World War I intervened or this purely Austrian event might have gone from strength to strength judging by its success in 1914. In 1926 it reappeared as a jointly organised rally that later spawned the largely French Alpine Rally. The revival of the Austrian Alpenfahrt as a rally came after World War II. For a time it was in the European Rally Championship and came to be one of the rallies in the first year of the World Rally Championship. But that 1973 event was marred by controversy and protest over a road blocked by the Alpine Renault team manager. The rally was not held in 1974 because of these problems, plus a fuel 'crisis', and has not been held since.

■ To publicise Monte Carlo out of season in January, Antony Noghès proposed that the Société des Bains et Mer de Monaco should sponsor an automobile event starting from all the winter-bound capitals of Europe and converging on the Principality. The first Monte Carlo Rally in 1911 was a great success. The early Monte Carlo rallies had relatively undemanding road sections from the starting town to Monaco, where final points were gained for Concours d'Élégance. But the winter weather encountered was often severe enough to eliminate even the better crews. In 1928, only 24 of the 65 starters were classified. In its heyday in the early 1950s, over 300 would start and there would be 250–70 at the finish. But even then, bad weather could play havoc, as it did in 1965 when only 22 finished from 237.

Interrupted by World War I, the Monte started again in 1924 and ran without break until World War II. It did evolve in those years, mainly in the field of formulae to try and equalise the different routes and the different cars. Some people built special cars to try and win, and there were always the eccentrics with cars on skis.

The main thing is that the Monte preserved its reputation and its multi-start format to spring anew in 1949 to lead the postwar European love affair with cars and rallying. The formulae were still around which gave Maurice Martin his win in 1961 with a Panhard, ahead of two similar cars – the only winner of whom almost no one had a photograph. In 1956 a common route was instigated between, on this occasion, Paris and Monaco, while in 1960 this was much shortened (Chambery–Monaco) and a final mountain circuit held in the hills behind Monaco for the 90 best classified cars. That has dropped to 60 but is still held today. In the same year special stages were introduced, but still formulae were applied and it was not until 1964 that they disappeared for good.

But in 1966 the FIA introduced new technical regulations for Group 1 cars and the Monte was the first event. The Minis, Ford Cortinas and Imps were excluded for allegedly contravening the lighting regulations and the Monte led the way again – this time in scandal. It says something for the strength of the event that it has survived this, a petrol crisis in 1974 and the attempts of FISA to stop it in 1985.

The most successful drivers on the Monte are Sandro Munari with wins in 1972 (Lancia Fulvia), 1975–7 (Lancia Stratos) and Walter Röhrl 1980 (Fiat

Abarth), 1982 (Opel Ascona), 1983 (Lancia 037) and 1984 (Audi Quattro). Röhrl must be considered to have the edge as he has won it in four very dissimilar cars.

MONTE CARLO RALLY OVERALL WINNERS

Year	Crew	Car
1911	Rougier	Turcat-Méry 25 hp
1912	Beutler	Berliet 16 hp
1924	Ledure	Bignan 2 litre
1925	Repusseau	Renault 40 hp
1926	Hon V. Bruce/Brunell	A.C. 3lx
1927	Lefèvre/Despeaux	Amilcar 1098 cc
1928	Bignan	Fiat 509A 990 cc
1929	Dr Van Eijk	Graham-Paige 4.7 litre
1930	Petit	La Licorne 905 cc
1931	Healey	Invicta 4.5 litre
1932	Vasselle	Hotchkiss AM 2.5 litre
1933	Vasselle	Hotchkiss 620 3.5 litre
1934	Gas/Trevoux	Hotchkiss 620 3.5 litre
1935	Lahaye/Quatresous	Renault Nervasport
1936	Zamfirescu/Cristea	Ford V8 3.6 litre
1937	Le Begue/Quinlin	Delahaye 135 3.5 litre
1938	Bakker Schut/Karel Ton	Ford V8 3.6 litre
1939	Trevoux/Lesurque	Hotchkiss 686 3.5 litre
	Paul/Contet	Delahaye 135 3.5 litre
1949	Trevoux/Lesurque	Hotchkiss 686 3.5 litre
1950	Becquart/Secret	Hotchkiss 686 3.5 litre
1951	Trevoux/Crovetto	Delahaye 175 4.5 litre
1952	Allard/Warburton	Allard P 4.3 litre
1953	Gatsonides/Worledge	Ford Zephyr 2.3 litre
1954	Chiron/Basadonna	Lancia Aurelia GT
1955	Malling/Fadum	Sunbeam MkIII 2.3 litre
1956	Adams/Bigger	Jaguar MkVII 3.4 litre
1957	No rally due to the Suez crisis	
1958	Monraisse/Feret	Renault Dauphine
1959	Coltelloni/Alexandre	Citroën ID 19
1960	Schock/Möll	Mercedes-Benz 220 SE
1961	Martin/Bateau	Panhard PL 17
1962	Carlsson/Haggbom	Saab 96
1963	Carlsson/Palm	Saab 96
1964	Hopkirk/Liddon	Cooper S 1071 cc

Year	Crew	Car
1965	Makinen/Easter	Cooper S 1275 cc
1966	Toivonen/Mikander	Citroën DS 21
1967	Aaltonen/Liddon	Cooper S 1275 cc
1968	Elford/Stone	Porsche 911 T
1969	Waldegaard/Helmer	Porsche 911
1970	Waldegaard/Helmer	Porsche 911 S
1971	Andersson/Stone	Alpine Renault 110
1972	Munari/Manucci	Lancia Fulvia 1600 cc
1973	Andruet/'Biche'	Alpine Renault 110
1974	No rally thanks to 'petrol crisis'	
1975	Munari/Sodano	Lancia Stratos
1976	Munari/Maiga	Lancia Stratos
1977	Munari/Maiga	Lancia Stratos
1978	Nicolas/Laverne	Porsche Carrera 3 litre
1979	Darniche/Mahe	Lancia Stratos
1980	Röhrl/Geistdorfer	Fiat Abarth 131
1981	Ragnotti/Andrie	Renault 5 Turbo
1982	Röhrl/Geistdorfer	Opel Ascona 400
1983	Röhrl/Geistdorfer	Lancia Rallye 037
1984	Röhrl/Geistdorfer	Audi Quattro
1985	Vatanen/Harryman	Peugeot 205 Turbo 16
1986	Henri Toivonen/Cresto	Lancia Delta S4
1987	Biasion/Siviero	Lancia Delta HF
1988	Saby/Fauchille	Lancia Delta HF
1989	Biasion/Siviero	Lancia Delta Integrale
1990	Auriol/Occelli	Lancia Delta Integrale
1991	Sainz/Moya	Toyota Celica GT4
1992	Auriol/Occelli	Lancia HF Integrale
1993	Auriol/Occelli	Toyota Celica Turbo 4WD
1994	Delecour/Grataloup	Ford Escort RS Cosworth

■ While rallies were reviving strongly in Europe after World War I, things in Britain were more oriented to the race track. The 1925 Scottish Six Days' Trial had to be cancelled while the SMMT saw fit to ban 'trade' involvement in UK trials and rallies.

■ A collaboration between the Austrians, Swiss, Italians and French resulted in a revival of the Alpine Rally. This 1926 event started and finished in Milan and stuck to the idea of giving out cups for unpenalised runs. Every finisher got one that first year but it gradually expanded and got more difficult. The Germans joined in in 1928 and by 1931, when Donald Healey won one of seven Coupes in his Invicta, it was a full six days of hard motoring in the Alps starting from Munich and finishing in Berne.

At this stage, individual entrants could win Glacier Cups for their unpenalised performances

Mini on the Monte – Aaltonen and Liddon heading towards a particularly satisfying win in a Mini-Cooper S in 1967, the year after the organisers' questionable decisions deprived the BMC team of victory.

while Alpine Cups were awarded to teams of unpenalised cars. For example, when the 1932 rally terminated in San Remo, the Talbot 105 team won an Alpine Cup, a performance repeated in 1934. This was the heyday of British drivers such as H. J. Aldington (Frazer Nash), Tommy Wisdom (MG Magnette and Talbot 105), Sammy Davis (Armstrong Siddeley) and the Rileys in cars of their own make.

The Alpine Rally was cancelled in 1935 because the German drivers were not allowed to send money to the French organisers! But in 1936 it went ahead under Swiss organisation; both Donald Healey (Triumph Vitesse) and Tommy Wisdom (SS 100) won Glacier Cups but otherwise German domination was almost total and the remaining events preceding World War II were not well supported by other nationals.

After the war it fell to the Association Sportive de l'Automobile Club de Marseille Provence to step in and in July 1947 it organised the first of a series of events that were known as the Coupes des Alpes, or just the Alpine Rally. The Coupe or Cup was awarded for individual performances. A later innovation was to give a silver Coupe to someone who had won three Coupes non-consecutively, and a gold Coupe to a person who won three Coupes in consecutive years. Only four drivers ever won silver Coupes: Don

Morley (Healey 3000) 1961, 1962 and 1964; René Trautmann (Citroën DS) 1960, 1962 and 1963; Paddy Hopkirk (Sunbeam Rapier and Mini Cooper) 1956, 1959 and 1965; and Jean Rolland (Alfa Romeo) 1963, 1964 and 1966. Three drivers won gold Coupes: Ian Appleyard (Jaguar XK) 1951, 1952 and 1953; Stirling Moss (Sunbeam Talbot) 1952, 1953 and 1954; and Jean Vinatier (Alpine Renault) 1968, 1969 and 1971 – the 1971 result was allowed to count as there was no rally in 1970. In any case, Vinatier qualified for a silver Coupe with an additional Alpine Coupe in an R8 Renault won in 1965.

The Coupes des Alpes flourished but it needed the high cols free of snow, and so had to run in mid-summer when the costs of closing roads and the disruption to tourism caused by professional crews recce-ing for weeks on end brought it into difficulties that only increasing sums of money could cure. In 1970 it was cancelled and in 1971 the last Coupes des Alpes had 35 starters – not enough to qualify for the FIA Championship.

■ After organising several fairly short car and motor-cycle events the Royal Motor Union of Liège launched a longer endurance event. Their first such event, held in 1927 under the title of Marathon de la Route, went from Liège to Biarritz and back. All six cars that finished were equal on zero penalties and the club decided to make things harder.

So well did they succeed in that aim that, under the direction of Maurice Garot, they produced a rally that normally had few finishers, none of them unpenalised. Only on one famous occasion in 1951, when the bandleader, Johnny Claes, partnered by Pascal Ickx (father of Jacky), drove to victory in a Jaguar XK120, did the winner finish with no penalty points. Claes distinguished himself further two years later when he won again in a Lancia Aurelia, but this time it was for driving almost all of the non-stop event single-handed after his co-driver fell ill. It was said of M Garot that his ideal rally would be one with just one finisher. He never achieved that but he did get it down to single figures twice.

The big problem with this grandest and toughest of rallies was in finding countries hospitable to its open-road, endurance format. In the early 1960s Yugoslavia and Bulgaria provided a *laissez-faire* use of their roads but, with the gradual increase in tourism, even they could not allow fast cars freedom of movement in August and September. The last Marathon to be held on the open road was the rally to Sofia in 1964. The name survived a further five years

attached to an endurance event held at the Nürburgring, only finally to die, mourned by the rally fraternity, after the 1969 event.

■ In 1932 H. J. Aldington took one of his legendary TT Replica Frazer Nash cars to the Alpine Trial and was rewarded with a Coupe des Glaciers for a penalty-free performance. He repeated that success in 1933 and 1934 which would have entitled him to a postwar Coupe d'Or.

■ The 1936 Monte Carlo Rally was won by a most extraordinary car, the Ford V8 special of the Rumanians Zamfirescu and Cristea. Based on a light 1932 chassis with a 1935 radiator shell and bonnet (to attract sponsors), it had a doorless three-seat body built of aviation ply and the spare wheels were mounted inside the wheelbase ahead of the rear wheels. The steering and front brakes were linked to skid the car round turns. Cristea had practised the final driving test to perfection and, using the unique braking system with great skill, won the final test and the rally by 1.5 seconds.

■ The Swedish Rally started life as a Monte Carlo clone in the summer of 1950. The event was known as the Rally to the Midnight Sun. It had three starting points in the south and finished in Kiruna towards the Arctic Circle. It was a summer rally until 1965. A special stage was run down a mine in Kiruna during the 1963 event.

The 1965 winter event was called the Swedish Rally, started at Orebro and finished in Stockholm. From 1966 the rally has been based in Karlstad, except for the start in 1971 which went to Gothenberg to honour its 350th anniversary. One notable experiment was carried out in 1973 when studded tyres were banned; it has not been repeated, though the continued use of studded tyres on the snow-ploughed forest roads often breaks through the ice and the rally runs virtually on gravel.

It has been won by Swedes from its inception until 1981, when Hannu Mikkola of Finland gave Audi its first World Championship win and the first win for four-wheel drive. The most successful driver is Stig Blomqvist who scooped a hat-trick of victories for Saab in 1971–3, won it again for them in 1977 and 1979 and then added two victories for Audi in 1982 and 1984.

■ From 1932 until 1939 the RAC held a national rally called the RAC Rally. This was the successor to the old 1000 Miles Trial. It had no overall classification and the event did not feature hard motoring on public roads but was settled by 'tests' held normally at the finish. After World War II it was revived in 1951 as an international rally, but was still decided by what were really manoeuvrability tests. As it progressed through the 1950s, hill climbs and difficult navigation sections were added. In 1957 the rally missed a year, while in 1958 snow in March led the organisers to shift the date to November for 1959, when snow drifts in Scotland led to protests and problems for the organisers.

It was that same year that Jack Kemsley took up the organisation and by 1961 he had moved the event into the forests, where it has largely stayed ever since. It was won by Scandinavian drivers for 11 straight years until Roger Clark took a home win in 1972; his second win, in 1976, was the only other one by a non-Scandinavian until the two wins by Spain's Carlos Sainz in 1990 and 1992. Hannu Mikkola has been the most successful driver in the event, winning it four times (1978, 1979, 1981 and 1982) and finishing second four times (1977, 1980, 1983 and 1984).

The rally has chosen a host of starting places around Britain, including London, to satisfy commercial and regional pressures, but most recently has favoured York, Chester, Bath, Birmingham, Nottingham and Harrogate.

■ The first international 1000 Lakes Rally in 1951 was the brainchild of those Finns who had been to the postwar Monte Carlo rallies. They called their event the Jyväskylan Suurajot (Grand Prix of Jyväskyla), since it was centred on the town of Jyväskyla in central Finland where it is still based. It was always a summer event and within two years it was using special stages over the famous jumping dirt roads for which the area is famous.

In the late 1950s works teams started to come from abroad and won the event a couple of times, but the Finns soon re-established their grip on it and only Stig Blomqvist (1971), Michael Ericsson (1989), Carlos Sainz (1990) and Didier Auriol (1992) have managed to wrest it from them. Certainly there is a special skill in negotiating the roller-coaster roads and committing to memory or to paper the way each crest and bend follows the other. Simo Lampinen, Timo Makinen, Hannu Mikkola, Markku Alen and now Timo Salonen have won the rally 22 times between them.

Sydney Allard with his immaculate P-type saloon – and suit and tie – at the prize presentation after the 1952 Monte Carlo Rally.

■ British rally fans had plenty to shout about when Sydney Allard won the 1952 Monte Carlo Rally in a P-type saloon bearing his own name and powered by a 4.3-litre American V8. After that, big engines, and V8s in particular, went out of fashion as rally winners, partly due to the Monte formulae. In 1964 Ford America came with V8 Falcons and one, driven by Bo Ljungfeldt, finished second overall. In 1965 Peter Harper survived the blizzard to put a V8 Sunbeam Tiger in fourth place, but since then the largest engine to win a Monte Carlo has been the 3-litre Porsche of Jean-Pierre Nicolas in 1978. Henri Greder used one of the Falcons from the Monte Carlo to win the Geneva Rally in 1964.

Big saloons seem improbable cars for the Monte Carlo Rally, but Ronnie Adams borrowed this erstwhile racing Mk VII from Jaguar to win in 1956 (right). Ford USA took a class win with a Falcon Futura Sprint in 1963 (below), and placed one car second overall in 1964.

■ To commemorate the coronation of Queen Elizabeth II, rally enthusiasts in Nairobi secured the sponsorship of a Kenyan newspaper and ran an event called the Coronation Safari in 1953. There were starting points in Kenya, Uganda and Tanzania along Monte Carlo lines, but the classes for the cars were based on their East African price rather than cubic capacity. There were no special stages, since the African roads were enough, and so it has remained until the 1990s.

In 1955 it was sanctioned by the RAC as Kenya had no motor sport body, but finally went international in 1957. The name was changed to the East African Safari in 1960 and the international cubic capacity class system adopted. Already it was on the calendar for European manufacturers and they all discovered that, every time, a local driver won. Admittedly, Bert Shankland broke the Kenyan run with his win in 1966, but he was from nearby Tanzania. Eventually Hannu Mikkola was the first European to win the Safari, for Ford in 1972.

Twice the rally has had only seven finishers, in 1963 and 1968, both times due to heavy rains and on both occasions it was won by Nick Nowicki in a Peugeot 404.

In 1974 the rally was run entirely in Kenya and has stayed that way ever since. To correspond, the title was shortened to Safari Rally in 1975. The most successful driver is Shekhar Mehta with a win for Datsun in 1973 (when he tied on penalties with Harry Kallstrom in another Datsun and the tie was resolved on the first to incur penalty) and his four straight wins, also in Datsuns, from 1979 to 1982. The win by the Toyota Celica Twin Cam Turbo in 1984 was unique in that it was the team's first attempt at the Safari, though team boss Ove Andersson had won it for Peugeot in 1975 and Henry Liddon, his number two, had been competing there since 1965. Bjorn Waldegaard (1977, 1984 and 1986), Joginder Singh (1965, 1974 and 1976) and Juha Kankkunen (1985, 1991 and 1993) have won the rally three times.

■ With rallies springing up all over postwar Europe, it was no surprise to find the Acropolis Rally amongst them. With the most gorgeous settings in Europe and some of the toughest rally roads, the Acropolis has always been a challenge and a pleasure.

Among its early winners was Johnny Pezmazoglou, the Opel importer, who had won the original ELPA national rally held in 1952 as a precursor of the international event. Pezmazoglou had an unbroken record of competing in the Acropolis from the first in 1953 until 1985. It became a very popular rally with foreign teams and private competitors who were offered help by the Greek Tourist agency.

By the early 1960s it had established its name and was part of the championship year. In 1966, Paddy Hopkirk lost, due to a penalty for alleged illegal servicing, but returned in 1967 finally to give the Mini Cooper the victory for which it had striven for five years. In 1975 Walter Röhrl gave Opel its first World Championship victory and went on to win the Acropolis three times – the other two were 1978 (Fiat) and 1983 (Lancia). This record has been equalled by Miki Biasion who has won the Acropolis Rally in 1988 and 1989 (Lancia Delta Integrale) and in 1993 (Ford Escort Cosworth).

■ The European Rally Championship for Drivers was created in 1953 and survives to this day. It was the only major rally championship recognised by the governing body, then the CSI, but it has now been surpassed in importance by the World Rally Championship Drivers' title. To start with, the European Championship had the pick of the European events but for obscure reasons often ignored major events like the Liège. When the major European rallies became aspirants for inclusion in the World series, the European Championship was spread over some 40-odd lesser events, categorising them so that the points scored on each event were proportional to their perceived status.

In the period immediately prior to the creation of the World series in 1973, the European Championship reached its zenith in importance, with drivers like Harry Kallstrom, Pauli Toivonen and Jean-Claude Andruet winning major events and the championship. Since then, it has been the domain of works-assisted teams with only a few drivers seriously following the entire championship.

WINNERS OF THE EUROPEAN RALLY CHAMPIONSHIP

Year	Driver	Car
1953	H. Polensky	Porsche
1954	W. Schluter	DKW
1955	W. Engel	Mercedes-Benz
1956	W. Schock	Mercedes-Benz
1957	R. Hopfen	Saab and Borgward
1958	G. Andersson	Volvo

Year	Driver	Car
1959	P. Coltelloni	Citroën and Alfa Romeo
1960	W. Schock	Mercedes-Benz
1961	H-J. Walter	Porsche 356
1962	E. Böhringer	Mercedes-Benz
1963	G. Andersson	Volvo
1964	T. Trana	Volvo
1965	R. Aaltonen	BMC Mini Cooper S
1966	L. Nasenius	Opel Rekord
	S. Zasada	Porsche 911 T
	G. Klass	Porsche 911 S
1967	S. Zasada	Porsche 912
	B. Soderstrom	Ford Lotus Cortina
	V. Elford	Porsche 911 S
1968	P. Toivonen	Porsche 911 S
1969	H. Kallstrom	Lancia Fulvia HF
1970	J-C. Andruet	Alpine Renault A110
1971	S. Zasada	BMW 2002
1972	R. Pinto	Fiat 124 Abarth Spyder
1973	S. Munari	Lancia Stratos
1974	W. Röhrl	Opel Kadett
1975	M. Verini	Fiat Abarth
1976	B. Darniche	Lancia Stratos
1977	B. Darniche	Fiat Abarth 131
1978	T. Carello	Lancia Stratos
1979	J. Kleint	Opel Kadett GTE
1980	A. Zanini	Porsche 911
1981	A. Vudafieri	Fiat Abarth 131
1982	T. Fassina	Opel Ascona 400
1983	M. Biasion	Lancia Rallye 037
1984	C. Capone	Lancia Rallye 037
1985	D. Cerrato	Lancia Rallye 037
1986	F. Tabaton	Lancia Delta S4
1987	D. Cerrato	Lancia Delta HF
1988	F. Tabaton	Lancia Delta HF
1989	Y. Loubet	Lancia Delta Integrale
1990	R. Droogmans	Lancia Delta Integrale
1991	P. Liatti	Lancia Delta Integrale
1992	E. Weber	Mitsubishi Galant VR-4
1993	P-C. Baroni	Lancia Delta Integrale

■ The first International Tour de Corse was won by a ladies' crew, Mmes Thirion and Ferrier in a Renault Dauphine. Its original title in 1956 was the Rally of the Ten Thousand Corners which may have been accurate in the beginning but was soon to be exceeded as the severity and length of the event increased. Traditionally held in November, at the end of the tourist season, it often encountered snow and,

in 1961, René Trautmann won the event by being in the lead when it was stopped on the Col de Vergio by snowdrifts. Since 1981 it has been run in the spring.

To emphasise its toughness, an award was donated each year to the crew that should complete the rally without road penalty. This accumulated each year that it was not claimed. The men who came closest to collecting the by-then enormous sum were Sando Munari and Luciano Lombardini whose Lancia Fulvia lost but a single minute on the road in 1967.

Since becoming a World Championship event at the inception in 1973, the Tour de Corse has become the host to epic battles between French and Italian teams. So far the score is twelve to the Italians and four to the French though the wins of Jean-Luc Therier (Porsche) in 1980, Bernard Beguin (BMW M3) in 1987 and Didier Auriol (Ford Sierra) in 1988 and (Toyota Celica) in 1994 could easily be claimed as French. In 1986 the sad accident which claimed the lives of Henri Toivonen and Sergio Cresto in the Lancia Delta S4 triggered off the Group B controversy which led to the Group A World Rally Championship which exists today.

■ Pat Moss won the first of eight outstanding Coupe des Dames on the Monte Carlo Rally, spanning a period from 1959 until 1972. Her co-drivers and cars were as follows: Ann Wisdom, Austin A40 (1959–60); Ann Wisdom, Morris Cooper (1962); Ursula Wirth, Saab 96 (1964); Liz Nystrom, Saab 96 (1965); Liz Nystrom, Lancia Fulvia (1968–9); Liz Crellin, Alpine A110 (1972).

■ The most memorable result ever from a ladies crew came in 1960 when the world's toughest rally, Liège–Rome–Liège, was won by Pat Moss and Ann Wisdom in a factory-entered Austin-Healey 3000. It was also the first time that a European Championship rally had been won by a ladies' team, and it was the first time that this most difficult of rallies had been won by a British crew or car.

■ San Remo inaugurated its International Rallye dei Fiori (Rally of the Flowers) in 1961. It marked an upsurge of interest in rallying within Italy which has survived 25 years and was provoked by the loss of events like the Mille Miglia.

International interest grew, and teams like Saab, Ford and Renault came to join the local Lancias. By 1968, when it was a counter for the European Championship, it started to be called the San Remo Rally. There was a period when it combined with the Sestriere Rally to become the Rally of Italy (1970–2) but then it was re-established as the San Remo and as a World Championship rally.

Its doses of controversy have been fairly well spaced: Vic Elford's Ford was disqualified from victory in 1966 (its homologation form was wrong and it did not comply with it!); then all the works Lancias ran into the same fuel feed problem within kilometres of the start in 1970 and sabotage was suspected: finally, in 1986, the Peugeot works team was excluded during the rally, a decision ruled to have been wrong and the San Remo results were struck from the World Championship results.

On the more positive side, the 1969 event saw Lancia perform the first planned tyre change in the middle of a special stage, 1974 saw the Lancia Stratos win its first World event after homologation, and, in 1981, the San Remo was the first World Championship rally to be won by a lady, Michele Mouton in an Audi. Markku Alen is the most successful driver, having won the San Remo three times (1978, 1983 and 1986).

■ It is not often that the same make and model of car wins major races and rallies in the same year, but in 1962 Sunbeam Rapier MkIIIs won the Scottish Rally (Andrew Cowan) and the Circuit of Ireland Rally (Paddy Hopkirk) and the Touring Car race supporting the Belgian GP at Spa (Lucien Bianchi).

■ In the absence of a true world championship from FIA, the RAC decided to award a 'World Cup' for manufacturers in 1963. It comprised five events, the Liège–Sofia–Liège, Midnight Sun, RAC, Canadian Shell 4000 and the East African Safari. It was won by Ford, using the Cortina GT and the Anglia on the Safari.

■ In 1963 the Tour de France Automobile was won for the fifth consecutive time by a Jaguar. It was won in 1959 by Ramos in a 3.4 MkI and then an incredible four times in a row by Bernard Consten in Jaguar 3.8 MkIIs.

■ The first international rally to be won by a plastic-bodied car was also the first major win for Jean Redelé's firm of Automobiles Alpine. The rally was the 1963 Rally des Lions in France and the 1000 cc

Alpine 108 was driven by Jose Rosinski and navigated by a lady, Michele Dubosc.

■ The smallest car ever to win a European Championship rally was the 650-cc Steyr Puch driven by Sobieslaw Zasada and his wife, Eva, on the Polish Rally of 1964.

■ The result of the 1965 RAC Rally – and of the European Rally Championship – was decided on a small hill in Cropton forest. It was covered in snow and many cars were stuck including the Healey 3000 of Timo Makinen. The Mini Cooper of Rauno Aaltonen passed him on the hill and maintained that advantage to the end of the rally.

■ The Portugal Rally was first held in 1967 when it was known as the TAP Rally. Portugal's enthusiasm for motor sport and its need for tourism were linked when TAP, the Portuguese airline, sponsored a rally in 1967. With several starting points and a common run into Lisbon featuring navigational sections and special stages, it was firmly following in the Monte Carlo tradition. Its large prize fund and generous support for foreign entries soon brought prestige entries and, in only its second year, it was won by Tony Fall with Paddy Hopkirk second. By the time the World Rally Championship was instigated in 1972, it was worthy of a place and has stayed there ever since.

It has had its problems, with Tony Fall being excluded after the finish in 1969 for allegedly carrying a passenger – his wife – on part of the route – the last yards to the last time control. Regrettably, in 1986 it came back to controversy when a car crashed on the first stage, killing four spectators, and the factory drivers went on strike because they said that the spectators were not properly controlled.

The navigation element was discarded in 1972 and the concentration runs in 1974 and it has been a straightforward special-stage rally ever since. Through the 1970s it concentrated these on rough and rugged dirt roads but in the 1980s more tarmac miles were included with the intention of coming nearer to the 50–50 of San Remo. It sponsors since 1975 have been the port wine companies.

The most successful driver here is Markku Alen with four wins (1975, 1977, 1978 and 1981), all at the wheel of Fiats, and one with Lancia (1987).

■ The first plastic-bodied car to win a European Championship rally was the Alpine Renault A110 with a 1300-cc engine and driven by Jean Vinatier on the 1968 Czechoslovakian Rallye Vltava.

■ The FIA introduced an International Rally Championship for Makes in 1968, comprising nine major rallies. The majority were in Europe but by the time it was ready to become the World Rally Championship in 1973, three of those nine were from outside (Safari, Morocco and Press-on-Regardless).

Winners: 1968 Ford of Great Britain; 1969 Ford of Europe; 1970 Porsche; 1971 Alpine Renault; 1972 Lancia. It was largely ignored by the press since it was neither a world nor drivers' championship.

■ Gerard Larrousse was set to win the first major rally for Alpine Renault with his A110 1300 cc on the 1968 Monte Carlo Rally when spectators threw snow on the Turini stage and he went off, giving the victory to Vic Elford's Porsche. The French team had to wait until Jean Vinatier won the Coupe des Alpes that same year to claim their first major win. Monte Carlo spectators' odd idea of entertainment persists!

■ Bob Neyret won one rally whilst competing on another. He took a break between the European and South American sections of the World Cup (London to Mexico) rally in 1970 to enter the Moroccan rally in a works Citroën and won it outright.

■ One of the few appearances by the Porsche 914/6 was on the 1971 Monte Carlo Rally in the hands of Bjorn Waldegaard, who had won the two previous Montes with a Porsche 911. He did not like the neutral handling and finished third equal with Jean-Claude Andruet's Alpine Renault A110.

■ The Renault Alpine 310 first appeared in production in 1971, but it was not until 1974 that this 1600 cc successor to the World Championship-winning A110 won its first rally. This was the Vercors–Vivarais where it was driven by Bernard Darniche/Alain Mahe. The 310 was later produced with a Renault V6 engine, of which the first were made in 1976. This model won its first international rally with Guy Frequelin at the wheel on the Criterium Neige et Glace in 1977.

■ The 1972 Acropolis Rally had only one brief halt in its 53-hour northern loop and consequently most crews were falling asleep before getting back to Athens. One co-driver even fell asleep while drinking a bottle of lemonade in the car! This and other incidents led to the formation of the Sleeping Co-drivers' Association whose first act was to lobby for proper rest halts.

■ The ultimate in severity – the Bandama Rally, shortly to become the Ivory Coast Rally – had no

finishers in 1972. Actually one car, the Peugeot 504 of Tony Fall, did finish within the time limits but then the Renault team protested and the results of the event were scrapped. Shekhar Mehta in a Datsun 240Z did complete the route but was definitely out of time. There had been 52 starters, most of whom described the rally schedule as 'ludicrous'.

■ Some 61 years after the first Monte Carlo Rally had been held, the International Sporting Commission (CSI) of the Fédération Internationale de l'Automobile (FIA) decided that rallying was worth its own world championship. They changed the old International Rally Championship for Makes into a properly titled World Championship for Rallies. The one thing they did forget was a drivers' section of this World Championship which, until 1977, was exclusively for manufacturers.

FIA WORLD RALLY CHAMPIONSHIP

Year	Manufacturer	Driver
1973	Alpine Renault	
1974	Lancia	
1975	Lancia	
1976	Lancia	
1977	Fiat	
1978	Fiat	
1979	Ford	Bjorn Waldegaard (Ford Escort RS & Mercedes 450 SLC)
1980	Fiat	Walter Röhrl (Fiat Abarth 131)
1981	Talbot	Ari Vatanen (Ford Escort RS)
1982	Audi	Walter Röhrl (Opel Ascona 400)
1983	Lancia	Hannu Mikkola (Audi Quattro)
1984	Audi	Stig Blomqvist (Audi Quattro & Quattro Sport)
1985	Peugeot	Timo Salonen (Peugeot 205 T16)
1986	Peugeot	Juha Kankkunen (Peugeot 205 T16 E2)
1987	Lancia	Juha Kankkunen (Lancia Delta HF)
1988	Lancia	Miki Biasion (Lancia Delta HF & Delta Integrale)
1989	Lancia	Miki Biasion (Lancia Delta Integrale)
1990	Lancia	Carlos Sainz (Toyota Celica GT4)
1991	Lancia	Juha Kankkunen (Lancia Delta Integrale)
1992	Lancia	Carlos Sainz (Toyota Celica Turbo 4WD)
1993	Toyota	Juha Kankkunen (Toyota Celica Turbo 4WD)

*First rally supercar – a Lancia Stratos crewed by
Munari and Maiga in the 1977 Monte Carlo Rally,
the year that Munari and Lancia completed a hat trick
of wins in the event.*

■ Best recovery on an event? Markku Alen went off
on the first day of the 1973 RAC Rally with his Ford
Escort RS and fell to 175th overall. By the end of the
event he was back up to third overall. This was
rivalled, but not beaten, by Colin McRae's rise from
164th to 10th on the Monte Carlo Rally of 1994.

■ The two works Ford Escorts of Timo Makinen and
Roger Clark failed to progress more than a few stages
through the 1975 San Remo rally because the truck
carrying their Dunlop tyres had broken down in
France. The team ran as far as they could on the tyres
they had, but when these wore out they had to stop.

■ When FISA modified the Group 2 rules for 1976 it
was suddenly realised that rallies would lose a lot of
competitors, so they allowed the 'old' Group 2 cars to
run in rallies as Group 4 cars. Originally, Group 4
had been derivatives of two-seater Group 3 cars, but

now more manufacturers saw that they could homologate their saloon cars into a category for which the production number was only 400 per annum. The first company to realise this had been Hillman which had put the Imp into Group 4 many years previously.

■ On the 1978 Criterium du Quebec, John Buffum and Doug Shepherd were disqualified at the finish for coming to the end of a special stage with crash helmets off and seat belts unfastened. They had suffered a puncture in the stage with their Triumph TR8 and when the wheel was changed had leapt in and continued without bothering with the safety equipment.

■ Bjorn Waldegaard was denied victory on the last night of the 1979 Monte Carlo Rally when spectators put rocks in the road and damaged his Escort. The delay allowed Bernard Darniche to go on to win with a French-entered Lancia Stratos.

■ When he won the 1980 RAC Rally, Henri Toivonen (24) was the youngest driver to have won a World Championship rally. This result was also the first World win for the Sunbeam Lotus which went on to

Four-wheel drive was brought to rallying by Audi in 1981, with the Quattro that was based on the front-wheel drive Coupé. It was heavy and not over-powerful, but in 1982 Audi gained the Makes Championship with it. This car is in the Rallysprint series that presented the kernel of stage rallying to a TV audience. The driver is Hannu Mikkola.

win the World Championship for Talbot in 1981. It effectively died when the new masters of the company, Peugeot, started the design and development of the 205 Turbo 16 in 1982.

■ The disqualification of the works Audi Quattros on the 1981 Acropolis rally created quite a sensation. It was alleged that the bodywork round the headlamps and two of the four lamps themselves had been removed during the rally to improve cooling. What was alarming was that Audi were not allowed to continue, pending the hearing of their appeal against the organiser's decision.

■ The 1982 Tour de Corse marked the debut of Lancia's new 037 but one driven by Attilio Bettega crashed and he was out of action for the rest of the season. On the same rally in 1983 he was fourth and then in 1984, with his new co-driver, Sergio Cresto, he was seventh. But in Corsica in 1985 he left the road, again with an 037, and was killed by a tree branch coming in through the window. Cresto survived that accident unhurt but was to be killed with Henri Toivonen in a Lancia Delta S4 in 1986 in Corsica.

■ At a mini-rally in Sarlat, Dordogne, in 1983 to commemorate the death of Jean-François Piot, the Peugeot 205 T16 had its public competition debut driven by Jean-Pierre Nicolas who had done most of the test driving. The World debut for the car was in Corsica in 1984 where Ari Vatanen crashed and Nicolas came in fourth. They both retired on Acropolis but then Vatanen had three wins in a row – 1000 Lakes, San Remo and RAC (Peugeot did not contest New Zealand, Argentina or Ivory Coast).

■ The rally with the most one-upmanship was the 1984 Portuguese event. Firstly, Lancia entered young Henri Toivonen to incite Markku Alen to greater things but Toivonen crashed on stage 6. But Alen's Lancia led and he started first on the very dusty stages. Hannu Mikkola had to battle through dust until he and Audi team-mate, Walter Röhrl, discovered that they could give Mikkola a clear run if Röhrl stopped in the stage and let the leading Audi through. This worked to good effect and it was Mikkola who now led but Alen was still first on the road. Lancia gave him all the help they could by noting both his and Mikkola's intermediate times in a stage from their team helicopter and then relaying it to ground crews who gave Alen 'pit signals'. In the end, the rally went to Mikkola by just 27 seconds from Alen after 425 miles/684 km of stages.

■ Stig Blomqvist's win in Argentina with the Audi Quattro in 1984 gave him the unique distinction of being the first man to win three consecutive World Championship rallies (Acropolis, New Zealand and Argentina). This was soon equalled by Ari Vatanen (RAC 1984, Monte and Swedish 1985) and exceeded by Timo Salonen in 1985 (Acropolis, New Zealand, Argentina and 1000 Lakes). Both Vatanen and Salonen were driving Peugeot 205 Turbo 16s.

■ The fifth Rally of Argentina in 1985 was to bring to an end the World title chase of Ari Vatanen who had already won Monte Carlo and Swedish for Peugeot. A high speed encounter with an uncharted bump on just the second stage led to a terrifying crash from which he emerged very close to death. He was to be out of rallying for almost 18 months, making his 'comeback' by driving a Peugeot as course car on the 1986 San Remo Rally, then winning Paris–Dakar four times for Peugeot and Citroën (1987, 1989, 1990 and 1991) as well as competing in WRC events for Ford, Mitsubishi, Subaru and, most recently, Ford with the new Escort Cosworth 4 × 4.

■ In June 1985 FISA announced that the current crop of four-wheel drive, evolution Group B cars were too fast. For 1987 they would be banning the evolutions to the production model that gave so much power and would introduce a Group S with power controlled to 300 bhp which would gradually replace Group B in the World Rally Championship. Less than one year later, when Group B was itself axed, Group S was also abandoned – the best-received and shortest-lived international formula that never turned a wheel. Opel built a car to

Mid-1980s supercars. Peugeot won the 1985-6 Makes series with the 205 Turbo 16, a mid-engined 4-wd car (opposite top, in its 1986 Evolution 2 form). Ford followed, with the RS200 (opposite bottom), which came for 1986, when 'supercars' were to be banned).

Group S regulations; Peugeot designed one and sued FISA for the money they had wasted.

■ Did Audi swap cars for Michele Mouton on the 1985 Ivory Coast Rally? It was not proved to the international stewards' satisfaction but then the media seemed to have all the evidence and published it afterwards. Also, Roland Gumpert, Audi's popular team manager, departed at the end of the season to take up other responsibilities.

■ The Lancia Delta S4 was homologated into Group B on 1 November 1985 and by the end of the month had won its first World Championship rally, the RAC, with Henri Toivonen. Another S4 driven by Markku Alen was second and another debutante, the Austin-Rover MG Metro 6R4 driven by Tony Pond, was third.

■ In May 1986 FISA announced a hasty ban on all Group B cars effective from January 1987, and that even Group A cars would have to submit to a limit on maximum power for rallying. Initially, this was poorly received by manufacturers who reckoned that the cars were being blamed for lack of spectator control and bad rally organisation, but they later split into two camps thus allowing FISA to go ahead with the proposal.

The FISA decision had been triggered by the deaths of Henri Toivonen and Sergio Cresto a day before the announcement. Their Lancia Delta S4 had gone off the road and burnt out. But there was never any direct connection made between the accident and the fact that the Lancia was a Group B car. Certainly, the actual accident could have occurred to any car and the fire was more likely to be due to the preparation of the individual car rather than the fault of the Group into which it was homologated. In short, the decision was more emotional than rational.

■ Markku Alen experienced the nightmare of every rally driver in New Zealand in 1986 – he met a non-competing car on a special stage. Fortunately, he was able to stop his Lancia in time, but the effect on his subsequent performance in the rally was marked and his second place – to Kankkunen – contributed to his losing the World Championship.

■ The 1986 1000 Lakes Rally became the first international rally where four-wheel drive cars filled the first ten places overall.

■ At the start of the 1986 San Remo Rally, the Manufacturers' World Championship was already Peugeot's for the second year running, but the Drivers' Championship could still go to either Markku Alen (Lancia) or Juha Kankkunen (Peugeot). During a rally which exhibited organisational faults that were not really acceptable at World Championship level, pressure was put on the harassed organisers to take action against the Peugeots for what were alleged to be aerodynamic devices fitted under the cars. The San Remo men went too far, threw out all three works Peugeots before the last night and would not allow them to continue under appeal.

Lancias were then in the first three places and Massimo Baision and Dario Cerrato, who were leading Alen, slowed up on team orders to let him through and win. Naturally, Peugeot appealed but before all that could be settled there were the RAC and Olympus rallies on both of which Alen beat Kankkunen. So the result of the San Remo appeal would decide the Championship for Drivers. Just before Christmas, after appeals heard in Italy and Paris that said the Peugeots should not have been excluded but failed to rule on the legality or otherwise of the Peugeots, it was left to the FISA Executive, supported by an overwhelming majority of the manufacturers, to take the results of the San Remo out of the count for the World Championship and thus decide that Kankkunen was champion for 1986 and that Alen's 11-day reign should come to an end.

With Peugeot's World Championship activity coming to a halt with the end of Group B, Kankkunen departed to sign a Lancia contract for 1987 where his team-mate was fellow countryman, Alen.

■ The first winner of the new-look Group A World Championship in 1987 was Lancia with the newly homologated Delta HF. Massimo Biasion was credited with first place on the Monte Carlo Rally but only because Juha Kankkunen who took second place in another Lancia had been instructed to let Biasion pass him by slowing down on the last special stage.

■ The first front-wheel drive car to win a WRC African rally was the VW Golf 16v of Kenneth Eriksson/Peter Diekmann which swept to victory on the 1987 Ivory Coast Rally. This was by no means the first win for a front-wheel drive car on a World Rally Championship event as that honour went to Stig Blomqvist's Saab 96 V4 on the 1973 Swedish Rally, the second rally ever to count for the WRC. Saab have won four WRC events, all on the Swedish Rally, with their front-wheel drive cars. The only other manufacturers to clock up wins in the WRC with a front-wheel drive car have been Renault, who won the Press-on-Regardless in Michigan, USA, with Jean-Luc Therier in a Renault 15 in 1974, and Opel who won the New Zealand Rally with Sepp Haider in a Kadett GSi in 1988.

■ Mazda gained its first WRC victory when Salonen/ Harjanne won the 1987 Swedish Rally in a 323 4WD.

■ The first four-wheel drive car to win the East African Safari was the Audi 200 Quattro of Hannu Mikkola/Arne Hertz in 1987. Audi was also the first manufacturer to win a World Rally Championship event with a four-wheel drive car when Mikkola and Hertz won the Swedish Rally in 1981 with the original Audi Quattro. The same year, Michele Mouton became the only lady driver to win a WRC event when she won the San Remo Rally in an Audi Quattro. Audi was very nearly upstaged by Gene Henderson in a Jeep Waggoneer who won the Press-on-Regardless Rally in 1972, the year before the WRC was created. And they were not the first people to rally a 4WD car on a WRC event since, in the East African Safari of 1980, Rob Collinge/Anton Levitan finished 15th in a Range Rover while a diminutive Subaru Hatchback came 18th and won the Group 1 category.

■ Hannu Mikkola became the first driver to compete in a hundred WRC events in the 1987 Acropolis (he finished third in an Audi Quattro).

■ At the end of the RAC Rally of 1987, Per Eklund's private Audi Coupé Quattro was excluded from second place overall for having an inlet manifold on which some of the holes were slightly oversize. The decision to exclude was almost as bizarre as that in 1966 when Peter Harper's works Sunbeam Tiger was denied its GT victory on the Coupe des Alpes because its exhaust manifold was fractionally undersize.

■ The Portuguese Rally of 1988 saw the first use in competition of Michelin's ATS tyres. These have a container fitted under pressure which releases a quick setting mousse if the tyre is punctured. The tyres fitted with ATS did not perform as well as those without and thus were reserved for very rough stages where punctures were likely.

■ Rallying in the USA suffered a double blow in 1988 when leading driver Jon Woodner was killed in a private aeroplane accident, and the Olympus Rally, the surviving American contribution to the World Rally Championship, attracted the smallest entry yet seen on a WRC event – 29 cars – after being forced by FISA to drop its long-time sponsor, Toyota.

■ The 1988 Argentine Rally was the first WRC event to be won by a Latin-American driver, Jorge Recalde (Lancia).

■ The first finish on a World Rally Championship event by a four-wheel steering car was the Mitsubishi Galant VR-4 of Michael Lieu from Hong Kong who came tenth on the 1988 Olympus Rally in the USA.

■ The end of an era came in March 1989 when Cesare Fiorio, the director of Lancia's rallying efforts since 1965, was appointed to run the Ferrari Formula 1 team. He was replaced by Claudio Lombardi who also left Lancia to go to Ferrari in May 1991 to replace Fiorio. Giorgio Pianta took over the reigns at Lancia but by the end of 1992 the Lancia presence in rallying was confined to the Jolly Club. The last semi-works Lancia to compete in the World Rally Championship was the Jolly Club/Repsol Integrale driven by Carlos Sainz on the 1993 Catalunya Rally where he failed to finish. In twenty years of the World Rally Championship, Lancia had been victorious ten times.

■ The Autoglass Tour of Britain held in 1989 was the first FISA international rally for cars running exclusively on lead-free fuel.

■ The boss of the Peugeot cross-country rally team, Jean Todt, caused great controversy when he chose to toss a coin to decide which of his two leading drivers, Ari Vatanen or Jacky Ickx, would allow the other to win the 1989 Paris–Dakar. The winner was Vatanen and this was to be the first victory of a hat trick between 1989 and 1991.

■ At the insistence of FISA, the East African Safari included special stages for the time in 1989. It was a 'Europeanising' experiment that only lasted three years before the rally reverted to its traditional format of timing controls to the minute.

■ The Swedish Rally, traditionally the only World Rally Championship event to be 100 per cent sure of snow, had to be cancelled for lack of it in 1990.

■ If there is going to be a scandal, it normally seems to attach to the Monte Carlo Rally. This was certainly so in 1990 when the Toyota team alleged – with photographs to back up their assertions – that Lancia had swapped their supposedly sealed turbos during the event in which Didier Auriol (Lancia) beat Carlos Sainz (Toyota). The FIA dismissed Toyota's appeal, but it did lead to increased vigilance by FISA scrutineers.

■ Louise Aitken-Walker, Ladies' Rally Champion in

1989, was the victim of a horrifying accident on the Portuguese Rally of 1990 when her Opel Kadett GSi aquaplaned off the road in a thunderstorm and plunged into a lake. She and co-driver, Christina Thorner, only saved themselves by kicking out the rear window and swimming for it.

■ For the first time, FISA proposed in 1990 a low-key specification for practice cars used on major events in an attempt to reduce the annoyance to the general public. This was finally introduced for the 1992 season together with a restriction on the number of days' practice that was allowed for each rally.

■ The RAC Rally organisers permitted pace notes to be used over all its special stages for the first time in 1990 including all the forestry stages, after a limited experiment with pace notes on the spectator stages the previous year. They allowed each crew to drive slowly over each special stage twice to make notes.

Lancia developed the Delta theme from 1985, through to the HF Integrale in 1992. Juha Kankkunen won the Championship with a Delta HF in 1987 (here in the Olympus Rally).

■ By winning the 1991 Catalunya Rally as co-driver to Armin Schwarz in the works Toyota Celica GT4, Arne Hertz of Sweden became the oldest person to win a World Championship Rally at the age of 52. At the other end of the scale, Samantha Haldane of New Zealand was only 17 years 1 month when she co-drove a Daihatsu Charade to victory in the Ladies Award on the 1992 New Zealand Rally.

■ In 1991 the Paris–Moscow–Peking marathon rally was cancelled thanks to political problems on the original route, but it went ahead in 1992 and was won by Pierre Lartigue in a Citroën ZX Rallye Raid, an evolution of the original Peugeot 205 T16 rally car.

Rally-raid cars. The Porsche 959 seemed an unlikely basis for a desert 'raid' event car, and was hardly handsome on those large wheels, but in 1986 René Metge drove this one to victory in the Paris–Dakar (above). The Citroën ZX Rallye Raid, based on Peugeot rally cars, won the 1992 Paris–Beijing Rally.

The Paris–Dakar changed its name for one year to Paris–Le Cap; it went to Capetown and was won by Hubert Auriol in a Mitsubishi Pajero. Auriol had the distinction of having won the old Paris–Dakar twice before in the motor cycle section.

■ In 1992 Lancia scored its 13th San Remo Rally win since the inception of the World Rally Championship 20 years previously.

■ More new rules from FISA in 1993 saw World Rally Championship contenders having to make do with one spare turbocharger per day and one spare gearbox for the whole rally. Most chose to carry the spare turbocharger with them so that moving up to

the new minimum weight limit of 2640 lb/1200 kg was relatively easy.

■ To police all the new rules and to be able to take fuel samples at random during an event, FISA took to using a helicopter to transport its technical officials around WRC rallies. It was first used in Corsica in 1993, just two months after FISA levied a fine of

Ford rallied Sierra variants with little success in the late 1980s and early 1990s, then returned to the forefront with the Escort RS Cosworth. In Portugal in 1993 François Delecour drove this car to Ford's first championship rally win for five years.

US$300 000 on Toyota for breaking the servicing rules on the Swedish Rally. Didier Auriol had been given two cans of oil by someone in an area designated 'no service' where crews could only work on the car themselves with no outside assistance.

■ By winning the 1993 New Zealand Rally in his works Subaru Legacy, Colin McRae became the second British driver to win a World Championship rally. Until then, Roger Clark, who won the RAC Rally in 1976 driving a works Ford Escort, was the only person who could claim that distinction. By contrast, 29 World Championship rallies have been won by British co-drivers.

■ World Champion in 1993 for the fourth time in his career, Juha Kankkunen achieved that result with no less than three different co-drivers. The early part of the season, including his third victory on the Safari Rally, was undertaken with Juha Piironen. But Piironen fell ill with a brain haemorrhage at the start of the Argentine Rally and, at short notice, Nicky Grist was flown in to replace him. Kankkunen won Argentina and came fifth in New Zealand but could not use Grist on the 1000 Lakes as Grist was contracted to do that event with Armin Schwarz in a Mitsubishi. Kankkunen won the 1000 Lakes with Denis Giraudet, but then Grist got permission to leave Mitsubishi and joined Kankkunen for wins in Australia and the RAC Rally.

■ 1993 was the 21st year of the World Rally Championship and saw Toyota pull off a double win with their driver, Juha Kankkunen, taking the Drivers' title and Toyota taking the Manufacturers'. The most successful model of car in the WRC to date has been the Audi Quattro with a total of 21 wins to its credit. Lancia's Group A Delta has won 46 times but it underwent four model changes during that period. However, Lancia is the most successful marque in the WRC with a total of 74 wins to its credit and its nearest rival is Toyota with 33. His 1993 season propelled Juha Kankkunen to equal Markku Alen's total of 20 WRC victories and with Alen without a factory drive and Hannu Mikkola (18 wins) virtually retired, Kankkunen pulled ahead into a clear lead when he won the 1994 Portuguese Rally.

■ François Delecour's win on the 1994 Monte Carlo Rally in an Escort Cosworth gave Ford its first win on that event since Maurice Gatsonides victory in a Ford Zephyr in 1953. It was also a personal triumph for Delecour who had so nearly won the event twice before for Ford. In 1990 he was leading with one stage to go when the rear suspension of his Ford Sierra Cosworth failed and put him back to third overall; then in 1993 on the debut event for the Escort Cosworth, he was unable to resist the last-minute charge of Didier Auriol in the Toyota Celica 4WD and had to be content with second place.

The Monte Carlo Rally hit the headlines yet again when on stage 3 of the 1994 event the rally leader, Armin Schwarz (Mitsubishi), and second place man Colin McRae (Subaru) both left the road on snow thrown by spectators. The first time this happened to the leader of the Monte Carlo was in 1968 when Gerard Larrousse hit spectator snow on the descent of the Col de Turini and went off, wrecking his Alpine Renault A110 and his chances. This time, both Schwarz and McRae got back on the road and were actually classified 66th and 164th overall on penalties at the start of the next special stage. They drove like men possessed, winning several of the remaining 19 stages outright, and to such effect that Schwarz finished seventh overall and McRae tenth.

THE DRIVERS

Rauno Aaltonen, Finnish (b. 1939). The original Flying Finn, Aaltonen made his mark co-driving with Eugen Böhringer in the Mercedes team in 1961. He went to BMC and won the Liège–Sofia–Liège with an Austin Healey 3000 in 1964, the European Rally Championship in 1965 and the Monte Carlo Rally of 1967 with a Cooper S. His later drives were for Lancia, BMW, Fiat and finally Datsun and Opel. He has finished second four times on the Safari Rally (1977, 1980, 1981 and 1984) but never won it. Nowadays, he trains other drivers for rallies and competition driving.

Markku Alen, Finnish (b. 1951). In more than 20 years of top level competition, Markku Alen has competed in 129 World Championship rallies and won 20 of them. He started by driving Volvos and then Ford Escorts but moved to the Fiat empire in 1974. He stayed with it for 15 years, driving the 131 Abarth as well as every kind of Lancia. He has won the 1000 Lakes no less than six times and in Portugal five times, but victory on the Monte Carlo and the Safari have always eluded him. He is the only Scandinavian driver to have won the Tour de Corse (1983 and 1984). Alen was the winner of the FIA Driver's Cup in 1978 and, for 11 days, was the FIA World Rally Champion in 1986 before the Peugeot appeal took the San Remo from the WRC results. Most recently, he has driven for Subaru and Toyota.

Ove Andersson, Swedish (b. 1938). Ove Andersson started out driving his own Saab and when in 1962 he won six rallies, the BMC Sweden team offered him a Mini Cooper for 1963 in which he drove the Polish and RAC Rallies and finished fifth overall on the Swedish Rally. Saab then offered him some factory drives but real success came when he was signed up by Lancia in 1966 and finished third on the Monte Carlo, San Remo and Acropolis, and seventh on the RAC Rally. On the 1967 Monte Carlo he finished second and won the Spanish Rally before moving to Ford where he gave the Escort its debut on an international rally, finishing third on the San Remo. He stayed with Ford for three years and then drove for Alpine Renault, winning the 1971 Monte Carlo, Acropolis, Austrian Alpine and San Remo rallies. He continued to freelance and in 1975 won the Safari for Peugeot. In the meantime, he had become involved with Toyota, first as a driver and then running the entire operation, Toyota Team Europe.

Mario Andretti, American (b. 1940). Andretti's first 'victory of consequence' (his words) was in a 1962 midget race at Teaneck, NJ, he drove his first USAC race in a roadster in 1964 and was still competing at that level in CART in 1994. He was successful at the highest levels in US, Grand Prix and endurance racing, USAC national champion in 1965, 1966 and

Mario Andretti

1969, CART champion in 1984, World Champion with Lotus in 1978. Raced Alfa Romeo and Ferrari Formula 1 and sports cars with less success, also drove for the short-lived Parnelli team and Lola F5000 cars, co-drove Porsches with his son Michael at Le Mans and was often in competition with him on US tracks. The father–son pair made up the front row in the 1986 Phoenix start line-up, and later that year he beat Michael by 0.07 seconds at Portland. Won his 50th USAC/Indycar race at Phoenix in 1988, became the oldest winner (at 53) at the same track in 1993. Competed in 128 Grands Prix, won 12.

Alberto Ascari, Italian (1918–55). Son of Antonio Ascari, Alfa Romeo GP driver of the 1920s who was fatally injured in a 1925 French GP crash, Alberto Ascari was the archetypal Italian racing driver of the post-World War II era. He generally drove for Ferrari, winning 13 Grands Prix in 1951-3 and the World Championship in 1952-3. He also won the Mille Miglia for Lancia. Ascari died in a still-unexplained accident in a sports Ferrari he was unofficially testing at Monza.

Miki Biasion, Italian (b. 1958). Twice World Champion and once European Champion, for much of his career Massimo 'Miki' Biasion drove for Lancia in first the 037 and then the Delta. For 1983 he was invited to join the Jolly Club team for their attack on the European Championship, driving a Lancia 037. He won seven major rallies and the championship. The following year, he joined the Lancia works team and finished sixth on the Monte Carlo. His first big win was in the 1986 Argentina Rally driving the Delta S4. When Group A replaced the supercars in 1987, it seemed to suit him perfectly; he started by winning Monte Carlo and went on to win Argentina and San Remo. In 1988 he carried all before him winning the Safari, Portugal, Acropolis, San Remo rallies and the World Championship. He won the 1989 Monte Carlo, Safari, Portugal, Acropolis and San Remo rallies on his way to a second title. In 1992 he signed for Ford driving first the Sierra Cosworth and then the Escort Cosworth but has only had one win, on the Acropolis Rally of 1993.

Stig Blomqvist, Swedish (b. 1946). Stig Blomqvist started out in a Saab and he drove his first event in a factory car in 1967. His last rally for Saab was in 1981 and during the intervening years he won the Swedish Rally for them five times, the RAC Rally, the 1000 Lakes and the Cyprus Rally. He moved to the Sunbeam Talbot team for a year, and helped it to the World Championship by finishing third on the RAC Rally, but then he was signed for Audi where he teamed up with Hannu Mikkola and Michele Mouton to give Audi two Manufacturers' titles and win the Drivers' title in 1984. He won the Swedish Rally twice more at the wheel of an Audi and the RAC Rally once more. In the late 1980s he drove for Ford but a freelance drive on the Safari in 1989 brought him third place with a VW Golf GTi.

Eugen Böhringer, German (b. 1923). Always associated with Mercedes, for whom he won a Coupe des Alpes in 1960, the European Rally Championship in 1962 and the Liège–Sofia–Liège in 1962 and 1963, one of the diminutive German's best drives came at the wheel of a Porsche 904 with which he finished second overall on the blizzard-torn Monte Carlo Rally of 1965. After numerous successes for Mercedes in South American road races, Böhringer retired to his family hotel outside Stuttgart.

Sir Jack Brabham, Australian (b. 1926). The taciturn Australian was a bold racing driver with finely developed tactical skills and sound mechanical application, combined with shrewd business sense. He was three times World Champion, winning seven Grands Prix with Coopers and seven with his own Brabhams – in 1966 he became the first driver to win a World Championship race in a car bearing his own name, in the French race at Reims. In 1970 he retired from single-seater racing (he later raced other types occasionally) and sold his interest in the Brabham racing car company to his partner of many years, Ron Tauranac. He continued to be involved in racing, where his sons Geoff, David and Gary were successful in the 1980s and 1990s. Sir Jack competed in 126 Grands Prix, winning 14. He was knighted in 1979.

John Buffum, American (b. 1945). National service in Europe brought John Buffum into contact with rallying during 1968 and 1969 when he bought a Porsche. On his return to the USA he started competing in races but then tried rallies with ever-increasing success, first in a Ford Escort, then a Porsche, then a succession of factory Triumphs and finally Audi Quattros. He has won over 55 rallies in North America, ten USA championships and taken the 'CanAm' Rally Cup five times. He runs his rally shop in Vermont and prepares cars for his son-in-law, Paul Choiniere.

Rudolf Caracciola, German (1901–60). Often rated the top German driver of the 1920s and 1930s, this calm Rhinelander had a great success record, usually with Mercedes-Benz, whose cars he drove to six German Grand Prix victories. His career was interrupted by serious accidents, notably in practice for the 1933 Monaco GP and the 1946 Indianapolis 500; his last, in Mercedes sports car at Berne in 1952, ended his racing career.

Erik Carlsson, Swedish (b. 1929). The images of Erik Carlsson and a red two-stroke Saab 96 are almost inseparable. He started out driving his own car on rallies and was so successful that in 1957 he became a test driver for the Saab factory and drove works cars on rallies, winning the 1000 Lakes Rally at his first attempt. After that he won the RAC Rally three times in a row (1960–2) and the Monte Carlo Rally twice (1962 and 1963). It was his attempts to win the really difficult events in the little Saab that drew most acclaim, such as leading the 1963 East African Safari until he hit an ant eater, finishing second on the Liège–Sofia–Liège in 1963 and 1964, and finally winning a Coupe des Alpes in 1964.

Jim Clark, British (1936–68). A driver with immense natural talent, Clark was universally respected by his colleagues in motor racing and the wider sporting world. He started racing saloons and sports cars in local Scottish events in 1965 and four years later joined Lotus, to begin an outstanding partnership with Colin Chapman. First drove in Formula 1 in 1960, scored his first F1 win at Pau in 1961 and his first World Championship victory in Belgium in 1962, was champion in 1963 and 1965. That year he became the first European driver to win the Indianapolis 500 for 45 years. The next year his drive in the RAC Rally showed that he had other unexploited skills. Clark was killed in an insignificant Formula 2 race at Hockenheim. He started in 72 Grands Prix, and won 24.

Roger Clark, British (b. 1939). In a sport dominated by Scandinavian drivers from the 1960s, Roger Clark stands out as being one of the few British drivers to meet them on their own terms. He is still the only Briton to have won the RAC Rally since 1959 and has done so twice, in 1972 and 1976. He was British Rally Champion four times (1965, 1972, 1973 and 1975); these wins were at the wheel of Ford cars, but the factory never really gave him his head on the international scene though he did win the Shell 4000 for it in 1967 and the Tulip and Acropolis rallies in 1968.

Juan-Manuel Fangio, Argentine (b. 1911). Fangio learned the racing craft in the rough school of South American road racing, and became one of the great-

Juan-Manuel Fangio (centre) with Giuseppe Farina (right) and Luigi Fagioli

est single-seater drivers, with a Grand Prix start/ success ratio that has never been equalled: he started in only 51 GPs – from a front-row position in 48 – and won 24. He won his first World Championship with Alfa Romeo in 1949, won two more with Mercedes in 1954–5, a fourth with Ferrari in 1956, and a fifth driving Maseratis in 1957. He retired in 1958, but for many years after that was a regular visitor to Grands Prix and other events, and he demonstrated racing cars with great verve until health problems forced him to ease off. Fangio was universally admired as a great racing driver and a gentleman.

Giuseppe Farina, Italian (1906–66). Often appearing aloof, impetuous and temperamental, Farina could be brilliant and a classic stylist. He raced Alfa Romeos before and after World War II, winning five races with the 158 that complemented his driving in the year when he became first World Champion, 1950. He had some success with Maserati and Ferrari single-seaters, and had a fine record in sports car racing. Farina started in 33 Grands Prix, won 5. He was killed in a road accident in 1966.

Emerson Fittipaldi, Brazilian (b. 1946). The younger of two brothers who raced in Grands Prix, Fittipaldi entered racing with karts in Brazil, then attracted wide attention in Formula Ford in Britain in 1968. In 1970 he drove in his first Grand Prix, in Britain, and at the end of the year won his first Grand Prix, in the USA. He continued in Formula 1 with Lotus until 1973, winning his first World Championship in 1972. His second title came when he drove McLarens, in 1974. He persevered with his brother Wilson's un-competitive Copersucars in 1976–9, and in 1980 when they were named Fittipaldi. He turned to US single-seater racing, won his first CART race in 1985, was CART/PPG champion in 1989, won the Indianapolis 500 in 1989 and 1993. He started in 144 Grands Prix, won 14.

Anthony Joseph Foyt, American (b. 1935). 'A.J.' was the all-American driver of the 1960s and 1970s, talented, with abundant charm or fury, and chunky good looks. He started racing midgets in the 1950s, first raced at Indianapolis in 1958 and first won the 500 in 1961, naturally driving a 'roadster'. 'A. J.' accepted the new age of 'funny cars' with rear-mounted engines reluctantly, but eventually built his own Coyotes on those lines and drove one to win the 500 for the fourth time, in 1977. His last Coyote victory came at Silverstone in 1978. He was USAC/ Indycar champion seven times, started at Indianapolis

A.J. Foyt

35 times, 1958–92, was badly injured in accidents in 1990 and 1992. Foyt also drove NASCAR stock cars (winning the Daytona 500) and sports cars; in a rare race outside North America he won at Le Mans, with Dan Gurney in a Ford in 1967. He retired in 1993.

Mike Hawthorn, British (1929–59). The first British driver to win the World Championship, Hawthorn became prominent with his drives in an under-powered Cooper in 1952, and won his first Grand Prix in a Ferrari in 1953, out-driving Fangio in the French GP. He was also a successful sports car driver. Hawthorn was deeply upset by the death of his friend and team-mate Peter Collins in 1958, and retired at the end of that season, as reigning champion. Within three months he was killed in a road accident. Competed in 45 Grands Prix, won three.

Graham Hill, British (1929–75). Raced in the Grands Prix for 18 seasons, with enormous determination that brought rewards, primarily the World Championship in 1962 and 1968. First competed in a GP at Monaco in 1958, and he was later to win that race five times. First wins came with BRMs in 1962, he returned to Lotus for four years from 1967, then drove Brabhams, then Shadows and Lolas of his own team, as he worked towards becoming a constructor. As that was achieved, he was killed with members of his team, in an aircraft accident. Apart from GPs, won many races, outstanding among them the Indianapolis 500 and the Le Mans 24-hour Race. Graham's son Damon drove his first GPs in 1992, and he won three with Williams in 1993. Graham Hill started in 176 GPs, won 14.

Phil Hill, American (b. 1927). First American to win the World Championship, Californian Hill was a leading sports car driver whose Formula 1 career centred on four seasons with Ferrari. Consistent high placings brought him the title in 1960. His active racing career ended in 1967, when he retired from competition to concentrate on historic cars. Hill started in 48 GPs, won three.

Paddy Hopkirk, Irish (b. 1933). Originally a works driver for the Standard team, Paddy Hopkirk moved

to Rootes in 1959 and won his second Coupe des Alpes for them in a Rapier and notched up two wins on the Circuit of Ireland. At the beginning of 1963, he joined the BMC team and finished second on the Tulip Rally of that year before winning the Monte Carlo Rally outright in 1964 in a 1071-cc Cooper S. He had several wins with the Cooper S and with a Healey 3000, but his best year was 1967 when he was second in San Remo and won the Acropolis Rally and Coupe des Alpes. Since then, he has distinguished himself in long distance events, finishing second on the 1968 London–Sydney, fourth on the London–Mexico in 1970 and third on the London–Sydney in 1977. More recently, he has been in the vanguard of the historic rally revival, winning the RAC Golden 50 in 1982 and celebrating his own 1964 win by taking a modern Mini on the 1994 Monte Carlo Rally.

Denis Hulme, New Zealander (1936–92). Denny Hulme worked hard in secondary categories for five years before his first F1 drive, with Brabham in 1965. He won his first GP at Monaco in 1967, and that year won the championship. There was more success in GPs and CanAm with McLaren in the following seasons, with CanAm championships in 1968 and 1970. At the end of 1974 he retired from front-line racing, but picked up the circuit threads with saloons (in 1986 he was co-driver of the TT-winning Rover). He died of a heart attack at the wheel of a BMW during a race at Bathurst, Australia. Hulme started in 112 GPs, won eight.

James Hunt, British (1947–93). James' racing career was controversial, from his early years to his premature retirement in the middle of the 1979 season. There was a buzz to his first GP years with Hesketh – he won the team's only championship race, in Holland in 1975 – and to his season-long title battle with Lauda in 1976. His title defence in 1977 was at times spirited but his McLarens were outclassed, and so was the Wolf that followed. He later became an excellent TV commentator. Hunt started in 92 GPs, won ten.

Jacky Ickx, Belgian (b. 1945). A fine all-round driver, Ickx is chiefly recalled for his sports car successes, with Ford, Ferrari, Matra, Alfa Romeo and Porsche, above all perhaps for his six Le Mans victories. He also drove in Formula 1 for Brabham and Ferrari with some success, less happily for other GP teams. In the 1980s he was successful in rally-raids, was involved with the rejuvenation of the Spa-

Graham Hill

Francorchamps circuit, managed the victorious Mazda team at Le Mans in 1991. Ickx started in 116 GPs, won eight.

(Above) James Hunt

(Below) Juha Kankkunen

Alan Jones, Australian (b. 1946). Alan Jones' first GP drives came in 1975 after he served a dogged 'apprenticeship' in secondary single-seater classes through the early 1970s. Won his first GP in Austria in 1977, driving a Shadow, joined Williams in 1978 and won 11 GPs with the team in 1979–81. Was World Champion in 1980. He 'retired' from Formula 1 in 1982, but won Australian national sports car championships, then had a rather pointless 'guest' drive with Arrows before committing himself to a disappointing 1986 season with the Beatrice Lola team. Then he retired again. He started in 116 GPs, won 12.

Juha Kankkunen, Finnish (b. 1959). In a career of just 15 years, Juha Kankkunen has been World Champion four times and has won over 20 WRC events. His talent was recognised early by Toyota and he joined them in 1983 though it was not until he went for the first time to the Safari in 1985 that he gave them his first win. He made it an African double by winning the Ivory Coast Rally the same year but left to drive for Peugeot in 1986 when he was World

Champion after Markku Alen lost his points from San Remo. To show that it was no fluke, Kankkunen changed to Lancia for 1987 and was World Champion again. He then had two years back with Toyota, breaking in their new Celica GT4 but only winning once, in Australia in 1989, before returning to Lancia and taking another World Championship in 1991. In 1992 he was second in the championship and then moved to Toyota for 1993 where he swept to his fourth championship.

Nikolaus-Andreas Lauda, Austrian (b. 1949). Niki Lauda made his own way up the racing ladder to Formula 1, raising a bank loan to ease his way into the Grands Prix. Then, in 1974, he joined Ferrari and won his first GP, following that with the championship in 1975. He narrowly survived a fiery accident in the 1976 German GP, and regained the title in 1978. He won two GPs in Brabhams in 1978, then abruptly retired during practice for the 1979 Canadian GP. He came back to racing with McLaren in 1982, was champion for the third time in 1984, then retired again at the end of the 1985 season. He then concentrated on his airline, but in the 1990s became a consultant to the Ferrari team. Lauda started in 171 GPs, won 25.

Niki Lauda

Nigel Mansell, British (b. 1954). Determination and courage sustained Mansell through some difficult periods, and remained an essential part of his make up as a racing driver. He was successful in karts and F Ford, sometimes struggled in Formula 3. There was a Lotus test contract in 1980, and a first GP drive in Austria. His first rostrum finish was in the 1981 Belgian GP, his first victories came when he drove for Williams in 1985, and in the next two seasons he won 11 GPs. A debut win in his first Ferrari season ensured his popularity with Italian enthusiasts, but relations with his team-mate became strained. Mansell returned to Williams for 1991–2, won 14 GPs then as reigning World Champion he turned to Indycar racing in 1993. Against most expectations he carried off the series title in a Newman-Haas team Lola. Mansell had started in 181 GPs, and won 30.

Bruce McLaren, New Zealander (1937–70). The McLaren marque has been in the forefront for a quarter of a century, which tends to overshadow Bruce McLaren's career as a driver. He won his first GP in a Cooper in 1959, then led the team while his sports car interests built up – there was a win at Le Mans in 1966, and his orange McLaren cars dominated CanAm racing for four years from 1967 (McLaren also drove his own F1 cars to win two Grands Prix). He died in a sports car test accident at Goodwood. McLaren started in 101 GPs, won four.

Colin McRae, British (b. 1968). Not too many rallying sons have outshone their fathers, but Colin McRae put one over on his multiple UK Champion father, Jimmy McRae, when he won the 1993 New Zealand Rally and became the first Briton to win a WRC event since Roger Clark in 1976. It was also the first such win outside the British Isles. McRae's early career was marked by brisk work at the body shop after each event and he shot to fame by finishing sixth on the 1990 RAC Rally with a Ford Sierra Cosworth whose door was kept shut by a bolt from a pig-pen. He was invited to join the Subaru team and won the British Championship for it twice before making a foray into overseas events. His most incredible drive was to eighth place on the 1000 Lakes of 1992 when the car suffered three major accidents, including one before the rally.

Shekhar Mehta, Kenyan (b. 1945). To win the Safari once is an achievement but five victories is the amazing record of Shekhar Mehta. Originally from Uganda, he started rally driving in 1966 and by the early 1970s was part of the official Datsun team. He won his first

Safari for them driving a 240Z in 1973, spent a year with Lancia and then came back to Datsun in 1976, ending up with a string of four consecutive victories on the Safari (1979–82). He won the Cyprus Rally in 1976 and the Middle East Rally Championship in 1980 but left Datsun at the end of 1985 to become a test driver for Peugeot. In one of their 205 T16 Raid cars he had a very serious accident on the Pharaohs Rally of 1987 and has not driven competitively since. He currently chairs the FIA Committee on Cross Country Rallies.

Hannu Mikkola, Finnish (b. 1942). The man who has competed in more World Championship rallies than any other is still Hannu Mikkola though his score of outright wins stands at 18, short of Kankkunen and Alen. Mikkola's claim to fame lies with two major wins with Ford Escorts near the beginning of his career, the London–Mexico in 1970 and the East African Safari in 1972, and with his move to Audi in 1981 showing faith in the unproven Quattro 4WD concept that was to net him a World Championship in 1983. Seven wins on the 1000 Lakes Rally and four on the RAC Rally underline his ability on loose surfaces but, like Kankkunen and Alen, he has never managed to win the Monte Carlo (though his record

(Left to right) Alain Prost, Nigel Mansell and Nelson Piquet in 1986

(Below) Hannu Mikkola

is still pretty impressive with three second and two third places). In his 50th year, he drove a works Toyota on the 1000 Lakes Rally and finished seventh.

Stirling Moss, British (b. 1929). A great all-round driver and at one time a prominent rally driver, Moss was denied a world title. Started racing in the 500-cc Formula 3, and moved into championship racing in the years when it was run to F2 regulations. His performances in a semi-independent Maserati in 1954 earned a Mercedes-Benz contract, and he scored his first GP win in the British race; seasons with Maserati and Vanwall followed, then he drove Rob Walker's independent Cooper and Lotus cars, before a crash at Goodwood in 1962 ended his main-line career. He also had an outstanding record in sports cars, and returned after his accident to compete in saloons and historic cars, maintaining his close association with motor sport. Moss started in 66 GPs, won 16.

Pat Moss-Carlsson, British (b. 1935). It would be pointless to list the number of Coupe des Dames that Pat Moss won during her 20 years of rallying. And it was not those that she herself was interested in either. She was quite capable of taking on the boys at their own game and when, after an apprenticeship in Morris Minors and Riley 1.5s, she finally got her hands on a big Austin-Healey in 1958 she did just that, finishing eighth on the Alpine Rally and fourth on the Liège–Rome–Liège. The real joy came when she won the Liège in 1960, also in a big Healey, and was second overall on the Alpine. She won the Tulip and German Rallies of 1962 with a Mini Cooper. She had a year with Ford in 1963 but the same year, married Erik Carlsson and joined him at Saab in 1964. The Saab 96 Sport was no longer as competitive as it had been but Pat was rarely out of the top six with the red car. She had two seasons with Lancia during which she won the 1969 Sestrière Rally and was second in San Remo. Since the early 1970s, Pat has concentrated on her family and the ponies that gave her the first taste of competition.

Michèle Mouton, French (b. 1951). Starting in local French rallies with her own Alpine Renault A110 in 1973, the diminutive French girl had attracted the attention of the Fiat Group and in 1977 she finished second in the European Rally Championship with a Fiat Abarth 131 and won the Ladies' Championship, the first of four. In 1978, she won the Tour de France Auto and then in 1981 was invited to join the new Audi team. That same year, she made history by

Stirling Moss and Mike Hawthorn

Michèle Mouton

Tazio Nuvolari

becoming the first lady to win a World Championship Rally, the San Remo. The following year, she went on to win the Acropolis Rally and finished second overall in the World Championship. In 1986 she drove for Peugeot and took on the task of winning the German Rally Championship which she did with six straight wins. Since then, she has become the promoter of the annual Race of Champions, currently held in the Canary Islands.

Sandro Munari, Italian (b. 1940). Sandro Munari was the star who put Italian rallying on the map. He joined the nascent Lancia team in 1965 and in 1967 won all the rallies of the Italian Championship. Even more impressive was his win in Corsica where, but for a handful of seconds, he would have been the first driver ever to finish that rally unpenalised on the road sections. A crash on the concentration run of the Monte Carlo put him out for just over a year but he came back and in 1972 did something that none of the Scandinavians had managed with a Lancia Fulvia and that was to win the Monte Carlo. Out of that success was born the Stratos and Munari made the most of it, winning dozens of rallies and, most im-

portantly, completing a hat trick on the Monte Carlo (1975, 1976 and 1977). When the Stratos was replaced by the Fiat 131, Munari never seemed at home and virtually stopped rallying a few years later. He now works for Lamborghini.

Felice Nazzaro, Italian (1881–1940). Of all the early racing drivers, Nazzaro came closest to the modern pattern – he even built cars bearing his own name, and raced them in 1913–14. For most of his career he raced Fiats, winning the three main races of 1907, and taking the French GP in a vastly more sophisticated Fiat in 1922, his last racing season.

Tazio Nuvolari, Italian (1892–1953). Nuvolari epitomised the brave and skilled Italian racing driver of an era that is long in the past. He raced motorcycles, then a wide variety of cars, from Bianchi in the 1920s to Ferrari in the 1940s, but is most often recalled for his exploits with Alfa Romeos in the 1930s. Towards the end of that decade he abandoned his hopeless campaign with outclassed machines, drove Auto Unions to three GP victories. After World War II he led the 1947 Mille Miglia to within 90 miles of the finish. A sick man, he drove his last race in a

Cisitalia in 1950, but the legends about 'Il Maestro' flourished.

Richard Petty, American (b. 1937). Supreme NASCAR driver from the mid-1960s through to the 1980s, Petty was the son of three-times national stock-car champion Lee Petty. When he won the Firecracker 400 at Daytona in 1984 Petty also scored his 200th Grand National victory; when he retired from racing at the end of 1992 'The King' had started in 1185 NASCAR races in 33 years and won seven championship titles.

Nelson Piquet, Brazilian (b. 1952). Piquet followed a familiar path from karts in Brazil to Formula 3 in Britain, and first raced Formula 1 cars in 1978. His career really took off with Brabhams, winning his first GP with them at Long Beach in 1980 and the World Championship in 1981 and 1983. In 1986 he won four GPs in Williams, then three more and his third championship in 1987, before joining Benetton and winning three more GPs in 1990–1. He then turned to Indycar racing and was very seriously injured in an Indianapolis practice accident in 1992. Piquet started in 204 GPs, won 23.

Alain Prost, French (b. 1955). The first French driver to win the World Championship, Prost has stood out for his sophisticated techniques, for ultra-smooth driving with 'something in reserve'. He was a European kart champion and European Formula 3 champion before his first GP season with McLaren in 1980. In the next three seasons he won nine GPs in turbocharged Renaults, then drove for McLaren 1984–9, winning 30 GPs and the World Championship in 1985, 1986 and 1989. Two years with Ferrari were only slightly less rewarding, then came a sabbatical before a season with Williams brought a fourth world title in 1993. Prost started in 200 GPs, won 51.

Jean Ragnotti, French (b. 1945). Equally happy as a stunt man for films or as a rally driver, Jean Ragnotti started out driving for Opel, with whom he had some category wins on the Monte Carlo Rally in the early 1970s. After trying Formula 3 racing, he went back to rallying with the Renault team and won the French championship for it in 1980, before winning the Monte Carlo in 1981 with an R5 Turbo and the Tour de Corse twice, in 1982 with an R5 Turbo and in 1985 with the Maxi Turbo. More recently, he has been campaigning the Clio Williams, one of the first cars to be developed specifically for the Formula Two rally rules.

Jochen Rindt, Austrian (1942–70). A courageous and friendly driver, Rindt made his name in Formula 2 single seaters and with a Le Mans victory in 1965, but his first four Formula 1 seasons, with Cooper and Brabham, were poorly rewarded. With Lotus, he won his first GP in the USA in 1969; in 1970 he won five more but was fatally injured in a practice accident at Monza. His points score was not equalled before the end of that season, and he became the first driver to be awarded the World Championship title posthumously. Rindt started in 60 GPs, won six.

Walter Röhrl, German (b. 1947). If anyone deserves the title of maestro among rally drivers, it must be Walter Röhrl whose performances in a wide variety of cars are the envy of his peers. Starting out in an unlikely Ford Capri, he went to Opel in 1973 and won the European Championship in 1974. In 1978 he joined the Fiat/Lancia combine, driving a Fiat 131 and a Stratos. In 1980 he was World Champion, driving a 131, with wins on Monte Carlo, Portugal, Argentina and San Remo. For 1982 he was lured back to Opel, winning the Monte Carlo and Ivory Coast rallies on his way to a second World title but in 1983 he went back to Lancia and won Monte Carlo for the third time and finished second in the World Championship. In 1984 he signed with Audi, a relationship which only terminated in 1993, and promptly won the Monte Carlo for them. This made an amazing four wins on that event, all in very different cars. After the Group B cars were banned in 1986, Röhrl reduced his participation in rallies and now works for Porsche as a test driver.

Keke Rosberg, Finnish (b. 1948). Keijo – 'Keke' – Rosberg coupled flamboyance with fine car control, and for years was a journeyman driver in various categories, before his first frustrating Formula 1 seasons with uncompetitive cars. Joined Williams in 1982, won his first GP (the Swiss event at Dijon), and the World Championship. He won four more GPs with Williams, 1983–5, had a less successful final F1 season with McLaren, retired from top-line driving but remained active in other areas of motor sport. Started in 114 GPs, won five.

Bernd Rosemeyer, German (1910–38). Rosemeyer moved from motor-cycle racing straight into a Grand Prix team, raced the rear-engined Auto Unions for the first time in 1935, and won his first GP that year. In the following seasons he seemed to take on Mercedes almost alone, winning nine races. Then his life was squandered in a pointless record attempt.

Carlos Sainz, Spanish (b. 1962). The problem for Carlos Sainz is that he has made a very successful career look so easy. He started rallying with a Renault Maxi 5 Turbo and then moved to a Ford Sierra Cosworth with which he won the Spanish Championship in 1987 and 1988. During that second year, he had tried some World Championship events and finished fifth in Corsica, sixth in 1000 Lakes, fifth in San Remo and seventh in the RAC Rally. For 1989 he signed for Toyota and improved on his results, almost winning the RAC Rally. He then won the 1990 World Championship, with wins including the 1000 Lakes and RAC Rally – unheard of for a non-Scandinavian driver. In 1991 he was second in the World Championship, winning Monte Carlo, Portugal, Corsica, New Zealand and Argentina Rallies and then bounced back to be champion again in 1991 with a win on the Safari to add to his laurels. In 1993 he made a career mistake by going to the Jolly Club just as Lancia hit the skids. His best result was San Remo from which he was disqualified as the fuel sample from the car was found to be illegal. For 1994 he signed with Subaru.

Jody Scheckter, South African (b. 1950). The only South African to win the World Championship, Scheckter built up an impressive record in F Ford and Formula 3 before he first raced a GP car, in 1972, and that year he won the US F5000 championship. Scored his first championship race victory with Tyrrell in 1973, then scored the only GP victory for that team's six-wheel P34. Won three GPs with the then-new Wolf team in 1977, three more with Ferrari in 1979, his championship year. Retired at the end of a mediocre season in 1980. Contested 112 GPs, won ten.

Ayrton Senna, Brazilian (1960–94). Ayrton Senna da Silva was a precocious talent when he moved from Brazilian kart racing to win two British F Ford championships in 1981. His success in the British F3 series led straight to a GP contract with Toleman, and he came close to victory at Monaco in 1984. Drove for Lotus in 1985–7, he scored his first GP victory in Portugal in 1985 and won five more before he moved to McLaren in 1988. Through the next five seasons he won 30 GPs in the red and white cars, and the World Championship in 1998, 1990 and 1991. He won five GPs in 1993, in McLarens he rated unworthy of his talents, then he joined Williams. Senna was fatally injured in the third race of 1994, and was widely mourned.

Jackie Stewart, British (b. 1939). Stewart enjoyed a scintillating Grand Prix career, then shrewdly built another on the base of motoring and motor racing. Showed great natural talent from his earliest circuit days, spent his first three GP seasons with BRM (scoring his first GP victory in Italy in 1965) and from 1968 drove for Ken Tyrrell, in Matra, March and Tyrrell cars. He was World Champion in 1969, 1971 and 1973, retiring before the last race of that season as a mark of respect for his young team-mate François Cevert, who was killed in a US GP practice accident. Stewart started in 99 GPs, won 27.

John Surtees, British (b. 1934). Seven times world motor-cycle champion, John Surtees started racing cars (F Junior Lolas) in 1960, but was soon a Grand Prix driver, in Lotus, Cooper and Lola cars before he joined Ferrari in 1963. That year he scored his first GP win, in Germany, and in 1964 he was World Champion. He left Ferrari in 1966 to drive Coopers in GPs, and he won the first CanAm championship in a Lola. Drove for Honda in 1967, then for BRM, then set up as a constructor. His cars were successful in Formula 2 and F5000, but the only F1 victory was in a non-championship race. Surtees became increasingly disenchanted with racing, abandoning Team Surtees' F1 programme at the end of 1978, then the secondary programme. Surtees started in 111 GPs, won six.

Henri Toivonen, Finnish (1956–1986). Henri Toivonen was the eldest son of Monte Carlo winner and European Rally Champion, Pauli Toivonen. The most charismatic of the Finns, he was adored by rally fans and respected by the other drivers. His first works drive was with Sunbeam Talbot in 1980, and he won the RAC Rally, the youngest driver to win a WRC event. Two years with Opel saw a consistency of result but it was not until he drove a Porsche for Rothmans in 1984 that the wins started to come. In

(Opposite) Ayrton Senna

1984 and the first part of 1985 he had a wild ride with a Lancia 037, but when their Delta S4 made its debut on the RAC Rally of 1985, he was the man to give it the win, something he repeated on the 1986 Monte Carlo. Sadly, Henri and co-driver Sergio Cresto lost their lives when they crashed in the Tour de Corse.

The Unser Family, American. This American racing dynasty stemmed from Louis and Jerry, who built and raced their own dirt-track cars. Two of the second-generation brothers, Bobby and Al, had long and successful careers, but their brother Jerry died in an Indianapolis practice accident in 1959. In 1985 Al Sr took the Indycar championship from his son Al Jr by just one point in the last race of the year.

Bobby Unser (b. 1934). First raced in 1949 but did not become a full USAC competitor until 1964, started winning regularly with Eagles in 1967 and drove Eagles until 1975. Three-time Indianapolis 500 winner, USAC champion in 1968 and 1974, winner in spring and stock cars, and in the family tradition many times a winner of the Pikes Peak hill climb, breaking the record as recently as 1985, in an Audi.

Al Unser Sr (b. 1939). In 1985 the oldest driver to win the US championship, in overall terms Al Unser ranked third to Foyt and Andretti, and in 1988 he set a new record for laps led in the Indianapolis 500. Scored his first USAC win in 1968, won four times at Indianapolis, was the first driver to win all three Indycar 500-mile races in a single season (in 1978), was also successful in F5000, stock cars and CanAm.

Al Unser Jr (b. 1962). Was successful in secondary classes, won the CanAm title in 1982, moved on to Indycar racing and gained his first win in that category in 1984. Was CART series runner-up in 1985 and 1988, CART champion in 1990, won the Indianapolis 500 in 1992 and 1994, was IROC champion in 1986.

Ari Vatanen, Finnish (b. 1952). Ari Vatanen has had two rally careers and seen enough action to fill several books. His first is mainly a story of Ford Escorts which gave him his World Championship in 1981 and imprinted on the rally world his unique driving style. A season with Opel gave him a win on the Safari in 1983 and then he joined Peugeot to drive the new 205 T16. Once the programme got into its stride, Vatanen won five WRC events in a row between 1000 Lakes in 1984 and Sweden in 1985. A horrific accident on the Argentina Rally of 1985 nearly killed Vatanen and it was 18 months before he returned to driving. This was still at Peugeot for whom he won Paris–Dakar four times. He has also campaigned regularly in the World Championship, most recently for Subaru, with second placing on the 1000 Lakes in 1993.

Bjorn Waldegaard, Swedish (b. 1943). Bjorn Waldegaard would have fitted perfectly into Shakespeare's idea of a man of many parts. During 30 years of top line competition, he drove for no less than ten factory teams in World Championship events, winning 16 of them, including four East African Safaris. But before the WRC was born, he had won two Monte Carlo rallies and a hat trick on the Swedish Rally for Porsche. He was World Champion in 1979, alternating between a Ford Escort and Mercedes 450SLC. In the 1980s, he emerged as being something of an African expert, taking three of his four Safari wins and three victories in the Ivory Coast Rally for Toyota. An immensely popular driver, Waldegaard has most recently been seen at the wheel of a Porsche in historic rallies.

MOTORING MISCELLANY

■ The first motor car used for electioneering in Britain was an Arnold-Benz Victoria which J. E. Tuke of Harrogate used to carry the Liberal candidate for Bradford South, J. Dawson, to election meetings on 31 October 1896 and to take electors to the polls on 2 November. Incidentally, until 1992 it was legal in Britain to use an untaxed car to take voters to the polling station.

■ One of the most famous trademarks in the automotive field is the Michelin Man. He was devised in 1898 by Edouard Michelin who thought that a pile of tyres at an exhibition looked like an armless man and had his friend, the caricaturist O'Galop, create the first Michelin Man, who took his name 'Monsieur Bibendum' from a Latin drinking toast, *Nunc est Bibendum*. Since 1898, of course, Bibendum's contours have varied according to the change in tyre profiles.

■ The builders of early cars had little idea of standardisation (or ergonomics). The popular belt-driven Benz cars of the 1890s had seven or eight (according to type) hand controls but only one pedal, while the more powerful cars built by top pre-World War I companies like Mercedes, Delaunay Belleville and Gobron-Brillié sometimes had four or five pedals (accelerator, clutch, two brake pedals and exhaust cut out) to confuse the driver. The Briareus award, however, must go to the inaptly named Orient Express of 1898. This had ten hand controls but only one pedal (which rang the warning bell) and the hand brake was on the passenger side of the car.

■ The first public subsidy for automobile building was the $10 000 offered by the State of Wisconsin in 1875 for a 'cheap and practical substitute for the use of horses'. No sufficiently 'cheap and practical' vehicle materialised – despite the holding of the world's first motor race which attracted two steam-powered contestants (though their owners were given a joint $5000 for their trouble) – and the motor industry eventually centred itself in the neighbouring state of Michigan, anyway.

■ The idea of regular roadworthiness testing goes back to 1901, when the Spanish Ministry of Agriculture announced that 'all autocars in Spain must be subjected to examination by officially appointed experts and that certificates of efficiency must be obtained by all who desire to drive them'. Thirty pesetas was charged for the car examination; the driving certificate was 15 pesetas.

■ An iron anchor formed part of the standard equipment of the 1901 Huntingburg from the town of the same name in Indiana. A leather-thonged whip was also included in the package.

■ The first garage to employ a breakdown lorry was George & Jobling of Newcastle-on-Tyne, which in 1902 removed the rear bodywork of an Argyll car to enable it to transport a steam car with damaged steering.

■ The first garage to cater for commuters by car was the City Garage of 34 Queen Street, Cannon Street, London, which in 1902 offered 'most convenient and appropriate storage [for] automobilists who live within 20–30 miles of the city and would like to drive in and out on their cars'.

■ Pneumatic tyres were the Achilles heel of early cars, causing breakdowns and much expense. In 1902 it was reckoned that a carefully driven light car might cover 2000 miles on a set of tyres. Heavy, fast cars might do less than 1000 miles. In 1901 the tyre bill for newspaper magnate Alfred Harmsworth's stable of 'four cars of French construction, two of American, two of English and some others which are practically English' was £500 – about £25 000 in today's terms (and several of Harmsworth's cars were fitted with solid tyres)!

(Opposite) To keep out the dust, early motorists sometimes wore face masks: not all looked as sinister as this.

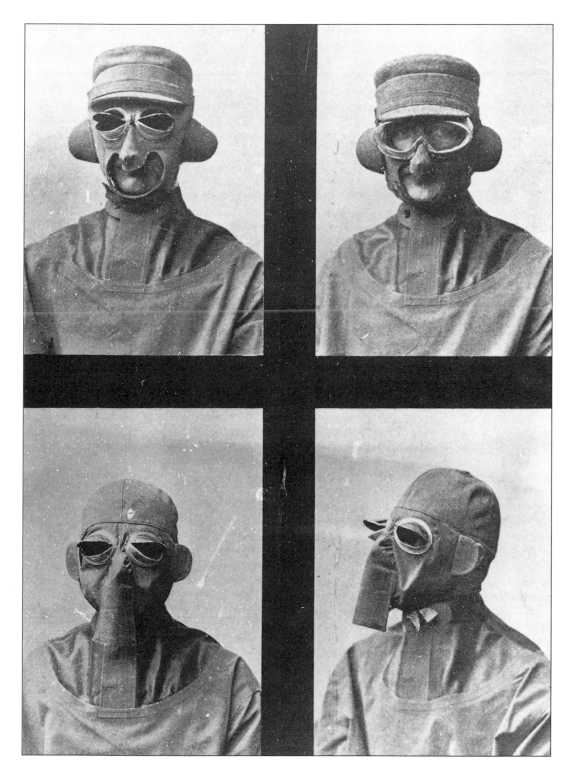

■ The first all-woman motoring organisation was the Ladies' Automobile Club established in 1903 and whose president was the *'grande dame* of automobilism in England', the Duchess of Sutherland.

■ The first standardised nationwide system of road signs was adopted in France in 1903.

■ The only person in the United Kingdom permitted to use a motor car without number plates is the reigning sovereign. However, some leading civic dignitaries were allocated 'zero' number plates for their official cars, including the Lord Provosts of Glasgow (G 0) and Edinburgh (S 0) and the Lord Mayor of London (LM 0).

■ The first car to take part in a US Presidential inauguration parade was a White steamer in the parade for Theodore Roosevelt in 1905. The first US President to drive an automobile was also Teddy Roosevelt, who drove a White steamer during a visit to Puerto Rico in 1906.

■ The Automobile Association was formed in October 1905 to warn motorists of police speed traps. AA scouts were provided for this purpose but this became illegal in 1906, so members were then instructed to stop a scout who failed to salute and ask the reason why. The scout would then advise the member to go slowly because of the road conditions if there was a speed trap ahead.

■ The first crossing of the Andes by motor car was made on 25 February 1905 by a single-cylinder Cadillac driven by José M. Piquero. The car crossed the 13 100-ft/3993-m pass from Las Cuevas, Argentina, to Los Andes, Chile, between 8 a.m. and 6 p.m. and was immediately dubbed 'The Tiger of the Andes'.

■ The first attempt by the US Congress to regulate motor vehicles was a bill introduced in 1905 which died in committee. So did a 1907 bill intended to regulate speed and registration of vehicles engaged in interstate travel.

■ The first roadside petrol pumps were installed in the USA in 1906.

■ The first major emergency in which motor vehicles gave humanitarian aid was the San Francisco earthquake of 1906. White steam cars were especially active in rescue work.

■ The first road in which motor vehicles were segregated from other traffic was the Champs-Elysées in Paris, which was divided into four separate tracks – the inner two for motor traffic, the outer two for 'horse vehicles, bicycles and nondescripts' – c. 1907.

■ The first two-way crossing of the USA was made by a Reo car in 1907.

■ Though Scotland Yard tentatively began replacing the horse-drawn cabs previously used by its detectives with motor cars in 1907, the first four cars put into service were heavy, sluggish landaulettes with small twin-cylinder engines. When the Metropolitan police proposed fitting taxis and motor buses with gongs which sounded when they exceeded the 20 mph speed limit, the only thing which prevented the proposal becoming law was the fact that Scotland Yard's cars were incapable of reaching 20 mph. The first 'flying squad' cars used by London's Metropolitan Police were RFC-type Crossley tenders, delivered in 1920.

■ 'Sleeping policemen' (or speed humps) were first used in Glencoe, Illinois, in 1907.

■ The idea of roundabouts with one-way gyratory circulation of vehicles to ease traffic congestion was first proposed in 1907 by a French civil engineer named Hénard.

■ The first family crossing of the United States was made by J. M. Murdock of Johnstown, Pennsylvania, who drove his wife and children from Los Angeles to New York between 24 April and 26 May 1908.

■ The first car to cross Australia from East to West was a 25-hp Talbot driven by Murray Aunger and Harry Dutton, who left Adelaide on 30 June 1908 and arrived in Darwin, some 2200 miles/3540 km distant, 51 days later, after crossing near-virgin territory, which included deserts and dried creek-beds. En route, they rescued and repaired a 20-hp Talbot which had stripped its drive gear on a previous attempt.

■ A convention on the international circulation of automobiles held in Paris in 1909 agreed the first internationally standardised road signs. The UK was not a signatory, having designated its own recommended system of road signs in 1903.

■ Pope Pius X was presented with an Itala as early as 1909, but refused to ride in it. The first Pope to use a motor car was Pius XI, starting with a two-tone purple Isotta-Fraschini – a gift of the people of Milan – in April 1928. Other gifts to him included a Fiat 525, a Mercedes 'Nürburg' and a Citroën donated by the Milanese agent for this French marque. All the brightwork was gold-plated, the radiator mascot was a solid gold Citroën emblem and a richly carved throne in the passenger compartment was upholstered in cloth of gold.

■ The first woman to drive across the USA was Mrs John R. Ramsey. She left New York at the wheel of her Maxwell on 9 June 1909 with three lady companions and arrived in San Francisco 53 days later.

■ The first concrete roadway in America was a 4-mile stretch on Woodward Avenue, near Detroit, laid in 1909 by the Wayne Country Road Commission.

■ The first attempt to build a car that could fly was made in 1910 by M. B. Passat, a Frenchman living in Wimbledon, whose flapping-wing ornithopter could be driven along the road with the bird-like wings folded back against its fuselage. Lack of finance kept the project on terra firma; as late as 1916 M Passat was still advertising in *The Aeroplane* in search of a backer. There have been intermittent attempts over the years to square this particular circle but the one-off flying cars that have been built – even by proper aeroplane manufacturers like Glenn Curtiss in 1917 – have only demonstrated the futility of the idea.

■ Perhaps the most extraordinary car ever was the 1910 Brooke Swan Car, built for an eccentric Scots millionaire from Calcutta. Its wooden body, carved

The amazing Swan car built by Brooke of Lowestoft in 1910 for a Scots millionaire, anxious to outdo Calcutta high society.

in the shape of a swan, incorporated gadgets ranging from a Gabriel Horn that played tunes to a nozzle in the beak that emitted scalding water. And a dump valve in the Swan's rear end dropped splats of white-wash onto the road.

■ Triplex safety glass was invented by accident when Edouard Benedictus, a French chemist, dropped a flask containing a celluloid mixture and found that it did not shatter. He patented the idea of safety glass laminated with celluloid in June 1910.

■ The most horrendous jump in taxation rates for private cars occurred on 1 January 1910 when cars were taxed on their RAC horsepower rating (which was based on the bore and number of cylinders) rather than on weight, as they had been hitherto. The increase was part of Liberal Chancellor Lloyd George's controversial 'People's Budget' and while taxes on smaller cars up to an RAC rating of 16 hp were either cut or remained much the same, taxes on the larger cars increased out of all proportion. At the upper end, cars of 60-hp rating or over had their annual duties increased eightfold, from a total of £5 5s 0d to £42 0s 0d (equivalent to over £2000 in modern terms). Lloyd George promised that the motor car tax would be used exclusively for road repairs and the building of village bypasses and a 'Road Board' was duly established.

■ The 'People's Budget' also imposed duty on petrol for the first time, at the rate of 3d a gallon, bringing the cost of a gallon to 1s 9d (8.75p); the tax was doubled in 1915 but repealed on 1 January 1921. It was little surprise when petrol duty was reimposed in the 1928 Finance Act at the rate of 4d a gallon; petrol duty has been with us ever since and today is by far the larger part of the price of motor fuel.

■ The first drive-in 'gasoline station' with island pumps was built in Detroit in 1910 by the Central Oil Company.

■ The first epidemic of automobile crime occurred in the spring of 1911 when the 'Red Hand' gang led by 'Tiger' Bonnot terrorised Northern France and Belgium. They stole high-powered cars (especially Delaunay-Bellevilles) which they used for highway and bank robberies. From the description of his methods – 'the auto would suddenly slacken its speed and turn completely around in a most incredible

Henry Alexander reaches the summit of Ben Nevis by Model T Ford in May 1911.

manner' – it sounds as though Bonnot ('The Demon Chauffeur') also invented the handbrake turn. He died in a shoot-out with the police in 1912.

■ The first central dividing lines on highways were painted in Wayne County, Detroit, Michigan, in 1911 under the supervision of Edward N. Hines.

■ Though Britain's highest mountain, Ben Nevis, had been climbed to within some 1200 feet of the summit by Dudley Grierson on an MMC-Werner motorcycle as early as 1901, it was not until May 1911 that the first successful ascent of the Scottish peak by motor vehicle was made. Henry Alexander, Ford agent at Edinburgh, made the ascent in a Ford Model T.

■ The world's first motor museum was founded in 1912 by Edmund Dangerfield, proprietor of *The Motor* magazine, in Oxford Street, London. It was transferred to Crystal Palace in 1914 and the collection was broken up at the outbreak of World War I, though many of the cars still survive.

■ The first driver to cross South America from coast to coast was Johnson Martin, who travelled across the Andes from Buenos Aires to Santiago in a two-year-old Model 28 Buick in 1914.

■ The car with the all-time least forward vision was the 1912 Blackiston, a one-off 90-hp roadster from Canton, Ohio, with a bonnet 5 ft 6 in/1.67 m high. The driver/constructor could only see forwards by leaning to one side (though he optimistically hoped to overcome this minor snag by a system of mirrors). Since the theoretical top speed was nearly 140 mph, one hopes he was successful.

■ The first petrol company to give away free maps was Gulf Oil of the US in 1913.

■ Britain's first roadside petrol pump was set up at Shrewsbury in 1913, though such pumps did not enter general use until 1921.

■ The first electric 'stop-go' traffic lights were installed in Cleveland, Ohio, in August 1914; the same year an illuminated stop sign, operated by a policeman, was used to control traffic in Detroit.

■ The first white lines on British roads marked dangerous bends on the London–Folkestone road at Ashford, Kent. They were the idea of Alderman Amos, a local farmer.

■ The idea of a motorway to link London with Liverpool was put forward by John, Lord Montagu of Beaulieu, in 1914, and got as far as a Private Member's Bill in Parliament before being dropped.

■ The young King Alfonso XIII of Spain was an enthusiastic motorist with a taste for fast cars which he drove 'like a cannonball in a cloud of smoke'. He patronised and encouraged the new Hispano-Suiza company, and their most famous pre-1914 sporting car was known as the 'Alfonso' in his honour after his young queen gave him an early example as a present.

■ It was an act of supreme optimism to open Iceland's first motor agency in 1914, selling Overland cars, for the market was the least promising in Europe. By 1936 just 784 cars were in use there.

■ In 1914 Francis Birtles, who had twice ridden round Australia on a bicycle, made the first north–south crossing of the continent from Burketown on the Gulf of Carpentaria via Sydney to Melbourne, a distance of 3500 miles/5630 km, in 21 days, accompanied only by his bulldog 'Wowser' (which he used as a towel after losing the supply of cotton waste which he carried to wipe oil off his hands) and living off the land. His diet included cockatoo, iguana and rock wallaby.

■ The Federal Road Act signed by US President Woodrow Wilson on 11 July 1916 was the first American law aimed at creating a nationwide network of interstate highways.

■ Before the Russian Revolution deprived him of his livelihood, Adolphe Kégresse – whose caterpillar-tracked Citroëns played a fundamental role in the motorised exploration of Africa and Asia during the period 1921–31 – was the manager of Czar Nicholas II's Imperial garages at St Petersburg, where the work surfaces were of marble. Kégresse originally devised his rubber caterpillar tracks so that the Imperial cars could run on snow. After the Revolution, Lenin revealed himself as a 'champagne socialist' by using a Rolls-Royce so equipped.

■ Motoring humour has its own coelacanth, a living fossil of a joke entitled 'Japanese Rules of the Road' which first saw the light of day on 3 September 1918 and is regularly quoted as though it were new-minted. It was featured, for instance, in the 1937 Ford film 'Milestones & Melodies' and was last 'sighted' on 21 January 1994 when wordsmith Nigel Rees recited extracts on the television word game show 'Countdown': 'When passenger of the foot hove in sight tootle the horn trumpet to him melodiously at first. If he still obstacles your passage tootle him with the more vigour and express by the word of the mouth the warning 'Hi, hi'.' This cobweb-shrouded jest was in fact written in a few moments by *The Motor* magazine staffman B. A. Hunt to fill a last-minute gap left by the wartime censor's scissors.

■ The first 'sneak picture' of a still-secret production model was published on 14 September 1921 when *The Motor* printed a photograph of the forthcoming 20-hp Rolls-Royce taken by Miles Thomas, then a staff member. He saw a badgeless prototype parked outside an hotel near Royce's home in Sussex, bought a camera in a nearby chemist's shop and snapped the car, which wasn't officially revealed until 13 months later.

■ The biggest six-cylinder private car of the vintage era was the Stoewer D7 of 1919; its 11 160-cc power unit was basically a World War I aero-engine.

■ Britain did not have an independent Ministry of Transport until September 1919: the first Minister was Sir Eric Geddes GCB GBE PC (1875–1937). The first Minister of Transport to become a member of the Cabinet was Herbert Morrison, on 19 March 1931.

■ The world's first three-colour traffic lights were installed in Detroit in 1919; two years later the city's police experimented with synchronised traffic lights.

■ The first transport of car spares by air took place on 19 June 1919 when parts for a racing Duesenberg were flown from Detroit to Indianapolis in a chartered biplane.

■ A Kodak Autographic camera and a compass were offered as standard equipment on the 1920 Templar touring roadster built in Cleveland, Ohio.

■ The inequities of the 'People's Budget' were compounded in the 1920 Finance Act, which changed the method of taxing cars from a banded system to a straight £1 per horsepower. This had the blatantly protectionist result of changing the annual road tax on the cheap and popular Model T Ford from £4 4s to £23, the same as a 3-litre Bentley or 20-hp Rolls-Royce. Within three years the Model T (widely regarded as American even though it had been built in

Manchester since 1911) was replaced as Britain's best-selling car by the Bullnose Morris, which was only taxed at £12. As a by-product of the 1920 Act, vehicle logbooks appeared for the first time in February 1921 and cars had to carry tax discs for the first time.

■ The first US President to ride to his inauguration by automobile was Warren Gamaliel Harding on 4 March 1921: the car was a Packard Twin-Six.

■ Though the motor car was featured in plays from very early on, the first full-length play centred on the automobile was 'Six-Cylinder Love', which opened at the Sam H. Harris Theater, New York, on 25 August 1921. Taken from the novel of the same name, it also appeared as a silent film version in 1923 and a talkie in 1931.

■ The 1921 motor vehicle laws in Pennsylvania forbade roller skaters from hitching a lift behind an automobile.

■ The first electrically synchronised traffic signals were installed in Houston, Texas, in 1922.

■ The first reflecting road sign in Britain was a direction sign for London put up in the Surrey village of Mickleham by the AA.

■ The first flashing illuminated road direction sign was erected on a fork at Wrotham Heath, Kent, to indicate the London and Sevenoaks roads. Light was provided by acetylene.

■ The 1922 Stoneleigh had a central driving seat with the passenger seats set back on either side, as does the McLaren F1 'supercar' of the 1990s. The prototype Julian of 1925, built by a wealthy eccentric from Syracuse, New York, apart from seats in arrowhead formation also had a rear-mounted radial engine in a backbone-type punt chassis.

■ The first British hotel to incorporate a car showroom was the Midland Adelphi Hotel, Liverpool, in conjunction with local dealers The Voss Motor Company during 1922.

■ Motorised perambulators were marketed by Dunkleys of Birmingham in 1922. Powered by 110-cc two-stroke engines, they travelled at 4 mph. There was a platform at the rear for the nursemaid to stand on and there was even a streamlined 'Saloon Pramotor'. The flaw was that English Law did not allow them to run on footpaths.

■ The first top-gear-only crossing of the USA was

PROTECT YOUR CAR

against theft

Locks may be picked or jimmied. Cars may be stolen in spite of them

BUT NO THIEF EVER ATTEMPTED TO STEAL A CAR WITH A MAN AT THE WHEEL

Bosco's COLLAPSIBLE RUBBER DRIVER

is so lifelike and terrifying, that nobody a foot away can tell it isn't a real, live man.

When not in use, this marvellous device is simply deflated and put under the seat. Easily inflated with your hand. or automatic pump. Price $15.

Order through your dealer or direct from

BOSCO. Inc., Akron, Ohio

Car crime is nothing new: this 'life-like and terrifying' anti-theft device dates from the mid-1920s. It was echoed in the inflatable 'passengers' of the 1990s.

made in 1923, when Erwin G. 'Cannonball' Baker drove an Oldsmobile Model 30-A touring car from New York to Los Angeles in 12 days 12 hours. The transmission was locked in 'high' and the rear wheels were jacked off the ground while refuelling so that the engine never stopped during the run.

■ The first British car whose seats could be converted into a bed (by using an optional ex-works £3 10s adaptor kit) was the 1923 Standard 13.9 hp tourer.

■ The number of motor vehicles (including motor cycles) in use in Great Britain first exceeded a million in 1923, but that figure for cars alone was not reached until 1930 (with 1 075 081). The number of cars registered in England alone exceeded one million in 1933. There were 2 073 404 cars registered in the UK in 1939; it took another 20 years to reach 5 080 510 cars, but the 10 million mark was passed in 1967. In 1993 there were 20 116 000 private cars on the roads of Britain.

■ *The Brooklands Gazette* (later *Motor Sport*) appeared in August 1924 and was the first British magazine dedicated to competition motoring.

■ The first north–south crossing of Africa from the Cape to Cairo was made by a party headed by Major and Mrs C. Court Treatt. They travelled in two 15/30-hp RFC-type Crossley tenders and left Cape Town on 24 September 1924. The direct distance was 7000 miles/11 200 km: the Court Treatts drove 12 732 miles/20 485 km, taking films and still photos en route and did not arrive in Cairo until 24 January 1926. Contrast their time with that of the first private car to make the trip from the Cape to London, a Chrysler driven by Gerry Bouwer. It left Cape Town on 6 February 1928 and arrived on 4 June.

■ The first year that there was not a single steam or electric car on display at America's National Automobile Show was 1924.

■ Work on the first motorway, the 21-km/13-mile Milan–Varese autostrada, started in June 1923 and the new road was opened in September 1924. By 1933 Italy had 12 500 miles/20 116 km of special motor roads, built at a cost of 2045 million lire.

■ The name 'motel' was coined by Arthur Heinman in 1924 and the first motel – the Motel Inn – opened at San Luis Obispo, California, on 12 December 1925.

■ In 1925 the Road Fund was raided by the Chancellor of the Exchequer, Winston S. Churchill. For the first time the money was used other than for road construction, the Exchequer tasted blood and the road fund tax was relegated to its continuing role as just another means of raising revenue for the government.

■ The first man to circumnavigate Australia by car was Noel R. Westwood, who left Perth on 4 August 1925 in a 5CV Citroën 'Cloverleaf' and returned on 30 December.

■ In March–May 1926 Frank Grey made the first crossing of Africa from west to east; his party used two 7-hp Jowetts christened 'Wait' and 'See'. It took them 60 days to complete the 'impossible' 3800-mile/6114-km journey from Lagos, Nigeria, to Massawa on the Red Sea.

■ Faxed photos are nothing new: the first 'photoradio' illustration to be sent across the Atlantic (to *Motor* magazine) depicted another first – the first Weymann fabric-bodied saloon built in America. It was a 'Safety' Stutz Vertical Eight shown at the New York Salon in January 1926. A further 'first' for the 1926 Stutz was the use of safety glass in the windscreen, which used a fine wire mesh embedded in the glass to render it shatterproof.

■ Britain's first one-way gyratory system defined by white lines and direction arrows painted on the road was inaugurated at Hyde Park Corner on 22 March 1926. A simple gyratory system had been in operation round the Victoria Memorial in front of Buckingham Palace for some months.

■ Manually-operated red-amber-green traffic lights went into operation in Piccadilly, London, in 1926.

■ Riding in a friend's sports car in Nice on 14 September 1927, free-loving dancer Isadora Duncan was strangled when her scarf caught in the car's rear wheel. But the car was an Amilcar, not the more glamorous Bugatti usually blamed for her death.

■ Scotland Yard's first high-performance vehicles were Lea-Francis 1.5-litre sports cars put into service in 1927.

■ The first London–Brighton Commemoration Run for Veteran Cars was staged on Sunday 13 November 1927 by the *Daily Sketch* and *Sunday Graphic*. Restricted to cars over 21 years old, it attracted 51 entries, of which 44 started and 37 finished. The 1928 and 1929 runs were sponsored by *The Autocar* and limited to cars over 25 years old. Since 1930 the Royal Automobile Club has been responsible for the event, which has been immutably restricted to cars made up to 31 December 1904.

■ The first woman motorist to drive round the world was Miss Violette Cordery on a 3-litre Invicta in 1927. She covered 10 266 miles/16 518 km, crossing five continents at an average running speed of 36 mph and was awarded the Dewar Trophy for her achievement.

■ The first overland journey from England to Australia by car was accomplished by Francis Birtles in his 14-hp Bean 'Sundowner'. He left London on 19 October 1927, and arrived in Sydney on 5 July 1928, having replaced the back axle and 12 tyres en route.

■ The first cloverleaf intersection was the Woodbridge Cloverleaf in New Jersey, constructed in 1928.

■ For a country which once had a fair-sized motor industry and produced three great automobile engineers – Birkigt, Roesch and Chevrolet – Switzerland has had a curiously ambivalent attitude to the automobile. Until 1 January 1933 each canton had its own individual motoring laws. The Grisons canton banned motorcars altogether until 1928 and the *loi dominicale* still banned Sunday motoring in much of the rest of Switzerland (except for doctors and veterinary surgeons) well into the 1920s. The national maximum speed limit of 25 mph was strictly enforced, urban speed limits were at the discretion of the local police and peasants were apt to stone cars as they passed.

■ Three-colour automatic traffic lights were first used in Britain at Wolverhampton in 1928.

■ Until the start of the Mussolini era, Italy had a wonderfully eccentric rule of the road. Motorists drove on the right in the country and on the left in towns until the law compelled a universal right-hand rule on 21 December 1923.

■ While twin tail lamps have only been required by law in Britain since 1956, they were a feature of several American makes as early as 1929.

■ The car used by the gang involved in the St Valentine's Day Massacre in Chicago on 14 February 1929 was a black Packard tourer with a bell on its running board, imitating the cars used by the detective bureau rather than the more popular Lincoln 'Police Special'.

■ The world's first old car club was the Veteran Car Club of Great Britain, which initially catered for pre-1905 cars. It was founded at the end of the London–Brighton Run in November 1930, over a drink at the Ship Hotel, Brighton. The three 'founding fathers' were S. C. H. Davis, J. A. Masters and J. A. Wylie.

■ Before the 1930 Road Traffic Act made them compulsory on 1 January 1931, motorists in Britain were neither compelled to take out third party insurance cover nor take an eyesight test when applying for a driving licence. The Act also compelled drivers to notify certain types of accidents and instituted Britain's first driving tests (though these were restricted to disabled drivers to prove that they were fit to drive safely). It also abolished the outmoded blanket 20 mph speed limit and replaced it with the offence of dangerous driving (there was no upper limit).

■ A law passed in the Australian state of Queensland in 1930 decreed that all complete cars had to be registered and charged an annual tax whether they were in use or not. Consequently, many dismantled Veteran cars have since been unearthed there.

■ The first murder trial in which a motor car played the central role was that of Alfred Arthur Rouse, who killed an unknown hitch-hiker at Hardingstone, Northants, and burnt his corpse in his fabric-bodied Morris Minor saloon on the night of 5–6 November 1930.

■ The first purpose-built cross-Channel car ferry, the 822-ton *Autocarrier*, operated by the Southern Railway, went into service between Dover and Calais on 30 March 1931. She carried 35 cars (which were lifted aboard on pallets) and 120 passengers.

■ The first ships with drive-on garage accommodation for motor cars – the *Victoria*, *Ausonia* and *Esperia* were in service in the Mediterranean in 1931.

■ Authoress Daphne du Maurier posed for the nude radiator mascot on the car of her actor-manager father, Sir Gerald du Maurier in 1931.

■ The first underground car park in the United Kingdom was opened at Hastings in December 1931.

■ The Highway Code was first issued by the UK government in 1931.

■ The first veteran car dealer was C. S. Burney, who in 1931 was offering 'a selection of relics at widely varying prices' from his premises at Brooklands.

■ Royal cars were not fitted with safety glass until 1931 as King George V was worried that discoloration in the glass might prevent people from seeing him.

■ The world's first concours d'elegance for veteran cars was held in Eastbourne in September 1931. It was won by E. de W. S. Colver's Arnold-Benz (now at Beaulieu).

■ France's first veteran car rally – a 30-mile run from Dreux to Versailles – took place in July 1931. Last one home took 24 hours.

■ Flashing the headlamps to warn fellow motorists of police traffic patrols was common practice in Britain as long ago as 1931.

■ The first car 'air-freshener' was the 'Autoemanatoré' deodoriser – a perforated cylinder containing a solid perfume block – sold by a Bradford company in 1932.

■ The seats in the Shakespeare Memorial Theatre, which opened in Stratford-on-Avon on St George's Day, 1932, were designed by Sir Herbert Austin.

■ When the Lord Mayor of London switched on the first 'robot' traffic lights, known as 'Eva' (for 'Electromatic Vehicle-Actuated Street Traffic Controller') at the junction of Cornhill and Gracechurch Street in the City of London on 14 March 1932, an explosion of sewer gas temporarily fused the system. Made by a London company, 'Eva' lights were in use by the autumn of 1933 at many major intersections in London and the provinces as well as in Paris, Berlin, Madrid, Barcelona, Milan, Zürich, Johannesburg, Durban and Sydney.

■ The first three-letter registration to be issued was 'ARF' (Staffordshire), in July 1932.

■ The pioneer of the modern automobile museum was Count Carlo Biscaretti di Ruffia of Turin. His Museo dell'Automòbile was first proposed in 1932. Biscaretti was appointed curator and began assembling exhibits which opened in temporary accommodation at Turin's Municipal Stadium in 1939. Work on a permanent museum in Turin's Corso Unità d'Italia began in 1957 but Biscaretti died in 1959, the year before the new museum opened on 3 November 1960.

■ The first pedestrian-operated street crossing lights were erected on the Brighton Road in Croydon, Surrey, in 1932.

■ The first sodium street lights were installed along the Purley Way, Croydon, in 1932.

■ The first drive-in cinema was opened at Camden, New Jersey, in 1933 and the first drive-in bank at Los Angeles, California, in 1937.

■ The world's oldest extant private automobile collection was started in 1934 by Dutch car dealer P. W. Louwman with a 1914 Dodge. The collection, which now numbers several hundred cars and is based at Raamsdonksveer, near Rotterdam, is today run by Louwman's son Evert as the Dutch National Motor Museum.

■ The Vintage Sports Car Club, originally intended as a protest against falling standards of sports car design, and restricted to cars built before the end of 1930, was founded in October 1934. Almost from the start the VSCC organised a special category for cars built between 1905 and 1915 which were known picturesquely (if inaccurately) as 'Edwardians'.

■ A splendid chap named Percy Shaw invented 'cat's eye' road studs after being saved from crashing by a cat's eyes reflecting the lights of his car one foggy night in 1933. The first reflective studs in British roads were laid at Market Harborough by a rival company in March 1934 but Shaw's cat's eyes – which were self-cleaning – were first tried the following month and proved so superior that they became universal. Mr Shaw, who made a well-deserved fortune from his major contribution to road safety, never married, rarely travelled from his native Yorkshire, and lived in the house in which he had been born. It had a separate TV set for each channel, no carpets and no curtains (which spoiled the view, he said).

■ Pedestrian crossings marked by dotted lines on the road and flashing striped 'Belisha Beacons' (named after Transport Minister Leslie Hore-Belisha) were introduced in Britain in 1934.

■ The 1934 Triumph Gloria was named after 'Miss Gloria', a mannequin at Selfridge's department store in London.

■ The smallest car ever to drive round the world was the 1935 98-cc Rytecraft Scootacar in which Surrey draughtsman Jim Parkinson circled the globe (at 10 mph!) in 1965–6.

■ America's first antique car club, the Antique Automobile Club of America, was founded in November 1935; it is now the world's largest organisation devoted to old cars. The Horseless Carriage Club of America followed in November 1937 and the Veteran Motor Car Club of America in January 1939.

■ The new standardised Ministry of Transport road signs which came into force in Britain in 1934 were the first to define 'major roads' and the precise significance of the red, amber and green signals on a traffic light.

■ The British urban speed limit of 30 mph came into force in March 1935.

■ The British Ministry of Transport introduced a driving test for the first time in May 1935 for those who did not already hold a licence: holders of provisional (learner's) licences had to carry L-plates at the front and back of their cars.

■ Vertically challenged dictator Adolf Hitler had a specially raised floor section in his open 5 ton armoured Mercedes 770K to make him appear 5 inches taller when parading before his jackbooted acolytes.

■ The first state official appointed to control motor sport and motor clubs was Fritz Hühnlein, named as Korpsführer of the Nazi NSKK ('Nazional Sozialistische Kraftfahr Korps', to which all Nazis owning cars or motorbikes belonged) in 1934.

■ The world's first parking meter was installed in Oklahoma City, USA, in July 1935, the invention of Professor H. G. Thuesen and Gerald A. Hale of Oklahoma State University. In August the Reverend C. H. North of the Third Pentecostal Church of Oklahoma City became the first person to be arrested for a parking meter offence.

■ Britain's first broken white line road markings appeared on a 70-mile stretch of the A30/A38 in Devon in 1935.

■ Flying cars have been tried, but the only car which was claimed to float as well was the 1935 Tri-Phibian built by a Greek immigrant named Constantios Vlachos. It blew up while being demonstrated in front of the Library of Congress in Washington before it could prove its three-element capability.

■ Germany's first Autobahn was opened between Frankfurt and Darmstadt in May 1935, although retrospective claims were made for 6 miles/9.8 km of dual-carriageway road, the Avus, southwest of Berlin, completed in 1921. The Hanover–Berlin motorway followed in 1936.

■ The longest solo marathon car run on record was accomplished by François Lecot – an hotelier from Rochetaillée, Lyon – in a Traction Avant Citroën. Between 23 July 1935 and 22 July 1936, he covered 400 000 km (c. 250 000 miles) in France at an average of 40 mph. He drove in daily spells of 19 hours, and even competed in the 1936 Monte Carlo Rally, finishing 50th overall. He had covered 100 000 km in a Rosengart (Austin Seven) in a similar run in 1931–2.

■ Britain's Transport Minister – rather than local or county councils – has been responsible for trunk roads since 1936.

■ The London Motor Show took place in the new Earl's Court building in October 1937 for the first time. Before that, the principal London show had been held at Olympia (since 1905).

■ Speedometers and safety glass were not compulsory on British-registered motor vehicles until 1937.

■ The first time that a statistical analysis of world motor vehicle taxation was undertaken, in 1937, it was found that motorists in the United Kingdom were the most highly taxed of all by a considerable margin. A family car of only 1.5 litres covering 12 000 miles a year paid £30.05 in tax whereas in the lowest-taxed country – Malaya – it would have paid just £4.90. The owner of a 3.5-litre car in the UK paid

£50.95; his counterpart in the USA would have paid only £8.23.

■ Petrol rationing was introduced in the United Kingdom for the first time on 16 September 1939, shortly after the outbreak of war. Headlamp masks, to cut out most of the light and thus be less obvious to enemy aircraft, became compulsory.

■ Great Britain's first flyovers were on the Winchester by-pass, opened in 1939, at the junctions with the Alton and Alresford roads, and with the old A33 road at Compton.

■ America's first dual carriageway, the Pennsylvania Turnpike, was opened in October 1940. It was built along a disused railway line.

■ The world's largest private collection of historic vehicles (1200-strong in 1993) was started in 1944 by Ghislain Mahy of Ghent, Belgium, with a 1921 Model T Ford acquired for 150 Belgian Francs. Many of the cars in the collection were restored by Mahy, who worked 12 hours a day, six days a week on the task until he was nearly 80. Some 325 of the outstanding vehicles of the Mahy Collection form the core of the Autoworld Museum in Brussels.

■ Petrol rationing was retained by Britain's postwar Labour government (which had a doctrinaire dislike of 'pleasure motoring') until 26 May 1950, after the Socialists had received a drubbing in the General Election. It was imposed again during the Suez Crisis (December 1956–May 1957). The 'basic' postwar petrol ration for private motorists varied from the equivalent of some 200 miles/320 km a month to nothing.

■ Though the horsepower tax ceased to be applicable to new cars after 1946, Chancellor Hugh Dalton failed to lift this impost from older models, which continued to be taxed under this punitive formula until 1951. The lowest rate charged during the currency of the horsepower tax was 15 shillings (£0.75) per taxable horsepower, from 1935 to 1938.

■ The first car firm to advertise on commercial network television in the USA is believed to have been Chevrolet in 1946. The first British company to advertise on commercial television was Ford, which advertised on the opening night of Associated Rediffusion on 22 September 1955, even though the only TV in the home of Ford managing director Sir Patrick Hennessy was in the servants' quarters.

■ Following a United Nations world conference on road transport in Geneva in 1949, 30 European countries adopted the standardised European system of road signs. Again, Britain displayed its independence by not adopting these Euro-signs until 1 January 1965.

■ The first regular car ferry service by air was started by Silver City Airways from Lympne, Kent, to Le Touquet in France at Easter 1949, using Bristol Freighters. A similar service was subsequently operated by Carvairs of British United Air Ferries from Lydd, Kent. The BUAF air ferry to the Continent ceased operation in November 1976.

■ Zebra crossings for pedestrians were first seen in Britain in October 1951.

■ The first car company to appoint a full-time product safety engineer was Ford (US), who hired former aviation engineer Alex Haynes for this purpose in 1952.

■ The Montagu Motor Museum was founded at Beaulieu, Hampshire, by Lord Montagu. Initially it had just five cars, displayed in the entrance hall of his ancestral home, Palace House, but within a decade it had over 100 vehicles in a purpose-built museum plus a library of motoring books, drawings and photographs.

■ The first 'non-club' British magazine devoted to vintage motoring was *The Vintage & Thoroughbred Car*, which first appeared in March 1953. It became *Veteran & Vintage* in 1956 and was absorbed into *Collector's Car* in 1979.

■ The modern interest in historic vehicles owes much to the 1953 film *Geneviève*, a comedy based on the annual London–Brighton Veteran Car Run, whose four-wheeled star was a 1904 twin-cylinder Darracq. The film caught the public imagination, played a major role in transforming the Brighton Run into the world's most popular motoring event and making the collection and restoration of antique cars the widespread hobby it is today. *Geneviève*'s owner, Norman Reeves, found the publicity more than he could handle and sold her. She spent the next 35 years in Australia and was acquired by the Dutch National Motor Museum in 1993. Her 'co-star', a four-cylinder Spyker, was redated as 1905 by the Veteran Car Club of Great Britain and became ineligible for the Run. It, too, is now in the Netherlands.

■ Before she was called 'Geneviève' (chosen as her 'stage name' because Geneviève was the patron saint of Paris, where the Darracq works were located) Norman Reeves' 1904 Darracq was known as 'Old Annie'.

■ Flashing indicators have only been legal in Britain since 1 January 1954. Twin rear reflectors became compulsory on 1 October that year, but twin rear lamps were not required until exactly two years later.

■ The world's biggest autojumble, held by the Antique Automobile Club of America in October each year at Hershey, Pennsylvania, now has over 10 000 separate stalls but started back in 1954 with just seven vendors.

■ The first non-stop run from Anchorage, Alaska, to Mexico City (6391 miles/10 283 km) was made in 1954 by Louis Matter of San Diego, California, and two friends.

■ The last US state to introduce driving licences was South Dakota in 1954.

■ In 1954 President Dwight D. Eisenhower authorised the creation of a permanent President's Action Committee for Highway Safety.

■ The first American state to make driver education compulsory before a driving licence was issued to under-18s was Michigan in 1955.

■ In an attempt to boost sales of the GT-350, Carroll Shelby's high-performance conversion of the Ford Mustang, 1000 examples of a special-edition black-and-gold GT-350H were added to the Hertz Rent-a-Car fleet during 1966, available for $17 a day to hirers who were over 25 and thus qualified for the 'Hertz Sports Car Club' (which also rented Chevrolet Corvette Stingrays).

■ America's 41 000 mile/66 000 km interstate highway system was approved in 1956 under the Highway Act which committed the federal government to meeting 90 per cent of the construction cost.

■ The first American motor show to be televised was the 1956 National Automobile Show (42nd in the series and the last to be held in the New York Coliseum). The hour-long TV show was seen by an estimated 21.6 million viewers and the speaker at the show banquet was Vice-President Nixon.

■ The first double white lines prohibiting overtaking appeared down the centre of roads in Britain in 1957, following a European Agreement.

■ Charles Faroux, technical editor of the French paper L'Auto, died in 1957, ending 53 years in that capacity. However, the longest-serving motoring journalist working for the same paper is William Boddy, Founder Editor of Motor Sport, who began writing for the magazine as a freelance in the mid-1930s, took over its editorship at the outbreak of war in September 1939 and, having passed his 80th birthday in 1993, was still contributing its veteran, vintage and classic content at the time of writing.

■ The Automotive Information Disclosure Act – or 'label law' – which came into effect in the USA on 1 October 1958 – compelled makers to fix a label to the windscreen or side window of every new car detailing its make, model, serial number, how it had been transported to the dealership, its price and the factory-installed options.

■ Britain's first motorway, the Preston by-pass, opened in December 1958. It is now part of the M6. The first section of the M1 opened in 1959.

■ The first parking meters in Britain were installed outside the American Embassy (very appropriately, as these wretched devices were an American invention) in London's Grosvenor Square on 10 July 1958. The Minister of Transport responsible was Harold Watkinson, not his publicity-seeking successor Ernest Marples.

■ Britain's first radio-telephone service for motorists was inaugurated on 29 September 1959 by the General Post Office. Initially, the service was restricted to parts of Lancashire and Cheshire and cost 2s 6d for a local call, with a quarterly rental of £7 10s. London did not have a car-phone service until 5 July 1965.

■ Britain's first conviction for speeding based on a radar trap was recorded in Lancashire on 19 August 1959. The alleged offender was fined £3.

■ Though Detroit has been the centre of the American motor industry since the early 1900s, it did not host the American National Automobile Show until 1960. Before that, it had been held in New York (1900–56).

■ The first auction of veteran and vintage cars was staged at the Montagu Motor Museum, Beaulieu, on 16 July 1960 by Southern Counties Car Auctions. Only a couple of cars (veteran examples of De Dion and Panhard) sold for over £1000 and a Speed Six Bentley changed hands for £330 (today's auction value would be in the region of £100 000).

■ The Ministry of Transport's annual Roadworthiness Tests for cars ten or more years old came into force on 12 September 1960. In April 1967 they were extended to cover three-year-old cars.

■ Britain's first self-service petrol pump went into operation at Southwark Bridge, London, in November 1961.

■ The longest road journey by a gas turbine-powered car was probably the New York–Los Angeles evaluation run made by a turbine-engined Dodge Dart in 1961.

■ The first solar-powered electric car was a 1912 Baker Electric fitted in 1962 with an International Rectifier solar panel on its roof.

■ A novel addition to the leisure market was the trailer caravan launched (literally) in 1963 by Stewart Coach Industries of Bristol, Indiana, which converted into a house boat.

■ Policewomen were employed for traffic control duties in Paris for the first time during 1964.

■ The Ford GT40 of 1964 was so called because its overall height was 40 inches.

■ Promoted as 'the most famous car in the world', a 1964 Aston Martin DB5 was fitted with some unusual extras by the special effects department for its role in the James Bond film 'Goldfinger' including 'machine guns' in the front wings, extending ram bumpers fore and aft, a retractable 'bulletproof shield' behind the rear window, three-way number plates, extending hub cap 'slasher spinners', hidden compartments behind the rear lights which drop oil and tyre-bursting spiked 'caltrops' to deter pursuing cars, a smoke-screen generator and an ejector seat for unwanted passengers.

■ The first British number plates to carry a letter suffix were issued in Middlesex in February 1964. The letter 'A' at the end of the number denoted the

year, which ran from January to December. In 1967, at the request of the motor industry, the year letter changed to 'E' on 1 January and to 'F' on 1 August. The idea was to boost sales in the traditionally slack summer season and worked beyond expectation, so that August is now the peak registration month. When the usable letters ('I', 'O', 'Q' and 'Z' are omitted) were exhausted, the year letter changed to a prefix in August 1983, starting with 'A' again.

■ The increase in traffic meant that the pleasant custom of AA patrols saluting cars carrying an AA badge was discontinued in 1965.

■ Announced during 1965, America's 'HELP' (Highway Emergency Locating Plan) enabled motorists in trouble to call 24-hour monitoring stations by Citizens' Band radio.

■ In Britain a 50-mph speed limit was imposed on 500 miles of roads in 1965.

■ The first transatlantic car-to-car radio telephone call was made by Richard Dimbleby to Max Kaufmann, a Montreal cab driver, in 1965. Both cars had Pye telephone equipment.

■ The National Traffic & Motor Vehicle Safety Act (designed to create a national safety programme and safety standards), the Highway Safety Act (to set up a nationwide coordinated road safety programme) and the Department of Transportation were all established in the United States during 1966.

■ A blanket 70-mph/112-km speed limit (including motorways) was imposed in Britain on 1 January 1967 as a temporary four-month experiment by Minister of Transport Tom Fraser. His non-driving successor Barbara Castle made it permanent, despite inconclusive results.

■ Safety campaigner Ralph Nader leaked news of what he claimed to be a major cover-up concerning the development of a 'highly-advanced electric car' by General Electric of America in 1967. Said to be a four-seater made from aluminium honeycomb, the GE electric was said to have a range of 200 miles/320 km, a top speed of 81 mph/130 kph and a hybrid fuel cell that could be recharged in 8 minutes, but was being kept secret 'because the oil companies and motor industry are major sub-contractors of General Electric'.

■ Sweden, the last mainland European country to retain the left-hand rule of the road, followed the Gadarene trend to the right in September 1967. The

change-over was eased by the fact that most Swedish cars were left-hand drive anyway. Iceland followed suit in May 1968. Those who advocate that the United Kingdom and Ireland should do likewise would do well to reflect on the fact that the right-hand rule of the road – like the metric system (and an extremely silly calendar, which was fortunately abandoned) – sprang out of the desire of the French revolutionaries to prove that they could order the universe better than God. Because the left-hand rule of the road had been sanctioned by Pope Boniface in the Middle Ages, the revolutionaries decreed that the opposite order should henceforth prevail. Revolutionary republics like the United States followed suit and other countries gradually switched over. But many countries – including the United Kingdom, Ireland, Japan (the world's leading car producer) and much of the former British Empire – still observe the left-hand rule. In Britain it was long believed that left-hand driving was a legacy of the preference of passing an approaching horseman or carriage right side to right side to facilitate right-armed defence against sudden attack or that Continental postillions were mounted on the rearmost left horse in a team and thus preferred to pass left side to left side. Oddly enough, in 1911 France's *Commission du Code de la Route* ('Highway Code') proposed that France should drive on the left 'because it is instinctive'.

■ Britain's first breathalyser tests were instituted on 9 October 1967. It became illegal for the driver of a motor vehicle to exceed 80 mg of alcohol per 100 ml of blood.

■ The largest private car offered since 1945 was the limited-production American Mohs Ostentatienne Opera Sedan, a $19 600 baroque extravaganza with a 8990-cc V8 engine announced late in 1967. It had a 270 degree windscreen, cantilever rear entrance door and safety seats that swung up on impact.

■ Britain's first four-level road junction was opened at the intersection of the M4 and M5 motorways at Almondsbury, near Bristol, in 1967.

■ US Federal Safety Standards came into force on 1 January 1968, following lobbying led by Ralph Nader. They demanded an exterior driver's mirror, lami-

The world's largest collection of Bugatti cars – over 120 of them! – was assembled by the Schlumpf brothers between 1957 and 1976; it now forms the core of the French National Motor Museum at Mulhouse (Alsace).

nated windscreen, collapsible steering column, two-speed windscreen wipers and front and rear seat belts. The extra equipment was inevitably reflected in higher car prices.

■ Computerised warning signs first appeared on British motorways in June 1968, on the Severn Bridge section of the M4. In spring 1969 the system was extended to the London section of the motorway.

■ In 1968 official figures claimed that highway travel in the United States had exceeded 1 000 000 million miles for the first time. The same year the American motor industry built its 250 millionth car.

■ The most expensive car ever built was the 1971 Lunar Rover, with a top speed of 10 mph/16 kph and a range of 57 miles/92 km – and a price tag of $19 million for a production run of four vehicles. Three of these were actually landed on the Moon as part of the Apollo space programme, and the lunar speed record of 10.5 mph/16.9 kph was set by astronauts Young and Duke during the Apollo 16 mission. They covered a total of 60 miles/96 km – equivalent to $320 000 a mile.

■ From the singularly appropriate date of 1 April 1974, all new cars on dealers' forecourts and showrooms in the UK were required to display official government fuel consumption figures.

■ America introduced the lamentable 'double-nickel' 55 mph blanket speed limit in 1977. The 88 kph metric conversion does not lend itself so easily to a nickname.

■ A specially built high-roof Rolls-Royce Phantom VI limousine was the British motor industry's gift to Queen Elizabeth II on her Silver Jubilee in 1977.

■ The British Motor Show was held for the first time at the new National Exhibition Centre in Birmingham in 1977.

■ EEC Type Approval applied to all new cars sold in Britain from 1 April 1978.

(Right) A muscular sports car in an old tradition, the Viper has a front-mounted V10 and a sparse cockpit. It carries Dodge badges in the USA, and is a Chrysler in other markets.

■ The world's longest recorded traffic jam occurred in 1980 when a queue of stationary vehicles 109 miles/175 km long formed on the autoroute linking Paris and Lyon. It was almost equalled in 1993 by a 100-mile jam from Hamburg to the Danish border on the German A7.

■ The British 'totting-up' system of driving licence endorsements was supplanted by a graded points system from November 1982. Accumulation of 12 or more points in three years resulted in automatic disqualification.

■ The wearing of seat belts by front-seat occupants of post-1964 cars and vans became compulsory in the UK from 31 January 1983.

■ The wheel clamp – known as the Denver Shoe in the USA where it originated – was introduced in London in May 1983 to immobilise illegally parked vehicles. Originally a special Metropolitan Police vehicle squad was responsible for clamping the vehicles but in 1986 the operation was handed over to private contractors, some of which became renowned for their tendency to act with more zeal than intelligence.

■ In 1985 computer boffin Sir Clive Sinclair introduced his C5 electric three-wheeler which needed no licence and could be used on the road by anyone over 14. Those were, it seems, its only plus points and it was soon withdrawn.

■ The world's largest collection of Rolls-Royce cars – 93 of them – was owned by Bhagwan Shri Rajneesh, an Indian mystic, who was deported from Oregon, USA, in November 1985; the cars were given to him by his disciples.

■ The world's longest urban ring road – the 120 mile/193 km M25 London Orbital Motorway – was completed on 29 October 1986. The planners were the only people surprised when peak traffic on the M25 considerably exceeded their predictions almost from the start.

■ Fixed penalty fines for minor motoring offences were introduced in Britain in October 1986. A scale of charges ranging from £12 to £24 covered some 250 offences, though motorists who denied guilt could still to go to court.

■ The highest-ever level of new car registrations recorded in Britain was 2 373 391, in 1989. That year also saw record car production of 1 299 082.

■ The world record price for a veteran car achieved at auction was £1.6 million paid for a 1903 60-hp Mercedes from the collection of the late Peter Hampton at a July 1991 Brooks (Auctioneers) sale in London. Auctioneer Robert Brooks had previously achieved the world record auction price for any pre-war car by selling a Bugatti Royale for £5.5 million at the Christie's Albert Hall sale in 1987.

■ The country with the highest percentage of exports in relation to total car production is Belgium, which in 1992 exported 1 018 200 cars out of its total output of 1 075 547, equivalent to nearly 95 per cent. The highest volume of exports was made by Japan, which exported 4 408 884 out of a total production of 9 378 694 that year.

■ European motorists spend a total of 32.6 billion hours in their cars every year, according to the industry-wide Prometheus programme. By 2010 the figure will have risen to 66 billion hours.

■ Britain's roads were safer in 1992 than at any time since records began in 1926, when there were 4886 road deaths. The 1992 figure was 4229. Britain is, indeed, by far the safest country in the European Community, with 187 deaths per million cars on the road: the worst is Portugal, with 916. Remarkably, Belgium, with 422 deaths per million cars, is far more dangerous than Italy, with 246.

■ The world's longest road is the 17 018-mile/27 381-km Pan-American Highway which links north-west Alaska to southernmost Chile.

■ The European country with most electric cars on the road in 1993 was Switzerland, with 1200; Japan had about 1000 electric cars, of which c. 60 per cent belong to government departments.

■ The world's largest car park – at West Mall, Edmonton, Alberta, Canada – has spaces for 20 000 cars plus overflow capacity for a further 10 000.

(Opposite) Two of the more extravagant 'super cars' of the 1990s were the Lamborghini Diablo (top), which failed to repeat the success of the Countach, and Jaguar's XJ220 (bottom), which also came when sales for costly high-performance cars were sluggish.

■ Britain's Driver & Vehicle Licensing Agency at Swansea, opened in 1974, holds the records for nearly 35 million drivers and 20 million vehicles, has a staff of over 4000 and sends out up to 350 000 documents every working day.

■ The most expensive number plate ever purchased was K1 NGS, bought at auction for £203 500 by an anonymous British buyer at Christie's of London on 11 December 1993. The previous record was the £176 000 paid for A1 in 1989.

Previous pages; The McLaren F1 brought advanced race-bred technology to a road car, with carbon-fibre construction and a 627 bhp 6.1-litre BMW V12 to give a top speed exceeding 230 mph. The price, some £540 000, also set a record . . .

(Opposite) The Ferrari 348 Spider (top) and the Aston Martin DB7 (bottom) represented sensible approaches to high-performance motoring for the second half of the 1990s. The 348 two-seaters had elegant Pininfarina bodies and V8 engines. The DB7 incorporates some Jaguar components, has a 'traditional' front engine/rear drive layout and was launched in coupé form.

■ The longest recorded trip in an antique car was undertaken in 1991–3 by the De Souza brothers of Valenca, Brazil. Driving the 1928 Ford Model A roadster he had owned since he was 13, Carlos de Souza (39) had covered over 47 200 miles/75 940 km via South and North America, Australia and Africa by the time he and his brother arrived in London in July 1993 and had a further 18 600 mile/29 925 km trip across Europe and Asia planned before the Model A was shipped back to Brazil from Portugal in the autumn of 1993.

■ The first 200 mph production car was the 1988 Ferrari F40. Using such a speed in virtually every country in the world would mean at best a huge fine, but 200 mph-plus cars were soon to be available from Jaguar, Bugatti, Lamborghini and McLaren as well.

■ The first attempt to drive 'overland' from London to New York began on Monday 27 December 1993 when two 4 × 4 Ford Mondeos (and a support team in off-road vehicles) set out from Westminster Bridge for the recently completed Channel Tunnel. The 15 000-mile journey did not achieve its objective when an amphibious vehicle failed to cross the Bering Straits between Asia and North America.

■ The fastest road car catalogued at the time of going to press was the McLaren F1 supercar, which during testing on the Nardo circuit in Italy was clocked at 231 mph/372 kph.

INDEX

Numbers in italic refer to illustrations

A
Aaltonen, Rauno, 204
ABS (anti-lock) braking, 180
AC cars: Ace, 81
　Cobra, 160
accelerator pedal: centre, 80
　starter actuated by, 67
accessories *see individual items*
accidents: fatal, 8, 9, 19, 117, 126, 156,
　157, 159
　first fine for, 9
　first recorded, 8
　racing, 117, 126, 156, 157, 159
　　first recorded, 115
　　Indianapolis, 127, 134
　　involving spectators, 139, 155
　　Le Mans 1955, 134
　　worst, 156
　rallying, 191, 196, 198, 200, 203
Achères LSR runs, 117
Acme cars, 22
　'perpetual guarantee', 43
Acropolis Rally, 190
　1972, 193
　1981, 196
　1987, 199
Adams, Ronnie, *189*
Adams 40/50-hp car, *84*
Adams V8 engines, 83
Adams-Farwell car, 84
Adelaide street circuit, 139
Ader, Clément, 123
Ader V8 racer, 83
advertising: on racing cars, 180
　television, 231
aerodynamics: bodywork, 63, 66
　'ground effects', 170
　'negative lift', 167
　'wings', 160
　see also streamlining
Africa: first north-south crossing, 227
　first west-east crossing, 227
Agnelli, Gianni, 98
Agnelli, Giovanni, 32, 98
Aintree circuit, Lancashire, 155
air bag experiments, 71
air conditioning, 68
air-freshener, 229
'Airfoil' lamps, 68
Airmobile cars, 92
airscrew-driven car, 91, *92*
Aitken-Walker, Louise, 199
Alaska-Mexico City non-stop run, 232
Aldington, H. J., 187
Alen, Markku, 192, 194, 196, 198, 203,
　204
Alexander, Henry, 222-3
Alfa Romeo cars: 158/159 GP cars, 147,
　152
　177 GP car, 170
　Bimotore, 141
　P2 GP car, 137
　saloon-car racing, *174*
　Tipo B ('P3'), 140, *142*

Type 512, 147
Alfa Romeo company, 29, 101
Alfa Romeo GP engines, 169
Alfa Romeo team, 170
Alfonso XIII, King, 224
Allard, Sydney, 161, *188*, 189
Allard P-type saloon, *188*
Allison, Bobby, 179
Allison, Davey, 179
Alpine Rally *see* Coupes des Alpes
Alpine Trial *see* Coupes des Alpes
alternator, 95
Alvis cars, 85
　12/75 sports car, 80
American Automobile Association, 140,
　156
American Bantam Jeeps, 49
American Grand Prize, 126
American Hot Rod Association, 153
American Motor League of Chicago, 22
American Motors company, 29
American National Automobile Show,
　232, 233
American Racing Series ('Mini-Indy'),
　178
American Underslung cars, 112
Amon, Chris, 162, 171
Amphicar, 52
Anderson Special, 85
Andersson, Ove, 190, 204
Andes, first crossing by car, 220
Andretti, Mario, 152, 179, 180, 204, *204*
　and family, 179
Andretti, Michael, 168, 205
anti-theft devices, 71, *226*
Antique Automobile Club of America,
　230
antique cars, longest recorded trip, 243
Apperson, Edgar and Elmer, 99
Ardmore circuit, New Zealand, 155
Argentine Grand Prix: first, 154
　1958, *145*, 157
　winners, 154
Argentine Grand Prix of the Roads, 127
Argentine Rally: 1985, 196
　1988, 199
Argyll engines, 86
Ariel, 44
Ariès 'Windora', 47
Arnold-Benz car, 218
Arrol-Aster engines, 86
Arrows team, 168, 170
Artioli, Romano, 30
Ascari, Alberto, 150, 205
Ascari, Antonio, 137, 205
Aspendale track, Victoria, 126
Association Internationale des
　Automobile Clubs Reconnus
　(AIACR), 123
Aston Martin cars: DB5 ('James Bond'
　car), 233
　DB7, *242*
　Lagonda, 71
Aston Martin company, 29, 100
Auburn-Duesenberg-Cord company,
　101

Audi cars, 90, 187, 198
　Quattro, *195*, 196, 199, 203
Audi company, 29
　badge, 50
Auriol, Didier, 203
Austin, Henry, 13
Austin, Sir Herbert, 41, 99, 229
Austin, Pat, 153
Austin cars: 10/4, 67
　American, 67
　Mini prototype, *53*
　Sheerline, *87*
　see also Mini-Cooper
Austin company, 29
Australia: car industry, 52
　circumnavigation of, 227
　first cars, 13
　first east-west crossing, 220
　first north-south crossing, 224
　first purpose-built circuit, 126
　Queensland registration law, 228
　see also England to Australia
Australian Grand Prix: first, 139
　1938, 143
　1985, 175
　1991, 179
Australian Horseless Carriage
　Syndicate, 13
'Australia's Own Car', *51*
Austria, early vehicles, 12
Austrian Automobile Club, Alpenfahrt,
　184
Austrian Grand Prix, 157
　first, 160
　1984, 173
　winners, 160
Austro-Daimler company, 29
Auto Avio Costruzioni, 147
Auto Union cars: A type, 141
　C-type, *132*
　D-type, *144*
autobahn, first, 230
Autocar, The, 24
autojumble, Hershey, 232
Automobile, 19
Automobile Association, 220, 233
　origins, 17
Automobile Club de France (ACF), 22,
　115
　1899 show, *22*
Automobile Club de l'Ouest, 134
Automobile Club of America, 22
　New York to Buffalo trial, 182
Automobile Club of Great Britain &
　Ireland, 23, 108, 112
　1000-Miles Trail, 182
　Easter tour 1898, *23*,
　see also Royal Automobile Club
Automotive Information Disclosure
　Act, 232
*Automotor and Horseless Vehicle Journal,
　The*, 24
Automotor Journal, 24
'Autopsy', steam omnibus, 9
Autoworld Museum, 231
Avon Park drag strip, 161

Avus circuit, Berlin, *132*, 138
axles, rear: hyploid, 80
  swing-axle 79

B
Back Bay Cycle & Motor Company, 24
badges and emblems, origins of, 43
  see also individual companies
Baker, Erwin G. 'Cannonball', 227
Baker Electric car, 58, 233
Baker headlamp system, 94
Balestre, Jean-Marie, 179
Balfour, A. J., 23
Ballot 2LS car, 85
Ballot-Léna, Claude, 163
Bandama Rally 1972, 193
bank, drive-in, 229
Barber, Robert, 176
Barber gearbox, 91
Barnard, John, 99, 171
Barnato, Woolf, 140
Barnfather Patent Tyre Sustaining
  Pump, 77
Barrett, Stan, 170
Bateman steam tricycle, 21
Bathurst circuit, Australia, 143
Battery Box (electric car), 169
batteries, concealed, 67
Bazzi, Luigi, 141
Beatrice Lolas, 159
'Belching Amphibian', 8
Belgian Grand Prix, 137
  first, 137
  1973, 161
  winners, 137
Belisha Beacons, 230
Bell, Derek, 173
Bell, Ray, 175
Ben Nevis: first successful ascent, 224
  1911, *222-3*
Bendix clutch, 93
Benetton B193B car, 180, *181*
Benetton team, 171, 176
Bentley, Walter Owen, *98-9*, 99
Bentley cars, *134-5*
  first, *98-9*
Bentley company, 29
Benz, Carl, 12, *16-17*, 99
Benz, Frau Berta, 15
Benz cars: 200 hp, 46
  dog carts, 23
  GP cars, 133
  three-wheeler, *12*
  Tropfenwagen, *144*
  'Viktoria', 42
Benz company, 29
  see also Arnold-Benz; Mercedes-Benz
Bernstein, Kenny, 153
Bettega, Attilio, 196
Bexhill-on-Sea, speed trials, 117, 124
Bégot-Mazurie cars, 44
Biasion, Massimo 'Miki', 190, 205
Biddle car, 47
Bignan-Sport cars, 47
Birabongse of Siam, Prince, 142, 147
Birch cars, 44
Birglow indicator, 66
Birkigt, Marc, 32, 99
Birmingham, England, 178
  National Exhibition Centre, 236
Birtles, Francis, 224, 228
Black, Sir John, 99
Black Prince cyclecar, *78*

Blackbushe Airport, Hampshire, 161
Blackiston car, 224
Blériot, Louis, 94
Blomqvist, Stig, 196, 205
'Bluebird', *120*
'Blue Flame', *121*
BMW cars: 328 coupé, *146*
  2002 Turbo, *87*, 90
  saloon-car racing *174*
BMW company, 29, 38
BMW engines, 171
board tracks, 127
Boddy, William, 232
body design: bonnet flutes, 43
  closed cars, 49
  'Roi des Belges', 25
  see also seating; stylists
bodywork, 58-71
  all-metal, 58, 59
  detachable, 59
  fabric covered, 63
  first unitary-construction, 68
  glass fibre, 70
  monocoque construction, 130, 159
  other materials, 62, 63
  pillarless, 62
  Pininfarina, *242*
  plastic, 69, 192
  stage-coach, *61*
  stainless steel panelling, *71*
  streamlining, *64*
  transformable, *61*
  unit construction with chassis, *79*
  welded all-steel, *60*
  'wind-cutting', 117
Boillot, André, 131
Boillot, Georges, 129, *130*
Bois de Boulogne, Paris, 147
Bol d'Or, 133
Bollée, Amédée *fils*, 29, 99
  Type E, 84
Bollée, Amédée *père*, 29, 99
Bollée, Léon, 99
bonnet release, first dashboard-
  operated, 68
Bonnier, Jo, 161
boot release, driver controlled, 69
  electric, 70
Borderel-Cail six-wheeled car, 74
Bordino, Virginio, 10
Bouillon, Pierre, 154, 156
Bouton, Georges, 21, *103*
Boyer, Joe, 136
'Boyle Special', 146
Böhringer, Eugen, 205
Brabham, Sir Jack, 137, 154, 155, 159,
  205
Brabham cars: first, 159
  BT20, *162*
  BT46, 170
Brabham team, 180
Brakes, 71-3
  air, 71
  anti-lock, 73, 180
  anti-skid, 73
  asbestos linings, 72
  disc, 71, 72, *72*
    first ventilated, 73
    racing, 143, 154
  dual-circuit, 72
  electronic systems, 68
  four-wheel, 85, 129
  front-wheel systems, 71

  hydraulic, 72
  parking, 72
  self-adjusting, 72
  servo-assisted, 72, 85
  brake transmission, 72
  'umbrella-handle' levers, 80
  vacuum, 72
  water-cooled, 72
Brandon, Eric, 147
Brands Hatch circuit, Kent, 151
  BOAC 500 race, 163
Brazil: first races, 143
Brazilian Grand Prix: first as world
  championship, 168
  1986, 176
  winners, 168
breakdown lorry, first, 218
breathalyser tests, 235
Breedlove, Craig, *120*
Bremer car, 11
Bremgarten circuit, Berne, 141, 143
Brescia-Cremona-Brescia race, 122
Brighton Road Motor Patrol, 17
Brighton Speed Trials, 124
Briscoe, Benjamin and Frank, 99
Briscoe roadster, 62
Bristol 404 car, 69
Britain: 1986 street-circuit meeting, 178
  first motoring charge, 18
  first south-north journey, 23
  history of motoring in, 8, 10, 21, 24
  motor vehicle numbers in, 227
  oldest motoring organisation, 23
  Ministry of Transport 225
British Grand Prix, 122, 126, 155
  1926, 137
  1971, 167
  winners, 138
British Ideal cars 81
British Leyland million-car production,
  57
British Motor Corporation, 110
British Motor Show, 236
British Rallycross GP, 152
BRM: GP cars, 152, 154
  V16 engine, 143
  see also Rover-BRM
Brno circuit, *174*
Broadley, Eric, 100, 156, 159
Brockhouse Turbo-Transmitter, 94
Brooke swan car, 221, *221*
Brooklands Gazette, The, 227
Brooklands Motor Course, Surrey, 126,
  132, 137
  Double Twelve race, *132*, 140, 171
  last races, 146
  outer circuit record, 142
  radio experiments, 96
Brooks, Tony, 156, 157
Brown, Samuel, 10
Brown, Sir David, 100
Brundle, Martin, *164-5*
Brush Runabout, 74
Bucciali cars, 47
  Double-Huit 50
Budd, Edward Gowan, *60*
Budd bodywork, 59
Budweiser Rocket tricycle, 170
Buehrig, Gordon, 68
Buenos Aires 1000-km race, 155
Buffum, John, 195, 205
Buffum Model G Greyhound, 83
Bugatti, Ettore, 100

Bugatti cars, *139*
  largest collection of, *234-5*
  Type 13, 85, 131
  Type 30 'Tank', *64*
  Type 35, 80
  Type 35B, *139*
  Type 41 Royale, 49
  Type 47, 85
  Type 53, 140
Bugatti company, 29
Bugatti Owners' Club, 146
Buick, David Dunbar, 43, 100
Buick cars, 32
Buick company, 30
bulbs, twin-filament, 94
bumpers, first, 59
Burman, Bob, 127
Burney, C. S., 229
Burt, Patsy, 167
Bush cars, 44
Butler, Edward, 11

C
cab fleet, first, 26
Cadillac, 'Le Sieur Antoine de la
    Mothe', 43
Cadillac cars, 32, 92, 94, 95, 220
  16-cylinder, 85
  El Camino, 69
  Model 452, 85
Cadillac company, 30, 110
Caesar's Palace Grand Prix, 172
Caffrey steam carriage, 90
Cagno, Alessandro, 124
California 500 1972, 168
Caloric cars, 81
Campbell, Sir Malcolm, 50, *120*
camshafts: overhead, 83
  twin-overhead, 85
Canada: early cars, 13
  history of motoring in, 8
Canadian Grand Prix: first, 158
  winners, 158
Canadian Shell 4000, 192
Canadian-American Challenge Cup
    (CanAm) series, 162
Cannstatt Daimler car, 42
Cannstatt Daimler company, *20-1*
Caracciola, Rudolf, 205
caravan cum house boat, 233
carburetter installations, multiple, 81
Carhartt company, 45
Carless, Capel & Leonard, 19
Carlsson, Erik, 206
Carrera Panamericana race, 152, *152*
CART, regulations, 170
Carter Two-Engine, 44
cassette players, 97
Catalunya Rally 1991, 200
'cat's eye' road studs, 229
CD players, 97
Cevert, François, 215
Chadwick, Lee Sherman, 100
Chadwick cars: racing, 126
  Six, 83
chain drive, 129
Championship Auto Racing Teams
    (CART), 170
Championship of Makes, World, 154
  winners 155
Chaparral sports-racing cars, 159, 160
  2D, 161
  2F, 160, 163

2J, 167
2F, 160
Chapin, Roy, 100
Chapman, Colin, 33, 100, *100*, *149*, 156
Charron, Girardot & Voigt engine, 81
Charron cars, 91
Chasseloup-Laubat, Comte de, 117
chassis, 73-81
  monocoque construction, *78*, 80, 130
  carbon-fibre, 171
  pressed steel, 74
  stainless steel, 81
  'twin chassis', 171
  vanadium steel 75
  wooden, 74, 163
Cheever, Eddie, 178
Chenard & Walcker 'Tank', 66
Chevrolet, Louis, 101
Chevrolet cars, 32
  'Baby Grand', 74
  'Copper-Cooled', 48
  Corvair, 80
  Corvette, 70, 88, 96
  first, *30-1*
Chevrolet company, 30
  annual production, 54
  emblem, 43
Chevrolet Indycar engines, 127
Chicago *Times-Herald* contest, 114, 182
China, People's Car, 52
Chiron, Louis, *142*
Christie, John Walter, 90, 101, 123, 125
chromium plating, 66
  ban on, 68
Chrysler, Walter Percy, 101
Chrysler cars, 80
  70 model, 72
  1937 model, 68
  Airflow, 67
  gas turbine, *87*
  key start system, 68
  Turbo Dart, 88
  Viper, *236-7*
Chrysler company, 30
cinema, drive-in, 229
Circuit des Ardennes, 122
Circuit du Nord, 122
circuit race, first, 122
circumnavigation, world: by a woman,
    228
  smallest car, 230
Cisitalia GP car, 150
Citroën, André, 101
Citroën cars: 2CV, 79
  DS19, 73
  'La Petite Rosalie', 140
  Traction Avant, 80, 230
  ZX Rallye Raid, *201*
Citroën company, 30
  badge, 47
City & Suburban Grand Victoria, *82*
City Garage, London, 218
city-to-city races, 127, 182
  first 117
  see also specific races
Clark, Jim, 161, 162, *162*, 206
Clark, Roger, 194, 203, 206
Clément, Adolphe, 101
clutch, automatic, 93
Coatalen, Louis, 101
Cobb, John, 142
Cole Series 890 car, 72
Colombo, Gioacchino, 101

Columbia Six car, 85
Commission Sportive Internationale
    (CSI), 123
companies: first selling standardised
    cars, 21
  oldest surviving, 19
  origins of, 43
  see also individual companies
computers, first on-board, 67
Confederation of Australian Motor
    Sport (CAMS), 154
Connaught cars, 156
Construction & Use Regulations, 15
Constructors' Championship:
  introduction of, 157
  winners, 157
Continental Beacon, 50
Continental Tyres Aqua Contact, 81
controls, early, 218
'convertible', 59
  powered mechanism, 67
cooling systems, 'sealed for life', 88
Cooper, John, 123
Cooper cars *149*
Cooper cars: 500-cc, 147, 151
  Alta, 154
  Climax powered 157
  first World Championship victory,
    145
  'Redex Special', 166
  T20, 154
  T54, 158
  see also Mini-Cooper
Cooper engines, 84
Copeland, Lucius D., 21
Copersucar GP cars, 169
Coppa Acerbo 1923, 137
Coquille, Emile, 134
Cord, Erret Lobban, 101
Cord 810 model, 68
Cordery, Violette, 228
Cork Grand Prix, 143
Cornelian cars, 74, 130
Coronation Safari, 190
Corsica, Tour de Corse, 191, 196, 198
Cosworth company, 102
Cosworth engines: DFX engine, 143, 163
  Indycar, 127
  see also Ford-Cosworth
Cotal gearbox, 94
Cotta steam carriage, 90
Country Club car, 91
Coupe de l'*Auto* 1912, 129
Coupes des Alpes, 186
  1926, 185
  1932, 187
Course du Catalogue, 122
Coventry Climax engines, 156
Coventry Daimler car, 23
Cowey cars, 74, *78*
crash helmets, 131, 141, 154
crash-testing, 68
Cresto, Sergio, 191, 196, 198
crime, 223, *226*
Criterium du Quebec 1978, 195
Crosby, Frederick Gordon, 50
Crosley station wagons, 52
Crossley cars: RFC-type, 220
  six-wheeled limousine, 74
Crown-Magnetic cars, 91
Crystal Palace circuit, London, 28, 122,
    143, 183
Cuban Grand Prix, first, 156

Cugnot, Nicolas-Joseph, 7, 8
Cugnot *fardier*, 7, 8, 90
Cuneo-Col de Madelena hill climb, 123
Cutler-Hammer transmission, 93
Czech Grand Prix, first, 140

D
Dagmar cars, 48
Daihatsu Charade Turbo, 90
Daimler, Gottlieb, 13, 101, *102*
Daimler, Paul, 29
Daimler cars, early 22, 23
    double sleeve-valve engines, 86
    early heaters, 58
    'Patent Motor Wagon', 13
    royal, *46*
    see also Coventry Daimler cars
Daimler Motor Company, 19, 30, 42
    Conquest, 52
Daimler Motor Syndicate, 112
Dangerfield, Edmund, 224
dangerous driving, 17
Danner, Christian, 175
Darniche, Bernard, 195
Darracq, Alexandre, 101
Darracq car, 231
Datsun cars, 49
    1935 roadster, *36*
Datsun company, 35
Daytona 500 race, *179*
Daytona Beach, Florida, 123
Daytona International Speedway,
    Florida, 158
DB GP car, 156
De Dietrich six-wheeled car, 74
De Dion, Bouton & Trépardoux, 19
De Dion-Bouton cars, 22, 44, 81, 91
    Model CL, 84
De Dion-Bouton company, 21, 30
De Dion-Bouton tricycle, 16
De Fillipis, Maria Teresa, 157
De Knyff, Chevalier René, 182, *183*
De Lorean cars, *58*
De Palma, Ralph, 131
De Paolo, Peter, 137
De Portago, Marquis Alfonso, 157
De Soto cars, 68
dealers, first independent, 19
Decauville car, 28
defrosters, built-in, 68
Delâge, Louis, 101
Delage GP cars, 133
Delage company, 30
Delahaye company, 31
Delamarre-Deboutteville, Edouard, 12
Delecour, François, *202*, 203
demister, 67
Denmark, early vehicles, 13
'Denver Shoe', 238
design: worst early, 28
    see also bodywork
diesel cars, first British, 88
differential, limited-slip, 94
Dino Ferrari autodrome, Imola, 171
Dion, Albert Comte de, 21, 30, 101, *103*
direction indicators, 66
    first built-in, 59
    self-cancelling, 67
distribution, by air, 51
distributor, Renault substitute, 175
Divila, Richard, 169
divisions, electric, 68
DKW 1931 twin-cylinder, 81

Doble, Abner, 101
Doble Model E, 86
doctor, first to use a car, 25
Dodge, John and Horace, 102
Dodge cars: bodywork 59
    Dart, 233
    Senior, 96
    Viper 90, *236-7*
Dodge company, 30, 31
Doherty, Tom, 14
Donington Grand Prix, 141
    1938 *144*
Donohue, Mark, 178
door handles, recessed, 68
door locks: anti-burst, 69
    electrically-controlled, 69
    vacuum, 70
doors, gullwing 68
drag racing, 148, 153, 160
    300 mph exceeded, 170
    1983 US Nationals, 173
    first A-class lady, 163
    first British, 161
Dreyfus, René, 143
Driver & Vehicle Licensing Agency, 243
drivers, minimum age, 17
driving licences: cost of, 17
    endorsements system, 238
    introduction of duties, 15
    US, 232
driving mirrors, 60
    adjustable from inside, 70
    automatic dip, 70
    see also rear-view mirrors
driving test, 228, 230
    first 18
    first lady to pass, 18
Du Maurier, Daphne, 229
Duckworth, Keith, 102, 163
Ducourage, Gérard, 173
Dudgeon, Richard, 8
Dudgeon steam carriage, 9
Duesenberg, Frederick and August, 104
Duesenberg cars, 72
    1921 GP car, 131
    Model A, 85
    Model J, 67
Duesenberg racing engines, 136
Duncan, Isadora, 227
Dunk, A.O., 47
Dunlop tyres, 80
Durand, Georges, 134
Durant, William, 30, 104
Duray, Arthur, 126
Duryea, Charles, 13, 42, 104
Duryea, Frank, 13, 104, *116*
Duryea cars *116*
Dutch Grand Prix *see* Netherlands
    Grand Prix
Dutch National Motor Museum, 229
Dynaflow transmission, 94
dynamo: first, 73
    see also alternator

E
Earl, Harley, 104
East African Safari, 190, 192
    1987, 199
    1989, 199
Eastman steam car, 58
Eccles trailer caravan, 47
Ecurie Ecosse, 175
Edge, Selwyn Francis, 104, 122

Edward VII, King, 24
Egerton, Hubert W., 27
eight-wheeled car, 74
Eireann Cup, 140
Eisenhower, President Dwight D., 232
Eklund, Per, 199
Elcar cars, 49
electioneering, first car used for 218
electric cars, *119*, 233, 238
    solar-powered, *90*, 233
electric carriage, *82*
electrical system, low-tension, 175
Elliot, Bill, 175
Ellis, Hon. Evelyn, 15, 19
'Emancipation Act', 15
Emancipation Run *see* London to
    Brighton run
emergency flashers, 70
EMF car, 44
emission control, 88
    testing facility, 54
Endurance Championship of Drivers,
    World, 154
    sports cars, 172
    winners, 155
Endurance Championship of Makes,
    World, 154
    winners, 155
endurance races: early, 187
    Group C2 cars, *175*
    regulations, 175
    see also individual races
Engineer, The, 1897 trial, 182
engines, 81-90
    16-cylinder, 85
    3-litre V8 GP, 163
    air-cooled racing, 123, 159
    aluminium components, 58
    De Dion, 21
    'dual-expansion' three-cylinder, 83
    early, 10
    eight-cylinder, 83
        first eight-cylinder in-line, 81
    exchange scheme, 50
    four-cylinder in-line, first, 81
    five-cylinder, 90
    'free-piston', 88
    gas turbine, *86-7*, 88, 160, 166, 167,
        233
    Grand Prix 143, 167, 169, 178, 179
    largest, 126
    turbo, 150
    Indycar, 127
    land speed record, *120*
    opposed-piston, 26, 84, 123
    power outputs, 81, 86
    rocket, 170
    rotary, 84, 88
    rubber mountings, 21
    six-cylinder, 82
    sleeve-valve, 86
    straight-12, 86
    straight-nine, 85
    supercharged racing, 133, 136
    supplied by De Dion-Bouton, 21
    transverse, 81
    turbo diesel, 90
    turbocharged *89*
        racing, 169, 171, 173
    twin-overhead camshaft, first, 85
    two in one car, 141
    V4, 81
    V6, 88

V8, 83
  Antoinette, *84*
V10, 90
V12, 83
  first production, 85
  racing, 133
V16, first production, 85
see also cooling systems; lubrication;
  and individual makes
England to Australia, overland, 228
'Enterprise' steam omnibus, 9
Entz electro-magnetic transmission, 91
Eureka car, *91*
European Grand Prix, 133, 152
  winners, 134
European Hill-Climb Championship,
  157
Euroracing team, 170
Evans, Oliver, 8
Exhaust emissions: 1896 regulations, 15
  monitoring, 88
exhibitions, early 21, 22
Exner, Virgil, 104

F
face masks, *219*
factories: first female labour, 21
  first managed by a woman, 48
  first reinforced concrete, 43
Fagioli, Luigi, *202*
Fall, Tony, 192, 193
Fangio, Juan-Manuel, 155, 206, *206*
Farina, Giuseppe, *202*, 207
Farman, Maurice, 122
Faroux, Charles, 134, 232
Ferguson cars, 79
  P99, 159
Ferrari, Enzo, 104, *104-5*, 137
Ferrari cars, 101
  125 sports-racing car, 147, 150
  348 Spider, *242*
  640 transmission system, 179
  Dino 246, 158
  F40, 243
  Thinwall Special, 154
  traction control, 179
  V12 GTB4, *56-7*
  Vettura 815, 147
Ferrari company, 31
  badge, 104, 141
  see also Auto Avio Costruzioni;
    Scuderia Ferrari
Ferrari engines: Tipo B, 141
  Formula 1 programme, 180
Ferrari racing team, 106, 141, 142
  100th World Championship victory,
    179
  500th World Championship race, 180
Ferrari: badge 104
ferry: air service, 231
  first cross-Channel, 228
Fédération Internationale de
    l'Automobile (FIA), 123, 179, 193
  Sports-Car Championship, 155
    winners, 155
  'World Cup', 192
Fédération Internationale du Sport
    Automobile (FISA), 123, 150
  presidency, 179
  rallying regulations, 194, 196, 198,
    199, 200, 202
Fiat cars: 1500, 68
  1900 model, 69

600 'Multipla', *69*
805, 133
  GP cars, 133
  last, 139
'Topolino', *32*, 108
Fiat company, 19, 32, 99
  Lingotto factory test track, 48
  name, 47
fines: first for accident, 9
  first recorded for drunken driving,
    18
  first recorded speeding, 19
  fixed penalty, 238
Fiorio, Cesare, 199
fire extinguishing system, integral, 67
Firestone tyres, 80
Firman, Ralph, 176
Fisher, Carl G., 127
Fisher 'No-Draft Ventilation, 67
Fittipaldi, Emerson, 128, 167, 169, 207
Fittipaldi, Wilson, 167
Fittipaldi GP cars, 169
five-wheeled cars, 79
flag signals, racing, 122
Flanders, Walter, 106
Florio, Vincenzo, 124
Flyer, Thomas, 59
flying cars, 221
  amphibian, 230
'flying squad' cars, 220
flyovers, first, 231
fog lamp, first, 94
foot-warmer, 58
Footwork team, 170
Ford, Edsel, 106
Ford, Henry, 13, 33, 46, 50, 106, *106-7*
Ford, Henry II, 106
Ford Air Transport Service, 48
Ford cars: 200th BTCC victory, 181
  10 millionth car, 48
  50 millionth vehicle, 52
  Aeroflow ventilation, 70
  Classic, 73
  Cortina, 70
  crash-testing, 68
  Edsel, 52
  Escort, 49
    RS Cosworth, *202*
  GT40, 161, 166, 233
  'Life Guard' seat belts, 69
  Mark One Consul/Zephyr, 80
  Model A, 32, 49, 243
  Model T, 32, 44, 46, 48, *75*, 96, *97*, 222-
    3, 224
    price, 48
  Model Y Popular, 50, 108
  Mondeo, 243
  Mustang, 232
  rally successes, 203
  RS200, *197*
  saloon-car racing, *174*
  Sunliner convertible, 67
  Tempo, 71
  Zephyr, 203
Ford Motor Co., 32
  emblem/logo, 43, 113
  fully-automated plant, 52
  production in one year, 48
  purchase plan, 48
  safety engineer, 231
Ford engines, 88
  DFV, *162*, 163
  DFY, *162*

exchange scheme, 50
  V8, 50, 54
  see also Ford-Cosworth
Ford Museum, 49
Ford of Britain, 108, 111
Ford USA Futura Sprint, *189*
Ford-Autolite 'Lead Wedge', 166
Ford-Cosworth DFV engine, 162, 163
Forghieri, Mauro, 106, 179
Formula 1 racing, 148
  Constructors' Association, 172
Formula 2 racing, 148, 154, 175
  Bogota races, 167
  last-ever race, 178
Formula 3 racing, *149*, 151
Formula 3000, 148, 175
  1993 Championship, 180
Formula 5000, 169
Formula Ford, 163, 176
Formula Junior, 157
Formula Vee, 160
Foss, George Foote, 13
Fouillaron transmission, 91
four-wheel drive, *93*, 140
  first purpose-built car, 92
  GP cars, 159, 166
  rally cars, 196, 199
    first win, 187
  with four-wheel-steer, 93
Four-Wheel Drive company, 90
four-wheel steering car, 199
Foyt, Anthony Joseph, 170, 172, 207, *207*
France, history of motoring in, 7, 11,
    17, 21, 22, 24
Franklin, Herbert, 106
Franklin cars, chassis, 74
Franklin racing engines, 123
Frazer, Joseph W., 106
French Grand Prix, 133
  first, 125
  1908, 126
  1912, 129, *130*
  1913, 129
  1914, 130
  1921, 131
  1923, *64*
  1924, 137
  1926, 138
  1951, 153
  1953, 155
  1962, 160
French National Motor Museum, *234-5*
Friderich, Ernst, 131
front-wheel drive, early, *91*
fuel: consumption figures, 236
  endurance race allowance, 175
  GP allowance, 173
  liquid air, 26
  paraffin (kerosene), 42
  random sampling during rallies, 202
  see also diesel; gas; gasoline; petrol;
    steam
fuel injection, 81, 88
fuel pumps, electric, 85
Fuji International Speedway, 161
funeral, first motor, 27
FWD cars, 92

G
Gabelich, Gary, *121*
Galloway Motors, 48
Garage, 19
garages: first purpose-built private, 26

shipboard, 228
see also parking
Gardner-Serpollet steam cars, 44
Garlits, Don, 153, 160, 161
Gary Taxicab Company, 44
'gas-buggy', 13
gas turbine cars, 86-7
Gas-au-Lec car, 83
gasoline: first drive-in 'station', 223
origin of name, 19
see also petrol
gear shift: 'H'-pattern, 91
pneumatic, 91
gear system, early, 74
gearboxes, 91
electrical, 93, 94
first synchromesh, 93
preselector, 93
gears: constant-mesh, 91
overdrive, 93
Gendebien, Olivier, 140, 173
General Electric car, 233
jet engine, 120
General Motors cars: 100 million
vehicles, 54
air bags, 71
annual model change, 49
General Motors company, 32, 41, 101,
104, 112
General Motors-Holden, 32
General Motors engine, 'free-piston', 88
generators, first high-output, 86
Hydramatic transmission, 94
Geneva round-the-houses circuit, 147
Geneviève (film), 231
George N. Pierce Company, 42
German Grand Prix: first, 138
1935, 141
winners, 138
Germany, early vehicles 12
Gethin, Peter, 167
Giacomelli, Bruno, 175
Giacosa, Dante, 108
Gilmore Special car, 143
Ginther, Richie, 160
Glas S1004 car, 88
glass: safety, 66, 223, 229, 230
tinted non-glare, 68
Gobron-Brillié cars, 26
competition cars, 123
engine, 84
Gold Leaf Team Lotus, 166, 167
Goleta drag strip, 148
Goodwood circuit, Sussex, 148
Goodyear tyres, 80
GP successes, 179
Gordon, Alexander, 10
Gordon Bennett Trophy race, 104, 122,
123
1903, 82-3, 183
Graham, D. F., 82
Graham Blue Streak car, 67
Graham-Paige transfer machine system,
49
Gran Premio Brescia della Mille Miglia,
146
Gran Premio Nacional, Argentina, 127
Grand Prix de l'Automobile Club de
France, see French Grand Prix
Grand Prix Drivers' Association, 159
Grands Prix des Nations 1946, 147
Grands Prix of the United States,
winners, 169

Grands Prix: closest-ever finish, 176
fastest, 167
first, 122, 124-5
first all-turbo, 173
first British victory, 133
first lady driver to score points, 169
longest, 153
'national firsts', 155
pit stops, 173, 175
record speed, 137
record wins, 178, 180
regulations, 125, 131, 141, 173
Formula 2, 154
postwar, 148, 150
riding mechanics, 137, 143
safety cars, 180
shortest, 179
'super-licence' form, 172
winners, 125
youngest winner, 158
see also individual races
Gransden Lodge circuit, 147
Gregorie, Eugene, 108
Grégoire cars, 61
Group 44, 172
GT Championship, 154
winners, 155
guarantees, life, 43, 47
Guinness, Kenelm Lee, 137
Gulf Miller car, 146
Gurney, Dan, 160, 167
Guthrie, Janet, 128
Gwalia cars, 79
GWK cars, 92
gyratory system, 227

H
Hahne, Armin, 179
Haldane, Samantha, 200
Halfords Birmingham Super Prix, 178
Hammel, Albert, 13
Hancock, Walter, 8
Harriman, Sir George, 108
Harrison starting system, 83
Harroun, Ray, 128
Hawthorn, Mike, 137, 155, 207, 212
Hayes infinitely variable gear, 94
Haynes, Alex, 231
Haynes, Elwood, G. 99, 108
Head, Patrick, 108
headlamps: automatic dimmers, 95
central, 95
dipping, 94
dual, 94, 95
flashers/flashing, 95, 229
pop-up/retractable, 68, 96
sealed-beam, 95
set-in, 94
swivelling, 96
Healey, Donald, 108, 185
heaters: early, 63
catalytic-type petrol, 69
Heath, George, 123
Hedag direction indicators, 59
Hedlund, Roger, 169
Heinrich of Prussia, Prince, 184
Henderson, Gene, 196
Hennessy, Sir Patrick, 108
Herdtlé & Bruneau motorised roller
skate, 44
Herkomer Trophy, first, 183
Herrmann, Hans, 166
Hertz, Arne, 200

Hertz Car Rental, 44
Hesketh 308B car, 168
Highway Code, 229
Highway Safety, President's Action
Committee for, 232
Hill, Damon, 137, 180, 208
Hill, Graham, 140, 152, 160, 207, 208
Hill, Phil, 161, 163, 208
hill climbs: first, 117
first British, 122
see also individual venues
hire purchase schemes, early, 25
Hispano-Suiza cars, 44, 99
'Alfonso', 224
H6, 49
H6B, 72
Hispano-Suiza company, 32
mascot, 47
Hitler, Adolf, 230
Hockenheim, Germany, 138
new circuit, 162
Holden cars, 32, 52, 74
48/215, 51
Holden company, 32
Holverter cars, 93
Honda, Soichiro, 108
Honda cars: first GP car, 161
RA 163-E, 173
RA302, 160
Honda company 33
Honda engines: assists Ferrari, 180
Indycar, 180
V10 racing, 178
Hopkirk, Paddy, 208
Horch, August, 29
Horch demister, 67
horns: bulb, 59
multi-tone, 71
steering-wheel mounted button, 62
Horseless Carriage Club of America,
230
Horstman cars, 48
Hubbard, Miriam Warren, 47
Hudson cars, 73, 100
Hulme, Denis (Denny), 162, 208
Humber company, 33
Hungarian Grand Prix: 1936, 142
winners, 142
Hunt, James, 168, 208, 209
Huntingburg cars, 218
Hutton cars, 91
Hühnlein, Fritz, 230
Hyundai, 57

I
Iacocca, Lido, 108
Iceland, 224
Ickx, Jacky, 140, 166, 173, 208
ignition keyholes, illuminated, 67
ignition: automatic advance, 81
electronic, 88
Ilmor engines, 163
Indycar, 127
IMSA GT championship, 167
in-car entertainment, 96-7
India, first recorded motoring event,
183
Indianapolis 500, 170
closest finish 173
first, 127, 128
1919, 131
1923, 134
1924, 136

1925, 137
1936, 143
1939, 146
1954, 156
1960, 158
1962, 160
1965, 161
1967, 166
1981, 172
1987, 178
1991, 179
1992, 180
winners, 128
Indianapolis Speedway, 124, 127
indicators, flashing, 232
Indycar races: 1993, 180
regulations, 170
instrumentation, fully electronic, 71
insurance, 228
first policies, 19
Intercontinental Formula, 158
Iris, 43
Irish Grand Prix, 140
Isle of Man circuit, 123
Isotta-Fraschini cars, 65, 129, 221
Israel, first production car, 53
Issigonis, Sir Alec, 108, 109
Itala cars, 221
transformable body, 61
Itala Type 11, 138
Italian Grand Prix, 159
first, 131
1921, 125
1971, 167
1986, 176
winners, 133
Italy: first race in, 122
rule of the road, 228
Ivory Coast Rally, 193
1985, 198
1987, 198
'Izzer' car, 45

J
jacks, integral screw, 67
Jaguar cars: C-type, 153, 154
E-Type, 56-7
Le Mans successes, 153
Mk VII, 189
saloon-car racing, 174
XJ220, 239
XJR-5, 172
XJR-6, 178
XJR-9, 164-5
XK120, 51
Jaguar company, 33, 110
and Daimler, 30
mascot, 50
Jaguarsport Intercontinental Challenge, 179
'Jamais Contente', 119
Jano, Vittorio, 108, 137, 155
Japan: first cars, 13
first exports 49
Japanese Grand Prix: first, 161
1987, 178
1989, 179
'Japanese Rules of the Road', 224
Jarama circuit, Spain, 163
Jarrott, Charles, 17, 122, 123
Jarrott & Letts cycle patrol, 17
Jeantaud electric vehicle, 117
Jeep, 49

Jeep Waggoneer, 196, 199
Jeffery, Thomas B., 108
Jenatzy, Camille, 117, 119, 123
John o'Groats to Land's End, 27
Johncock, Gordon, 173
Johnson, Claude, 108
Jones, Alan, 139, 209
Jones, Parnell, 160, 166
Jones, Stan, 155 Jordan, Edward, 108
JWA team, 166

K
K-D car, 45
Kaiser Allstate car, 44
Kaiser safety harness, 69
Kaiser-Frazer company, 106
Kane-Pennington cars, 22
Kankkunen, Juha, 190, 198, 200, 203, 209, 209
Kégresse, Adolphe, 224
Kettering, Charles F., 108
Kelly, John B., 8
Kemsley, Jack, 188
Kenworthy Line-O-Eight, 85
Kia car, 90
Kimber, Cecil, 33, 48, 108
King, Charles Brady, 13, 108
Kingsford-Smith, Sir Charles, 79
Knight, John Henry, 18
Knight cars, 11
three-wheeler, 18
Kogyo, Toyo, 33
KRIT car, 44
Kurtis-Kraft cars, 156
midget, 143
Kyalami circuit, South Africa, 158

L
L'Automobile Journal, 24
La France Automobile, 24
La Locomotion Automobile, 24
Ladies' Automobile Club, 220
Lago, Antonio, 108
Lagonda cars, 1913 model, 79
Lagonda company, 100
'Lambda sensor', 88
Lambert, John William, 13
Lambert, Percy, 129
Lamborghini cars: Diablo, 239
Espada, 34
Jarama, 34
Miura, 34
Lamborghini company, 33
Lamborghini GP engine, 179
Lanchester, Frederick, 109
Lanchester, George, 109
Lanchester cars, 59, 63
construction, 79
early, 11
Forty, 85
four-cylinder, 82
Lanchester company, 33
Lancia, Vincenzo, 109
Lancia cars: 037 rally car, 196
Aurelia, 88
D50, 156
Delta, 203
Delta HF, 198, 200
Delta S4, 198
rally successes, 202
Stratos, 194
Lancia company, 33
end of rally programme, 199

Land Rover: 1948 model, 39
County Station Wagon, 39
Land Speed Record, 117, 120-1, 126, 173
forerunner of, 117
holders, 50
venues, 117–119, 123
Land's End to John O'Groats, 23
Larrousse, Gérard, 159, 193, 203
Lascelles, Hon. Gerald, 52
Lauda, Niki, 173, 210, 210
Laumaille, Madame, 117
Laurin & Klement Type FC runabouts, 45
Lautenschlager, Christian, 126, 130
Lawson, Harry J., 109
Le Mans 24-hour Race, 140, 166
first, 134
1927, 134-5
1950, 152
1951, 153
1952, 154
1955, 156
1965, 87
1966, 162, 163
1971, 167
1980, 171
1982, 173, 176
1984, 175
1987, 178
1988, 179
1991, 177
1992, 177
winners, 134
Le Mans voiturette race, 131
Lea-Francis cars: 1.5-litre sports, 228
S Type, 85
Leader cars, 81
Lecot, François, 230
Ledwinka, Hans, 40, 109
left-hand drive, 49, 63
Legros & Knowles, 43
Leland, Henry M., 30, 33, 42, 110
Lenoir, J-J. Etienne, 11, 110
Lentz, Rea, 131
Lentz hydraulic transmission, 91
Leopold II, King of the Belgians, 24
Levassor, Emile, 74, 110, 114, 114-15
Lever engine, 49
Leyat car, 91, 92
Liddon, Henry, 190
Liège-Rome-Liège Rally, 187
1960, 191 Liège-Sofia-Liège rally, 192
lighting, 94-6
see also bulbs, and individual lights
Ligier GP cars, 169
Lincoln Zephyr, 112
Lincoln company, 33
Lion-Peugeot company, 37
'Liquid Air' car, 26
Loasby, Mike, 71
Locke-King, Hugh, 126
Lockheed hydraulic brakes, 72
Locomobile, 24, 42
Locomotives on Highway Act, 10, 15
log books, 225
Lola company, 100
Lola racing cars, 156, 159
Lombardi, Claudio, 199
Lombardi, Lella, 169
London Electrical Cab Company, 26
London Motor Show, 47, 230
London Orbital Motorway, 238
London to Brighton run, 228, 231

first, 15
'London Carriage', 8
London-New York, overland, 243
Long Beach, California, 126, 169
long-distance journeys, first, 15
Lord, Sir Leonard, 110
Lord Mayor's Show, 15
Lotus cars, 170
  2 trials car, *149*
  12 F2 car, 156
  16 GP car, 157
  25 GP car, 161
  38 car, 161
  49 GP car, *162*, 166
  56 car, 166
    56B car, 167
  88 GP car, 171
  94T GP car, 173
  active suspension, 178
  Elite, 70
Lotus company, 33, 100
Lotus, Team, 166, 167
Loughead, Malcolm, 72
Louwman, P. W., 229
lubrication: high-pressure, 82
Lucas 'Startrix', 68
Lunar Rover, 236
Lyons, Sir William, 110, *110*

M
Macpherson strut suspension system,
  80
magazines, first, 24
  see also individual magazines
Magny-Cours circuit, France, 179
Mahy, Ghislain, 231
mail order cars, 44
Maki F101 car, 168
Makinen, Timo, 194
Mansell, Nigel, 140, 141, 180, *181*, 210,
  211
manufacturers: acronyms, 44
  most popular name, 43
manufacturing subsidies, 218
maps, free, 224
marathon car run, longest, 230
Marathon de la Route, 187
March racing cars, 166
  Indianapolis cars, 173
March Indianapolis successes, 178
Marimon, Onofre, 156
Marion cars, 112
Marko, Helmut, 168
Marks-Moir cars, construction, 79
Markus, Siegfried, 12, 110
Marmon cars: 16-cylinder, 85
  Wasp, *128*
marque names, 44, 47
  'American', 43
  first production car, 42
Marriott, Fred, 126
Marseilles-Nice race 1898, 117
Marseilles-Nice-la Turbie race, 115
Martin, Johnson, 224
mascots: 'Spirit of Ecstacy', 23
  see individual companies
Maserati cars: GP cars, 138
  8CTF, 146
  Sedici Cilindri 140
Maserati company, 33
mass production, term first used, 49
Mathis '*pistomètre*', 67
Mathis cars, 80

Matra racing cars, 161
Matra-Simca Bagheera, 50
Maxwell, Jonathan Dixon, 110
May, Michael, 160
Maybach, Wilhelm, 101, 110
Mazda cars, 88
  787 B, *177*
  RX-7 Turbo, *87*
Mazda company, 33
McKinley, President William, 24
McLaren, Bruce, 126, 158, 162, 167,
  210
McLaren cars, 99, 161
  electronic throttle, 180
  F1 'supercar', 225, *240-1*, 243
  GP successes, 178
  M2B, 161
  M8 sports-racer, 162
  MP4, 171
  MP4/7, *181*
McLaren engines, 172
McLaren team, 173
McRae, Colin, 194, 203, 210
Mears, Rick, 173, 178
Mehta, Shekhar, 190, 193, 210
Mercedes cars, 42
  1903 60-hp, 238
  Connecticut-built, 42
  Mercedes, 42
  racing cars, 129, 133
Mercedes-Benz cars, 85
  260D, 86
  300D, 88
  300SL, 68, 88, *152*
  'Nürburg', 80
  W25, 141
  W125, 143
  W196, 155
Mercedes-Benz company, 19, 33
  Sauber associations, 180
Mercer Raceabout, 111
Mercury 1956 model, 69
Mercury company, 33
Metge, René, *201*
Metropolitan Police, 220
Metzger, William E., 19
Mexican 1000 Rally, first, 166
Mexican Grand Prix, first, 159
MG company, 33, 108
  badge, 49
  name, 48
  Air Pollution Control Centre, 54
  MGA, 52
Michelin, André and Edouard, 110
Michelin Man, 218
Michelin tyres, 170, 199
  'X', 80
midget cars, 143
  racing, 140
Midnight Sun, Rally of the, 192
  first, 187
  see also Swedish Rally
Mikkola, Hannu, 187, 188, 190, *195*, 196,
  199, 203, 211, *211*
Milan Grand Prix 1927, 139
Milan-Varese autostrada, 227
Mille Miglia, 146
  first, 138
  1957, 157
  'substitute', *146*
Miller, Harry, 111, 143
Miller GP car, 143
Miller, Sammy, 170

million-car production: Britain, 51, 52,
  57
  Europe, 52
  USA, 48
Minardi team, 179
Mines Field, California, 141
Mini-Cooper S, *186*
Minoia, Fernando, 138
'Mistproof Plate' heater, 63
Mitchell, William, 111
Mitsubishi cars: Galant VR-4, 199
  Sigma, 57
Mitsubishi company, 35
Modoc cars, 44
Mohs Ostentatienne Opera Sedan, 235
Monaco Grand Prix: first, 139, *139*
  1933, 140
  1982, 172
  winners, 140
monocoque body/chassis construction,
  78, 80, 130
Mont Tremblant circuit *see* St Jovite
Mont Ventoux hill climb, 123
Montagu Motor Museum, 231, 233
Monte Carlo Rally, 193
  Coupe des Dames, 191
  1911, 184
  1936, 187
  1952, *188*, 189
  1956, *189*
  1967, *186*
  1971, 193
  1977, *194*
  1979, 195
  1990, 199
  1994, 203
  winners, 185
Montlhéry autodrome, France, 136
Montreal, Ile Notre Dame circuit, 158
Monza circuit, Italy, 133, 156
Morandi, Giuseppe, 138
Morel, André, 133
Moreno, Roberto, 139
Morgan, H. F. S., *76*, 111
Morgan cars, 74, *76*
  4/4, *35*
Morgan company, 35
Moroccan Grand Prix, first 137
Morris cars: direction signals, 66
  Eight Series E, 94
  million cars built 51
  Minor, 50, 52
    '£100' Minor *36*
  six-wheeled, 74
  see also Mini
Morris Motors, 35, 48
Morris, William (Lord Nuffield), 111
Mors 1897 model, 73
Mors V4 engine, 81
Morse company, 45
Mosley, Max, 123, 179
Mosport Park circuit, Canada 158, 159
Moss, Myer, 8
Moss, Stirling, 137, 138, 154, 155, 156,
  157, 159, 212, *212*
Moss-Carlsson, Pat, 191, 212
motel, 227
Moto-Cycle Manufacturing Company,
  21
Motor, The, 225
Motor, 24
'Motor car', 19
Motor Car Act 1903, 17

Motor Car Club, The (MCC), 22
Motor Car Journal, 24
motor club, first, 10
Motor Sport, 227, 232
motoring magazines, first 9
  see also individual magazines
motoring organisations and clubs,
  world's oldest 22
motorway: first, 227
  British 232
  proposal for 224
  see also autobahn
Mount Washington, New Hampshire,
  122
Mouton, Michèle, 131, 192, 196, 198,
  199, 212, *213*
MRD Formula Junior car, 159
Muldowney, Shirley, 163
Munari, Sandro, 184, 213
murder trial, 228
Murphy, Jimmy, 131, 136
Murray, Gordon, 111
Museo dell'Automòbile, 229
museums: largest private collection, 231
  oldest private, 229
  Turin, 229
  world's first, 224
  see also individual museums

N
Nader, Ralph, 233, 235
Napier, Montagu, 111
Napier cars, 104
  six-cylinder, 82
NASCAR, 147
  1985 Grand National, 175
Nash, Charles W., 111
Nash cars: 600 model, 68
  Rambler, 68
Nash company, 35
National Automobile Show,
  America, 22, 227
National Hot Rod Association, 153
National Motor Museum, 231
National Off-Road Racing
  Association (NORRA), 166
National Traffic & Motor Vehicle
  Safety Act, 233
Nazional Sozialistische Kraftfahr
  Korps, 230
Nazzaro, Felice, 130, 213
Netherlands Grand Prix: first, 152
  1960, 159
  1967, *162*
  1985, 173
  winners, 152
New York-Paris race, 126
New Zealand Grand Prix, first 155
New Zealand Rally: 1986, 198
  1992, 200
  1993, 203
Neyret, Bob, 193
Nice Speed Trials, 117
Nicholas II, Czar, 224
Nicolas, Jean-Pierre, 196
Nissan company, 35
Nobel, Richard, *121*, 173
Noghes, Antony, 184
NSU Wankel Spider *55*, 88
Nuffield, Lord, 111
number plates, 17, 220
  first American, 19
  first integrally illuminated, *95*

first issued, 17
first with letter suffix, 233
most expensive, 243
reflective, 235
  see also registration
Nuvolari, Tazio, 141, 142, *144*, 146, 213,
  213
Nürburgring, Germany, 138, 162
  1000-km race 1966, 161
  new circuit, 175

O
l'*Obéissante* steam carriage, *11*
Offenhauser engines, 143, 156
oil cooler, 85
oil pressure warning light, 66
Olds, Ransom Eli, 25, *26*, 35, 111
Oldsmobile cars, 25, 32, 66
  88 Holiday Coupé, *70*
  Curved Dash, 37
  'Merry', 25, *26*
  Toronado, 57
Oldsmobile company, 19, 35
Olympus Rally: 1987, *200*
  1988, 199
Opel cars, 32
  Olympia, 80
  rally cars, first World Championship
    victory, 190
Opel company, 37
Orbital two-stroke engine, 88
Orient Express car, 218
Orsi, Omer, 33
'Orukter Amphibolos', 8
Otomos cars, 49
Oulton Park circuit, Cheshire, 154
  Gold Cup, 159, 166
overdrive, 92
  automatic, 94
Owen-Magnetic cars, 91
Österreichring, Austria, 158, 160

P
Packard cars, 80
  Model B, 81
  Super-8 One-Sixty, 68
  tourer, 228
  Twin-Six 85, 225
  V12 racing, 131
Packard company 37
Packard factory 43
paint: acrylic lacquers, 69
  cellulose, 66
  choice of colours, 66
  iridescent, 67
  metallic, 68
Pan-American Highway, 238
Panhard cars, 117, *183*
  Dyna, 54 69
  Dynamic, 50
  twin-cylinder, *114-15*
Panhard company, 37
Panhard double sleeve-valve engines,
  86
Panhard & Levassor cars, 22, 25
  5-hp car, 15
  four-cylinder, 81
  1892 model, 74
  free patrol service, 17
Paris-Amsterdam-Paris race 1898, 117
Paris-Beijing Rally 1992, *201*
Paris-Berlin race 1901, 117
Paris-Bordeaux-Paris race, 114, 122

1895, *114-15*
Paris-Dakar Rally, 202
  1986, *201*
  1989, 199
Paris-Le Cap Rally, 202
Paris-Madrid race 1903, *116*, 117
Paris-Marseilles-Paris race, 115
Paris-Moscow-Peking Rally 1991, 200
Paris Motor Show, 1899, *22*
Paris-Ostend race 1899, 122
Paris-Rouen Reliability Trial, 114, 182
Paris-Toulouse-Paris race 1900, 117
Paris-Trouville race, 117
Paris-Vienna race, 182
  1902, 117
'Parkmobile', 67
parking meters, first, 230
  first British, 232
parking problems 66
parks: first underground, 229
  largest, 238
Parks, Wally, 153
parts and parts distribution: by air,
  48
  first US company, 24
  first recycled plastic, 90
Passat, M. B., 221
Pathfinder cars, 93
Patrese, Riccardo, 180
Pau Grand Prix, 122
pedestrian crossings, 230, 231
Pedrables circuit, Spain, 129
Peerless cars, 43
  chassis, 74
Peking-Paris 'race', 126
Pennington, Edmund Joel, 111
Pennington 'Raft' car, 28
Pennsylvania Turnpike, 231
Penske, Roger, 168
Penske cars: PC9, 172
perambulators, motorised, 225
Perry, Sir Percival, 16, 111
Pescara straight-ten project, 86
Pescara Grand Prix 1923, 137
Pescarolo, Henry, 140, 173
Petersham Hill, Surrey, 122
petrol: duty on, 223
  early use of, 42
  leaded, 85
  octane rating system, 85
  origin of name, 19
  rationing, 231
  unleaded, 88
petrol can, 26
petrol car, first, *12*
petrol pumps: roadside, 220, 224
  first self-service, 233
Petty, Richard, 214
Peugeot, Armand, 111
Peugeot cars, 22, 43, *130*
  205 T16, 196
  205 Turbo, 16 *197*
  905 model, *177*
  1894 model, 77
  1912 GP car, 129
  Baby voiturette, 17
  convertible, 67
  L'Eclair, 74
Peugeot company, 19, 37
'Phaeton Moto-Cycle', 21
'Phianna', 47
Phoenix Park, Dublin, 140
Pianta, Giorgio, 199

Pierce-Arrow cars, 42, 44, 94
  V12 'Silver Arrow', 65
Pierce-Arrow company, 37
Pike's Peak hill climb, 131, 147
  first climb of, 24
Pininfarina, Battista, 111
Pioneer car, 13
Piquet, Nelson, 211, 214
pits, 126
  see also Grands Prix
Planchon, Charles, 133
Plass, Reuben, 13
Plymouth cars, 30
Plymouth company, 37
pneumatic systems, 84
Pocono 500 car, 172
police pursuit by car, first, 18
policewomen 233
Polimotor plastic engine, 88
Pontiac cars, 32
Pontiac company, 37
Pope, Albert Augustus, 111
Pope Manufacturing Company, 15
Pope Pius X, 221
Pope Pius XI, 221
Porsche, Dr Ferdinand, 29, 38, 111, 141,
  184
Porsche, Ferry, 38
Porsche cars: 356 roadster, 38
  904 GP car, 159
  914/6, 193
  917, 162, 168
  956 model, 176
  959, 201
  Le Mans successes, 178
  TAG engines, 172
  Type 360, 150
Porsche company, 37
Porsche racing engines, 143, 172
Porter, Finley Robertson, 111
Portuguese Grand Prix: first, 154
  winners, 154
Portuguese Rally: first, 192
  1984, 196
  1988, 199
Postlethwaite, Harvey, 169
Prescott hill climb, 143
press launch, first 15
Press-on-Regardless rally 1972, 196,
  199
Prinz Heinrich Fahrt, 184
'private car', first, 8
product recall, first known, 45
production: Ford assembly lines, 45
  fully-automated, 52
  highest export figures, 238
  'just-in-time', 48
  moving line, 42
  Japanese, 49
  transfer machines, 48, 49
    automatically controlled, 52
  see also mass-production
production cars, first 200 mph, 243
production landmarks, 54-7
Prometheus programme, 238
Prost, Alain, 139, 173, 179, 179, 180, 181,
  211, 214
Proton, 57
Protos F2 car, 163
Prototypes Championships, 154
  winners, 155
Pullinger, Dorothée, 48
Pullman cars: 32hp, 93

six-wheeled, 74
Pungs-Finch Limited car, 83
Puritan Machine Company, 47

Q
quartz halogen lamps, 96

R
RAC Grand Prix see British Grand Prix
RAC Rally, 187, 192
  1965, 192
  1980, 195
  1990, 200
  see also Tourist Trophy
race, circuit, first, 122
  city-to-city, 127, 182
Race of the Two Worlds, Monza, 156
  winners, 157
races: first true, 114
  24-hour, 133
  see also individual races
racing: 132
  flag signals, 122
racing drivers: cooling system, 172
  first permanent school, 157
  strike, 172
radar trap, 232
radiators: air intakes, 69
  thermostatic shutters, 85
radio telephones, 68
  first British service, 232
  first car with, 96
  transatlantic, 233
radios, 96, 97
  first, 97
Radley, James, 184
Ragnotti, Jean, 214
Rally Championship, European: 1965,
  192
  smallest car to win, 192
Rally Championship, World, 192
Rally Championships, World: 21st year,
  203
  1986 exclusions, 198
  consecutive winner, 196
  first four-wheel drive win, 199
  first four-wheel steering win, 199
  most successful marque, 203
  winners, 193
    first ladies' victory, 196
    oldest, 200
    youngest, 195
  youngest competitor, 200
Rally Championship for Drivers,
  European, 190
  winners, 190
Rally Championship for Drivers,
  World, 190
Rally Championship for Makes,
  International, 193
Rally des Lions 1963, 192
Rally-raid cars, 201
Rallycross, 160
Rallye dei Fiori, first, 191
rallying: four-wheel-drive, 195
  Group 2 rules, 194
  Group 3 bans, 196, 198
  pace notes first used, 200
  supercars, 197
  first, 194
Rallysprint series, 195
Ralt cars, 171
Rambler cars, 29, 108

Ramsey, Mrs John R., 221
Rapson, F. Lionel, 79
rear-engined cars, first racing victory,
  157
rear-view mirror, 59, 128
  compulsory, 67
  early, 60
Recalde, Jorge, 199
record players, 97
records, non-stop: first car to cover 1000
  miles, 28
records, speed: 100 miles in an hour,
  129
  closed-circuit, 178, 180
  diesel car, 171
  electric car, 166, 169
  Grand Prix, 137
  wheel-driven car, 179
'Red Flag Act', 10
'Red Hand' gang, 223
Redman, Brian, 169
Reeves Octoauto, 74
reflectors, rear, 232
Regazzoni, Clay, 141
registration, 17
  British, 28
    record, 238
  cost of, 17
  first three-letter, 229
Reims-Gueux circuit, 137
Renault, Louis, 111
Renault cars: Alpine 310 model, 193
  Alpine A110, 192, 193
Renault company, 19, 37
Renault racing engines, 169
  EF15, 175
  V10, 178
rental, first, 24
Reo transmission, 94
Resta, Dario, 137
Reutemann, Carlos, 172
Reventlow, Lance, 158
reversing light, automatic, 94
Reynard, Adrian, 168
Reynard cars, 180
Ricart, Wilfred, 147
Rickenbacker, Eddie, 131
right-hand drive, 49
right-hand rule of the road, 235
Rigolly, Louis, 123
Riley company, 38
Rindt, Jochen, 167, 175, 214
Riverside International Raceway,
  California, 157
road markings: broken white lines, 230
  dangerous bends marked, 224
  double white lines, 232
  first dividing lines, 224
road signs: computerised warning, 236
  first standardised, 220
    British, 230
    European, 231
    internationally, 220
  flashing illuminated, 225
  reflecting, 225
road tax 15
Road Traffic Act 228
roads: cloverleaf intersection, 228
  first British four-level junction, 235
  first British one-way system, 227
  first concrete, 221
  first US dual carriageway, 231
  improvements in surfaces, 28

interstate highways, 224, 232
longest urban ring road, 238
Preston by-pass, 232
reflective studs, 229
responsibility for trunk roads, 230
world's longest, 238
see also motorway; road markings
roadworthiness testing, 218, 233
Roberts, Dr Thomas, 25
Rodriguez, Pedro, 137
Roesch, Georges, 111
Rolland-Pilain Type CRK, 72
Rolls, Hon. Charles Stuart, 112, 122, 182
Rolls-Royce cars: 'Alpine', 184
largest collection, 238
overdrive, 92
Phantom VI limousine, 236
'sneak picture', 225
see also Royce cars
Rolls-Royce engines: Avon jet, 121
V8, 83
V12, 120
Rolls-Royce company, 38
badge, 50
'Spirit of Ecstacy' mascot, 23
Romeo, Nicola, 104-5
Rondeau, Jean, 171
Rondeau sports cars, 171
Roosevelt Field, New York, 123
Rootes, Sir William, 112
Rosberg, Keke, 175, 214
Rosemeyer, Bernd, 132, 143, 214
Rosier, Louis and Jean-Louis, 152
Rothschild & Cie, coachbuilders, 25, 59
roundabouts, first, 220
Rover cars: 1905 model, 73
BRM sports car, 88, 160
gas turbine, 87, 88
'JET 1', 86
see also Land Rover
Rover company, 38
Royal Automobile Club, 23, 108, 112
see also RAC
Royal Motor Union of Liège, 187
Royce, Sir Henry 38, 112
Royce cars, 39
Röhrl, Walter, 184, 190, 214
Rumpler, Edmund, 62-3
Rumpler car, 63, 79
Russell, Jim, 157
Russia, Imperial Garages, 224
Rytecraft Scootacar, 230

S
Saab company, 38
SABA cars, 93
Sabra car, 53
Safari Rally, 190
safety belts, 59
compulsory, 71
seven-point, 69
safety glass see glass
safety padding, 68
Safety Standards, US Federal, 235
safety statistics, 238
see also accidents
Sainz, Carlos, 215
Sala, Luis, 178
Salonen, Timo, 196
saloon-car racing, 174
San Giusto cars, 80
San Marino Grand Prix: first, 171
1982 boycott, 172

winners, 171
San Remo Rally, 191
1975, 194
1981, 196
1986, 198
1992, 202
Santa Pod drag strip, 161, 166, 170
Saostat Cup, 140
Sauber team, 180
Scarab GP car, 158
Schaudel cars, 81
Schebler V12 car, 83
Scheckter, Jody, 169, 215
Schlumpf Collection, 234-5
Schumacher, Michael, 181
Schwarz, Armin, 200, 203
Schwitzer, Louis, 127
Scotland Yard, 220, 227
Scott Sociable, 74
Scottish Automobile Club, Glasgow to
London trial, 183
Scottish Six Days Trial 1925, 185
Scripps-Booth Model C, 62
Scuderia Ferrari, 106, 141, 142
Scuderia Italia, 159
SEAT, 40
seat belts, 59, 68
1956 Ford range, 69
automatic, 71
compulsory, 70, 238
first European, 69
first fitted, 58
fitted as standard, 70, 71
see also safety belts
seating, three-abreast, 50
seats: convertible, 227
foam-filled, 68
power-operated, 68
Sebring circuit, Florida, 126, 152
Segrave, Henry, 133
Sekine cars, 48
Selanger 800 race, 175
Selden, George Baldwin, 13, 112
car, 14
patent, 13
Sénéchal, Robert, 137
Senna, Ayrton, 140, 171, 173, 178, 179,
181, 215, 216
Sentul circuit, Indonesia, 181
Serpollet, Léon, 18, 112
Serpollet steam cars, 44
Sestriere Rally, 191
Shadow Grand Prix team, 168
Shaw, Percy, 229
Shaw, Wilbur, 146
Shearer car, 13
Shelby, Carroll, 232
Shelby AC Cobra car, 160
Shelsey Walsh hill climb, 123
showrooms, 225
Siffert, Jo, 166
'Silent Knight' engine, 86
Silverstone 1000-km race, 178
Silverstone circuit, Northants, 148
Silverstone International Trophy: first
150
1956, 156
1974, 168
Simms, Frederick R., 19, 59, 112
Simms-Welbeck cars, 59
Sinclair, Sir Clive, 238
Singer SMX roadster, 69
Singer company, 40

Singh, Joginder, 190
'Six-Cylinder Love', 225
six-wheeled cars, 74
Sizaire-Naudin car, 76
'skirted fenders', 67
Skoda cars, 49
predecessor of 45
'sleeping policemen', 220
Sloan, Alfred P., 112
Smith Flyer, 79
Smith's 'Jackall', 67
Snetterton 24-hour race, first, 171
Sneva, Tom, 128
Society of Motor Manufacturers &
Traders, 112
Sommer, Raymond, 147
Sonolux stop light, 94
Sorensen, Charles, 112
South African Grand Prix, 141
1984, 173
winners, 141
South America, first coast to coast
crossing 224
Southern Cross cars, 79
Spa 24-hour Race, first 137
Spa-Francorchamps circuit, Belgium,
137
Spanish Grand Prix: first, 129
1975, 169
1986, 176
winners, 129
spare wheels see wheels
spares, air transportation of, 225
spark plugs, 25, 85
Spaulding 'Sleeping Car', 47
speed humps, 220
speed indicator, average, 69
first, 63
speed limit: British, 233
urban, 230
enforcement of, 16, 17
first, 10
maximum raised, 15
speed traps, 220, 232
earliest, 16
first photographic, 19
speedometers, 230
Spence, Mike, 163
Spice, Gordon, 175
'Spirit of America', 120
Spirit team, 173
sponsorship, racing, 122, 166, 167
see also advertising
Sports Car Championship, World, 154
winners, 155
see also Endurance Championship
Sports Car Club of America (SCCA),
147, 178
sprint championship, first British, 167
sprint meeting, first, 117
Spyker cars, 232
C4 life guarantee, 47
St James, Lyn, 128
St Jovite circuit, Canada, 161
St Petersburg-Moscow race, 126
St Valentine's Day Massacre, 228
'Standard', 43
Standard cars, 67
Vanguard, 88
Standard company, 40
Standard-Triumph cars, 99
Stanley, Francis E., 112
Stanley, Freelan O., 112, 122

Stanley Cycle Show, 21
Stanley Motor Carriage Company, 42
Stanley Steamer, 122
Star cars, 67
  station wagon, 63, *66*
Star company, 66
starters: accelerator-actuated, 67
  Bendix quick-thread, 74
  first electric, 73
  Harrison system, 83
  key system, 68
  kick starters, 48
  pneumatic 73, 84
station wagon, first 63, *66*
Steam Carriage Company of Scotland,
  9
steam cars, 7, 42, 44
  fastest 126
  last 86
  see also Locomobile; Stanley; White
'Steamin Demon' steam-powered car,
  176
steering: electronic controls, 68
  four-wheel, 180
  power, 74, 80
  rear-wheel, *92*
steering wheel, horn button on, 62
Steinway, William, 42
Stella, Ugo, 29
Stewart, Jackie, 161, 166, 215
Steyr Puch 650-cc rally car, 192
Stirling 'hot air' engine, 88
Stoneleigh car, 225
stop lamps, first, 94, *95*
street lights, sodium, 229
Streiff, Philippe, 175
Stroewer D7 car, 225
Stuck, Hans, 141
Studebaker cars, 42
  Avanti, *55*
  'Rockne', 50
Studebaker company, 40
Sturmey, Henry, 23
Sturtevant cars, 91
Stutz, Harry C., 112
Stutz Vertical Eight car, 227
stylists, first woman, 47
Subaru company, 40
Sukuka circuit, Japan, 178
Sunbeam cars, 94, 129
  GP cars, 133
  Rapier MkIII, 192
  Toodles V, 85
Sunbeam company, 40, 101
Sunbeam Mabley car, 28
sunroofs: first electric, 71
  first sliding, 60
supercars, *194*, *197*, *239*
supercharged cars: first, 83, 85
  GP cars, 133
supercharger, forerunner of, 126
Surfer's Paradise, Australia, 180
Surtees, John, 159, 162, 166, 215
Surtees cars, 166
surveyor, first to use a car, 28
suspension: active, 178
  hydropneumatic, 80
  independent: front, 74, *76*, 80
    all-round, 74, 80
    pneumatic springs, *78*
    self-levelling, 79, 80
    air, 74
  swing-axle rear, 79

Suzuka circuit, Japan, 160
Swallow Sidecars (SS), 33
swan car, 221, *221*
Sweden, right-hand driving in, 233
Swedish Grand Prix 1978, 170
Swedish Rally: 1987, 199
  1990, 199
Swiss Grand Prix: first, 141
  1936, 143
  winners, 141
Switzerland, attitudes to motoring, 228
Sykes, Charles, 23
Syracuse Grand Prix 1955, 156
Szisz, Ferenc, *124-5*

T
1000 Miles Trial, 122
  first 23, 182
  1903, 183
  successor to, 187
1000 Lakes Rally: first 188
  1986, 198
24-hour races, 123
  see also individual races
TAG GP engines, 172
tail lamps, 228
Takuri car, 13
Talbot cars, indicators on, 66
Talbot company, 40, 108, 111
TAP Rally, 192
tappets, first hydraulic, 84
Targa Florio, 146
  1906, 124
  1919, 131
TARK cars, 175
Tasman series, 160
Tatra cars, *54*, 109
  Type 77, 50
Tatra company, 19, 40
Tauranac, Ron, 159
tax discs 225
taxation, 231
  on horsepower rating, 225
  rates of, 223
  Road Fund, 227
  world comparisons, 230
taxicabs, first, 44
Taylor, Henry Seth, 8
Teague, Al, 179
'Tear-drop car', *62-3*
Templar roadster, standard equipment,
  225
terminology, early motoring, 19
test drives by press, 15
Thackwell, Mike, 151, 171
Thomas, Edwin Ross, 112
Thomas, Miles, 225
Thomas-Detroit company, 100
Thompson, Mickey, 160
Thomson car, 13
three-wheeled cars, 74
throttle, electronic, 180
Thrust 2, *121*, 173
Thruxton circuit, *174*
Tiga GC85 car, 175
Tincher cars, 71
Tjaarda, John, 112
Todt, Jean, 199
Toivonen, Henri, 191, 195, 196, 198, 215
Toleman team, 171, 176
Tour de Corse: first, 191
  1982, 196
  1986, 198

Tour de France Automobile, 182
  1899, 117
  1963, 192
Tour of Britain 1989, 199
Touring Car Championship, British,
  first, 158
Tourist Trophy, RAC, 123
Toyota cars: Camry, 57
  Corolla, 57
Toyota company, 40
  employment, 57
Trabant cars, 62
tracks, banked, 126, 132, 137, 142, 146
traction control, 179
traffic control, by police, 233
traffic jam, longest, 238
traffic lights: first electric, 224
  first 'robot', 229
  manually operated, 227
  by pedestrians, 229
  synchronised, 225
  three-colour: automatic, 228
  first, 225
transmission, 90-4
  automatic, 94
  early, 91
  first production car with, 91
  selector positions, 94
  dual-ratio, 94
  expanding pulley belt, 93
  friction drive, 92
  hydraulic convertor, 94
  pre-selective, 93
  semi-automatic, early, 91
Trautmann, René, 191
'Travelling Engine', 8
Trevithick, Richard, 8
Tri-Phibian, 230
Triplex safety glass, 223
Tripoli Grand Prix 1933, 141
Trippel, Hans, 52
Triumph cars. Gloria, 230
  Herald, 80
  TR3, 73
  TR4, 71
  TR5, 88
  TR8, 195
Triumph company, 40
Trojan Type XL, 80
Tropfenwagen, *62-3*, 144
Trossi, Count Felice, *142*
Trossi GP car, 141
Tucker, Preston, 112
Tunbridge Wells exhibition of motor
  vehicles, 22
turbocharged cars, *89*, 90
Turin-Asti-Turin reliability race, 122
turn indicators, amber, 96
Turnpike Act, 15
'Twilight Sentinel' headlamps, 95
Type Approval, EEC, 236
tyres, 73-81
tyres: 1896 specification 15
  'balloon', 80
  changing early, *75*
  Grand Prix, 179
  guaranteed life, 79
  improved weather grip, 81
  Michelin ATS, 199
  pneumatic, 73, 114, 218, 73
  first car with, *77*
  radial, 81
  Grand Prix, 170

radial ply, 80
repairing punctured, 77
'run-flat', 80
slick, 167
tubeless, 73, 80
two-ply, 80
Tyrrell, Ken, 161
Tyrrell GP cars, 167
Project 34, 169

U
Ulster Trophy 1946, 147
United States Auto Club (USAC), 156
races in Britain, 156, 170
record race wins, 172
regulations, 170
United States Grand Prix, 172
first, 173
winners, 172
United States Motor Company, 100
Unser, Al, 217
Unser, Al Jr, 180, 217
Unser, Bobby, 128, 131, 168, 172, 217
Unser, Louis, 147
Unser, Robby, 131
US Grand Prix: first, 126
forerunner see American Grand Prize
winners, 127
USA: 250 millionth car, 236
first crossings of, 24, 25
by a family, 220
by a woman, 221
Pathfinder, 93
top-gear-only, 225
two-way, 220
first recorded woman motorist, 18
first true race, 116
'HELP', 233
history of motoring in, 8, 13, 18, 19,
22, 24
'label law', 232
motor vehicle laws, 225
nationwide road network, 224
production figures, 47

V
'Velie' cars, 47
'Villa des Cyclistes', Poissy, 16
valves/valve timing: electrically
controlled, 83
pneumatic, 84, 175
variable exhaust, 81
Van Diemen racing cars, 176
Van Lennep, Gijs, 168
Van Winkle car, 92
Vanderbilt Cup, 123, 126, 143
eliminating trials, 123
Vanwall racing cars, 137, 156, 157
Varzi, Achille, 142
Vatanen, Ari, 196, 217
Vauxhall cars, 32, 43
10-hp model, 80
GP cars, 133
Vauxhall company, 41
ventilation systems, 70
disc brakes, 73
early attempts, 67
see also air conditioning
Vercors-Vivarais rally, 193
Veteran & Vintage, 231
Veteran Car Club of Great Britian, 228
veteran cars: auction record price, 238
first auction, 233

first concours d'elegance, 229
first dealer, 229
first rally, 229
see also antique cars
Veteran Motor Club of America, 230
Villeneuve, Gilles, 158, 161
Vinatier, Jean, 192
Vintage & Thoroughbred Car, The, 231
Vintage Sports Car Club, 229
Voisin, Gabriel, 113
Voisin cars: GP cars, 133
'Laboratoire', 64
Volkswagen cars: ARVW, 171
Beetle, 41, 51
millionth, 52
20 millionth, 57
Formula Vee, 160
Golf 16v, 198
'hybrid', 47
Volkswagen company, 41
annual production, 54
factory automation, 52
Volvo cars, seat belts, 70
Volvo company, 41
saloon-car racing, 174
Von Trips, Wolfgang, 159
Vukovich, Bill, 156

W
Wagner, Louis, 137
Walbeck-Rousseau, René, 24
Waldegaard, Bjorn, 190, 193, 195, 217
Walex disc brake, 72, 72
Walker, Rob, 145
Walter car, 43
Wankel, Felix, 113
Wankel rotary engine, 88, 89
first production car with, 55
warfare, first car used in 24
Warwick, Derek, 178
Waterman Arrowbile, 50
Watkins Glen circuit, New York, 126,
148
Watson, John, 171
Watson cars, 161
wedding, first motor for, 27
Weigel Grand Prix car, 126
Welbeck Park, Nottinghamshire, 122
Welch 30/35hp car, 83
Westbury, Peter, 159
Weymann fabric body, 63
Wheatcroft, Tom, 142
wheelchair-accessible car, first, 58
wheel clamping, 238
wheels, 73-81
aluminium, 121
cast spoked, 80
concealed spare, 62
detachable, 79
interchangeable, 74
stainless steel wire, 80
wood, 80
see also tyres
White, Windsor, Rollin and Walter, 113
White steamer, 24, 220
Whitehead, Peter, 143, 150
Williams racing cars, 108, 168, 181
active suspension, 178
traction control, 179
Willis engine, 85
Wills, Childe Harold, 113
Wills St Claire car, 94
Willys, John North, 113

Willys-Overland company, 106
Wilson, Charles, 113
Wilson transmission, 93
Wimille, Jean-Pierre, 147
Windham, W. G., 16
Windham detachable bodies, 59
windows: curved side, 69
electric, 68
retractable rear, 69
safety glass, 66
wind-up, 63
see also windscreens
windscreen washers/wipers, 67, 71
automatic, 63
concealed, 71
early, 59
first mechanical, 62
hand-operated, 63
windscreens: demister, 67
early, 59
curved, 67
heated, 63
Windsor cars, 48
Winton, Alexander, 19, 113, 123
Winton 'Bullet' team, 82-3
Winton cars, 24, 25, 84
Wisconsin contest 1878, 182
Wisdom, Anne, 191
Wolf WR1 GP car, 169
Wolseley cars, first, 99
Wolseley company, 41
emblem, 67
wood: chassis, 74, 163
integral construction 79
wheels, 80
see also bodywork
Woodner, Jon, 199
Woods Dual-Power car, 47
World Championship of Drivers: 151
Prost's record points score, 180
see also individual races
World Championship rules, 148
world speed record, 117
Wyer, John, 166

Y
Yellow Cab, 44
York Dragway, 161
Yugoslav Grand Prix, 146

Z
Zandvoort circuit, Holland, 148
Zasada, Sobieslaw, 192
Zebra crossings, 231
Zeltweg circuit, Austria, 157, 160
ZF gearbox, 94
ZF-Soden gearbox, 93
Zhu Hai circuit, China, 181
ZIL straight-eight, 88
Zink, John, 160
ZIS cars, 51
Zolder circuit, Belgium, 161